EAST EUROPEAN JEWS IN TWO WORLDS:

STUDIES FROM THE *YIVO ANNUAL*

EAST EUROPEAN JEWS IN TWO WORLDS:

STUDIES FROM THE *YIVO ANNUAL*

EDITED BY DEBORAH DASH MOORE

NORTHWESTERN UNIVERSITY PRESS
AND THE
YIVO INSTITUTE FOR JEWISH RESEARCH

Northwestern University Press
Evanston, Illinois 60201

Printed in the United States of America

Library of Congress Cataloging-in-Publication Data

East European Jews in two worlds : studies from the YIVO annual / edited by Deborah Dash Moore.
    p. cm.
   ISBN 0-8101-0847-X. — ISBN 0-8101-0848-8 (pbk.)
    1. Jews—Europe, Eastern—History. 2. Europe, Eastern—Ethnic relations. 3. Jews, East European—United States—History.
4. Immigrants—United States—History. 5. Jews—United States—History. 6. United States—Ethnic relations. I. Moore, Deborah Dash, 1946– . II. Yivo Institute for Jewish Research. Annual.
DS135.E8E24 1989
947′.004924—dc20   89-25536
                                                CIP

Contents

Preface

The *YIVO Annual of Jewish Social Science* began publication in 1946 under the editorship of Max Weinreich, Research Director of the YIVO Institute (then called the Yiddish Scientific Institute). The purpose of this new English-language publication was to bring the best of Yiddish scholarship to American academics and to American Jews, both largely English-speaking groups. The destruction of European Jewry by the Nazis in World War II deracinated Yiddish cultural activity, removing it from its sources. The decision to start an English-language publication reflected the Institute's efforts to establish new roots for Yiddish scholarship and to recreate an intellectual community in the United States for social scientific research on Jews. From the first issue, the *YIVO Annual* published original research on East European Jews in the New World, thus signaling the Institute's interest in the largest remaining population of East European Jews and their descendants and its desire to integrate the study of the Old World with that of the New.

The *YIVO Annual* quickly achieved prominence. It published translations of the foremost historians, sociologists, ethnographers, and linguists of East European Jewish life and culture as well as nurturing a new generation, many of whom are now among the leading figures in contemporary Jewish scholarship. This collection includes essays from the first sixteen volumes. The articles indicate the breadth and originality of the research produced. Many introduced new areas of study or pioneered in innovative methodologies. The collection also includes a sample of the range of scholars associated with the YIVO. However, in order to preserve a measure of thematic unity, many notable essays written by important figures had to be excluded.

The volume opens with Abraham Joshua Heschel's depiction of the Eastern European era in Jewish history. Heschel originally delivered this talk in Yiddish at YIVO's annual conference in January 1945. When he finished speaking, the audience of several thousands was moved to tears, and a spontaneous Kaddish was uttered by many who were committed secularists and nonbelievers. The essay first appeared in Yiddish in *YIVO Bleter* 25 (1945), the same issue that included Abraham Ain's pioneering ethnography of a Jewish town in Eastern Europe. Ain's reconstruction from memory of the details of everyday Jewish life represents an early effort to retrieve material about a community that had been completely destroyed. Yekhiel Shtern's description of a Jewish elementary school is similarly unmarred by nostalgia. The article is drawn from his book *Kheyder un bes-medrash*, a study of Jewish education in Eastern Europe. These first three essays draw upon the authors' memories and personal experiences. The following articles utilize a range of methodologies reflecting their authors' diverse backgrounds.

Dan Miron is among a group of young scholars who came to the YIVO to study Yiddish literature. He originally presented his essay on Mendele Moyker-Sforim, one of the "fathers" of Yiddish literature, at the YIVO annual banquet in 1971. Written at the beginning of his academic career, the article presents a revisionist interpretation of Mendele and the periodization of modern Yiddish literary history. Bernhard Brilling's historical analysis of the struggle for the Jewish right of religious worship in Breslau anticipated contemporary interest in Jewish politics. Brilling's case study of the *Vaad Arba Arazot*, the Jewish Council of Four Lands, during a period when Jews had little formal political power, continues to be appreciated by students of East European Jewry. Jacob Lestchinsky, one of the founders of Jewish demography, originally published his sociological portrait of modern Polish Jewry in succeeding issues of *YIVO Bleter* 20 (1942) and 21 (1943). His focus on urban Jewish life includes comparative analyses. Raphael Mahler's contribution on the economic background of Jewish emigration from Galicia was drawn from a two-volume collaborative study of the Jewish labor movement in the United States. Initiated by the YIVO Institute under Elias Tcherikower, the history stresses the important continuities between East European Jews in Europe and America. Mahler's essay integrates immigration and labor history. Liebman Hersch's statistical comparison of Jewish and non-Jewish criminality also broke new ground. The essay examines a controversial topic—in 1989 no less than in 1942 when it first appeared in *YIVO Bleter* 20—with dispassion. Like Hersch, Isaiah Trunk approaches an emotion-laden subject with scholarly rigor. Trunk's examination of Jewish religious, educational, and cultural problems in the ghetto indicates the enormous possibilities for researching the Holocaust and the use of scholarship for understanding this catastrophe. The YIVO Institute's pathbreaking role in initiating serious study of the Holocaust appears also in Philip Friedman's essay. Friedman's question "Was there an 'Other Germany' during the Nazi period?" anticipated by more than a decade similar scholarly queries.

The New World section begins with an essay by Horace M. Kallen that draws upon his learning to place the American Jewish experience into the broader context of modern Jewish history. Like Heschel's evocation of East European Jewish life, Kallen's overview reflects his personal perspective. Kallen originally delivered this address at the 1957 YIVO annual conference. The subject of the Jewish labor movement, first identified as an important research topic for historians of American Jews by the Tcherikower project, receives reinterpretation by a leading historian of East European Jews, Ezra Mendelsohn. Mendelsohn studied at YIVO and later edited the special issue of the *Annual* in which his essay first appeared. His article on the Russian roots of the American Jewish labor movement documents continuities between East European Jews in Europe and the United States. It also represents the fruits of a new generation producing Jewish history in the English language. Rudolf Glanz's contribution to the study of East European Jewish immigrants introduces a new source. Glanz examined the American press, particularly the muckraking journalists who exposed social and political ills, to explore how Jews were seen by a select group of outsiders. Like Glanz, Tamara K. Hareven looks at the press to provide a window on immigrant Jewish life.

Hareven's study of the socialist *Jewish Daily Forward* won first prize in the Institute's student essay competition, one of the ways the Institute encouraged young scholars to study East European Jews.

These fourteen essays were chosen with the help of the *YIVO Annual* editorial board. Board members assisted the editor in identifying the most compelling essays and then helped in the difficult task of paring down the long list. It is hoped that this volume will serve to introduce some of its treasures to those too young to know the *YIVO Annual* and that it will offer those familiar with the *Annual* a useful one-volume compilation. To all, may it provide a diverse, enticing, and rewarding introduction to the study of East European Jews.

Deborah Dash Moore
Editor

THE EASTERN EUROPEAN ERA IN
JEWISH HISTORY

By Abraham Joshua Heschel

Originally published in the *Yivo Bleter*, XXV (1945). This paper was read at the annual conference of the Yivo in New York, January 7, 1945

In the last thousand years the spiritual hegemony in Jewish life was divided between Sephardic and Ashkenazic Jewry. Earlier in the period the primacy went to the Sephardic group; in the latter half the Sephardim were superseded by the Ashkenazic group. All Ashkenazic Jews in the areas bounded by the Rhine and the Dnieper, the Baltic and the Black Seas, and in some neighboring states as well, comprised up to the nineteenth century a culturally uniform group. The beginnings of the cultural sphere go back to Rashi and Judah the Pious and his disciples. The zenith of its spiritual development was attained in eastern Europe, particularly in Hassidism.

The attempted appraisal of the Eastern European era is in the perspective of history; thus, events that loomed important only in recent years are considered in the aspect of their importance for the entire period, which extended over eight hundred years. Our task is to characterize those traits that, in our opinion, express the essence of the era; adventitious traits we must perforce ignore. Neither shall we attempt to analyze the causes that led to the assumption of its particular physiognomy by the era under consideration. That problem requires a special study. Nor shall we describe the various accomplishments of the era, such as the development of the Yiddish language, the rise of the *Wissenschaft des Judentums,* the spread of Hassidism, Haskalah, the revival of the Hebrew language, the modern Hebrew and Yiddish literatures, Zionism, Jewish socialism, the establishment of new centers, the rebuilding of Palestine, the various attempts to modernize Jewish life and to adapt it to changing conditions.

1

I

How do we appraise the historic value of an era? What standards do we use in measuring culture? It is customary in the modern world to appraise an epoch on the basis of its cultural progress, the quality of its books, the number of academies, the artistic accomplishments, and the scientific discoveries made therein. We Jews, the first nation in the world that began not only to mark, but also to appraise and to judge, the generations, evaluate eras on the basis of different criteria, namely, how much refinement is there in the life of a people, how much spiritual substance in its workaday existence, i.e., how much metaphysics in its material aspect? To us culture is the style of life of a people. Our gauge of culture is the extent to which the people, and not only individuals, live in accordance with the dictates of an eternal doctrine—the extent to which inwardness, mercy, beauty, and holiness are to be found in the daily life of a people.

The pattern of life of a people is more important than the pattern of its art. What counts most is not expression, but existence itself, the source of expression. The key to the source of creativity lies in the will to cling to spirituality, to be close to refinement, and not merely in the ability of expression. Creativity comes from responsive merging with infinite reality, not from an ambition to say something. To appraise properly the meaning of the Eastern European era in Jewish history, we must not merely dwell upon its contribution to literature, science and the arts, but upon its life-feeling and life-style. We shall then find that it was the era in which our people attained the highest degree of inwardness. From that point of view we are justified in saying that it was the golden period in Jewish history, in the history of the Jewish soul.

Jewish culture of the Hellenic and Sephardic eras is the product of a fusion, of a symbiosis of Jewish tradition with Greek or Islamic culture. Life is frequently oriented to the outer world. Literary forms, scientific methods, philosophical criteria, and even theological principles are adopted from others. The attempt is made to stress the elements Judaism has in common with the surrounding cultures, frequently overlooking its own specific, peculiar contributions. Often, the writing and thinking are in a foreign pattern, endeavoring to compromise with the theories of the great thinkers; at times even an apologetic note is sounded.

In the Ashkenazic era the spiritual life of the Jews is lived in solitude, among primitive Germanic and Slavic peoples. Spiritually above their neighbors, the Jews developed a unique Jewish collective life, based upon its own traditions, upon the cultivation of the indigenous and the personal, to the utter disregard of the outside world. They borrowed from other cultures neither substance nor form. Their literature was written by Jews and for Jews; no apologies were offered to philosopher or historian. No commendation was asked of either prince or penman. No comparisons with others were indulged in, no energy wasted in rebuttal of hostile prejudices.

Sephardic Jewry often lacked folk traits. Its culture was derived from above. Jewish men of learning of the Sephardic school were inspired by Arabs; Arab poetry and philosophical morality were frequently the prototype of their teachings. In the main, they devoted themselves to scholarship; their books being frequently designed for individuals or limited groups. Their Jewishness was aristocratic; their poetry was frequently written in a language intelligible only to the scholar. Many of the great among the Sephardim did not find complete self-fulfillment in their Jewish environment. Sephardic men of letters wrote many of their books in Arabic, including Responsa and commentaries on the Bible, the *Mishna* and the *Gemara.* The like is inconceivable in Poland, or even in Germany, among Ashkenazic Jewry. No one could imagine the *Toledot Yakov Yosef* (a Hassidic work of the 18th century) in Polish, or the Talmudic novellae of the "Pne Yehoshua" (Talmudic authority of the eighteenth century) in German.

A synthesis of Torah and people is attained by Ashkenazic Jewry. Eastern European Jews speak Yiddish, a language of their own. Hebrew, too, emancipates itself of its rhetorical artificialities, becoming simple and natural as in Midrashic times. Because the collective life of the Jews is wholly pervaded by Jewishness, the relations among all the components of the Jewish community, between the saint and the untutored, the Yeshiva student and the farmer, are intimate, organic. The wholesome earthliness of villagers, the geniality of ordinary folk, and the ingenuousness of the *magid,* the popular preacher, penetrate the *Bet-Midrash.*

In eastern Europe the Jewish people has come into its own. It does not live like a guest in somebody else's house that must constantly keep in mind the ways and customs of the host. The Jews live their own life without disguise, outside of their homes no less than within them. The people itself becomes a source of Jewishness; it can truly say, "In my flesh I shall see God." The Jews begin to sing. Their fancy takes wings. The *pilpul* indulges in fictitious situations, the sermons of the preachers abound in parables. Everywhere one finds cryptic meaning and allusions. The author of *Megalleh Amukot,* in the 17th century, interprets the portion of the Bible (*Vaethanan*), in which Moses pleads with God for permission to enter the Holy Land, in 252 different ways. The manifest becomes occult; dialectic is joined with Kaballah, and in the *Hoshen Mishpat* (the part of the *Shulhan Aruk* dealing with civil and criminal law) one begins to discover profound mysteries. Even names of towns and countries contain allusions. The name Poland is allegedly derived from the two Hebrew words *Po-lin* ("here abide"), which was inscribed on a note descended from heaven and found by the refugees from Germany on their eastward journey at the time of the Black Death and the attendant massacres of Jews. On the leaves of the trees, the story goes, are inscribed sacred names and in the branches are hidden errant souls seeking deliverance through the intermediation of a pious Jew, who in passing would raise his voice in praise to the Creator.

Sephardic literature is distinguished by a strict, logical orderliness; it is written in accordance with a clear-cut scheme, in which every detail has its assigned place. Ashkenazic writers renounce clarity for the sake of profundity; the contours of their thoughts are not very clearly marked; the thoughts, however, are direct, moving, and natural. Sephardic literature is like classical architecture; Ashkenazic literature, like a painting by Rembrandt, profound and full of mystery. The former prefers the harmony of a system; the latter, the tension of dialectic. The former is sustained by a balanced solemnity; the latter, by impulsive inspiration. Frequently, in Ashkenazic literature, the form is shattered by the overflow of feeling, by passion of thought, and explosive ecstasy. Sephardic literature is like a cultivated park; Ashkenazic, like an ancient forest. The former is like a story with a beginning and an end; the latter has a beginning, but turns frequently into a tale without end.

The Sephardim, interested in preserving the spiritual heritage, classify and synthesize the material that has accumulated in the course of the centuries. The Ashkenazim are eager to discover the new, to probe deeper. The important thing with them is not to remember and to know, but to discover and to understand. Not the final decision is important, but the syllogisms whereby it was derived. The *Mishneh Torah* of Maimonides, the Sephardic Jew, classifies the laws according to logical concept, and reduces the stream of precepts and laws into an abstract system. The *Turim* ("Rows") of the Ashkenazic Jew (Rabbi Jacob, son of the R'o'sh, d. 1340), which forms the basis of the *Shulhan Aruk,* arranges the precepts in accordance with the daily program of the Jew, beginning with the rising in the morning and concluding with the night prayer of *Shema.* Maimonides' arrangement is logical; the *Turim* reflects the workaday life.

The Sephardim aspire to personal perfection, tranquility of soul, inner peace and contentment, attempting to express their ideal in rational concepts. Their ethic is frequently bourgeois, full of practical wisdom and prudence, advocating the golden mean as the best policy. The Ashkenazic ethic knows no perfection that is definable; its aims are: *seek higher than that.* The Ashkenazic moralist or Hassid is exalted. He yearns for the transcendental, the preternatural. Not for him the tranquil contemplation, the gradual ascent! Ecstasy without end, prayer, study without limit: these appeal to him. And although in effect one is engaged in a persistent struggle with the material, with the finite (one cannot escape one's self), one can at least aspire to self-abnegation.

II

A unique Jewish person has evolved, whose habits and taste are not in accordance with the classical canon of beauty, but who, nevertheless, possesses a specific charm. He is not like a page in an open book, static in its own lines and in the proportion of text and margin. He is different. His soul is a book whose pages are constantly turning. He that dislikes being motionless, that has a quick grasp and is not seized with dizziness at the sight of constant change, will enjoy the beauty of genuine mobility. There are few artists that can both perceive and appraise this "Jewish nature." When this mobility takes shape in crystallized deeds and word, we find in these a certain "kink" for which there is no definition.

The charm of East European Jewry derives from their inner richness, from the polarity of reason and feeling, of joy and sorrow. Everything in their life is fixed according to a pattern; nothing is left to chance. But they have enough vitality to constantly modify the accepted pattern. New customs are continually added to, and a new "kink" introduced into, the old pattern. The deeds, the forms, are passed on from generation to generation, but their meaning and their motivation change. Thus, the source of perennial freshness never runs dry.

The pattern of life was not limited to religious activities. Not only what is to be done on the Sabbath, but also what is to be done in the course of the week, has a definite form. The pattern prescribes the kinds of food to be eaten on certain days, the manner of putting on and off the shoes, the deportment in the street. Every part of the liturgy, every prayer, every hymn, has its own tune. Every detail possesses its own physiognomy, each object bears its individual stamp. Even the landscape is judaized. During the penitential season the fish in the streams tremble; on Lag b'Omer (scholars' festival in spring) the trees rejoice. The spirit of a Jewish festival is felt even by the domestic and wild animals. The nightingale sings with a choir. And a magpie on a branch appears in the distance "as if wrapped in a small white *tallis* ... bowing in supplication." [1]

Eastern European Jewry was a people with a common will and destiny. It was not merely a uniform group, a homogeneous tribe; but a multiform society, uniform in its variety: one language, with many dialects. Social existence was complex, frequently dominated by centrifugal forces, but there was a common center and in most cases also a common periphery. There was even a social dynamic that created groupings in its own fashion. Hassidim, adherents of one "Rebbe," regardless of the geographic and economic distance separating them from one another, were a distinct group, with a specific way of life, specific customs and interests, which were so intensive that they affected their economic position. On the other hand, economic divisions often imposed their stamp on religious institutions. Artisans of a class established their own places of worship, making themselves independent of the community synagogue.

III

An important factor in the development of Ashkenazic Jewry was the democratization of Talmudic study. In the first five centuries following the redaction of the Talmud, the Babylonian Gaonate had the hegemony over Jewish life. They explained equivocal passages in the Talmud and rendered legal decisions. It was not until the twelfth century that the Occident began to emancipate itself. By the compilation of compendia of laws and commentaries to the Talmud, the Jews in the distant parts gradually achieved independence from Babylonia. The first commentaries, however, were merely to isolated

---

[1] Mendele Moikher Sforim, *Fishke der Krumer.*

passages, and the first compendia were not sufficiently inclusive. Only Maimonides' *Mishneh Torah* and Rashi's commentary on the Talmud rendered the Jewish people independent of the *Gaonim*; no longer was it necessary to refer questions to Babylonia.

Rashi and the *Tosafists* were particularly instrumental in making the people culturally self-sufficient. Without Rashi the Talmud was an esoteric lore; through him, the paths to its understanding were opened, for Rashi explained the meaning of words rather than discoursed on methodology and dialectic. He democratized Jewish education; he brought the Bible, the *Gemara* and the *Midrash* (exegetical homilectical commentary on the Bible, 4th-12th centuries) to the people, and made the Talmud a popular book, everyman's book. In him was effected a fusion of the Palestinian and the Babylonian legacies. Scholarship ceased to be the monopoly of the few and became widely disseminated. In many communities, the untutored became the rare exception.

A Jewish township

> is a place of learning of old standing, where practically all the inhabitants are scholars, where the House of Study is full of men and young men busily pursuing their studies..., where at dusk, between the *Minha* and the *Maariv* services, artisans and other simple folk gather around the table to listen to a discourse on the *Midrash*, the Bible, *Hobot Halebabot* ("Duties of the Heart," a moralistic book of the 11th century) and similar ethical and philosophical works . . . where on the Sabbath and on the holidays one hears fiery sermons kindling the hearts of the listeners with love of the Divine Glory, interspersed with words of comfort from the prophets, with wise parable and keen aphorism of the sages, in a voice and a tone that penetrate the entire being.[2]

Poor Jews sit like intellectual magnates. They possess a wealth of ideas and of knowledge, culled from little-known passages in the Talmud. One raises a question about a difficult passage in Maimonides; the other outdoes him in his answer, in the subtlety of his dialectic. The stomach is empty, the home overcrowded; but the heads are full of spiritual and cultural riches, and the Torah is free and ample.

For recreation one goes not to the tavern, but to the House of Study. Passions seek no outlet in gambling, drinking, and other dissipations, but in the desire to act as precentor in the synagogue.

What other nation has a lullaby to the effect that "study is the best of wares"? At the birth of a child, the school children come and

---

[2] Idem, *Shloime Reb Khayims.*

chant the *Shema* in unison around the cradle. The child is taken to school for the first time wrapped in a *tallis*. School children are referred to as "sacred sheep," and a mother's pet name for her little boy is "mayn tsadikl" (my little saint). Hence, one is ready to sell all household belongings to pay tuition. Women work all their lives to enable their husbands to devote themselves to study. One shares his last morsel of food with a Yeshiva *bokher*. And when the melancholy sweet tone of Talmudic study penetrates the poor alleys, exhausted Jews on their pallets are delighted, for they feel they have a share in that study. Unable to devote themselves to study because of economic exigencies, they draw comfort from the thought of supporting the students. The ambition of every Jew is to have a son-in-law a scholar. Nowadays we speak disparagingly of the institution of *kest* (supporting a son-in-law). But what institution has done more to promote the spiritual development of large numbers of people than *kest*?

Study was a song of longing, a pouring out of the heart before the Merciful Father, a sort of prayer, a communion and an ardent desire for a purified world. Inwardness has assumed super-real forms. Jews immersed in a discussion of the laws pertaining to the "merchants of Lydda" at the same time suffer the anguish of the Divine Glory in Exile. They are endeavoring to unravel an obscure passage in the MaHaRSha (Talmudic authority of the 16th-17th centuries), and at the same time feel the affliction of the world.

Study was a technique of sublimating feeling and thought, dream and syllogism, of expressing pain in a question and joy in a solution found to a difficult problem in Maimonides. The tension of the spirit found an outlet in the contrivance of subtle, practically insolvable riddles, in yearnings and expectations, in the invention of new logical devices. The greatest joy was to find an answer to gnawing doubts. A world of suppressed gayety and frolic lies in their dialectic. The conscious aim, however, is not self-expression. One does not want to exploit the Torah; one uses it as an ornament. The people are enamored of study, therefore, they put mind, heart and soul into the *Gemara*. Borne up by the tune, one soars in the pure spiritual realm of thought, far from the world and its objects, its facts and aims, away from the boundaries of here and now, to the place where the Divine Glory listens to what Jews recreate anew in the study of the Torah. There was holiness in their acumen; the psalmist's "my soul thirsteth for God" filled the entire being.

Every Jew felt himself a partner in the Torah. He struggled over a difficult question and, because of his kinship with the Torah, felt entitled to an opinion. He received the apparatus of study, consisting of various methods, and attempted to evolve a system of his own, in addition to the acquisition of data. The result was that he became a thinker, not merely a guardian of facts.

The Jews studied those parts of the Torah that had no relevance to their daily life no less eagerly than those that had a direct bearing on it. They busied themselves with studies that were not actual, even far from the banal course on living. Their study was non-utilitarian, free from pragmatic design; not practical, esthetic. He that studied for the purpose of becoming a rabbi was the subject of ridicule. However, the weighing of subtle opinions and the addition or subtraction of a nuance made the student feel as if he were the guardian of the treasures in the temple of the Torah. It was a kind of service that enchanted the spirit. Its priestly glory lay in the mere act of doing, not only in the results achieved. The *Gaon* of Vilna told his disciple, R. Khayim Volozhiner, that at times "heavenly mentors" came to him, desiring to impart to him sacred mysteries, but he refused their offer. He would rather struggle over the Torah and attain the truth unaided.

The *pilpul* was a continuation of the disputation of the *Gemara,* a development and elaboration of the unending tradition. One could dispute with the authorities of the past. The boundaries between yesterday and today were obliterated. If there is a discrepancy between R. Akiba Eger of the 19th century and R. Isaac Alfasi of the 11th century, a Warsaw scholar of the 20th century reconciles it with a novel view on the issue in question. There is no desire to solve actual problems, merely to continue the study of the *Tannaim* and *Amoraim,* of the early and the later teachers. One is less interested in the solution of the problem than in its devising.

It is easy to belittle such a mentality and to dub it unworldliness. The soul is sustained by impracticality. The unpractical experiences are the heart of culture, the spring of energy of humaneness. A civilization that concentrates merely on the utilitarian is essentially not greatly different from barbarism.

The plain meaning of the Torah is too superficial for these Jews. They, therefore, delve into the words and find hidden thoughts in their depths. The simple idea of a principle, the straight line of a law, are too narrow and too confining to contain their glance. The storm of the soul held under control becomes a mighty impetus of the intellect. The inner restlessness finds expression in intellectual passion. Thinking becomes charged with strength. The mind breaks down the forms of the Talmudic thoughts and recasts them in fantastic molds, zigzags, in which the thought at first becomes snarled but finally succeeds in disentangling itself.

Just as acumen in thought is the favorite of those that study the "manifest teachings," so economy of expression is the forte of those that are absorbed in mystic lore. A style evolves that skips the hypothesis and at once reaches the conclusion. The aphorism aiming directly at a thought, instead of approaching it slowly and gradually, is the literary form most adequate to express the thought of Eastern European Jews. They speak briefly, precisely, concretely, almost in a hint.

Ideas are like precious stones. The thought animating them brings out a wealth of nuances and distinctions, as the ray of light passing through a prism produces the colors of the spectrum. Upon rotation, the multiform ideas emanate a light that changes in accordance with the direction in which they are placed against the light of reason. The alluring gracefulness, the variety of polished ideas, enlighten the intellect and dazzle the eye. The concepts become dynamic; they give forth colors and meanings that at first thought seem to have no connection with one another. Full of original devices, the joy of their discovery quickens the heart of the discoverer. This is no realistic thinking; but art, too, does not consist in imitating nature, nor is mathematics an imitation of something that already exists.

IV

We must understand the life-feeling that dominated Eastern European Jewry in order properly to appraise the fact that the majority of their best intellects were devoted to the study, the interpretation, and the development of the Law. To them the world was no treasure that the Creator had left ownerless. Life to them was not merely an opportunity for indulgence, but a mission that God entrusted to every individual. Life is at least as responsible an enterprise as, let us say, the management of a factory. Every man constantly produces thoughts, words, deeds. He supplies these products to the Powers of Holiness or to the Powers of Impurity. He is constantly engaged either in building or in destroying. It is incumbent upon man to restore to perfection that which has become impaired in the cosmos.

Therefore, the Jews are engaged in the Service of God. They are rarely dominated by a desire for rigorism, or a tendency to irrational discipline. In the main, they are borne up by a sense of the importance of their mission. The world could not exist without the Law. This sense lends to their tone the magic of an artistic act, in which the material is not stone or bronze, but the mystic substance of the cosmos.

Scientists devote their lives to the study of the properties of plants or the life processes of insects. To science every trifle is significant, and its votaries inquire diligently into the most intricate properties of matter. The pious Ashkenazic scholars investigated with similar passion the laws that should govern the Jew's conduct. The devotion and honesty invested in their work have their parallel in scientific research. They wish to banish chaos out of human existence and to civilize the life of man on the basis of the *Halacha.* They tremble over every move, every breath; no detail can be treated lightly; everything is important. Hence, additional laws, new restrictions, are instituted. They are passionately striving to attain the maximum of piety. As the self-sacrificing devotion of the scientists seems torture to the debauchee, so the poetry of rigorism jars on the ears of the cynic. But, it may be, the question as to what benediction to pronounce upon a certain type of food, the problem of matching the material with the spiritual, is as important as the determination of the melting point of a certain metal.

V

As Rashi had democratized Jewish education, so, in the twelfth and thirteenth centuries, Judah the Pious and his disciples democratized the ideals of mystic piety. To attain to them, no high theoretical conceptions are necessary, the main requirements being faith, the heart, inwardness. Piety is more important than wisdom, naïveté ranks higher than speculation, the God-fearing man is above the scholar. By their apotheosis of simplicity, of warm faith, of humaneness and desirable moral qualities, they paved a way to God for the ordinary man.

Prayer, the outpouring of the heart before the Creator, is considered by them the basis of the Service of God. The *Siddur,* the folk-book of our literature, is dear and sacred to them; every word in it a precious jewel. They count the words, for in them are contained mysteries no end. Thence they attempt to uncover the old secrets that the prophets[a] transmitted to their disciples, which were later passed on orally and revealed only to the chosen few, the God-fearing.

In reality, however, the concentration upon the secrets is not the major aim. The heartfelt prayer of the simple untutored man frequently ranks higher than the prayer of the man of learning. A God-fearing Jew who does not understand Hebrew, but wants to pray with the proper devotion, may pray in the language with which he is conversant. A well-known legend tells of a simple Jew who, in the time of the persecutions, saved a community from imminent destruction through the merit of his recital of the Psalms.

The times are bad for the Jews; they are persecuted and hunted on all sides. Massacres are a daily occurrence; Jews are led to the slaughter like sheep; but all this is accepted willingly in submission to the Divine Will. With superhuman fervor they sacrifice themselves for their faith. The *Sefer Hassidim* ("Book of the Pious") finds it necessary to comfort those that "die on their beds" and have not merited death for the Sanctification of the Name. Life at its best is a battlefield. Man must constantly struggle with the Evil Inclination, "for Man is like unto a rope, one end of which is drawn by God and the other end by Satan." Hence one learns the tactics of this war, consisting, in the main, of eschewing all but the essentials of life, and in overcoming temptation. Lapses can be atoned for by fasts, which purge the soul of its stain.

The "Pious Men of Ashkenaz" attach great importance to the daily conduct of prominent Jews, or even ordinary Jews; to usages that are not the result of scholastic sophistication, but improvised instinctively; to customs that derive from the feelings, from the moods. They begin to commit to writing the various customs. Books appear aiming to teach the people tact, social refinement, proper religious practice. In this spirit books especially designed for the ordinary folk are written, poetic and tender in style, abounding in folk-tales and parables. They do not speak of high ideals in the abstract; they are didactic. There arises a literature in "Taytsch"—Yiddish, for women. For centuries they read the *Lev Tov* ("Good Heart") and the *Ts'eno Ur'eno* ("Go out and see") and pour out their hearts in the *Tehinot* (devotional prayers) written by women for women.

---

[a] According to R. Eliezer of Worms, the author of *Rokeah* (13th century).

VI

In the 17th century, the mystic teachings of the *Zohar*, and of R. Isaac Luria began to penetrate Poland. These esoteric books were reprinted, and the people were seized with a desire to study the mystic teachings which had heretofore been known only to individuals but were by this time made available to all. The spread of mysticism had a profound influence upon the life-feeling of East European Jewry. The Kabbalah breathed into them the consciousness of the importance of their actions for all worlds; all that takes place "above" in the upper spheres, depends upon man "below." It made every Jew somewhat of a Messiah. According to its teachings, redemption is not a thing that will take place all at once at the end of days; it is a continual process, taking place every minute. Man's good deeds are single acts in the long drama of redemption. Furthermore, redemption is not a process affecting merely the Jewish people; all the world is in need of redemption.

The sense of man's life lies in his perfecting the world. He has to distinguish, gather, and redeem the Sparks of Holiness scattered throughout the darkness of the world. This service is the motive of all precepts and good deeds. But the Jew, upon whom the deliverance of the world is incumbent, is in a position not merely to build but also to destroy. Endowed with gigantic powers, he can by means of the proper consecration ascend to the highest spheres. His spirit can create heavens. At the same time he must not forget, however, that his feet are upon the ground, close to the Powers of Darkness. It is quite conceivable that instead of ascending to the heavens, he may by Evil Inclination be cast down into the abyss. Hence, the Jews attempt to subdue the foe, matter, fasting every Monday and Thursday and undergoing other mortifications to purify the self. And the Evil Inclination pursues with a sharp ax; one wrong move, and the ax comes down. This feeling leads to both enthusiasm and sadness. One feels the infinite beauty of the heavens, the sacred mysteries of the precepts, but one is also aware of the gloom of the world. Man is so unworthy and sinful; the heavens are so exalted and far. What has man to do in order not to sink into the Nethermost Pit?

VII

Then came the Hassidim and brought down heaven upon the earth. They banished melancholy from the soul and uncovered the great fortune of being a Jew. Jewishness meant rebirth. Customs and quotations suddenly took on a breath like that of new grain. A new prohibition was added: against being old. The spirit grew younger. One was enamored of God, one felt "the unbearable longing for God." One began to feel the infinite sweetness that comes from fulfilling the precept of hospitality, or from donning *tallis* and *tefillin*. What meaning is there to the life of a Jew, if not the acquisition of the ability to taste the joys of Paradise? He who does not taste Paradise in the performance of a precept in this world, will not feel Paradise in the world to come. No sooner has one come to feel life eternal in a sacred ritual, or in the Sabbath, than these and the world to come are identical.

The Jews became so refined that they ceased being afraid of the body. Commenting upon the passage, "Hide not thyself from thy own flesh" (Is. 58.7), the Baal Shem Tov said: "Do not mortify the flesh; pity it." One can worship God even with the body, even with the Evil Inclination; one merely has to be able to distinguish between dross and gold. For the significance of this world lies in the fact that a little of the other world is mingled with it. Without refinement, matter is full of darkness. The Hassidim have always maintained that the joys of this world are not the highest attainable; they, therefore, kindled in them the desire for spirituality, a longing for the world to come. Only its bliss, *Olam Haba,* was perfect.

The story is told of a *melamed* making a wintertime pilgrimage afoot to his "Rebbe." The town's rich man passed by in a sumptuous coach, drawn by four horses. Seeing the *melamed,* he asked him into the coach. The *melamed* consented, and was soon snugly tucked away in a corner, covered with heavy warm blankets. The rich man then offered him some brandy, cake, even some roast goose. Suddenly, the *melamed* turned to the rich man, saying: "Pray, tell me, what is your this-worldly joy, your *Olam Hazeh*?" The rich man was astonished: "Don't you see the luxurious coach and the expensive foods? Are they not enough of this-worldly joy?" "No," replied the *melamed,* "these are your other-worldly joys, the acme of your joys, your *Olam Haba,* but what is your *Olam Hazeh*?"

It was like the miracle that took place at the passage of the Red Sea, as told by our sages. An ordinary Jew frequently began to perceive what the scholars had so often failed to sense. And do not really a contrite sigh, a little inwardness, a little self-discipline and self-sacrifice, outweigh the merits of him that is full of both learning and pride? When study becomes an aim in itself, it may turn into a sort of idol worship. Excessive *pilpul* may dry up the spring of the soul. Hence the scholar who shuts his *Gemara* and sets out upon a self-imposed "exile," to live far from home, to bear humiliation, to taste the cup of privation.

The story is told of a scholar who once came to a "Rebbe." "What have you done all your life?" inquired the "Rebbe." "I have gone through the Talmud three times," replied the scholar. "But what of the Talmud has gone through you?" countered the "Rebbe."

From sheer piety one can forget the Creator. The main object is to feel the soul, in one's self, in the Torah, in the world. Man is no mere reflection; he is a spring. Divesting himself of the husks, he can illuminate the world. Hence the fate of his "dear people of Israel" is of such concern to God. He is the endless, no thought can conceive Him; yet in ecstatic contemplation of His infinity, the Jew exclaims, "Sweet Father!" It is incumbent upon the Jew to obey his heavenly father; He in turn is bound to take pity on His children. Everyone knows that God loves even the most wicked in Israel with a love surpassing our love for the most saintly in Israel. But when the suffering of exile is most severe and heavenly aid does not appear, R. Levi Yitskhok of Berdichev summons God to stand trial, as it were.

In 1917-18, during the pogroms in the Ukraine, a friend of mine engaged in recording those events was struck by the fact that a certain town directly in the path of the passing hordes had in the various pogrom waves been persistently spared. My friend expressed his surprise to a resident of the town in question, who offered the following explanation: "We had been promised safety. Centuries ago there lived in our town a great saint. It came to pass that on a certain Friday he had to go, for the sake of a *mizvah,* to a neighboring town. The saint hesitated for a while. How set out on a journey on the day preceding the Sabbath? But the distance was small, the trip urgent, and he departed. Unfortunately, the journey took much longer than he had expected. Finally, when he arrived in the town, the Sabbath candles were gleaming in Jewish homes. The saint was wroth with God, as it were, that He dealt thus with him. In his indignation he refused to recite the *Kiddush*—the blessing over the wine. The heavenly spheres were, of course, duly impressed with the saint's form of remonstrance. But the saint would not be placated easily, not until he was promised that there would never be a pogrom in his town. Only then he proceeded to usher in the Sabbath.[4]

The Jews had always known piety, the Sabbath, holiness. The new thing in eastern Europe was the introduction of a part of the Sabbath into the week-days. One could taste life eternal in the fleeting moment. In such environment it was not difficult to maintain the Additional Soul. No beautiful synagogues were erected; instead, bridges were built leading from the heart of God. There were no concerts or operas; instead, the third Sabbath meal was attended with such feelings that music was not sufficiently refined to express them.

The present overflowed its bounds. Life became more than life. One lived vertically, not horizontally, being with the great men of the past not only in narrating tales about them, but also in feeling and dream. Every Jew felt a kinship with R. Akiba and R. Simon b. Yohai. Jews studied the Talmud, and saw Abaye and Raba before their eyes. Elijah the Prophet attended their circumcision ceremonies, their *sukkas* were visited by the Holy Guests. History never ceases, in such vertical life. Among such Jews there live the thirty-six hidden saints. In that environment one is always ready to welcome the Redeemer. If Isaiah were to rise from his grave and were to enter the home of a Jew, the two would easily understand one another.

Korzec, Karlin, Bratslav, Lyubavitch, "Ger," Lublin—hundreds of towns—are like holy books. Every place is a pattern, an aspect, a way in Jewishness. When a Jew utters the name of Mezhbuzh or Berdichev, it is as if he were to utter a holy name. A splendor emanates from ordinary acts. "Why do you make a pilgrimage to the 'Rebbe'?" an eminent scholar was asked. "In order to see how he laces his shoes." Hassidim tell how the "Rebbe" opened the door, how he tasted of the food: ordinary events, yet full of mystery.

It is superfluous to speak of faith, for who does not feel the presence of God filling the entire universe? To preach to those Jews the necessity of observing the 613 precepts would be banal; to live according to the *Shulhan Aruk* became second nature. But the Jews wanted more. They wanted to be higher. The old Rabbi of Slobodka used to say: "If I knew that I should remain what I am, I would lay hands on myself. But if I did not hope to become like the *Gaon* of Vilna, I would not be even what I am." This longing for the higher

---

[4] Told by David Koigen.

spheres endowed them with almost superhuman powers. Everyone knows what beauty is and can conceive it with his senses. In eastern Europe holiness, the highest of all values, became so real and so concrete that it could almost be felt as one feels beauty.

Notwithstanding the life of poverty and humiliation that Jews lived, inwardly they bore the sorrow of the world and the vision of deliverance for all men and all creatures. There were Jews from whose spirit the suffering of the generations and of their times never departed. Yet, this did not interfere with their continuous festive mood. For there is no despair, says R. Nakhman of Bratslav. "Fear not, dear child, God is with you, in you, over you, around you. Even in the Nethermost Pit one can be close to His Blessed Name." The word "bad" does not come upon their lips. Trials do not terrify. For "all can be taken from me—my house, the pillow from underneath my head—but not God within my heart."

Miracles no longer startled the people, and it was believed that men endowed with the Holy Spirit were not uncommon. The later generations were no longer considered inferior to the earlier, no longer looked down upon as epigons. On the contrary, there were Hassidim who believed that it was easier to attain the Holy Spirit in their own day than in the days of the *Tannaim*. For there are two sources from which the Holy Spirit emanates: the Temple and the Complete Deliverance. And we are closer to the time of deliverance than the *Tannaim* had been to the time of the Temple. The splendor of the Messiah appears in advance. Pity Abraham Ibn Ezra! His period was far from both the Revelation at Sinai and the Messiah; hence his sober tone.

A discussion was being waged in the Middle Ages, whether man is higher than the angels. Saadiah Gaon maintained the affirmative; Abraham Ibn Ezra, the negative. In the Eastern European period there was unanimous agreement on man's superiority. The angel knows no self-sacrifice, he needs not rise above obstacles, he has no choice in his course of action. Furthermore, an angel is stationary, remaining in the category in which he was created. Man, however, is a wayfarer, he goes forward or backward. He cannot remain in one place. More than that. Man is not merely the crown of creation, he can become a participant in the act of creation. Hassidim know the responsibility they bear, they know that entire worlds wait to be delivered from their imperfections. Not only are we in need of heaven, but heaven needs us as well.

VIII

No classical works were created in eastern Europe. The *Gemara* and the *Mishneh Torah,* the *Zohar* and the *Shulhan Aruk,* the *Guide to the Perplexed* and the *Ez Hayim* (of the mystic Hayim Vital, d. 1620), had their origin elsewhere. Eastern European Jewry had no ambition to create final forms of expressions. Their works are so unique and so rooted in a world apart that they are less accessible to the modern man than the works of the Sephardic scholars. The Ashkenazic Jews are but little interested in creating literature; their works are notes that they have made in the cause of their teaching. They are the product not of the writer's desk, but of the lecture hall, of the discourse delivered before the students. But their simplicity and humility conceal their great creative accomplishments. Their *obiter dicta* are like perfume. Their life was spirit; there arose in them an infinite world of inwardness, a Law within the Heart in addition to the Oral and Written Laws. They develop like artists that know how to fill the week-day hours with mystic beauty. They write no poetry. Their life is a poem. When Jews stand prepared to receive the Additional Soul, becoming enamored of God anew, and from their heart a song of rapture wells—what poetry can compare with this communion, this beauty?

The Jews did not disparage secular education without reason. They resisted the stream that sought to engulf the small province of Jewishness. They did not despise science. They believed, however, that the daily recitation of the prayer "Lord, guard my tongue from evil" was more important than the study of physics, that meditating upon the Psalms inspires a man with greater compassion than the study of botany. They had no confidence in the secular world. They believed that the existence of the world is conditioned not upon museums and libraries, but upon Yeshivas and Houses of Study. To them, the House of Study was not important because the world needed it; but, on the contrary, the world was important because the House of Study existed in it. To them, life without the Law and the precepts was chaos. A dweller in such a life was regarded with a sense of fear. Harassed and oppressed, they carried deep within their hearts a contempt of the "world" with its power and glory, its tumult and boasting. Jews that rose at midnight to devotions and spent the day peddling trinkets were not insulted by the scorn of the wicked, nor affected by his praises. They knew the world and did not turn it into an idol. Progress did not deceive them, and the magic of the twentieth century did not blind them. They knew that the Jews were in exile, that the world was unredeemed. Their life was oriented to the spirit; they could, therefore, ignore its external aspects. Externally, a Jew might have been a pauper; inwardly, he felt akin to royalty. The inner strength and freedom of a Jew wrapped in *tallis* and *tefillin* can be grasped only by him who has undergone that experience.

There are more attractive literatures and profounder philosophies than those that have arisen among the Eastern European Jews. In the pages of the latter, however, the light of the image of God was never extinguished. There were Jews who claimed that they could recall the time when their souls witnessed the Revelation at Sinai. Their will constantly resounded: "We will do and obey." Rarely was this affirmation uttered more fervently. Fiery young men would break into the streets and proclaim aloud: "There is none beside Him!"

When was there more light among the Jews in the last two thousand years? Could it have been more beautiful in Safed or in Worms, Cordoba or Pumbedita?

The story is told that once the Baal Shem with his disciples came to Berdichev to see the famous R. Liber. The latter was not at home, for it was the day of the fair, and he had gone to the market. Arriving at the market place, they saw R. Liber conversing with a peasant. "Do you know with whom R. Liber is speaking?" the master queried. "It is Elijah," he said, and beholding the amazement of the disciples, he added: "It is not R. Liber that is privileged to have a revelation of Elijah, but Elijah that is privileged to have a revelation of R. Liber." This story perhaps best expresses what happened in that period. In the days of Moses the Jews had a revelation of God; in the days of the Baal Shem Tov God had a revelation of Israel. Suddenly there was revealed a holiness in Jewish life that had accumulated in the course of many generations. In the final analysis "We will do and obey" is as important as "I am the Lord thy God," and "Who is like unto Thy people, one nation" as important as "the Lord is one." Who would have believed our report: One looked at the Jews and beheld the Divine Glory!

IX

It is easier to appraise the beauty of the older Jewish life than the revolutionary spirituality of the modern Jew, of the *Maskil*, Zionist, or socialist. The Jews of older days frequently overlooked this world, because of the other world. Between man and world there stood God. In the meantime, however, decrees and pogroms shattered the ground under the feet of the Jews. They had no peace, nor the means to gain a livelihood. Then came young men with new tidings. There arose the Haskalah, the Jewish socialist movement, Zionism, the *Halutzim* movement. How much of self-sacrifice, of love of Israel and of the Sanctification of the Name are to be found in these modern Jews, in their will to suffer in order to help! The zeal of pious Jews was transmitted to their emancipated sons and grandsons. The fervor and yearning of Hassidim, the ascetic obstinacy of Kabbalists, the inexorable logic of Talmudists, found their reincarnation in the supporters of the modern Jewish movements. Of the pair, Torah and Israel, they accepted Israel. Even those who have abandoned tradition, even those whom the revolutionary impetus has carried to the antithesis of tradition, have not separated themselves, like the sects of previous days, but have remained within the fold. The powerful urge to redemption continued in them. The Satan of assimilation is very seductive; but the Jews who have not capitulated, who have not deserted Jewish poverty, who have relinquished careers, favor, and comfort in order to find a healing for the hurt of their people: these have been like new wine in old bottles.

The modern Jew in eastern Europe, with certain exceptions, of course, has not only repudiated assimilation, but has developed a militant attitude as well. Both religious and free-thinking Jews fight for Jewish honor, for a dignified existence, striving to assure the rights of the community, not merely those of the individual. They manifest a collective will for a collective aim. With lightning rapidity they straightened their backs, mastering the arts and the sciences; over three thousand years of history have not made them weary. Their spirit is animated by a vitality that frequently leads them into opposition to monumental traditions. They want to begin anew, refusing to live on bequests. Not until recently have they begun to long for a union of the present with the past, a synthesis which has not yet been realized.

In the dreadful anguish of these days, a bitter question sears our lips: What will become of us, the surviving? Shall we, Heaven forbid, be subject to the fate of Sephardic Jewry after the catastrophe of 1492: fragmentized groups in Turkey and Morocco, stray individuals in Amsterdam, magnificent synagogues and fossilized Jewishness? Shall we permit our people to be lost in the multitude? Our Sabbath to be dissipated in the week-days?

Rich stores of potential energy, of intellectual resilience and emotional depth, gathered in the course of generations of a disciplined mode of life, are now contained in us. Much wisdom and much refinement are frittered away in intellectual trash, a good deal of the soul is lost to Satan.

We must retain the Jewishness of our fathers and grandfathers. Their Law within the Heart was not a matter of esthetics. Romantic portraiture of Hassidism, nostalgia and piety, are merely ephemeral; they disappear with the first generation. Solidarity with the past must become an integral part of our existence. We are in need of Jews whose life is a garden, not a hothouse. Only a living Judaism can survive. Books are no more than seeds; we must be both the soil and the atmosphere in which they grow.

The present generation is still in possession of the keys to the treasure. If we do not uncover the treasures, the keys will go down to the grave with us, and the storehouse of the generations will remain locked forever. The Eastern European era can become a source of inspiration for all of us. It is incumbent upon us never to forget the Jews that sanctified their lives by their proximity to heaven.

Mankind is now attracted by chaos. It has strayed into a desert with but few oases. We might have to be sustained by drops of manna.

When Nebuchadnezzar destroyed Jerusalem and set fire to the Temple, our grandfathers did not forget the Revelation at Sinai and the words of the Prophets. Today the world knows that what transpired on the soil of Palestine was sacred history, from which the nations draw their inspiration. A day will come in which the hidden light of the Eastern European era will be revealed. This era was the Song of Songs (which according to the rabbis is the holiest of Holy Scripture) of Jewish history in the last two thousand years. If the other eras were holy, this one is the holy of holies.

SWISŁOCZ: PORTRAIT OF A JEWISH COMMUNITY IN EASTERN EUROPE

By Abraham Ain

Originally published in the *Yivo Bleter,* XXIV (1944) and XXV (1945)

The area bounded by the Dnieper and the Vistula, the Baltic and the Black seas contained before the slaughtering of six million by the Germans over eight million Jews. Part of the general community in their respective lands, these Jews also developed their own specific forms of life, which in addition to religion embraced many other spheres of activity, such as philanthropy, recreation, and the like. Some of these forms of Eastern European Jewish life were incorporated, with proper modifications, in the basic pattern of the Jewish community in America, a fact that bears eloquent testimony to their vigor and effectiveness.

I. General Aspects

Population and Appearance

Swisłocz (Yiddish name: *Sislevich*) was considered one of the larger towns (*shtetl*) in the district of Grodno. According to the census of 1847, there were 997 Jews in Swisłocz. Fifty years later, the town numbered 3,099 persons, of whom 2,086 were Jews. In the beginning of the present century the population again increased substantially. A leather industry of considerable size sprang up and a railway was built, linking the town with the industrial centers of Western Russia. Jews and non-Jews from surrounding villages flocked to the town. In 1906, the town had some 600 families, of whom 400 were Jewish. In addition to the permanent inhabitants, there were a number of temporary residents in town, such as the students of the teachers' seminary and the ailing seeking medical aid from the local physicians.

The town consisted of a market, five large and a dozen small streets and alleys, and a synagogue yard. The market covered an area of about two city blocks in the center of the town. It housed all the town's business places. All larger streets, which extended on the average to three or four city blocks, began in the market and terminated in the suburbs. These streets were known after the towns to which they led. Thus the Grodno Street led to the Grodno highway. Two of the larger streets, the market, and the synagogue yard were inhabited by Jews. The other large and most of the small streets were inhabited by both Jews and non-Jews. The non-Jews consisted of White Russians, Poles, a score of Russian civil servants and, to complete the picture, a dozen or so Moslem Tartars. The Jews were "townspeople" and were registered in the lists of the town administration (*meshchanskaya uprava*). The president and the secretary of the town administration were Jews. Most of the non-Jews were "villagers" and were registered in the lists of the village administration (*volostnaya uprava*).

At the end of every larger street, at the entrance to town, was a huge gate. Once upon a time the town had been surrounded by a deep moat. At the entrance to the large streets there was no moat, so that passage was only through the gates. In the daytime the gates were open; at night they were closed, and no one could then enter or leave town. In my days only three of the large streets had gates; the others were in ruins. Three of the large streets had cobblestone pavement; the other streets and the market were unpaved. On rainy days the mud was ankle-deep and crossing the market was no pleasant undertaking. In 1904, the chief of police ordered every property owner in the market to pave the street fronting his property to a depth of twelve feet. This was the sidewalk of the market.

At the eastern approach to the town were ruins of massive stone walls. These ruins were called the stores and represented the remains of a street, two city blocks in length, that had burned down. The stores had been erected by Polish noblemen, owners of the town, in order to encourage trade. Several times a year fairs had been held in town, each lasting four weeks. In the 1830's a conflagration destroyed the stores. The owners of the town, involved in the insurrection of 1831 against Russia, fled abroad, and there was no one to rebuild the ruins. Conflagrations were no rare events in the towns. In the course of the nineteenth century the town burned down to the ground twice. In 1910 half of the town was destroyed by fire again. Hence, the town was continually being rebuilt anew and its external aspect improved. Many of the houses were substantial two-story brick structures, adorned with balconies. Some of the newer houses had hardwood floors and papered walls.

In the center of the market was a concrete square pillar, some fifty feet high, twelve feet square at the base tapering off to two feet at the top. From the top of the post extended a brass bar, about a foot long, supporting a round brass ball some two feet in diameter. No one knew the age of the post. Tradition had it that the owners of the town had formerly erected the post. On the significance of the post there were several theories. One maintained that it was constructed as a lightning-rod. Another version claimed that the Russians had hanged on that spot several Polish noblemen for participation in anti-Russian activities, and their colleagues had erected the post as a monument to them. A third account had it that the brass ball contained ancient documents about the history of the town.

How Old Was the Town?

There were no records to indicate the age of the town, or the age of its Jewish community. The Holy Burial Association (*Khevre Kadishe*) formerly had a *pinkes,* a minute-book, but it was destroyed in one of the periodical fires, and no other source for the history of the Jews in town was left.

The Jewish cemetery was divided into a new and an old burial ground. On the old cemetery, near the entrance, the tombstones had collapsed, so that it was difficult to tell that the place had once been a burial ground. Farther down, the tombstones protruded half-way from the ground, but the inscriptions on them were obliterated. On the new cemetery the graves and tombstones were in better condition. But even the new cemetery had probably been used for centuries, for in the first World War it was filled up and ground was broken for another cemetery.

In 1903, when a railway was being built through the town, a large number of human skeletons was unearthed. These skeletons were laid out in rows, close to one another, at a depth of about three feet. There were no clues for closer identification of the skeletons, nor was there any real interest in them. Apparently, the town had a long history, which was completely obliterated from the memory of the inhabitants.

The Vicinity

The immediate surroundings of the town were dotted with villages. Their inhabitants, chiefly White Russians, were, in the main, poor peasants who had to supplement their meager incomes by doing chores in town or laboring in the forests. Some of them worked in the leather factories in town; others were engaged in hauling timber from the forests to the railway depot. In the villages close to the forest skillful peasants carved all sorts of articles out of wood: pails, kneading troughs, felloes, yokes, and shingles. These articles they brought to town for sale, and with the money thus realized they purchased not only farm implements, but occasionally also flour and barley, for some peasants had so little land that they could not raise enough food for their families. There were also in the vicinity several large and small estates that belonged to Polish landlords.

Nearly every village and estate had a Jewish family. These families were engaged as millers or lessees. On the eve of the first World War there were practically no more Jewish millers in the villages, for two Jews, former millers in a village, by installing two motor mills in town rendered the village miller superfluous.

Administrative Authorities

Administratively and juridically the town was linked with Woł-kowysk, the county seat, which was at a distance of some twenty-eight versts. Economically, however, the town was closely bound up with Białystok, some seventy versts away. In 1906, the railway through our town was completed, and a closer contact was established with Woł-kowysk and other nearby towns.

To maintain order the town had a chief of police and a constable (*uryadnik*). In 1905 this force was augmented by eight policemen. The chief of police (*stanovoy pristav*) was the ruler of the town; his word was law. Frequently, this official would tyrannize over the town, but a way was always found to placate him. As a rule, he was not averse to a little gift. . . . In 1903, a new chief of police came to our town. Forthwith he launched a vigorous campaign against "subversive" elements, particularly among the young people. His zeal knew no bounds. Once, encountering on the outskirts of the town two young men reading a book, he had them arrested and questioned for two weeks. Subsequently, they were released. Another time, he raided a meeting of the clandestine Jewish Labor Organization "Bund" in the forest and arrested ten young men and three girls. The arrested maintained that their gathering was in the nature of a harmless outing and as no forbidden literature was found on them, they were released. The young bloods of the town decided to teach the chief of police a lesson. On a dark night they set fire to the woodshed of a school on the outskirts of the town. The regulations called for the chief of police to be present at a fire. A group of young people lay in wait for him and gave him a thrashing. This experience considerably diminished his zeal for discovering conspiracies. The constable, too, who began to peer into closed shutters, was given a beating, while in a somewhat intoxicated state.

The town had, moreover, a justice of the peace (*zemski nachalnik*), who adjudicated minor litigations of the rural population, and three excisemen, who supervised the manufacture and sale of alcoholic beverages.

Controversies in Town

The town, consisting exclusively of *misnagdim* (opponents of Hassidism), had a Synagogue and three Houses of Study (*besmedresh*), in which services were conducted three times a day. The Houses of Study possessed rich collections of books, and at dusk, between the *minkhe* (late afternoon) and the *mayriv* (evening) services, numerous groups could be seen busily pursuing their studies of the Scriptures, the Talmud, or some ethical text. The untutored had a teacher who instructed them in the weekly portion of the Bible on Friday evenings and Saturdays. The older folks were pious but tolerant toward the young generation, which was largely heterodox in its religious views. The young people, too, refrained from publicly offending the religious sensibilities of the orthodox.

On one occasion, however, a sharp conflict broke out between the young and the old generations. An itinerant preacher came to town. He was a man of eloquence and power and opposed to the "progressives," whom he attacked in his sermons. These sermons led to strained relations between some of the parents and their children. Once several young people entered the House of Study and interrupted one of the preacher's customary diatribes against them with catcalls. Some of the older people rose to the defense of the preacher and a fight ensued. During the altercation a butcher called out that the young people were justified in deriding the preacher because he was sowing discord in the community. The older folks avenged the slight to the preacher by prohibiting the butcher from selling kosher meat. The prohibition would have ruined the butcher, had not the Jewish Labor Organization "Bund" sent an ultimatum to the trustees of the Houses of Study to repeal the prohibition, or it would adopt strong measures. The trustees were frightened and complied with the request of the organization.

There were also deep-seated and prolonged dissensions within the camp of the orthodox. They began toward the end of the past century, when the old rabbi of the town, Rabbi Meyer Yoyne, died, leaving a son, Rabbi Motye, who aspired to the position. Although he had been duly ordained and was qualified for the rabbinate, the old and prominent members of the community opposed his candidacy. The reasons for their opposition were that the deceased had not left a will designating his son as successor and that, furthermore, the aspirant because of his youth and familiarity would not command the respect due to that office. They, therefore, selected one Rabbi Shneyer Zalman as rabbi. The artisans and small tradesmen, however, sided with Rabbi Motye and argued that since he was qualified for the position, the fact that he was a local man or that he was not well advanced in years should not be exploited to his detriment. And so he, too, remained rabbi in our town. Rabbi Shneyer Zalman was a quiet and tactful person, and the tension between the two factions was kept at a minimum.

In 1903, Rabbi Shneyer Zalman died and Rabbi Joseph Rosen was chosen as his successor. The conflict flared up anew with increased bitterness. The young people remained largely outside of the struggle, although their passive sympathy was on the side of Rabbi Motye. Shortly before the first World War, Rabbi Motye died and his adherents chose no successor. After the war, Rabbi Joseph Rosen left for America, and the two factions were reconciled and agreed on one rabbi.

The Community Council

The Community Council administered all religious and community affairs. It gave financial aid to the various religious and charitable associations, paid the salaries of the rabbi and other functionaries, and maintained the ritual bathhouse (*mikve*) and the poorhouse (*hekdesh*). The budget for these activities came from the tax on kosher meat known in our parts as *korobke*. The *korobke* was usually leased by one person, or by several partners, called the tax lessees. The *shokhtim* (ritual slaughterers) could not slaughter an animal or a fowl without a permit from the tax lessee. The permit for a chicken cost three kopeks; it was somewhat higher for a duck, goose, and turkey. The permit for a calf was sixty kopeks. For slaughtering a cow or an ox there was a certain tax, and an additional tax was levied on the meat, exclusive of the lungs, the liver, the head, and the legs. To guard against the importation of meat from nearby towns, the rabbis prohibited the sale and consumption of such meat. In cases where this prohibition proved ineffective, recourse was had to the police, who confiscated the imported meat.

Some twenty or twenty-five prominent members in the community, who were the trustees of the Houses of Study and the various associations, constituted the Community Council and ruled the community. They were the choosers and the chosen. The elections took place in the following way. By order of the rabbi a meeting was called, to which the Houses of Study sent delegates. The delegates were chosen in this manner. The trustee of the House of Study told the sexton to call out the name of the delegate. The sexton called out: "Rabbi Shmuel, son of Rabbi Mendel, first delegate! Will anybody second the motion?" The prominent members chorused, "Second." The sexton then called out: "Rabbi Mendel, son of Shmuel, second delegate! Will anybody second the motion?" The same members responded again, "Second." And so on, till the required number of delegates were "elected." The delegates met and elected the Community Council or passed upon matters of policy under discussion. Popular dissatisfaction with their decisions did not affect them.

Thus the Community Council ruled the town up to the first World War. During the German occupation of the town, the tax on meat was abolished. After the war, the Community Council was elected in a more democratic manner.

Associations

The Holy Burial Association (*Khevre Kadishe*) played a leading role among communal institutions in town. Its membership consisted of old and pious Jews. Membership in the Holy Burial Association was restricted. Admission took place in one of the following ways: first, members could enroll their children or grandchildren as minors and upon attaining maturity they became full-fledged members; or, second, an adult wishing to be admitted to the association had to serve for a year as a sexton, whose duties were the calling of the membership to meetings and attendance at funerals. The association purchased the site for the cemetery and took care of the surrounding moat (the cemetery had no fence). It obtained the necessary funds from the families of the deceased, in accordance with their financial abilities. To the credit of the association be it said that it never wronged these families. It was fair and reasonable in its demand and always conciliatory in its dealings.

The most popular of the organizations in town was the Nursing Association (*Khevre Line*). The function of this association was to provide nursing service for cases of prolonged illness. The constant attendance on the patient, in these instances, would leave the other members of the family exhausted, and this service would give them an opportunity for a brief rest. The association sent two members—to a male, two men, and to a female, one man and one woman—to attend to the patient from ten o'clock in the evening to seven o'clock in the morning. The association had its medical supply department that lent thermometers, icebags, heating pads, and similar sick-room needs to poor patients. The very poor were also supplied with medicine and nourishing food. The association had an ice cellar, supplying the sick with ice in case of need. The association obtained its funds from weekly dues paid by practically every adult in town, from special pledges in the synagogue, from the collection on the eve of the Day of Atonement, and from grants of the Community Council. The administration of the association was elected at a meeting of the entire membership.

Two types of visitors came to town frequently: poor Jews who went begging from door to door and itinerant preachers. The former were lodged in the poorhouse and the latter in a specially provided guest house (*hakhnoses orkhim*), consisting of a large room with several beds in it. The sexton would arrange for their meals in some household. The more distinguished preachers and the collectors for charitable organizations (*meshulokhim*) usually stayed at the inn.

The small merchants were always short of money and in need of a loan. Most of them had to resort to a private lender who charged usurious rates. For a loan of twenty-five rubles for a period of a half-year he charged four rubles, interest, which he deducted initially. Repayments had to be made from the first week, at the rate of one ruble a week. There was in a town a traditional loan association, *Gmiles Khasodim,* granting loans up to twenty-five rubles without interest. But many people refused to apply to the *Gmiles Khasodim,* for they regarded such a loan as a form of charity.

In 1908-1909, a cooperative savings and loan association was established with the aid of the Jewish Colonization Association (ICA) in St. Petersburg. The members of the association could borrow money at the rate of 8%. The state bank gave the association a loan of several thousand rubles. The people had confidence in the association and instead of depositing their savings in the savings bank, they deposited them in the association, which paid 6% interest. Even the non-Jewish population did business with the association. In time the private lender with his usurious rates was banished from the scene.

Sanitary and Hygienic Conditions

Sanitary conditions in town were far from satisfactory. Some inhabitants had to attend to their needs in the open. The wells were not covered, and dust and dirt would find their way into them. Before the war some wells were covered, and the water was obtained by means of a pump.

The Jewish community had a bathhouse, which was too small for the needs of the population. On Fridays it was badly overcrowded, particularly in the winter. In the summer time conditions in the bathhouse were better, since a number of people bathed in the river. All types of disease were prevalent in town, though they rarely attained epidemic proportions. Only during the German occupation in the first World War and immediately thereafter, epidemics of dysentery and typhus raged in town.

The economic situation of the town was fair; the people were well-fed and well-dressed. As a rule, they had adequate medical attention. The town had a municipal hospital, with one physician, one assistant (*felcher*), and a midwife. Hospital service was free to all, and the non-Jewish population made use of it. The Jews, as a rule, avoided the hospital, although they occasionally used the services of the physician and the assistant in the capacity of private patients. In addition there were two physicians (Poles, who had estates in the vicinity), an assistant (a Jew), and two Jewish midwives in private practice. The physicians enjoyed an excellent reputation in the entire district. One of them, a surgeon and gynecologist, attracted patients from points hundreds of miles away.

Education

At the age of five, a boy was sent to a school (*kheyder*) where he was taught the alphabet and reading. In the *kheyder* the boy usually spent a year or a year and a half, and was then promoted to a higher grade, where he took up the study of the Pentateuch and the rest of the Bible. The next step in his education was the study of the Talmud. Some teachers (*melamdim*) also instructed their pupils in writing and in the elements of arithmetic. Thus, at the age of ten, a Jewish boy knew a little of the Bible, could write Yiddish, had a smattering of elementary arithmetic, and was studying the Talmud.

For the study of Russian there was a special teacher. Some boys studied in *kheyder* only part of the time and devoted several hours daily to the study of Russian, arithmetic, and writing.

The *kheyder* was ordinarily in the home of the teacher. Study hours, except for beginners, were from nine in the morning to nine in the evening, with an hour for lunch. In the winter time every pupil had to contribute a pint of kerosene for the lamp.

For children whose parents could not afford the fee, there was a Talmud Torah, in which the fee was very low or tuition was altogether free. The Talmud Torah had three classes. In the first class instruction was given in reading, the Pentateuch, and the rest of the Bible; in the second class, in Bible, Talmud, and in writing Yiddish and Russian; in the third class, in Talmud, writing Yiddish and Russian, and in arithmetic. Instruction in the secular studies was given by two teachers who came for that purpose to the Talmud Torah for two hours daily, except Friday and Saturday. One teacher taught Yiddish writing and arithmetic and the other, Russian.

The years between twelve and fourteen were years of decision for the boys. Most of them entered at that age the leather factories, or were apprenticed to artisans. A small number of ambitious and promising boys left for the Yeshivas. The boys from the wealthier homes helped their parents in their factories or stores and simultaneously continued their education with the aid of a private tutor.

The education of girls was delayed to the age of seven or eight. It began with instruction in reading Hebrew and Yiddish. Thereafter came instruction in writing Yiddish and Russian, and in the elements of arithmetic. At the age of thirteen or fourteen girls were usually apprenticed to seamstresses. The poorest became domestics. Some girls

worked as saleswomen in their parents' stores part of the time and
continued their education.

At the turn of the century a general public school, of four grades,
and a modern Hebrew school were opened in town. These schools
gave the foundation of a systematic education to a number of Jewish
children. Moreover, some of the well-to-do parents began sending
their children to secondary schools in the larger cities. At the time of
the first World War, under German occupation, a secular Yiddish
school was opened. After the war the old-fashioned type of *kheyder*
became practically extinct. It was replaced by a net of Yiddish and
Hebrew schools, which existed till the second World War.

Educational facilities for the non-Jewish population were provided
by the Russian government. It maintained two elementary schools,
one for boys and one for girls, and a seminary for the training of
teachers for the elementary schools in the villages. The seminary had
some 300 students. These students came from the entire district of
Grodno and were provided with board and lodging by the school.
Together with the faculty and staff the seminary population comprised
some 350 people, who were a considerable economic factor in town.

Political Parties

The first political party in our town was the Zionist organization.
On a winter eve, some time in 1898 or 1899, the Jews were summoned
to the House of Study, where an out-of-town preacher and some local
men addressed them and Hebrew songs were sung. As far as I recall,
the speakers appealed to the audience to become members in the
Zionist organization, and the response was good. The work of the
organization consisted mainly in collecting money for the Jewish
National Fund. Before every Zionist congress there was some activity
in town in connection with the election of delegates. The Zionist
organization also opened and maintained the Hebrew school in town.

From 1905 to 1907 the town had an organization of Zionist
Socialists, known by the abbreviated Russianized name of S.S. The
leadership of the group consisted of some temporary residents in
town: a teacher and several workmen. Upon their departure, the
group dissolved. The town also had an anarchist club. In that organization, too, the leader of the club was from out of town and upon his
departure, the club closed its doors.

The Jewish Labor Organization "Bund" had its beginnings in our town about 1900. By 1905 it had grown into a powerful organization. Its membership was drawn from all classes of the Jewish population. The organization called and conducted the strikes in the leather factories and in the shops. The organization helped elect to the first Duma a "Bund" representative, who received some 80% of the Jewish votes cast in our town. The years 1907 and 1908, the period of political reaction in Russia, saw a decline of the organization in our town. Some active members left town; others became disillusioned and gave up political activity. In 1909, the group was reorganized, concentrating mainly on cultural activities: symposia, lectures, discussions, and similar enterprises.

The heroic period in the history of the Jewish Labor Organization "Bund" in Swisłocz was the year 1905. In the fall of that year a peculiar tension was felt in town. People awaited eagerly the arrival of the mail to obtain the latest news. Rumors of pogroms spread and there was talk of organizing a Jewish self-defense. Money was needed for the procurement of arms; and the following way of obtaining the required sum was decided upon, although the organization was in principle opposed to confiscation.

The town had two government stores for the sale of liquor. It was decided to stage an attack on one of these and to take its money. Once a month there was a fair in town, to which peasants and merchants from the neighboring villages and towns would come. During the fair the government stores took in considerable sums of money. The day of the fair was, therefore, deemed ideal for such an enterprise. Some time in October, 1905, in the evening following the day of the fair, as soon as the front door was closed, several of the most active members of the organization entered the store and, intimidating the salesgirls, departed with the money. Although the street was full of people and police (the chief of police summoned for the fair the police forces of the neighboring towns), no one noticed what had happened. When the salesgirls raised an alarm that they had been held up, no one believed them. Rumor had it that they embezzled the money and that the story of the burglary was an invention. It was only after the "Bund" published a proclamation taking the responsibility for the act that suspicion of the salesgirls was allayed.

The attack was well organized, save for one serious slip. The participants entered the store undisguised, and the salesgirls identified two of them. One fled abroad; the other was arrested, and faced a long term at hard labor. After several months' imprisonment, he was freed on bail of five hundred rubles and likewise fled abroad. With the aid of the chief of police a false death certificate of the arrested was secured. The certificate was submitted to the district attorney and he released the bail. In the final analysis, the affair cost considerably more than it had brought in.

Theatre

Formerly, Joseph and Esther plays, in Yiddish, were given during the Purim season. The actors, who were young men, took the parts of both men and women. Some time in 1905 or 1906 the first Yiddish play was given in which women, too, acted. This play was sponsored by the "Bund"; it was followed by several Yiddish plays given by the Zionist Socialist group.

Great difficulties were involved in these dramatic presentations, mainly in securing the requisite permission for them, which the chief of police was very reluctant to grant. Another difficulty was finding a suitable place. For a time a large barn was used, later on, a vacant factory loft. Under the German occupation and thereafter, dramatic presentations in Yiddish were given more frequently, with the dramas of Jacob Gordin enjoying great popularity.

Folkways

At the ceremony announcing the engagement of a couple to be married, plates were broken. After the engagement the bride and groom were invited to the houses of their future in-laws for a holiday or a weekend. On such occasions relatives and friends would send wine to the house entertaining the guest, with a greeting, "Welcome to your guest!" (*Mit lib aykh ayer gast.*)

Wedding festivities began on the Saturday night prior to the wedding. The bride's girl friends would gather in her house for dancing and merrymaking. This gathering was called the prelude (*forshpil*). The wedding proper commenced at dusk, with a reception for the bridegroom, in which, as a rule, the older people participated, and with the ceremony of "seating" the bride (*bazetsn*), at which the young folks danced. After the reception, the bridegroom was led to the house in which the bride was "seated," where he performed the ceremony of veiling the bride. If the bride was an orphan, a memorial prayer was recited for her deceased parents.

The wedding ceremony was usually performed in the synagogue courtyard. The bride and groom were led to the ceremony to the accompaniment of music. First, the musicians led the bridegroom under the canopy and afterwards the bride was brought. After the bridegroom pronounced the marriage formula and the appropriate benedictions were recited, the young couple were taken back to the house where the bride was "seated." At the entrance of the house the couple were met by someone holding a tray with wine and cake. Since both bride and groom fasted on their wedding day, they were taken into a separate room, where they were given a light repast.

After the ceremony the older folks sat down to the wedding supper. At the supper, the wedding gifts were announced by the sexton or the jester (*badkhn*) in the traditional formula: "A gift from the bride's [or groom's] relative!" The young people danced after the ceremony. When the elders finished their meal, the young folks had theirs and afterwards continued dancing.

On the following morning, the bridegroom served brandy and cake. On the Sabbath following the wedding, the traditional "seven benedictions" were pronounced three times: Friday night, Saturday morning, and Saturday afternoon. Saturday morning the bridegroom was led by a group of men to the synagogue. The bride was similarly led by a group of women. A bride and a lying-in woman were not permitted to be alone in the house or on the street. After the bride had been led to the synagogue and the lying-in woman had gone to religious services, the restriction was lifted. On the walls of the room in which there was a lying-in woman, talismans, known as *shir hamay-lesn,* after their opening words, were hung, containing psalm 121 and a number of incantations.

At the birth of a child, for the first seven days of confinement, the beginners in *kheyder* would come at sunset to the house of the lying-in woman and recite in unison several passages from the Bible, for which they were rewarded with sweets. If the newborn infant was a boy, a celebration called the *sholem zokher* was held on the Friday night following his birth, at which the guests were served boiled peas and broad beans. Some considered it particularly beneficial to have the child circumcised in the House of Study.

In case of death, the *Khevre Kadishe* was notified, and its representatives came and "lifted" the deceased, that is, strewed a little straw
on the floor and placed him with his feet at the door. The grave digger
was ordered to bring the coffin and dig the grave. Female members of
the *Khevre Kadishe* sewed the shrouds. The sexton was sent to call out
through the town, *"mes mitsve!"* implying that attendance at the
funeral was requested. While these preparations were going on, a
group of men would recite psalms in the house of the deceased. The
Khevre Kadishe then washed the body, dressed it in a shroud, placed it
in the coffin, covered it with a black cover, and carried it to the
cemetery. One of the members of the *Khevre Kadishe* descended into
the grave and put away the body, placed potsherds over the eyelids
and two forked twigs in the hands, and boards over the body.

On the eve of Sabbath or holidays the people were summoned to
the synagogue by the sexton. His summons served to indicate to the
women that it was time to kindle the Sabbath candles. As soon as his
powerful baritone voice was heard thundering, "To the synagogue!"
the tradeswomen quickly closed their shops and rushed home to usher
in the Sabbath. The people were also summoned to the synagogue
when a preacher came to deliver a discourse in the synagogue.

The women believed in the evil eye, which they greatly feared. If
a child was ill, particularly if it yawned, the mother immediately concluded that the child was given the evil eye. The only remedy for the
evil eye was exorcism. For that purpose the women had several Yiddish
incantations. One of them was, in translation:

> There are three cracks
> In the ceiling wide.
> There the child's evil eye
> Will depart and hide.

Another incantation was:

> Three women sit on a stone.
> One says: "The child has the evil eye."
> The other says: "No!"
> The third says: "Whence it came
> Thither it shall go."[1]

The incantation was followed by spitting three times.

---

[1] This incantation is reminiscent of one of the oldest German incantations and
is frequent in the folklore of many peoples. See K. Müllenhoff and W. Scherer,
Denkmäler deutscher Poesie und Prosa aus dem VIII-XII Jahrhundert, Berlin,
1892, I, p. 15.

Daily Fare

Like every other town, Swisłocz, too, had a nickname: *sislevicher krupnik.* The town fully deserved that nickname. For there was not a day, except the Sabbath and the holidays, when *krupnik* was not on the menu of every jewish home in town. What is *krupnik?* It is a thick soup of barley or groats mixed with potatoes. In the winter time, when meat was cheap, a slice of lamb or veal was added to the mixture. In the summer time, when meat was expensive, only the wealthy could afford to season their *krupnik* with meat. The average population had to be content with a little beef fat in their *krupnik,* to which onions were added as a preservative.

For the Friday breakfast the *krupnik* was prepared differently, as a rule with stuffed gut. It was eaten with fresh rolls, which nearly all Jewish women baked on Friday. Friday was also graced with potato pudding. Advantage was taken of the fact that the oven was kindled for the baking of Sabbath bread (*khale*). Some families had potato pudding twice on Friday.

Another popular dish was *lekshlekh bulve,* peeled potatoes, thinly sliced and boiled with meat. The dish was prepared in the morning, placed in the oven, and eaten for lunch or for supper. Likewise popular were potatoes boiled in their jackets (*sholekhts bulve*). The wealthy ate the potatoes with herring; the rest of the population, with herring sauce. On the whole, potatoes were a staple in the diet of our district, both among Jews and non-Jews. It was not without a measure of justification that the district of Grodno was known in Russia as "the Grodno potato."

II. ECONOMIC ASPECTS

Occupationally, the Jews of the town were divided, in the main, into three categories: leather manufacturers and workers, merchants, and artisans.

The Leather Industry

The leather factories were the backbone of the Jewish economic life in town. Some 70% of the Jewish population were directly or indirectly connected with the leather industry. Its beginnings date from the 1870's, when Pinkhes Bereznitski opened a factory, in charge of a

German master craftsman. Thereafter a number of other Jewish employers established factories. From 1900 to the German occupation (1915), the leather industry was the decisive factor in the general economic life of the town. At the beginning of this century the town numbered eight leather factories employing between forty and fifty workers each, and a dozen or so smaller shops employing from six to twelve workers.

The factories were divided into wet tanneries and dry shops. They produced leather from horse hides, which was used in the making of leggings and uppers for shoes and boots. The process of converting a raw hide into leather took about three months. The hide was taken into the wet tannery, soaked, scoured, and set out ready for the dry factory. These several steps took some ten weeks. In the wet tanneries the work was mainly unskilled, and most of the workingmen were non-Jews. In the dry factories it took another three weeks or so to curry, grain, wash, and otherwise make the leather ready for the use of the cobbler. Here the work was entirely skilled, and most of the workers were Jews. The work in both the wet tannery and the dry shop was done without machinery. It was hard work, the lighter tasks being performed by boys fourteen or fifteen years old. The big employers owned both wet tanneries and dry shops. The capital invested in such an enterprise was from twenty to forty thousand rubles. The business was conducted in a modern way. The raw hides were purchased in Białystok with payments by drafts made out to a Białystok bank. The leather was sent by freight to the leather merchants and the receipts for it were discounted in the Białystok banks.

Practically all the manufacturers had to resort in part to borrowed capital to operate their businesses. Some capital they obtained in the banks and some from private individuals on promissory notes. The interest private people charged on such loans ranged from eight to ten per cent. Every big employer went once a week to Białystok to purchase raw hides and to settle his accounts with his banker. The smaller operators had no wet tanneries. They purchased half-finished hides in town or in nearby towns and finished them. The capital involved in such a business was between two and three thousand rubles.

The finished product was sold to merchants all over Russia. The biggest customers were the merchants in Poland. The transactions were negotiated chiefly by mail. The town had several brokers who took commissions from merchants out of town. They purchased the merchandise and supervised its packing and shipment. From time to time the out-of-town merchants would come to town and their brokers would accompany them to the factories.

Earnings of factory workers were good. From 1904 to 1908 earnings were the highest. An apprentice earned from two to four rubles a week; a semi-skilled worker, from eight to twelve rubles; skilled workers, from sixteen to twenty-five rubles. In 1908 and 1909 earnings declined about one-third. This lower level of earnings obtained up to the first World War. From 1904 to the first World War the working-day was eight hours: from eight o'clock to twelve o'clock and from one o'clock to five o'clock, with the exception of Friday, when the workers quit at three. Jewish workingmen did not work on Saturdays. Since the workers in the leather industry earned good wages, their standard of living was comparatively high. They were well-fed, well-clothed, and contributed freely to many a charitable cause. Frequently they extended loans of small amounts to hard-pressed merchants.

Merchants

There were some sixty stores in town, mostly small establishments, whose stock was worth fifty to a hundred rubles. Some of them, a dozen or so, were operated by women, with the husbands engaged in another occupation, such as tailoring, bricklaying, and the like. However, most of the merchants drew their entire sustenance from their stores. A few stores there were whose stock was valued at ten thousand rubles. These enjoyed the patronage of the landowners, officials, and leather manufacturers.

The big merchants took several business trips in the course of the year to Białystok or Warsaw, where they purchased some of their stock. Otherwise, they purchased what they needed through a kind of commission merchant who did a two-way business. These commission merchants bought in town such farm products as butter, eggs, mushrooms, and the like and shipped them to Białystok on hired peasants' carts, usually on a Monday. Simultaneously, they took from the merchants in town orders for their immediate needs. On Tuesday mornings they would leave by train for Białystok, attend to the orders given them, and sell the farm products that had in the meantime arrived in the city. On Thursday they would dispatch the carts back to town laden with merchandise and then go home the same evening by train. There, usually with the aid of wife and children, they delivered the merchandise to those who ordered it. Several of the more enterprising commissioners purchased some wares on their own account and sold them later on to the local business people.

Up to 1898 there were in town a dozen or so tavern keepers. After 1898, when the sale of liquor became a state monopoly, there were no more Jewish taverns. Several Jews obtained a license for a beer-hall (*raspivochno*), where bottled beer, tea, and a light bite were sold. Several Jews were grain dealers, buying from the landowners and the rich peasants. Part of the grain they ground to flour and sold it to the bakers, and part of it they sold to wholesale merchants.

The district around the town abounded in forests; some were state owned and others the property of Polish landowners. (The Białowież forest, the property of the Czar, was a distance of fourteen verst from town.) A number of Jews were engaged in the timber business, some of them on a very large scale. The big timber merchants employed managers to supervise the work; the small merchants, who bought strips of forests (*otdelianka*), usually did all the work themselves. Occasionally, two or three small merchants formed a partnership. The better types of logs were floated down the Narew to the saw mills or to Germany. The others were used for railway ties. Defective logs were cut into fire-wood.

Artisans

There were two types of men's tailors in town: those that catered to the town's trade and those that worked for the peasants in the vicinity. The former were generally proficient in their trade and comparatively well-paid. Frequently, they employed two or three apprentices. The latter were less fortunate. In the summer time, when the peasants were busy in the fields, the tailors depending on them for work had a slack season. They had to resort to supplementary occupations, such as orchard-keeping and selling the fruit. (The latter was usually the task of the wife.) Even in the winter time, when these tailors were fully employed, their earnings were meager. The materials they received from the peasants were home-made rough cloth, or sheepskins for coats. These materials could not be sewn by machine, but had to be, for the most part, stitched by hand.

The town had several women's tailors. Some of them employed one or two apprentice seamstresses. These tailors sewed bridal wardrobes, ladies' coats, or worked on orders for the wives of the landowners. They were proficient and well paid. There were, furthermore, a few seamstresses who sewed blouses and skirts for the town women. Other women sewed blouses or jackets (*kurtka*) for the peasant women. The remuneration for this work was very low: twenty or twenty-five kopeks per blouse. In addition, a few women were engaged in sewing underwear, pillowcases, and the like.

The shoemakers catered almost exclusively to the town population. Because the peasant went barefooted in the summer time, a pair of boots lasted many years. The shoemakers made their wares to order. The uppers were cut according to measurement by the cutter (*zagotovshchik*). The soles, shanks, and heels were purchased in a store. The well-to-do shoemakers would purchase these supplies in larger quantities, and the poor, for each pair of shoes individually. A few wealthy shoemakers purchased leather for both uppers and soles in large quantities. These shoemakers employed several apprentices. During slack times, when orders were few, they kept on working, preparing a stock of shoes, and selling them later on, in the busy time, such as the preholiday season. Before the first World War, two merchants began to import shoes from Warsaw. The local shoemakers saw in this step a threat to their existence. They banded together and declared a boycott on the imported shoes: they refused to repair them. Some of the shoemakers were truly masters of their trade. They made a pair of shoes that vied in attractiveness with any displayed in the stores of the large cities.

There were several joiners in town. Their season was in the summer, when new homes were being built. They finished the wood work in the houses. In the winter time, they took to cabinetmaking, producing chiefly inexpensive household furniture and the wooden furnishings for the leather factories. Expensive furniture was imported from Białystok.

The few blacksmiths in town catered, in the main, to the village population. They put rims on wheels, hammered out plows, and sharpened scythes. In the winter time, work fell off. It was practically limited to putting iron runners on sleds or shoeing horses. Some blacksmiths would purchase wheels in the winter time, put rims on them and sell the finished wheels in the summer, when there was great demand for them.

The town had eleven bakers. Two baked black bread, four baked both black and white bread, rolls, and *khale* for the Sabbath. Five baked cake, cracknels, and pastries.

The town also had a number of Jews without a definite occupation, shifting from one calling to another, or engaging simultaneously in two callings or more. Thus, such a man would own one or two cows and sell milk, bake bread for sale, fatten geese, and bake matza for Passover. These tasks were carried out by the women. The men would go to the market, buy a measure or two of grain, and resell it to an export merchant. In the winter time, some of them would buy a calf or a lamb, have it slaughtered and sell the skin and the meat, retaining the head and the legs and other minor parts. Others would buy from the peasants skins of foxes and martens, wool, bristles, mushrooms, and berries, and resell them to export merchants.

These Jews without a definite calling were indirectly engaged in agriculture. The Jews who kept cows or horses had manure. The peasants in the vicinity were always short of manure. Those who owned fields near the town would sublet a strip of land for two years to a Jew who had manure. The Jew would hire laborers to strew the manure on the field and to plant potatoes. The following year, he would plant barley, oats, or buckwheat. On the third year the field was returned to the peasant in a fertile state, ready for planting rye. The Jew, in turn, would have enough potatoes and barley, or any other cereal planted, for his use, and even a small quantity for sale. The straw, chaff, and very small potatoes served as food for the cattle.

An Attempt at Statistics

Knowing the town well, its streets, houses, occupants, and their calling, I traversed, in memory, the entire town, house by house, street by street, and recorded the callings of the people. I did the same with the factories. Here, however, the task was more complicated. In a factory with several dozen employees, it is difficult, according to my system, to indicate the number of workers with absolute accuracy. It is especially difficult in the case of the assistants and apprentices. Figures for them as well as for the factory workers are approximate. From 1902 to 1914 the number of artisans did not change. The following table covers that period.

TABLE 1

Artisans and Apprentices

OCCUPATION	ARTISANS		ASSISTANTS AND APPRENTICES	
	JEWS	NON-JEWS	JEWS	NON-JEWS
Shoemakers.......	22	4	3	14 [2]
Men's Tailors....	12	—	9 [3]	1
Women's Tailors..[4]	4	—	12	2
Joiners..........	9	1	6 [5]	1
Blacksmiths......	9	2	1	1
Coppersmiths.....	2	—	—	—
Tinsmiths........	2	—	—	—
Shoe-Stitchers...	3	—	2	—
Bookbinders......	3	—	—	—
Bricklayers......	4	—	—	—
Dyers...........[6]	5	—	—	—
Harness-Makers...	3	—	—	—
Glaziers.........	2	—	—	—
Carpenters......[7]	4	— [8]	—	—
Bakers..........	11	—	1	—
Watchmakers......	2	—	1	—
Capmakers.......[9]	4	—	—	—
Locksmiths.......	1	1	—	—
Potters.........[10]	1	1	—	—
TOTAL	103	9	35	19

When we compare the figures for Jewish artisans, assistants, and apprentices with those for non-Jews we are struck by the disparity in one aspect. For 103 Jewish artisans there were 35 assistants and apprentices, that is about one Jewish assistant or apprentice to three

[2] All non-Jewish assistants and apprentices were in Jewish shops.
[3] Several of them were the children of the owners.
[4] All but one were women.
[5] Several of them were the children of the owners.
[6] They dyed the home-made yarn, spun by peasants from flax and wool. Two of them had machines for carding wool.
[7] They built new frame houses and shingled roofs.
[8] There were several non-Jewish carpenters whose number I don't know.
[9] They used to make fur caps and hats, with the entire family helping.
[10] They made earthen and glazed vessels.

Jewish artisans, whereas for every non-Jewish artisan there were two non-Jewish assistants or apprentices. Why was the number of Jewish artisans' assistants and apprentices so small? The Jewish youth was attracted by the leather factories. As an apprentice, he had to work the first year for a very low remuneration and, occasionally, without remuneration. In the factory he received seventy-five kopeks a week as a beginner and after six or eight months, two rubles a week and even more. The effects of the disparity in the numbers of Jewish and non-Jewish artisans' assistants and apprentices became manifest later on. The number of Jewish artisans began to decline and that of non-Jews to rise, as is shown in the following table.

TABLE 2
Jewish and Non-Jewish Artisans

OCCUPATION	1902 — 1914		1919 — 1920	
	JEWISH ARTISANS	NON-JEWISH ARTISANS	JEWISH ARTISANS	NON-JEWISH ARTISANS
Shoemakers........	22	4	12	9
Men's Tailors.....	12	—	9	1
Women's Tailors...	4	—	1	—
Joiners..........	9	2	7	3
Blacksmiths......	9	1	6	1
TOTAL	56	7	35	14

In 1919-20, the number of Jewish artisans in the categories under consideration declined by 37.5%, whereas that of the non-Jews increased 100%. In 1902-14, the Jews comprised 88.9% of these occupations and in 1919-20 only 71.5%. Particularly great was the decrease in the number of Jewish shoemakers. In 1919-20 their number declined 45.5%, whereas the number of non-Jewish shoemakers rose from four to nine.

Strikes and Lockouts

Up to the turn of the century, working conditions in the leather industry were very bad. The working-day was fourteen or fifteen hours and even more; wages were very low. Gradually, conditions improved. The number of factories increased and some of the smaller establishments expanded. More workers were needed, and wages rose. The higher wages attracted a number of young people from well-to-do homes, who deemed it below their dignity to become artisans. (These usually entered the more specialized branches of the trade, such as trimming and cutting, which were better paid.) Also young people from the vicinity came to work in the leather factories.

At about that time, a branch of the "Bund" was in the process of formation. In 1900-1901 the "Bund" called the first strike in the leather factories in town. Members of the organization assembled a large number of workers and together they formulated their demands. These included a raise of wages, and a twelve-hour working-day, from seven in the morning to seven in the evening, with an intermission of one and a half hours for breakfast and one hour for lunch. Thereafter, a general assembly of the workers was called, at which these demands were discussed. A strike committee was appointed and a resolution adopted that no one should resume work until all demands were granted by the factory owners. This resolution was confirmed by an oath taken on a pair of phylacteries by each worker.

When the strike committee presented the demands to the factory owners, the latter remained unimpressed. They were inclined to regard the entire affair as a boyish prank. On the following day, however, when not a single worker reported for work, the factory owners began to take a serious view of the strike. They attempted to break the solidarity of the workers by promising higher wages to the older workers. Some of these workers remained unmoved by the tempting offers. In the case of others, the oath on the phylacteries acted as a powerful deterrent. The strike lasted only a short time and ended in the complete victory of the workers. The factory owners granted fully their demands.

A second general strike in the leather factories took place in the summer of 1904. This was during the Russo-Japanese war, when the profits of the factory owners were high and the cost of living had gone up. The "Bund" was by that time firmly entrenched in town, conducting systematic organizational and educational activities among the workers. It was therefore no difficult task to call the strike. The "Bund" called a general assembly of leather workers in a forest, Vishnik, one verst and a half distant from town. To impress the assembled, a speaker from the neighboring town of Wołkowysk was invited. The speaker presented the demands formulated by the "Bund" to the assembled for their approval. These demands were: 1) a raise of about 35% in wages; 2) a working-day of nine hours, from eight to five;

3) tenure of job, that is, no worker was to be discharged without sufficient cause; 4) medical aid: the employer was to pay the medical bills of the ill employee.

That evening the demands were presented to the factory owners. They were ready to negotiate a reduction in working hours and a raise of wages, but would not consider the other two demands. They were particularly incensed by the demand for tenure of job, which to them appeared highly arbitrary. The strike committee refused to negotiate their demands piecemeal, and a strike was called. It lasted three weeks and again ended in a victory for the workers. The newly acquired working conditions were in effect till the end of 1907. The period 1904-1907 came to be regarded as the good years of the workers in the leather industry.

The political reaction, which set in after 1905, began to show its effects also in the economic sphere. The attitude of the employer to the employee changed. In November, 1907, the factory owners called a general assembly of their workers and put before them the following conditions: 1) a reduction of 35-40% in wages; 2) discontinuance of medical aid; 3) abolition of tenure of job. Refusal to accept these conditions, they threatened, would be answered with the closure of all factories. The workers rejected these conditions and countered with a strike. Although the "Bund" was then considerably weakened, it took over the direction of the strike.

In the first weeks of the strike it became evident that the developments had more than a local character. The leather factory owners of the entire district were anxious for a victory of their fellows, in which instance they would follow suit and put before their workers similar conditions. On the other hand, the workers of the entire region were hoping for the success of the strikers in Swisłocz. The Tanners Union of the district sent a professional organizer to advise and guide the strikers. He was an energetic young man and an eloquent orator, who inspired confidence. He also traveled throughout the district to collect funds for the strikers. The Tanners Union also enlisted the interests of the union in the district of Vilna and there, too, collections were made for the benefit of the Swisłocz strikers.

Most of the strikers did not require aid. Before the strike, they had earned decent wages and had managed to accumulate some savings. A few of them, the less skilled workers, whose earnings were considerably lower, were in need of aid. These were given one and a half rubles per week, if single, and three rubles, if married. To keep up the spirit of the strikers, daily meetings were necessary. Since it was in the winter time, and assemblies in the open were impossible, the strikers met daily, with the exception of Saturday, in the House of Study. The trustees of the House of Study raised no objection; the majority of the Jewish population was in sympathy with the strikers.

There were at first no difficulties with the police. At the time of the strike the chief of police was a quiet and liberal man. He gave assurance that as long as the strike was conducted peacefully, he would not interfere. It was difficult, however, to conduct the strike peacefully, and a clash between the strikers and the police occurred. The strikers had pinned their hope on the factory owners' need for money to cover their outstanding notes. When these notes became due, the factory owners decided to raise cash through the sale of half-finished leather. This transaction led to the clash. In the seventh or eighth week of the strike, the strikers were told that a factory was shipping half-finished leather to other towns. A group of strikers left for the factory to prevent the loading of the leather. At the entrance to the factory yard several policemen posted there denied entry to the strikers. When the latter attempted to force their way into the yard, the police fired a salvo in the air. The strikers retired and marched to the homes of the factory owners, demanding that the police be withdrawn from the factories. In the altercation that ensued, a factory owner was beaten up. The chief of police took a grave view of the situation and called for soldiers to patrol the streets. Tension mounted steadily. The organ of the Tanners Union printed a letter from Swisłocz reporting that the police had fired on the strikers. It was sued for spreading false rumors. However, strikers from Swisłocz testified in defense of the organ.

Fortunately, the strikers' committee kept cool heads. An ultimatum was presented to the factory owners to effect a withdrawal of the police and the military from the factories and the streets, or they would bear the responsibility for the consequences. Soon the police and military were recalled, and the strike again assumed a peaceful character.

On one occasion the factory owners succeeded in shipping half-finished goods. But the strike committee, which maintained connections with the railway workers, was informed of the destination of these goods. At the request of the committee, the workers of the town to which the goods were shipped refused to work on them. This solidarity of the workers discouraged the manufacturers of neighboring towns from buying half-finished goods in Swisłocz.

The strike continued into the ninth and tenth week. Some strikers began to feel discouraged. At the meetings of the strikers in the House of Study demands were made for opening negotiations with the owners. The strike committee decided to call a conference of the Tanners Union of the Białystok and Vilna districts. The conference met in Swisłocz in the twelfth week of the strike. (The chief of police might have known of the conference, for it met in the neighborhood of his office.) It lasted two or three days and was attended by delegates from a number of towns. After prolonged discussions, it was decided to continue the strike. Following the conference, a general meeting of the strikers was called at the House of Study. Several delegates addressed the strikers, moving the audience to tears.

When the strike entered its fifteenth week, the spirits of the workers flagged. Aid from the neighboring towns came irregularly. The Passover festival was approaching, and the needs of the strikers were great. The demands for a settlement became more urgent. The factory owners, too, were in a conciliatory mood. A week later the strike was settled with a compromise on wages. The workers won on the other points.

Essentially, however, both sides lost: the workers, sixteen weeks' wages; the factory owners, the loss of production and, above all, the loss of markets. During the strike, some of the merchants who had formerly bought their leather in Swisłocz sought out other sources of supply and retained these connections even after the strike was over. In fine, several factories closed and the others sustained heavy losses.

The Leather Industry from 1908 to 1919

A few weeks after the strike, the factory owners renewed their demands for the abolition of tenure of job under the threat of a new lockout. When the workers refused their demands, they carried out their threat. The "Bund" was then in a weakened condition and the workers were exhausted by the previous prolonged strike. After three weeks of the lockout, the workers capitulated and accepted all the demands of the owners.

The workers were quite demoralized. Since several factories had closed, a number of them were unemployed. Furthermore, the large factories began selling their product in half-finished form. This meant that the workers in the dry factories were left without work. Dry factories that had previously employed forty and fifty workers reduced that number to fifteen or ten. In these factories the percentage of Jewish employees was very high, and the growing unemployment affected chiefly the Jewish workers.

Some of the unemployed workers opened their own shops. Two workers·would usually go into business in partnership. The amount of capital required for such enterprise was not large. For about two thousand rubles they could rent a shop, hire a couple of workers, buy a quantity of half-finished leather and finish it. The small shops paid lower wages than the factories. Thus, a worker who had received before the strike some sixteen rubles a week in the factory, was paid for the same work in the small shop ten or nine rubles. Even at their best these small shops could give employment to only a small fraction of those who were out of work. A large number of workers decided on immigration to the United States and Canada.

The depression continued up to 1911. Then conditions improved slightly. In 1911-12, the "Bund" regained some of its former strength and renewed its activities. Its members helped in the organization of strikes in the smaller shops. From that time to the first World War conditions in the leather industry were fair. The first year of World War I was a boom year, with every worker employed.

Toward the end of the summer of 1915, the German armies entered Swisłocz. During the German occupation trade in leather was forbidden. At the end of 1918, when the Germans left town, a few factory owners resumed operations on a small scale. The source of supply of hides was limited and the demand for the finished product even more so. Swisłocz was cut off from Russia, previously the main market for leather. To meet the demands of the local market, several small shops began producing fine leather from calf skins. On the whole, however, the leather industry, the backbone of Jewish economic life in Swisłocz, never regained its former position.

Strikes in Artisans' Shops

There were practically no strikes in the artisans' shops, which as a rule employed few outside hands. Joiners, blacksmiths, and bakers worked alone with their children. The few tailors and shoemakers who employed outside help usually granted the demands of their employees and avoided strikes. Some recalcitrance was shown by the women's tailors. They employed young girls between fourteen and twenty years old. In season they worked from eight in the morning to ten in the evening, and even later than that. In 1901 and 1902 a demand was put forth for a regular working-day of twelve hours. The employers refused this demand and the girls were too timid to strike. As an act of solidarity the young leather workers notified the tailors that unless regular working hours were introduced the windows of their shops would be smashed. They carried out their threat, and the tailors yielded.

Emigration

Up to the turn of the century few Jews emigrated from our town. In 1896, several families left for Argentina to settle in the colonies of Baron de Hirsch. In the beginning of the present century there was a slight rise in emigration. After the depression resulting from the strike in 1908, the tempo of emigration quickened, with England, the United States, and Canada as destination. In 1916, under the German occupation, several groups of women went to America. Emigration assumed mass proportions after the first World War, chiefly to the United States. There was also considerable emigration to Canada, Palestine, and Argentina.

A KHEYDER IN TYSZOWCE (TISHEVITS)

By Yekhiel Shtern

Originally published in the author's *Kheyder un beys-medresh* (New York, Yivo, 1950)

The Appearance of the Kheyder

My *rebbe's* elementary school (*dardeki kheyder*) was called "*Gershon melamed's dardeki kheyder*," after the name of my teacher, Gershon. It stood across the *beys-medresh* on the west, an old decrepit little house whose walls caved inward at the roof. The old kheyder building sloped up-hill from north to south and joined at the rotting and moss-covered shingled roof with another little house that stood entirely on the hill. The rain would pour down from the roof of this other house upon our kheydr and then descend with violent downpour from our roof, making a long ditch alongside the north wall of the kheyder. In this ditch the school children would dance around in the summer time and beat back with the palms of their hands the long streams of rain coming down from the roof top.

We also would throw pebbles on the roof of the adjoining house and wait tensely for them to roll down on the roof of our kheyder, while we stood with outstretched hands ready to catch them. On more than one occasion this prank would end with the breaking of a small pane in the windows on the north wall. We would then get our due from the teacher. The teacher's wife would stuff up the open space with a rag or a small pillow. The glazier of the town, Isaac the deaf, had plenty of work to do, patching up the broken panes with pieces of glass.

On the outside of the windows there were heavy shutters, painted blue. They were covered with various carved figures and flowers and other decorations in baroque style. The school children would also play with these shutters, particularly in the summer mornings when the teacher was still in the synagogue. We would open and close the shutters and often break a window pane in doing so. All the

51

panes in the windows, therefore, were full of patches of different pieces of glass and we used to get a thrill out of listening to their clatter and rattle during a thunder storm. They would provide a real concert when the teacher would rap on the window with his pointer summoning the children outside to come in to class. The din of their clatter would only increase the fear we had of the teacher.

Near the east and north sides of the kheyder was a sort of fence, made up of several tall posts set into the ground. Placed across them lengthwise were two round beams which were joined together at right angles. There were always children roosting on this fence. The school boys would seat themselves in a row one behind the other. They would kick their legs, as when riding a horse, clap their hands on the beam and shout "gee-up," calling out all sort of names of horses at the same time. The more the shirt tails beat around the sides, and the earlocks blew in the wind, the more we jogged up and down, shouted still louder and were sure we were really riding.

On the other end of the fence we would turn somersaults, twine ourselves around the beam and turn around and around several times. The fence was rarely quiet. More than once we would tussle for a place on the beam and the teacher would have to end the fight. He would start tapping his pointer on the window pane and the gang would scatter in all directions.

There were two doors to the kheyder. One on the north, made of panes, was boarded up all winter and stopped up with straw. It was opened up only in the summer. The second door, on the south, led to a hallway. This door was never at rest. It always closed with a bang, so the boys would always open and close it and enjoy the rattling of the patched-up window panes caused by the banging of the door. This was only a winter sport. During the summer we would stop in the hallway in the early morning and listen to the sounds of the birds nesting in the attic. Some of the boys had a secret desire to clamber up to the attic to the birds but they never dared do it in the presence of the rest of the children because we were all sure that these were not birds but disguised souls or angels singing praises to God.

There were two doors from the hall, one on the west off to the right and the other east off to the left. On the right there was only the opening for a door, which led to the ruins of a house, four walls minus a roof, joined by two of its walls to the west wall of the kheyder. This was an unfinished house in which were stored stone and wooden tombstones. The teacher's son was a tomb-stone engraver and he would do his work here. The place was always full of youngsters who would follow the work of the engraver with curiosity and then try to imitate him by drawing with chalk on the walls either hands in the position of the priestly benediction or other figures found on tomb-stones. When the engraver was not present the boys would practice climbing on the stones.

The proximity of the tomb-stones to the kheyder gave rise to fantastic tales about ghosts and migrating souls. No one dared venture into the ruins at night. During the winter we had classes at night and we were afraid to go through the hall because of the tomb-stones. The reflection through the door of a white and snow-covered stone seemed certain to be a ghost in shrouds. The teacher, therefore, would lead the children out through the hall.

So much for the exterior of the kheyder.

The inside consisted of a large square room divided in two by a screen. Behind the screen was the teacher's bedroom and kitchen. We used to call it "the teacher's alcove." Over the opening of the alcove hung a red sheet covered with countless white dots. We would wrap ourselves in this sheet and play hide-and-seek. During the winter, at twilight, when the teacher and his helpers were in the synagogue and the schoolboys who studied at night were alone, this sheet was converted into a *tales* (praying shawl), and would-be magicians wrapped themselves around in it and imitated the cantor in the synagogue.

Through the second door-opening in the same screen one could see the dark kitchen with the rusty chimney-stove, full of dishes and kitchen furniture. There was alo a big belly-front buffet on which the youngsters would clamber. The room was always full of curious children who watched the teacher's wife putter around in the kitchen.

At the west wall, between the opening to the kitchen and the hall door, stood a big, wooden, closed alcove. It was a sort of pantry and the teacher's wife was always either taking something out of it and carrying it to the kitchen or bringing something back to it from the kitchen. We always watched her open and close it and almost every school-boy knew every piece of kitchenware she owned.

On the alcove were piled up old torn prayer books and Bibles which the teacher and his helpers would take down for class. In the corner near the same wall and not far from the door which led to the hall stood a large barrel of water and near it on a bench a big brass can. On the ground near the barrel stood a large wooden trough with two handles.

In this trough would be collected the left-overs of the children's meals, all kinds of paper which the children would throw into it, also the water from the brass can which the children used for drinking. This corner was always wet and slimy. Near the north wall stood a long wooden bench. During the winter the children would draw figures on it or play *"iks-miks-driks."* Behind the bench was a combination bench-bed, which served as a bench during the day and as a bed at night. The teacher would sit on a little pillow on this bench-bed, wearing a vest but no jacket and a skull cap on his head. He would set his twisted pointer into the prayer book or the Bible used by the children, who were seated near him on a long bench at the table along the east wall. At the other end of this table, which went all along the east wall, was a helper who taught another group of children. The east wall came to an end with the glass door which was used only during the summer.

The kheyder was as noisy as a fair, especially during the winter. The children ran around from one place to another; some would sit on the ground, clap their hands and sing: *"Joshe, Toshe, hentelekh! Di name vet brengen kikhelekh, ah—aw!"* Others just brawled or fought with each other and made a racket. Near the teacher on the bench-bed there would always be a new "little infant," brought to school for the first day and crying bitterly. The din was made all the greater by the slamming of the door which the children would open and close with a bang. The bedlam was particularly great when a beggar would come in. (The kheyder also served as a sort of lodging-house for wandering beggars.) The youngsters would surround him, help him unpack his bundle, count the lumps of sugar which he had collected going from door to door in the town. From amidst the uproar one could hear several children's voices, repeating in a sweet, sorrowful chant their reading lesson or the Bible: *"Aw, Baw, Gaw"* or *"Vayoymer*—and he said." When the noise became too great the helper would swish his rod in the air and the children, trembling and sobbing, would seat themselves on the floor and sit quietly for a few minutes, only to increase the uproar later. One can imagine what went on when one considers that there were 70-80 children in such a kheyder.

STAGES OF STUDY IN THE KHEYDER

The child's life became bound up with the kheyder from the day of his birth. The *Shir hamaalot* amulets, which were pasted up in the room of a mother in child-birth, were purchased from the teacher of the kheyder. On the seventh day after birth the helper would bring the school children, after class, to the home of the new-born and there read the *Shema* with them. For the ritual of circumcision a special kind of honey cake, called *reshete*, was prepared. This *reshete* was brought to the teacher before baking and the teacher would mark out on the dough the form of a little fish and the words *Mazl tov*. He also would make a lot of little holes over the whole cake. That is why it was called *reshete*, which means a sort of iron sieve. The little fish was supposed to indicate that Jews were to multiply like fish.*

When a boy became three years old, his parents would wrap him in a *tales* and bring him to the kheyder. The children in the kheyder would stand around, look at him and wait for candy or cookies that the parents would distribute. The teacher's wife would come in and wish the parents of the child "that he should be eager to learn." The teacher would then take the child to the table and show him the alphabet printed in large letters on the first page of the prayer book. The teacher would point out the letters ת מ, א, י, ד, ש; then he would combine them in the words " שדי אמת " (the Lord is truth) and the child would repeat it after the teacher. After class the teacher would let a coin drop on the table from on high. The sound of the coin on the table would startle the new pupil and the teacher would say: "An angel threw this down for you so that you should be eager to learn."

The child would study the above-mentioned letters every day for two weeks. He would then proceed to the alphabet in regular order. He would learn first not the sounds of the letters but their names. Later he was taught to distinguish the letters with a dagesh from those without, like ת ,ת ;ב ,ב ;כ ,כ etc.

In teaching the letters the *rebbe* would try to bring home each letter by comparing it to something already known to the child. The א, for example, was compared to a water-carrier with two buckets; a ב to a little hut with an open wall; a ג to a soldier putting left

---

* This allusion to fish is derived from *Gen.* xlviii, 17, where the words וידגו לרוב were traditionally translated "to multiply like fish".—Ed.

forward to march; a ד to a hammer with a handle; a ה to a man crippled on one leg etc. In pointing out the letter the teacher would outline the contours of each letter with his pointer. (This only refers to printed letters; writing was not taught in the elementary school.)

The second stage in the teaching of reading was the so-called *"komets-alef."* The alphabet was taught to each child individually. The *"komets-alef"* was taught to groups of two or more children. The teacher pointed to the prayer book and pronounced the names of the vowel points: *komets, pasakh, segl,* etc., and the children repeated after him. The vowel points were introduced in the same way as the letters. A komets (⟍) was represented as a stick with a beard; a segel (⟍) as three true friends always together; a kholem (˙) as a soldier looking down from a brick building, etc.

After the children learned to know the names of the vowel points, they were taught to combine them with the letters, *i.e.* to create simple syllables. The teacher, pointing into the prayer book, would call out first and the children would repeat after him: *"komets alef, aw; komets beyz, baw;* etc."

The next step was the so-called half-syllable. This differed from the *"komets alef"* in that the children would read the simple syllables by themselves without first calling out the names of the letters and

CHANT USED IN TEACHING OF READING

vowel points. After this they proceeded to "complete syllables." Here they learned to pronounce the unvocalized letters at the end of a word, as for example the final letters in אמת or עבד . Next they were taught the "final letters," ך, ם, ן, ף, ץ.

When the pupils became well-versed in the technique of reading, they would read without the help of the teacher. He would only follow the reading with his pointer and help them with a difficult word. The last stage in the teaching of mechanical reading was to pronounce the sheva in the middle of the word. We called it "pronouncing the *sheyvey*." The sheva in the middle of a word was pronounced as a *tseyre*. When we arrived at this final stage the teacher would always observe the following preliminaries:

> When there is a '*sheyvey*' at the beginning of a word, what do you do with it?"

> You have to catch it.

> When there is a '*sheyvey*' in the middle of the word, what do you do with it?

> You have to jump over it!

Various parodies were invented on this, as for example, "When a gentile boy is standing at the beginning of the village, what do you do with him?" etc. This completed the process of learning mechanical reading and it lasted about three terms. After that the child studied the order of prayers and at the same time began the study of the Pentateuch. This was taught only to boys.

The girls, after mastering mechanical reading, would begin to study *"ivre taych"* from the *"Tsene urene."** There were a few girls together with the boys in the kheyder. Most girls attended a special "girls' kheyder" with a woman teacher.

The commencement of the study of the Pentateuch took on a special ceremonial character. The teacher would appoint three older boys who had already begun to study the Pentateuch to act as *"benchers"* (blessers). These *"benchers"* were taught by the teacher the blessings they were to pronounce over the "beginner" at the ceremonial occasion. At the same time the child was coached in the first several verses of *Leviticus* (known as *"Torat Kohanim,"* the law of the priests).

---

* The *Tsene urene* was the traditional Yiddish version of the Pentateuch which was used by Jewish women. The language was old Yiddish with a high percentage of German words. Hence the term *"ivre taytch,"* which originally meant a translation of the Hebrew into German—Ed.

Preparations for the ceremony lasted several weeks. The actual ritual was carried out in the following fashion: A table was set with honey cake, brandy, nuts and candles; here the teacher sat. To his right sat the father of the child and all around sat the other invited guests. The women, including the mother of the child, stood off at a distance and looked on with delight. In the very center of the table stood the guest of honor, clad in holiday clothes and adorned with watches and other jewelry borrowed for the occasion. Near the youngster stood the *"benchers"* and they placed their hands on his head. All the boys were covered by a *tales* (a symbol of "the Lord arched the mount over them like a tank," at the receiving the Torah at Mt. Sinai).

Teacher: Little boy, little boy, what are father and mother doing now?

Child: My father and mother are having a grand celebration now.

Teacher: Is it because you are beginning to study the Pentateuch that your father and mother are making the grand celebration?

Child: Yes, teacher, that is so, you guessed right.

Teacher: Would you first like to recite something of the Torah?

Child: Of course, that is what I was created for. Although I am not fit to recite any Torah, nevertheless I shall say a few words:

Teachers and friends: Why does the Torah start with a "Beyz", *Bereyshis,* and not with an Aleph? Because when the Lord created the world, he blessed it to have permanence. *"Beyz"* stands for *borukh* [blessed] and aleph stands for *orur* [cursed]. Had the Lord created the world with an aleph there would have been no people of Israel.

Teachers and friends! I would like to add a few words more. Why did God give the Torah to Moses and not to Abraham?

The *"benchers"*: Because then there were few Jews and in the days of Moses there were many Jews.

Child: You gave the answer of the Torah. I will give you the answer for a child. There was no need to give the Torah in Abraham's time because then the generation was not bad.

There is another answer: If God had given the Torah through Abraham then the Jews would have forgotten it in Egypt.

First *"bencher"*: Bend your head and I will bless you: "You shall have a wife with twelve curls and each curl shall contain the sanctity of the tribes."

Second *"bencher"*: Even though when Jacob blessed Ephraim and Menasseh half of the blessing was realized and half was not, since Ephraim and Menasseh are not counted among the twelve tribes, yet you should have all your blessings come true. As you wear the watches on your heart and as we hold our hands on your head, so shall these blessings come true.

Third *"bencher"*: May that which the first two wished you come true, but I will give you another blessing: May your life and the life of your family be as sweet as the fine fruits of a tree near a spring.

The assembled guests, silent until now, would then shout: *"Mazl Tov!"* The women would shower candy and nuts on the boys on the table. The *"benchers"* then would get down from the table and the youngster would seat himself near the teacher before an open Bible. The following dialogue would then ensue:

Teacher: What are you studying, little boy?

Child: The Pentateuch!

Teacher: What does Pentateuch mean?

Child: Five.

Teacher: Five what?

Child: Five books in the sacred Scriptures!

Teacher: What are their names?

Child: Genesis is one; Exodus, two; Leviticus, three; Numbers, four; Deuteronomy, five.

Teacher: Which do you study?

Child: I study the third.

Teacher: What is its name?

Child: *"Vayikro"* (*Leviticus*).

Teacher: What is the meaning of *"Vayikro"?*

Child: He called.

Teacher: Who called, the rooster on top of the stove?

Child: No, God called to Moses, to tell him the law of sacrifices.

Teacher: What is the law of sacrifices?

Child: A lamb that has a blemish is not to be sacrificed on the altar.

Teacher: What is a blemish?

Child: A lamb with a blind eye or a broken leg, is said to have a blemish.

Teacher: And a lamb with a blind foot or a broken eye, is that a blemish?

Child: No!

The child would then begin to read from the first chapter in *Leviticus* and translate word for word, from the beginning up to *"lirtsono."*

The dialogue of the *"benchers"* and also that between the teacher and the child all proceeded in a set chant. This would conclude the grand ceremony and the guests would then enjoy the brandy and special cookies prepared for the occasion.

After having gone through such a ceremony the pupil was called *"khumesh yingl"* (Bible student), and every week he was taught the first section of the weekly portion of the Pentateuch. The translation was taught word for word as *e.g. vayeshev* he sat, *Yaakob* —one who was called Jacob, *beerez*—in the land, etc.

Bible students were put together in groups of four or five. When the Bible student had become adept in translating words he was then initiated into translating phrases or sentences. During this stage he was also taught some of the legendary and homiletical comments on the verses he was studying. Most of these comments were derived from the commentary of Rashi. Here are a few such examples. "I will go down now and see whether they have done althogether according to the cry of it which has come until me." (*Gen.* xviii, 10) was first translated literally, then came the following interpretation: "The cry," whose cry is referred to? The cry of Lot's daughter. She had given a poor man a piece of bread, for which the men of Sodom stripped her naked, smeared her body with honey and laid her on the roof. Thereupon the bees came and stung her to death. This was done to her because it was forbidden in Sodom to help the poor. The Lord says here, therefore, "Like her cry that came up to me; what they did, thus will I annihilate them.*

---

* The traditional translation of the word *"Kalah"* in this verse was "to annihilate," instead of "altogether."—*Ed.*

Another example is the homily on *Gen.* xlviii, 7, "And as for me, when I came from Paddan Aram."

> And I, even though I am instructing you to bear my remains for burial from Egypt to Palestine, I did not do this with your mother Rachel. I buried her in the middle of the road, even though there was still some distance to the city, as it is written in [in *Gen.* xxxv, 16] "And there was still some way to come to Ephrath." But I was told to do it this way. When Nebuzaradan will drive the Jews into exile, they will go by mother Rachel's grave and weep and wail. Then mother Rachel will emerge from her grave and cry and plead to God, as it is said: "Rachel weeps for her children." A voice will then come forth from heaven and cry: "Rachel, hold back thine voice from crying, there is reward for thy deeds. A day will come and your children will return to their borders. A day will come when the Jews will return to Eretz Yisroel." Therefore, I beg of thee, have no ill-will against me, and bear me and bury me in the land of Canaan, so that I shall not have to go through the ordeal of rolling from Egypt to Eretz Yisroel. For when the Messiah comes all the dead outside Eretz Yisroel will have to roll through the earth to Eretz Yisroel in order to be resurrected!

Of particular interest were the homilies on the *Song of Songs,* studied before Passover, and the Akdamoth, studied before Shabuoth. The love dialogues in the *Song of Songs* were interpreted as conversations between God, the beloved shepherd of the Jews, and the congregation of Israel, the beloved and chosen people. The obvious meaning of the words was completely ignored. We only studied the first two chapters in the elementary school. The following is an example of the interpretation of the first several verses:

> *Shir*—a song, *hashirim*—of all songs. The song that King Solomon sang was more beautiful, better and bigger than all other songs. Another song may be holy; this song is holy of holies. Another song was sung by a prophet; this was sung by a prophet, son of a prophet, king, son of a king, sage, son of a sage, singer, son of a singer, a righteous son of a righteous father. *Asher*—which, the song that King Solomon sang, *lishlomo*—to God blessed be He, who is called *Shlomo,* because Shlomo stands for *melekh shehashalom shelo,* the peace of the whole world is his. Then the congregation of Israel in *golus* (exile) says: *halvai yishakeni,* would that he would kiss me, *mineshikot*—from the kisses, *pihu*—of his mouth, let him talk to me mouth to mouth, as he spoke to me at the revelation at Mt. Sinai. *Ki*—because, *tobim,* are better, *dodekha*—your friendship, *miyayin*—from good wine, your friendship in giving us the Torah is much better than good wine. . . .

The last stage of study in the elementary school was the study

of Rashi's commentary. First one studied single letters and then entire words.* When the pupil mastered the reading of the Rashi type
he was taught a few verses of Rashi at the beginning of each week's
Biblical portion.

In addition the pupils in the kheyder were taught the blessings
for different kinds of food and for natural phenomena. The helper
would teach these to the children during the summer time, early every
evening before the children were sent home from kheyder. He would
gather them in a circle around him and order them around in the
following manner:

Helper: What do you say for a thunder?
Children: Blessed art Thou O Lord our God, King of the
Universe whose power and might fill the Universe!
Helper: What do you say for an apple?
Children: ....who has created the fruit of the tree!
And so on for all other blessings.

Every Sabbath the helpers would take the children to the synagogue. They would seat them near the pulpit where the cantor
was chanting the prayers on the steps before the holy ark. At every
blessing the helpers would signal the children to say *Borukh hu,
borukh shemoy* (Blessed be He, blessed be His name) and *Amen.*
If you add to all this the *Moyde ani* which the helper would recite
with each child every morning, you have the full program of the
kheyder, the purpose of which was to prepare the Jewish child for
the Jewish religious way of life.

HOLIDAYS AND THE SCHOOL CHILDREN

The kheyder pupils celebrated all the national and religious
holidays together with the grown-ups. They were prepared for the
holidays in the kheyder.

Before Passover they were taught the "Four Questions," with
Yiddish translation and the mnemonic signs, given at the beginning of
the Haggadah, which indicate the procedure of the *seder* service . . .
The coming of Passover was in the air several weeks ahead of time
because of the study of these things.

A few days before Passover the inter-session period began. It

* The Rashi commentary in the conventional Hebrew Bible is printed in a different kind of type from the Biblical text. It is cursive type, and hence has to be
learned separately.—*Ed.*

lasted until the intermediate days of the holiday, when the new summer session began. The intermediate days of Passover and of Sukkoth were the days when new pupils were enrolled. A school term lasted half a year.

An important holiday in the kheyder was Lag Be-omer. We began to prepare for this day on Passover. The helpers and the older boys who could carve made bows out of elastic sticks, tying both ends with a string, and wooden arrows that looked like hooks. The children would buy the bows and arrows from the helpers. We had school only half a day on Lag Be-omer. In the afternoon we ran around through the town, shouting and vying with each other in shooting the arrows far or high.

Several days before Shabuoth the children began to cut rushes for the holiday. The day before Shabuoth there was no school and the entire day was taken up with this occupation. We carried the bundles of rushes home and decorated the floors. We arranged them into squares, triangles or stars of David.

For Simhat Torah we made flags in kheyder, for Hanukah, spinning tops, and for Purim, noise makers. Playing spinning tops went on during the entire winter.

Even the fast days were holidays for the children since there was no school on these days. Of special interest was the Fast of Ab. There was no school and we played the special game of throwing burrs at each other. For the Fast of Ab we made wooden pistols and swords in the kheyder. The pistols were shot off with caps.

GAMES IN AND AROUND THE KHEYDER

The kheyder pupil spent the greatest part of the day together with the other pupils without either the teacher or his helper. For every child was at the teacher's table only two or three times during the day and only for a few minutes each time. The rest of the time was taken up with play. All the child's vivacity and creative fantasy, which found little outlet during the studies and which was suppressed by the severe discipline of the kheyder, found free expression in these games.

All the walls, benches and everything in and around the kheyder that would take chalk were covered with all sorts of figures and images drawn by the children. The shell of a house that stood next to the kheyder swarmed with children in the summertime who clambered over the walls, rode hobby-horse on the tombstones, kicked around, shouted, imitated the neighing of horses and filled the air with children's voices. The open space between the kheyder and the *beys-medresh* was also full of children playing. Here one would find a group playing the game *sheli-shelokh* (mine and thine). They played it in this fashion. The children would line up in a row side by side and take each other's hand. One child would stand in front of the line and face the children. He was called the "prince." The children in line would say: "What does the prince want?" The prince: "The prince wants to go to the princess in the palace." The children: "We are the palace guards and let no one enter." The prince: "But I, the hero prince, unsheathe my sword and go in." The children: "We will fight to the last drop of blood." The prince, spitting into his hands and making ready to attack: "Here comes the prince for the first time." The children, to each other. "Stand firm, hold fast!" The prince then would rush at the row of children standing with locked hands, attempt to crash through, then go back to his palace. The children: "But we won!" The prince: "Here comes the prince again!" Both the children and the prince would repeat their previous lines. The prince: "Here comes the prince the third time!" This time the children would let him break through. The prince would run off, all the children chasing after him and whoever caught him became the prince for the next round of the game.

In another corner of the open space one could find children in groups of five playing *"beknbroyt."* Four children would stand in a square and one in the center would go from one child to the other and beg for *"beknbroyt."* Each child would answer: "In the next row," and point to another child in the other corner of the square. The one in the center would thus be sent around from one corner to the other, and at the same time the other children would change places with each other. The child in the center would then attempt to occupy one of the corner places before any of the others got to it and if he succeeded in doing so the child left out would then take his place in the center. The game, of course, depended on swiftness of movement . . . *

Some of the children would play *kichke-pale* (this game is

---

* This is like the game called "pussy wants a corner."—*Ed.*

called *chizhekes* in Polesie).* The *"kichke"* was the name given to a small peg pointed at both ends, the *"pale"* was the longer stick. The *"kichke"* was placed on a higher spot, near a hole made in the ground. The player would hit the pointed end of the peg with the larger stick and send the peg flying into the air. He would run and try to hit the peg while it was in the air and send it farther away from the plate. The more times one hit the peg, the better player he was. The other player would run to get the peg and throw it to the plate. The peg was not to be struck on the return to the plate. But if it was not returned to the plate the first player then would strike the peg wherever it happened to fall, without changing its position. This continued on until the second player got the peg back to the plate, after which he became the batter and the other the catcher. The game went on until one of the players scored a given number of hits of the peg, decided on in the beginning. The number was usually twenty or thirty. The loser would then have to give the winner what was called a *"yarsh."* This meant that the winner would have the right to strike the peg even when it was being returned to the plate. He would, therefore, keep his stick over the plate and hit it back if it came close to the plate. The *"yarsh"* would end when the peg fell on the plate. It was considered quite a humiliation to have to give a *"yarsh."*

There were many such active games at the kheyder. The most popular one was playing horses.

Every once in a while the teacher or his helper would call one of the players to the table. This would disrupt the game for a while, but it would soon be resumed with greater impetus. There was also a code of morality attached to the games. If any one was dishonest in the game the rest of the players would surround him and shout at him *"shekernik, shekernik"* (dishonest one). This kind of treatment we called *men peret im,* or *men drikt im di gal.* In other regions it was called *yaden.*** Such a culprit was excluded from the games.

There were also various oaths and maledictions associated with the games, as e.g. "I should live so" (*kh'zol azoy lebn*), "Upon my word" (*oyf mayne nemones*), *khay-adoyshem,* (by the life of God); *"akn, bakn, brotn, brenen, ver es vet opnarn, der vet lign in gehenem"*

---

* This is like the game called "peggy."—*Ed.*
** These are Yiddish expressions for berating the culprit.—*Ed.*

(ache, bake, broil and burn, he who is dishonest will go to Gehenna).
We would hold our *tsitsis* (fringes) in our hands while uttering
these oaths to seal the oath. We also had many counting-out rhymes to
determine who was "it" in the various games. These of course had
no meaning by themselves. There were two that were most frequently used. *"Eyns, tsvey, dray; lozer, loxer-lay; okn, bokn, beyner-
shtokn; onk, bonk, shtonk."* The second one was widespread
throughout Poland. It went like this: "A peasant (*goy*) rode off
to the woods; he broke the axle of his wagon, how many nails
must he have to fix the axle?" The child on whom the word axle
came out, had to answer with a number. Then the number was
counted out among the children and the one geting the last number
was "it."

There were also quieter games at the kheyder. Youngsters would
sit on the ground and make mud pies and bake them in the sun.
Some would make figures of cats and dogs out of soft bread. Others
would make a little garden for themselves, fence off a little plot
with sticks, make little furrows, dig little holes in the furrows and
fill them with water. When there was not enough water some of the
boys would urinate into the holes and get a great kick out of so doing.
If the teacher noticed it from the window, however, the whipping rod
would spoil the fun.

Among the quieter games should also be mentioned burying
the potato bug in the ground. These bugs would be buried in the
ground together with some coins so as to have a treasure grow there.

Most of the quieter games were played in the winter, when
the children were forced to remain indoors and active games were
not possible. The most popular game then was playing with but-
tons, which would often be torn from our own garments. Very popular
too were games with penknives. The blade of the knife would be
opened and allowed to fall to the floor. Before dropping the knife
the question would be asked if so and so were one's enemy, e.g. "Is
the teacher my enemy?" If the point of the blade remained stuck in
the floor then it meant that the person mentioned was an enemy.
If the knife fell back down on the floor it meant he was not an enemy.
There were also several gradations of enemies. If the blade remained
standing vertically in the floor it meant the person was a great
enemy, if it inclined it meant he was not completely hostile.

Another game common during the winter was called *"iks, miks,* *driks."* * This was played by two players. Two vertical lines were drawn on a board and crossed by two horizontal lines. The players would alternately put dashes and ciphers in the compartments formed by the lines. The object of the game was to get a row of three dashes or three ciphers before the adversary did. The first to get a row won the game and then was said to "rub the chin" of the loser. The winner would wipe off the board with the palm of his hand and then rub his palm over the chin of the loser, taunting him at the same time with the words: *"iks, miks, driks, fonye mit der biks."* ** There would always be onlookers at the game who would enjoy taunting the losers. Not infrequently a fight would ensue and the helper would have to restore order with his whipping-rod.

Another game that was popular was "goats and wolves." At Hanukah time all these games were crowded out by play with the spinning top (*dreydl*). Girls in the kheyder had their own games. They made mud pies, played "house," "kitchen," "bride and groom" and hopscotch. They would also dance around in a circle for hours while singing the popular folk-song, *"hak meser, brok messer, mir gut, dir is nokh beser."* *** The girls would also gather in groups and sing folk songs sung by their parents.

The account of all these games in the kheyder, made up by the children themselves, should do much to dispel the commonly accepted picture of Jewish school children as being prematurely adult and lacking the playful character of the normal child.

The fantasy of the child's mind was expressed also in the various superstitions and old-wives' tales that were circulated. Here are a few: If you point with your finger at the stars in the sky you must bite the finger. If you look at a mirror too much during the day, the image of the mirror comes to choke you at night. The same thing is done by the shadow of a person if you play with it too much during the day. If you annoy an orphan his deceased parents will come and drag you away to their grave at night. That is why the orphan was a privileged child in the kheyder. He would always threaten the other children with his deceased parents.

Childish fantasy also fed upon the host of stories and legends

---

* The equivalent of tick-tack-toe.—*Ed.*
** Iks, miks, driks, *fonye* with the gun. *Fonye* was a derisive term used by the Jews for Russian tsarist soldiers.—*Ed.*
*** "Chop knife, cut knife; I feel good, you feel still better."—*Ed.*

that were current and transmitted by word of mouth. Each narrator would add a bit from his own imagination. The stories were about God, Gehenna, the Garden of Eden, robbers, princesses, princes, water creatures, hidden treasures that could be discovered by magic or *kabala* or by burying in the earth a coin with a potato bug. The latter would discover the treasure underground and it would then grow up from the earth by itself.

DISCIPLINE IN THE KHEYDER

Discipline in the kheyder was severe, even brutal. Corporal punishment was used in all its forms. The lash was always at work. Very, very rarely did it rest on the wall near the teacher. The children were so used to the strokes of the lash that no one cried when beaten. When too great a turmoil developed in the room the helper would lash out right and left among the children without regard for who was struck. The lash was also used during instruction. Both the teacher and his helper did not refrain from using their hands. Every mistake by the child was requited with a thump in the side. The teacher also would poke his snuff-box into the mouth of a pupil who yawned during instruction. A very severe punishment was whipping. The helper or the teacher would set the "culprit" on his knees and administer a drubbing to his buttocks. For more serious offenses there were special punishments, the mere mention of which made the children tremble. The most terrible of these were the following three: (1) whipping of the naked buttocks with wet, salted reeds; (2) stuffing the mouth with a wooden peg; (3) "to be made a bundle." The last of these was considered to be the most terrible punishment. There was a legend among the children that one pupil once died during this punishment. It was administered in the following way; The culprit had his outer garment and his hat turned inside out. His face was blackened with soot from the stove. Then his hands were tied and under one arm they placed a broom and under the other a paddle. On his back was tied a bundle of old rags, which was to give the impression that he was hunch-backed. The lad, got up in this way, was then carried around the room, set up on high places, like a table or cupboard and all the other children would stand around him, clap their hands and shout in chorus: "Bundle maker! bundle maker!" And the name stuck to the child for good. These three punishments were already discontinued in my time. The helper would only threaten us with them.[1]

THE PERSONNEL OF THE ELEMENTARY KHEYDER

The teacher was the owner and administrator of the school. Every inter-semester period he had the job of getting pupils enrolled for his school. He would canvass the homes that had eligible children and visit both the parents of the children that had attended his school previously and the parents of prospective pupils. He also had to arrange for his helpers and for the place for the school.

The teacher's income was derived from tuition fees that were paid in installments for the entire session and from holiday moneys which he got from the parents as gifts. He also would get a certain sum for every circumcision and for every celebration of beginning the study of the Pentateuch. These gifts were usually very small and depended on the generosity and prosperity of the donor.

Poor children who could not afford to pay tuition fees received instruction just like the wealthy children. The teacher was paid for these by the trustees of the Talmud Torah, who would collect contributions for this purpose. These children were known as "Talmud Torah children" even though there was no special Talmud Torah in our town.

The teacher also sold *tsitsis* and *shir-hamaalot* amulets for pregnant women. With all this, nevertheless, the teacher was quite poor and every Friday he would walk through the village with a red handkerchief in his hand and solicit charity donations. Officially he was supposed to be collecting these for the village poor but actually it was for himself.

The teacher had three assistants: a chief helper, an assistant helper and a messenger-boy. The chief helper would instruct the children together with the teacher. He and the assistant helper would take the children to synagogue every Sabbath and holiday morning and teach them the responses "Blessed be He, Blessed be His Name!" and "Amen!" All three assistants would take the children to the home of a new-born boy one day before the circumcision and read the "*Shema*" with them. The chief helper would board with the teacher

[1] A fellow-townsman of mine, of my age, told me that in his school—there were two elementary schools in our town—they once administered the "bundle" punishment as described here. My description of this punishment was based on data furnished me by older inhabitants of the town.

and received in addition a small salary for each term. He also had a
side income from the toys he made for the children for the holidays.

There was a custom in our region that the chief helper would
prepare the fish for every wedding. Often too he would be the
waiter at the wedding meal. Thus, in addition to his other qualifications, the chief helper had to know how to prepare fish and how to
wait on tables for a wedding. The helper would be paid for these
additional jobs. The position of helper was not considered very
reputable in the village. The word *belfer* even came to be used in
popular language as a term of insult. On the other hand it also
became synonymous with the words for "fop" and "dandy." The
helper would pay a great deal of attention to his clothes. We used
to speak of *geyn ongeton yoldish*[2] (be dressed like a dude). He was
one of the few in the village to wear a stiff collar and a tie, a short
coat, and a small cap on his head. He paid attention to the crease
in his trousers, trimmed his earlocks, combed his hair and kept his
young beard trimmed. He also had the reputation of being lax in ritual
observance. He dared allow himself minor transgressions.

The assistant-helper's main job was to go to the home of every
child every morning, help the child get dressed, say the *Moyde ani*
and the *Shema Yisroel* with him, and have him kiss the *tsitsis*. He
would sometimes substitute for the chief helper in instructing the
children and would help him in general with all his work He would
also bring on his back those children who could not or did not want
to come to kheyder. That is why he was hated by the children.
Towards evening he and the messenger-boy would take the children
home. The assistant-helper received a monthly fee from the parent of
every child whom he cared for in the morning. He also received free
meals regularly from the more wealthy parents.

Both the chief helper and his assistant were, as a rule, not natives
of the village in which they worked. They also very rarely remained
for more than a few seasons in the same kheyder. As a rule they
would leave for another village after every term. The messenger-
boy, on the other hand, was a poor boy of the village. He would
help out in the kheyder and received a few pennies as his fee. His
major job was to bring food for the children twice a day in a large
hand valise. He also ran errands for the mothers of the children and
they would usually compensate him with food or meals.

---

[2] In our area the word *frantish* was replaced by *yoldish.*

The Discovery of
Mendele Moykher-Sforim and the
Beginnings of Modern Yiddish Literature*

By DAN MIRON

The connection between the figure of Mendele Moykher-Sfo-rim and the beginnings of the so-called "new" Yiddish literature is a familiar theme. Indeed, it has become perhaps too familiar. The notion that Mendele is the fountainhead of modern artistic Yiddish literature (and, as many contend, of modern artistic He-brew literature as well), that he was a "first," an innovator, a found-ing father, etc. is commonplace. Sholem-Yankev Abramovitsh him-self stated, in an autobiographical sketch written in 1889, that his first Yiddish story, *Dos kleyne mentshele* (published in 1864), in which his Mendele had made his first appearance, was "the corner-stone" of the new Yiddish literature."[1] His statement has been ac-cepted and repeated with various embellishments *ad nauseam* by scores of critics, historians, writers, and banquet orators from the 1880's and 1890's to our own days. Nevertheless, it seems to me that the theme is worth reconsideration. Moreover, I think that it even calls for redefinition and restatement. In any case, I wish to redefine the two components of my title: Mendele Moykher-Sforim and the beginnings of modern "new" Yiddish literature. First, we should perhaps pause to ask what we mean when connecting the

---

* This paper was presented at the Annual YIVO Banquet on Nov. 14, 1971.
[1] See Abramovitsh's *Reshimot letoldotay. Kol kitve Mendele Mokher Sfarim* (ed. in 1 vol., Tel-Aviv, 1947), p. 5.

name of Mendele with the "beginnings of modern Yiddish literature." It was perhaps justifiable for Abramovitsh to proclaim his
literary parenthood in 1889, because so little was known about the
literary use of modern Yiddish before the 1860's; although even
then, one may suggest, a less arrogant writer would have paid trib-
ute to Shloyme Etinger's brilliant *comédie larmoyante, Serkele,* or
Yisroel Aksenfeld's novel *Dos shterntikhl* (both published a short
time before his *Dos kleyne mentshele*—in 1861 and 1862 respec-
tively—and written decades earlier), or to some of Ayzik-Meyer Dik's
naive but not unartistic novelettes. Today we know—thanks to the
labor of scholars and historians, who for more than sixty years
have been studying the early stages of the new Yiddish literature
—that when Abramovitsh made his debut as a Yiddish writer in
1864, there already existed something like a continuous development of a literature that was, by all standards, "new." It was: (a) a
literature based on the employment of modern, East European
Yiddish, and thus differentiated from the Old Yiddish literature,
which had flowered during the fifteenth, sixteenth, and seventeenth
centuries in countries in which Ashkenazic Jews spoke Western
Yiddish, and (b) a literature expressing a new, non-traditional,
even anti-traditional sense of life and set of values, and thus differentiated from the naive folk literature written in the modern
variety. Furthermore, it had existed for fifty or sixty years, and
had absorbed the talent of at least four writers of undoubted
literary importance: Sh. Etinger, Y. Perl, Y. Aksenfeld, and Ay.-M.
Dik. If we go on repeating the commonplace notion that somehow
the "real" beginning of modern Yiddish literature was Mendele,
we should qualify it, explain it in a way commensurate with our
present knowledge of the early development of the new Yiddish
literature. It is precisely such a qualification or explanation that
I intend to offer here; for I believe that the notion of Mendele
as a "first," as the pioneer who charted new courses for almost
everything which has followed in Yiddish fiction for more than a
hundred years, is, although hackneyed, true. With this in mind,
however, I must first make as clear as possible to whom reference
is being made when the name Mendele Moykher-Sforim is mentioned.

Mendele is neither the writer Sh.-Y Abramovitsh nor his
slightly disguised spokesman. He is a fictional character in his own

right, an artistic creation which must be distinguished—like all artistic creations—from its creator. Of course, it looms very large in the poetic world, wrought by Abramovitsh in his novels, novelettes, and short stories. It is, indeed, the pivot, the center, on which the whole artistic structure of this poetic world depends. Still, it is a fictional entity, an artifice, not to be confused with the artificer; at least not more than one is allowed to confuse Gulliver or Bickenstaff with Swift, or Marlow with Joseph Conrad. It goes without saying that like every creation central to its creator's work it expresses him in a significant way. However the expression is not a direct and personal one, but rather esthetic, i.e., objectively dramatized, indirect, and generalized. Even as such it is but a part of a wider and more comprehensive esthetic expression, which is the entire work of art with all its components, by which it is constantly conditioned. One should never select a sentence spoken by Mendele and present it as a direct utterance of Abramovitsh. It is the utterance of a fictional character in a dramatic situation; an utterance the meaning of which is subordinate to the more comprehensive meaning of the situation as a whole, and consequently to that of the whole work, of which this situation is only a part. What Abramovitsh had to say was nothing less than the entire story or novel as a unified, integrated poetic statement. Mendele is but one of the many components of which this statement is made, although it is certainly a component of crucial importance.

It should be realized, however, that Mendele, although an imaginary creation, is not a fictional character of the ordinary type like Fishke in *Fishke der krumer* or Hershele in *Dos vintshfingerl*, or for that matter, most of the characters, whether "flat" or "rounded," that we encounter in fiction. He is certainly the most vividly realized character in Abramovitsh's works and probably one of the most memorable figures in modern Jewish literature, but in many ways he is a severely limited fictional entity. Like some of Dickens's "flat" characters, for instance, his development as a fictional person is all but impossible. When we encounter him in the first version of *Dos kleyne mentshele* he is already a man of mature age, fifty years old or so, who has for many years been a bookpeddler and occasionally also a publisher of Jewish books, and when we take leave of him in Abramovitsh's last works, written fifty years later, he is still the same man. He does not get older; he has almost no personal past. Indeed, he has scarcely any existence beyond the limits of his function as a narrator, observer, and as a technical caretaker of the stories, which he is supposed to have published and sometimes also edited or even rewritten. The fact is that Mendele, as much as he is a living character, is basically a device, a stratagem, a fictional accessory that holds together the structural framework of each of Abramovitsh's major works as well as of his entire Mendele cycle as a unified Jewish comedy. He moves with an amazing, almost acrobatic skill, but he must balance himself all the time on a very narrow thread hung high in the air, for he is a figure confined to a particular and limited task in the stories, which is basically the task of explaining under what circumstances, how, and for what purpose a "true" story, i.e., a story which is supposed to be based on the non-fictional, literal truth, has achieved publication. All of Abramovitsh's works, in which the Mendele figure has a part (there are some from which he is absent, such as the early Hebrew novel *Haavot vehabanim* or the Yiddish melodrama *Der priziv*) are presented as reports of real occurrences told by the people who have been directly involved in them, and who, in all cases but one (the case of *Shloyme Reb Khayims*), are not professional writers. Whether this presentation is always meant to be taken seriously is not the point now. What is important is that this convention of presenting the public with stories which were allegedly nonfictional, "true to life," was invariably employed by Abramovitsh in all his major works throughout his long career. *Dos kleyne mentshele* is a "true" autobiography in a form of a confession. *Fishke der krumer* is the "true" story of a Jewish cripple, who unwillingly joined the underworld of itinerant paupers, told by himself. The drama *Di takse* is supposedly an accurate, *ad-hominem* portrayal of the criminal behavior of the leaders of a big Jewish community, written by an anonymous member of this community. *Di klyatshe* is presented as an authentic report of the aberrations of its protagonist, Yisrolik the Madman, written by himself and brought to Mendele for publication by his friend. *Masoes Binyomin hashlishi* is said to be a concise, somewhat simplified version of its protagonist's memoirs and travelogs. *Dos vintshfingerl* is based on the autobiography of its protagonist, who is supposed to be actually living in Germany. *Shloyme Reb Khayims* is also presented as its protagonist's autobiography and, since in this case Shloyme is a professional writer, is published intact by Mendele. The basic need Abramovitsh had for a Mendele was then a simple, technical one. Without him he could not maintain the fiction of non-fictional veracity. All those "true" stories, autobiographies, travelogs, and confessions needed a mediator, an entrepreneur, somebody who would collect them, prepare them, when necessary, for publication, and publish them, and that, in fact, is exactly what Mendele is. Of course, he is much more than that. In all of Abramovitsh's works, even the earliest and more juvenile versions of his stories, Mendele transcends the mere technicalities of his function; but he always remains firmly tied to his mechanism of non-fictional fiction. This, obviously, is the root of his literary existence, from which he can never be torn without immediate loss of artistic meaning and vitality and without causing the collapse of the whole fictional structure of Abramovitsh's works.

This is why he can never change his profession or grow out of it. He is not a Mendele who is also a book peddler, but rather Mendele THE Book Peddler. Selling and publishing books is not only his profession, or as he himself sometimes says, his vocation; it is his mode of fictional existence, his *raison d'être* in Abramovitsh's works. Only once in all these works did the author allow his Mendele, very briefly, and for special satirical effect, to dissociate himself from his profession. This happens in the Hebrew novelette *Bime haraash* in which Mendele, under the influence of Zionist propaganda, suddenly wishes to settle down as a comfortable farmer in the pastures of Judaea "under his vine and fig tree." This, however, is a momentary aberration. After the sobering experience of mixing with the Zionist enthusiasts of Odessa, Mendele goes back to his Glupsk and Kabtsansk, repurchases his old horse and once again becomes the book peddler he must be; all this, with the "relief of the frog when he returns weary and jolted to his native bog from a long journey on dry land..[2] Book peddling and publishing is Mendele's *métier* not because it suits his "character," but because it is only through this profession that he can carry the structural task, which basically *is*, among other things, his character.

---

[2] *Ibid.*, p. 419.

2

My title referred not only to Mendele and to the beginnings of modern Yiddish literature, but also to the "discovery" of Mendele, the implication being that through the Mendele artifice Abramovitsh somehow set in motion a literary development, which subsequently came to be known as the "new" Yiddish literature. It must be quite obvious that the device of a literary entrepreneur who presents his public with allegedly non-fictional, "true" stories, can by no means be considered a "discovery" of Abramovitsh. The modern European novel, i.e., the novel as it has developed from the beginning of the eighteenth century onward, is replete with literary mediators of the Mendele type, as well as with "true" stories or rather "true histories," as they are called. The urge to present works of fiction as such manifests itself everywhere during the development of the novel and is peculiarly typical of its early stages. Readers of English literature will remember that Defoe tried to impose on the public his "true histories," and that Richardson, posing as a mere editor, presented his *Pamela* as a collection of genuine letters. Readers of the French novel will remember, in this connection, Rousseau's *Nouvelle Héloïse,* Laclos's *Les Liaisons Dangereuses,* or Benjamin Constant's *Adolphe,* to mention only three conspicuous examples. The most prominent German example will undoubtedly be Goethe's *Sorrows of Young Werther,* while one can think of any number of famous Russian examples from Radishtshev's *Journey from St. Petersburg to Moscow,* to Dostoyevski's *Notes from the House of the Dead.*

The need to present fiction as literal truth, although enhanced and qualified in different literatures by specific circumstances and traditions (e.g., the objection of Puritan morality to "romances" and even to fiction, as such, in the cases of Defoe and Richardson), was, generally speaking, postulated in the early stages of the development of the modern novel by the very characteristic that distinguished it from its predecessor and rival, the romance, that is by its claim to be a true representation of daily life, as opposed to the allegedly false, sentimentalized, or spiritualized version of life-representation, typical of the knightly or courtly romance of the Renaissance. Since the writing of novels of the new kind was conceived of, as the critic Ian Watt puts it, as "the production of what purports to be an authentic account of the actual experiences of inviduals,"[3] it had to extend as far as possible the pretense of truth at least during the period before the new genre established itself. Later on, when novels were written under the impact of the cult of sensibility, the fiction of literal veracity was maintained for purposes of emotional immediacy and authenticity of sentiment. In any case, wherever the pretension of truth appears in the development of the novel, it always involves—ironically perhaps—the creation of two or even several fictions instead of one, since to the initial fiction, i.e., the main story (or as Mendele often calls it: *iker-hamayse*) a fictional frame or frames (in Mendele's terminology: *a mayse iber a mayse*) had to be added. Thus throughout the eighteenth century and the first decades of the nineteenth, a legion of imaginary editors, publishers, literary executors, etc., were indefatigably producing prefaces, proems, letters to patrons or to the dear reader, advertisements and diverse notes for this purpose. Again and again manuscripts were said to have been found in distant places, handed to the publisher by relatives and friends, etc., while serious editors and publishers felt it their duty to make them public and, on occasion, to describe the circumstances of their publication.

There can be no doubt that Mendele Moykher-Sforim is basically one of these mediators, one of these guarantors of literal authenticity with whom the literature of the European novel abounds. It is not difficult to understand how modern Yiddish fiction, in its early development, came to be as influenced by the urge to present itself as literally true as the modern novel in the major European literatures had been one hundred or one hundred and fifty years earlier. We encounter its manifestations everywhere. Perl's anti-Hasidic satires were actually accepted as authentic Hasidic documents. Aksenfeld insisted on the literal truthfulness of his plots in his doggerel-verse introductions to his four surviving plays and to his one novel. In the proem to the novel, for instance, he seems for a moment to be playing with other possibilities only to revert with redoubled emphasis to the pretense of complete veracity: *Oyb der bashrayber fun der mayse hot zikh dos oysgetrakht/ Iz es nokh mer tshikave, vi azoy er hot azelkhes gemakht;/ Nor, az me vet oysleyzn in gantsn gor,/ Veln ale moyde zayn, az alts vos shteyt iz vor.* ('If the recorder of the story has fabricated all of this/

---

[3] Ian Watt, *The Rise of the Novel* (Penguin Book ed., London, 1963), p. 28.

Then you should be even more curious to know how he did such a thing;/ But once you have read it through,/ Everyone of you will concede that whatever you find here is true.')[4] In the long and often rhyming subtitles which Dik gave to his numerous novelettes, the veracity of the plot was very often emphasized, and the stories were referred to as *zeyer vikhtik un zeyer rikhtik,* 'very important and very true.' Linetski, Abramovitsh's contemporary, presented each of his three larger works of fiction, *Dos poylishe yingl, Der litvisher bokher,* and *Der vorem in khreyn,* as his "true" autobiographies and was more than once taken at his word, although each of the three persons who tell their life stories in these works is distinctly different from the others. As late as the 1880's, when the notion of literal veracity laboriously began to sublimate itself into a primitive theory of fictional realism, young Sholem-Aleykhem persistently referred to his juvenile novels as *undzer rikhtike, nisht oysgetrakhte geshikhte,* 'our true, unfabricated story.'[5] Later, he presented his two masterpieces *Menakhem-Mendl* and *Tevye der milkhiker* as series of authentic letters and monologues, reproduced *vort-bay-vort* in their original form with the utmost fidelity. Abramovitsh himself emphatically differentiated his *magnum opus,* the novel *Dos vintsh-fingerl,* from other Yiddish novels as "a history of Jewish life" and not "just another story," "a doll to play with."[6]

This is not the place for an extended discussion of the special circumstances that made this need for non-fictional veracity so pressing in the case of nineteenth-century Yiddish literature. However, I shall pause to mention briefly one or two of them here. Modern Yiddish fiction had no romance of the de Scudéry type to contend with, but it was supposed to counter-balance the influence of popuar legendary literature, the Hasidic legends and hagiography, and also that of the still popular Old Yiddish epics and romances of the seventeenth century. (Cf. Elye Bokher's *Bovo-bukh* in particular.) In several instances in Abramovitsh's works, particularly in the early version of *Dos vintshfingerl,* this legendary literature is subjected to ridicule, while scientific truth is recommended as the only basis for the reorganization of Jewish intellectual and eco-

---

4 Y. Aksenfeld, *Dos shterntikhl,* ed. M. Viner (Moscow, 1938), p. 49.

5 See, e.g., Sholem-Aleykhem's early novel *Kindershpil* (1885), in *Ale verk fun Sholem-Aleykhem,* vol. XX (Folksfond ed., New York, 1917–1923), p. 71; or his *Sender Blank,* vol. XI (1887), *ibid.*

6 See Abramovitsh's letter to Sholem-Aleykhem of June 10, 1888, *Shriftn,* vol. I (Kiev, 1928), p. 251.

nomic life. The treatment of the Don Quixote motif in *Masoes
Binyomin hashlishi* is unintelligible if we examine it, as some critics do, out of this context. Of course, all this had to do with the
commitment of Yiddish (and Hebrew) writers of the time to the
ideas of the Haskalah (the Jewish Enlightenment Movement). As
maskilim most of these writers were imbued with rationalistic and
positivistic respect for logical analysis and for verifiable facts; hence
their immense interest in natural science, and the numerous books
and articles they wrote on subjects ranging from zoology and chemistry to geography. (Abramovitsh dedicated the best part of the first
decade of his literary career to the composition of an extensive zoology textbook, in Hebrew. He also intended to write a popular
encyclopedia of the natural sciences in Yiddish.) For many of them,
fiction, as such, was suspicious, a natural ally of superstition and
thus of Hasidism and backwardness. When the *maskilim* began to
write novels in Hebrew they had to face strong opposition from
their adherents. Yiddish *maskilic* fiction writers, however, were in
an infinite worse position in asserting their rights of fictionality;
for Hebrew novels could always be defended on the grounds of the
holy tongue's dignity and self-sufficiency, or as demonstrations of
its suitability to modern usage, while Yiddish, on the other hand,
was supposed to lack even the rudiments of stylistic dignity. The
one obvious merit a Yiddish narrative could possess, by the very
nature of the language it was written in, was fidelity to life. It
should then be quite clear that young Abramovitsh, switching in
1864 from Hebrew to the then "undignified" Yiddish, was very
anxious to emphasize the direct educational "usefulness" and importance of his stories as "true histories." For this purpose he had
to employ an imaginary literary entrepreneur, and thus the figure
of Mendele Moykher-Sforim came into being. This in itself, as we
saw, by no means entitled him to the status of a literary innovator,
not even within the narrow bounds of contemporary Yiddish literature. Even the very lively presence the figure of Mendele presented was not in any way new. Many of the prefaces and comments of imaginary editors or publishers of European "true" novels were written with an unmistakable flair for lively characteri-
zation and authentic speech. We may, for instance, compare the
liveliness and volubility of Mendele with that of Jedediah Cleish-

botham, the deliciously garrulous "schoolmaster and parish clerk of Gandercleugh," who is the "collector and reporter" of some of Scott's allegedly true Scottish novels and tales. Indeed, the comparison might reveal more points of resemblance than one would have thought possible. Like Mendele, Jedediah is a man of good sense and naive shrewdness, who sometimes likes to conceal his very practical common sense behind homiletic formulae. Like him, he is the literary mentor of a small, backwater half-feudal world, and as such entrusted with manuscripts that he makes public, as he insists, for the benefit of "his loving countrymen" (Mendele's "dearly beloved children of Israel"), and not for anything as gross as financial gain. Finally, like him, he finds the writing of his *Omar Mendele* 'Mendele sayeth' type of introductions too great a pleasure to be quickly done with, and he lets his natural chattiness carry him far beyond the mere call of a publisher's or editor's duty.

I am not trying to suggest that Abramovitsh was directly "influenced" by Scott, whose novels, for all their enormous European reputation, he may not have read. On the other hand he certainly was acquainted with the works of some of Scott's German and Russian "disciples," such as the young Gogol, whose construction of the *Evenings Near the Village of Dikanka* series with its unifying figure of the old garrulous narrator, the bee-keeper, Rudi Panko, was immediately recognized as a Scott-influenced one.[7] Far more important than the problem of possible "influences" is the realization that in such a literary creation as Mendele, Abramovitsh was following the intrinsic logic of the novel as a poetic form: an intrinsic logic that made the varied developments of the novel form in the different literatures of Europe undergo "phases," or progress through "stations," which are basically the same, even when these developments were separated from one another by many decades and by the great geographical and spiritual distances that make Glupsk and Kabtsansk so unlike Gandercleugh and Abbotsford. It is this intrinsic logic that leads different novelists to similar answers to similar literary problems they are somehow bound to face in the development of the genre.

---

7 See Viktor Vinogradov's *Etyudi o stile Gogolya* (Leningrad, 1926), pp. 42–50. I am thankful to Martin Horowitz, Bennington College, for having supplied this information.

3

What then is the "discovery" Abramovitsh made when he created and developed the figure of Mendele; a discovery, which I intimated, had such a decisive influence on the further development of Yiddish literature that it justified the widely accepted notion of the figure of Mendele as the fountainhead of this literature?

What Abramovitsh really discovered for Yiddish literature was not the Mendele-device *per se*, but rather the rich artistic resources which lay dormant in this character-device, and through which modern Yiddish fiction could, under very special and severely limiting circumstances, evolve into a great literary tradition. At the beginning of the present century, when the basic critical distinctions and formulae pertaining to Abramovitsh's works were formed, critics used to deny, with vehemence, the relevance of a European context to the understanding of Abramovitsh's art. Living then under the impact of a newly developed Jewish nationalism, they agreed that, with the exception of Don Quixote, the general tradition of the novel had no bearing on the art of a writer, who was then described as utterly original and quintessentially "Jewish."[8] As much as this was understandable as a manifestation of a very real need for national literary self-assertion, it was, when regarded from the critical and historical points of view, nothing more than

---

8 The two authorities who made this "doctrine" the basis of the conventional evaluation of Abramovitsh's achievement for more than fifty years were David Frishman, the major Hebrew critic at the time (see the appropriate passage in his seminal essay, "Mendele Mokher-Sfarim," *Kol kitve D. Frishman*, vol. VI [Warsaw-New York, 1931], p. 74), as well as the illustrious Hebrew poet Bialik (in his article "Mendele ushloshet hakrakhim"). Bialik went so far as to warn the prospective readers "not to forget the rules and theory of literature" when they came to study Abramovitsh, and even more urgently, "not to study him by comparison," for he constituted a separate category of literature (see *Kitve H. N. Bialik*, vol. II [Tel-Aviv, 1935], pp. 330–331). This absurd notion of originality has, of course, been challenged by critics who presented Abramovitsh's fiction as part of the European tradition of the novel. The Hebrew critic Sh. Tsemakh judiciously argued, as early as 1919, that if such definitions of Abramovitsh's art were to be trusted, it could "either be an art originating from the deep jungles along the banks of the Congo River . . . or not exist at all." If, moreover, one must believe that such an art "was created in the latter part of the nineteenth century by an artist who had written zoology textbooks and believed in the progress of civilization," one had every right to regard it with suspicion. See Tsemakh's article "Baavotot hahavay," in *Erez* (Odessa, 1919), p. 129. For examples of literary analysis starting from the realization of one European context of Abramovitsh's art see Y. Goldberg's "Der veg-roman un der intimer stil" in *Shriftn fun vaysrusishn melukhe-universitet, yidishe sektsye fun pedagogishn fakultet*, vol. I (Minsk, 1928), pp. 45–60 and M. Viner's various Mendele studies collected in his *Tsu der geshikhte fun der yidisher literatur in 19tn yorhundert*, vol. II (New York, 1946).

chauvinistic superstition. It not only blinded critics and historians, making them overlook the scores of obvious links connecting Abramovitsh's art throughout its development to the traditions of the European novel and satire; but it also made them insensitive to Abramovitsh's real originality, i.e., to his successful and creative responses to the special needs and difficulties of Yiddish literature. For, of course, it is only by comparison and through the realization of similarities that the uniquely dissimilar or meaningful different that often lurks behind the similar can be pointed out.

The Mendele-device is obviously a case in point. The very conventionality of the function performed by him indicates, on the one hand, that the tradition of nineteenth-century Yiddish fiction, which blossomed in the works of Abramovitsh and Sholem-Aleykhem, is not a literary Rod of Aaron, but rather a branch of modern European fiction. On the other hand, the importance this function assumed in Abramovitsh's and other writers' works (such as Linetski's and Sholem-Aleykhem's) indicates that a convention was used unconventionally here. We realize how unusually great the significance of the Mendele-device was, and how it kept growing, when we trace one of the many aspects in the development of Abramovitsh's use of Mendele: the changing relations between Mendele and the imaginary authors of the manuscripts he publishes. The range of this shifting relationship can be illustrated by the earliest (1864) and latest (1907) versions of *Dos kleyne mentshele*. In 1864 Mendele was commissioned to publish the protagonist Yitskhok Avrom's confession for purely technical reasons: "because he has printing experience and because he travels throughout Poland," and thus will be in the best position to circulate the printed book.[9] He was not supposed to interfere in any way with the manuscript; nor did he seem much concerned about its contents. By 1907 the nature of his commission changed considerably. Yitskhok-Avrom himself says here:

> For properly putting these papers in order, for correcting my crude errors, for adding to the chronicle some pepper and spice, so that it will make a tasty dish, for printing it in book form and then circulating it everywhere—for all these tasks I know no better man than Reb Mendele the Book Peddler.[10]

---

9 *Kol-mevaser*, 3rd year (1865), no. 6, p. 94.
10 See *Ale verk fun Mendele Moykher-Sforim*, vol. II (*Mendele-farlag* ed., N. Mayzl, Warsaw, 1928), p. 150.

The metaphorical terms in which Mendele's task is conveyed here are typical and highly suggestive. If in 1864 Mendele was a mere technical contractor, he is now not only a local celebrity, but a veritable expert, a literary *chef de cuisine*. Although he cannot supply the chronicle itself, it is his treatment of it, his spices and sauces that transform it from the raw piece of "real life" it must have been, into a "tasty dish." Of course, Mendele must also perform the cruder, preliminary task of "cooking," such as putting the manuscript in order, correcting grammatical and stylistic errors, printing, circulating, etc.; but he is much more than a printer and editor. He is the master about whose "finishing touch" there is always some air of wizardry. Mendele is, in fact, equated here with the artistic dimension of the story, with the "layer" of art that allegedly has been added to the "true history."

Mendele's progression from the status of a technician to that of an artist began very early. Already in Abramovitsh's second Yiddish story, *Dos vintshfingerl* (earliest version, 1865), Mendele intends to add his own notes to the manuscript of the imaginary author, Hirsch Rathmann, and when he is dissuaded from this (by the imaginary translator of a supposedly German original of this book), he compensates for this by adding an introduction and a conclusion which are almost as long as half of the original story. In the introduction to the play *Di takse* (1869), allegedly written by a frightened and harassed author, who remains anonymous, Mendele says that the manuscript was in such bad shape that he was obliged not only to edit it, but also to fill in some missing scenes. Besides, he says, the play intrigued him to such an extent, "I could not refrain from adding a few words to it here and there from what I myself have seen and heard on my trips." Here, then, Mendele enters the sphere of marginal authorship. In *Fishke der krumer* (first version, 1869) he goes much further. He still allegedly relates Fishke's own version of his "true history" with fidelity, but this takes only half of the story, covering the protagonist's life from his disastrous marriage to the present. The other half, which contains not only the earlier part of Fishe's story, but also a wealth of descriptions, comments, lyrical outbursts in the style of Sterne, and a portrait of the protagonist completely different from the one supplied by himself, is almost completely focused on Mendele. In the introductions to *Masoes Benyomin hashlishi* (1878) and *Dos vintsh-*

fingerl (second version, 1888), Mendele cunningly explains why although the original versions of the stories, as they were written by their protagonists, were excellent, he had to rewrite them completely. He intimates by different suggestive analogies that the manuscripts were not really as well written as he at first pretends to say, and that is why only very short quotations from them occur from time to time in the final text. Furthermore, this final version should be read as if written by Mendele himself, who is presented here as the great Jewish cook or the expert Jewish taylor, who can prepare a good meal or a respectable Jewish *kapote*, 'long coat' from almost anything. In most of Abramovitsh's later short stories it is Mendele himself who does the telling. It is only the professionalism of Shloyme Reb Khayims that makes Mendele refrain from interfering with his manuscript, so that here he must satisfy his literary ambition merely with a very long and brilliant *Omar Mendele* introduction. Mendele's importance, it is clear, grows from one work to the other, and from one version of the same work to the following version. He seems to slowly engulf the whole cycle of Abramovitsh's Jewish comedy and submerge in it his own vitality. Instead of being its humble caretaker he becomes the element within which it floats and which determines its climate, its very existence. Now this, as far as I know, never happens to the usual imaginary publisher or editor of the allegedly non-fictional works of fiction, and I submit that of all these mediators of world literature Mendele is the most memorable and brilliantly vivid. However, it seems to me that what made Abramovitsh so superior to most other novelists in bringing the character-device of the literary entrepreneur to life was not necessarily a superiority of talent, although there can be no doubt that he was a supremely gifted writer of fiction. Rather, it should be borne in mind that because of certain literary-historical circumstances of far-reaching significance, Abramovitsh was compelled or chose to invest an unusual portion of his artistic energy in developing this conventional device; it thus ceased to be a mere device, became an aesthetic end in itself, and grew to a brilliant creation of overwhelming dimensions. This amazing growth, to be sure, indicates a certain fundamental limitation or narrowness in the very basis of modern Yiddish literature that forced Abramovitsh's great talent to expand "disproportionately" in one direction, thus rendering the "frame" of Abramovitsh's works more brilliant and impressive than the picture in it, indeed, making the "frame" invade the picture and cover huge parts of it with its own unmistakable gilt.

It is beyond the ken of this paper to explain, in detail, the precise nature, causes, and consequences of the historical limitation I am referring to; but at least one of the major consequences of it must be obvious to those with some knowledge of nineteenth-century Yiddish literature. Until Abramovitsh, and to a large extent even after him, this literature was incapable of assuming the epic tone with any real artistic success. It was strictly confined to what is usually described in current literary jargon as "showing," while it was almost completely debarred from "telling." This generalization applies, of course, only to the consciously "new" literature created by the Yiddish *maskilim,* and it involves the very basic assumptions of the Haskalah literature concerning the Yiddish language. In the Hasidic and folk literature one can find as much "telling" as one cares for. The naive epic is the mode *par excellence* of this literature. The revolutionary Yiddish *maskilim,* however, had to resort from the very beginning to two non-epic techniques, which indicate the same basic assumption, i.e., that Yiddish is not the writer's own language, the medium through which he expresses his innermost thoughts and feelings, but rather "their" language, the language of the simple people, whom the writer is supposed to educate. The two techniques were those of parody (either in monolog or in epistolary form) and of scenic comedy. In the framework of parody and comedy the people could speak for themselves and exhibit their shortcomings through their own linguistic medium. The reader who will remember the major achievements of Yiddish writers in the nineteenth century will realize how widely applicable my generalization is: Y. Perl's *Megale temirin* is an epistolary parody; Malage's *Gedules Reb Volf* is a parody in monolog form; part I of Y. Levinzon's *Hefker velt* is a dialogue, or a symposium, while part II is in monolog form. Above all, the best Yiddish literary works in the first half of the century from Y. Aykhel's *Reb Henekh, oder vos tut men damit* through Etinger's *Serkele,* and Gotlober's *Dektukh* to Aksenfeld's *Genarte velt* or *Kaptsn-oysher-shpil* are scenic comedies, highly suitable for the stage. Aksenfeld's novel, *Dos shtern-tikhl* is basically a series of dialogs and comic scenes connected by short stage directions. Most of Linetski's output consists of series of comic or parodic monologs and dialogs. Sholem-Aleykhem reaches the pinnacle of his magnificent art not in the novel form, but in the epistolary series of *Mena-khem-Mendl,* in the *Monologn* series (including the monologs of *Tevye* and *Motl Peysi dem khazns*) and some of his scenic comedies. Only the less artistically conscious and the less *maskilic* writers such as Dik, Dinezon, or Shomer (Y. Shaykevitsh) constantly used the omniscient author and the third person technique in their stories; but for this they paid the heavy price of dragging Yiddish fiction back to its naive beginnings, to the *mayse-bikhl* and folktale, thus depriving their stories of any semblance of psychological reality in the modern sense of the term. It goes without saying that this situation did not allow much of a development in Yiddish belles lettres. For a real development of a modern fiction genre in Yiddish the barrier between "showing" and "telling" had to be successfully crossed, and this is exactly what Abramovitsh succeeded in doing through the Mendele medium. Mendele is, of course, a dramatic creation. He speaks; we actually hear his voice. However, by standing, as his function of literary mediator obliges him to, *outside* the immediate sphere of the story, by becoming by degrees its editor and manipulator, he slowly develops the presence of the epic raconteur. He becomes *the first narrating consciousness* of modern Yiddish literature, and he frees this literature from the limitations of parody and from the staccato rhythm of comic dialogue. Naturally Abramovitsh was very careful to protect his dramatic credibility. In most cases he did not try to overreach himself by defying the basic limitations of the age. However, he did everything possible within these limitations to widen the scope of Yiddish fiction, to make it absorb as many of the different elements of narrative as it possibly could at the time: detailed description, interior monolog and deliberation, lyrical digression, straight epic storytelling, as well as the monolog, the dialog and the polylog. For all these he was utterly dependent on the services of his Mendele, and that is why he let Mendele become the literary giant, who almost swallowed its own creator. That is also the reason why the notion that the Mendele figure is the real origin of modern Yiddish literature, at least of modern Yiddish fiction, is basically correct.

---

11 *Ibid.,* vol. IV, p. 8.

THE STRUGGLE OF THE *VAAD ARBA ARAZOT* FOR THE JEWISH RIGHT OF RELIGIOUS WORSHIP IN BRESLAU IN THE 17TH CENTURY

By BERNHARD BRILLING

1

After the expulsion of the Jews from Breslau in 1453, their three synagogues were confiscated.[1] Subsequently, the city permitted brief stays for Jews coming to the markets and fairs. At first few, their numbers gradually increased. As in other cities in which fairs were held and which had no Jewish communities and hence no synagogues, religious services conducted at the Breslau fairs[2] were at first largely unnoticed by the public.[3] Supervision of these services, as of all other matters pertaining to the Jews at fairs,[4] was maintained by the duly constituted Jewish authorities—in Breslau, by the *Vaad* of Poland (and later also by the *Veadim* of Bohemia and Moravia).[5] These central Jewish institutions also undertook to meet the threats to Jewish worship at

---

[1] On the synagogues of the mediaeval Jewish community in Breslau, see Brann, M., *Geschichte der Juden in Schlesien* (Breslau 1896) vol. i, p. 31-32. Cf., Heppner, A. and Brilling, B., "Geschichte der Synagogen in Breslau, I," *Breslauer jüdisches Gemeindeblatt,* vol. viii (1936) no. 12, p. 167-168.

[2] Meir ben Gedalia (MaHaRaM) of Lublin (1558-1616) writes of these fair services in his *Responsa* (no. 84) as follows: "It is a fixed custom to designate a specific place at each fair at which daily services are held. On the Sabbath there gather there wise men, the heads of the Yeshivot, the leaders of the provinces, and large assemblies." On the equipment of these synagogues at the fair, of which there is evidence dating back to the 16th century, see Suppl. X in the present article. Cf., Brann, M., "Geschichte des Landrabbinats," in *Grätz Jubiläumschrift* (Breslau, 1887) p. 226.

[3] Hence there were, at first, no complaints against them. In 1692 the Jews declared that their services at the fair in Breslau had been conducted and tolerated since time immemorial (Stadtarchiv Breslau, BoeA 73 f.296b).

[4] See Halpern, Israel, "Der vaad arba arotses in zayne batsiungn mit oysland," *Historishe shriftn,* Yivo (Vilna 1937) vol. ii, p. 69-71, on the *dayanim* and *shamashim* at the fairs. Cf., Weinryb, B., *Mehkarim letoldot hakalkala vehahevra shel yehude polin* (Jerusalem 1939) p. 35.

[5] See Brilling, B., in *Zeitschrift für die Geschichte der Juden in der Tschechoslowakei,* vol. ii (1931) p. 3f (Hereafter *ZGJT*).

fairs. As we shall see, the *Veadim* were called upon more than once to use their good offices in Breslau in the last quarter of the 17th century.

It was, to be sure, politically hazardous on the part of the *Vaad Arba Arazot* to venture beyond the borders of Poland and attempt to influence the non-Jewish authorities. The urgent imperative to defend the right of worship provided the motivation and the economic power of the Jewish fair merchants the force for the efforts of the *Vaad* leaders in this matter. (It should, moreover, be recalled that they could count on the support of the Polish nobility, who generally interceded on behalf of the interests of their Jewish subjects.) Obviously, the *Vaad Arba Arazot* did not have the means of political warfare of a state at its disposal, and was constrained to employ its sole weapon: an economic boycott.

With respect to the strictly religious aspect of the problem, the elders of the Polish *Vaad* took the precaution, as early as the last quarter of the 17th century, of submitting the prayerbooks used for worship at the fairs to Professor Johannes Acoluthus, Inspector of Churches and Schools of the Augsburg Confession, and to a certain *Magister* Friedrich.[6] Their inspection of the texts, of course, revealed nothing insidious which could serve as ground for barring their use.

2

The chief Breslau hostelries at which Jews would stay during— and, occasionally, between—fairs were located in the commercial squares and arteries extending from the former "Judenplatz" (later Karlsplatz and, until 1933, Lassalleplatz). Among them were Der Pokoyhof (referred to as early as 1624 as an inn for foreign Jews[7]), Die Fechtschule, Das Goldene Hirschel, and Das Goldene Rad. "It was here that the Jewish people began to dwell in our midst," wrote E. Scheibel, a local Breslau poet.[8] Frederick the Great had already designated these four inns, which lay between Antonienstrasse and

---

[6] See Suppl. I. On Acoluthus, see Zedler in *Universallexikon* (1732) vol. i, p. 362. Since he died in Breslau in 1689, he must have examined the prayerbooks some time before. His son Andreas (1654-1704) was the predecessor of Daniel Springer, to whom we refer below, as professor of Hebrew at the Breslau Elisabeth-gymnasium.

[7] Markgraf, H., *Die Strassen Breslaus* (Breslau 1896) p. 30.

[8] Quoted in Brann, M., "Ein Breslauer Gedenktag," *Jüdischer Volks- und Hauskalender für 1899*, ed. M. Brann (Breslau) p. 84.

Karlstrasse, as the sole places at which Jews coming to the fairs in Breslau could stay.[9]

The Jewish and, it is likely, commercial affairs, of the Jewish visitors to the fairs and markets were centered in and about these squares. Here, too, the earliest synagogues were probably located. Throughout the 16th and three-fourths of the 17th century there was no mention of prohibiting these synagogues or the worship of the visitors to the fairs. Such was the case in Danzig and Torun, Poland, as well.[10] On the other hand, in Leipzig, the other large city of the East in which fairs were held and which likewise attracted many Jews, attempts at forbidding Jewish communal worship were made quite early.[11]

3

There were two synagogues in Silesia in the 17th century: in Glogau and in Zülz (Upper Silesia, now Biala, Poland).[12] Here, Jewish religious worship was, if not expressly sanctioned by the authorities, at least tolerated. In Breslau, however, services could not be conducted in buildings specially constructed for this purpose, but were held in rented rooms. This pattern of worship was not patently public and attracted little attention for some time. Connivance was, moreover, economically advantageous, for the Jews, as the Breslau inhabitants themselves put it, were "noted" for controlling all of "the Polish and most of the Lithuanian and Russian trade."[13] The authorities preferred to compensate for the "oversight" by strictest enforcement of market

[9] Markgraf, *loc. cit.*

[10] See Suppl. I. On Danzig, see Kirschbaum, J., *Di geshikhte fun di yidn in dantsig* (Danzig 1926) p. 36.

[11] On relations in Leipzig, see Cohn, Gustav, in *Festschrift zum 75 jährigen Bestehen der Leipziger Gemeindesynagoge* (Leipzig 1930) p. 16-17. In Vienna, too, worship was permitted communally only "insofar as [it] could not be conducted alone or within the family"—Bato, L., *Die Juden im alten Wien* (Vienna 1928) p. 73-74.

[12] The synagogue in Glogau burned down in 1678 (Brann, *Geschichte . . .*, p. 219). A synagogue existed there in 1628, according to Berndt, *Geschichte der Juden in Gross-Glogau* (Glogau 1873) p. 22. Permission to build a synagogue was received in 1622 (*ibid.*, p. 43). The Zülz wooden synagogue is reported to "have been built perhaps in 1662" (Rabin, I., *Die Juden in Zülz* [Neustadt 1926] p. 27). It probably burned down, for negotiations were under way in 1686 for the purchase of a synagogue location in Zülz (Rabin, I., *Vom Rechtskampf der Juden in Schlesien* [Breslau 1927] p. 48, fn. 1). The synagogues in both cities in that century, incidentally, were wooden structures.

[13] Quoted in Rabin, *Rechtskampf . . .*, p. 61, fn. 1, in re: 1691.

ordinances.[14] The Breslau burghers included among the transgressions of these ordinances the attempt of several Jews to settle in or near Breslau.

Jews evidently began to settle in the suburbs of Breslau about 1665.[15] Among the early settlers were the founders of the Breslau branch of the Kuh family of Prague. This opportunity for settlement arose because the suburbs came under the jurisdiction of the Church rather than under municipal authority.[16] The former was concerned to reap the highest profits from its possessions. Moreover, it was not bound by Breslau's *Jus Judaeos non tolerandi.*

Lazarus Zacharias (Elazar ben Zerah Halevi) of Nachod, Bohemia, succeeded, in his capacity of minting agent for the crown since 1656,[17] in obtaining the right to settle, with his family, in Breslau itself. Thereafter, several other minting agents and later a number of functionaries of other Jewish communities (*shamashim*, 'beadles')[18] were allowed, although for a limited period of time, to live in Breslau. These two groups of Jews—in the suburbs and in the city itself—instituted religious services which were conducted regularly, and not only during fairs.

---

[14] For example, on the struggle with Prague Jews, see Brilling, B., "Die Prager Schammes in Breslau," *ZGJT*, vol. i (1931) p. 139-159.

[15] There is no evidence of any earlier settlement of Jews in the Breslau suburbs. Zimmerman, *Geschichte und Verfassung der Juden im Herzogtum Schlesien* (Breslau 1791) p. 27, was the first to hypothesize that Jews had settled in Breslau suburbs as early as 1630, i.e., in the middle of the Thirty Years' War. Zimmerman's further claim that Jews resided in Breslau in 1635, if it has any basis at all, probably rests on a misinterpretation of a charter issued by the Breslau Municipal Council on May 7, 1635, in which the Council reserved the right "in the course of the present war, and should it be in the best interests of the city . . . [to permit] this or that Jew to enter the city." BoeA 67, p. 617-620. This does not, however, refer to the permanent residence of Jews in Breslau, but to the authorization of foreign Jews to remain in the city for a brief period of time beyond the period specified in the charter. M. Brann (in "Etwas von der Schlesischen Landgemeinde," in *Guttmann-Festschrift* [1915] p. 22G) relies on Zimmerman in writing that Jews resided "in 1635 occasionally even in the inner city of Breslau." Rabin, in *Rechtskampf* . . ., p. 45, fn. 2, makes the same mistake. All these do no more than show that the wartime charter issued by the Municipal Council permitted those Jews coming to the fairs to remain for some time thereafter for business reasons. Perhaps 1657, which is referred to in a document of 1687 as the beginning of the "Judenschaden" (BoeA 72, p. 99b.), is to be considered as the first year of Jewish settlement in Breslau. See Rabin, *Rechtskampf* . . ., p. 40-41.

[16] Brann, "Geschichte des Landrabbinats . . .," p. 223-224.

[17] The name of Lazarus Zacharias is mentioned in the account books of the Breslau mint for the first time in 1656. He is also the first person whose death record bears the designation "aus Breslau." On him see also Brilling, B., in *Zeitschrift für die Geschichte der Juden in Deutschland*, vol. vii (1937) p. 109-112.

[18] On the role of the *shamashim* see Brilling, in *ZGJT*, vol. i, p. 138f., 149; vol. ii, p. 8f. Also, Weinryb, *op. cit.*, p. 35f.

4

The issue of prohibition of Jewish worship was raised in Breslau in 1676, for the first time after the Middle Ages. In a letter to the Municipal Council of October 23, 1676, complaining about profanation of Sunday, the Merchants' Guild also referred to the Jews, "who are now even permitted to go about their blasphemous, supposedly religious, worship undisturbed."[19] The reference here is presumably to services conducted in the city itself. In a letter of December 22, 1677,[20] from the merchants to the Breslau Council concerning foreign Jewish brokers and others who were arriving in Breslau from Poland, despite the epidemic raging there, complaints were made about the Jewish services in the suburbs. The Jews, they wrote, "go no further than the suburbs. They settle down, particularly in Elbing,[21] and remain in the dwellings which they have leased for lengthy periods, and—much to the chagrin of their Christian neighbors—conduct their religious services like in a filthy Jew town."

Year after year the burghers, corporations and guilds would lodge complaints against the Jews to the Municipal Council, and propose that Jewish religious worship be prohibited. This strategy was but a religious facade to mask the interests of commercial competition. In 1687 they wrote that the Jews "even conduct regular gatherings and services altogether freely, in order to pursue their Judaism and heresy."[22] Notwithstanding the fact that this charge was presented as subsidiary in the complaints against the Jews, it had prospects of consideration. Thus it came to pass that in conjunction with the deteriorating economic situation,[23]—which was, naturally, blamed upon the Jews—the Jewish synagogues were ordered closed, for the first time, in August 1692, just before the High Holy Days. The Jews had but one place to turn for assistance in this situation—the *Vaad Arba Arazot,* which could attempt to mobilize its political force.

[19] BoeA 69, p. 397-398.
[20] *Ibid.,* p. 684, 688.
[21] The quotation is from BoeA 69, p. 685-686. On the suburb of Elbing, which consisted of some municipal property (the so-called "Stadtgut") and estates of the Orders of St. Vincent and of St. Matthew, see Markgraf, *op. cit.,* p. 39-40. In 1696-97 there were nine families living on the municipal property near the Oder Gate, and eight families near the Ohlau Gate, "at the eleven boards." See BoeA 75, p. 87b—Klose J. A., 465. On the entire episode, see Brann, "Geschichte des Landrabbinats . . .," p. 223-224. On p. 224 he mentions a synagogue located in the suburb in 1727.
[22] BoeA 72, p. 101a (Complaint 6 of March 22, 1687).
[23] On the reasons for this decline, see Rabin, *Rechtskampf . . .,* p. 69.

The Jews of Great[24] and Little Poland constituted the great majority of Jewish visitors to the fair.[25] Their representatives, the leaders of the *Veadim*, protested sharply against the curtailment of religious worship. Above all, they pointed out that Jewish import and export business was of the greatest benefit both for the Breslau burghers and for the crown. This would cease, they implied, if the current situation continued, for Jews would be compelled to transfer their trade to Danzig or Torun. In the latter cities, although likewise Protestant, they could carry on Jewish worship unhindered. Moreover, they added, the debts owed by individual Jews and by the *Veadim* and Jewish communities would necessarily remain unpaid, since not a single Jew would be able to come to Breslau. Having presented their weightiest (economic) arguments, the *Vaad* leaders returned to the point that Jewish religious worship in Breslau was no innovation. Services had been conducted there ever since Jews had begun to participate in the fairs. Anticipating the charge of insidious material in the prayer books, they noted that they had taken the precaution of submitting the texts to Christian theologians. Breslau was the only Protestant city which had prohibited Jewish worship solely on religious grounds. No such restriction existed in Danzig, Torun, or even in Catholic Vienna, the seat of the crown, where Jews had not been allowed to reside after the expulsion of 1670. On the basis of all these arguments, the Jewish leaders of Great and Little Poland, in their petition of September 5, 1692, to the Breslau Municipal Council,[26] requested that the Jews retain the right of religious worship.

Since the Municipal Council could hardly ignore the economic arguments advanced in the petition, the representatives of the merchants, in turn, presented a memorandum, seeking to assure the continuation of the ban on Jewish communal worship. This was pre-

---

[24] That same year the elders of Great Poland requested the military leader of Great Poland, Leszynsky, to intervene with the Breslau Municipal Council on behalf of the Great Polish and Kalisz Jews, whose freedom of movement was threatened on account of the debts of Polish-Jewish *Veadim*. In 1690, acting without the elders of Little Poland, they had approached the military leader of Great Poland, Opalinsky, in a similar matter. Cf. Lewin, L., *Die Landessynode der grosspolnischen Judenschaft* (Frankfurt-a.M. 1926) p. 39.

[25] See, for example, the list of Jews participating in Breslau fairs from 1651-1738, published by B. Brilling in *Mitteilungen der Gesellschaft für jüdische Familienforschung* (=MGJF) no. 39 (1935) p. 678f.; no. 40 (1936) p. 711f. Ten years later, in 1702, both *Veadim* presented a joint protest to the Breslau Council against the latest anti-Jewish restrictions. See Rabin, *Rechtskampf* . . ., p. 75, fn. 3.

[26] BoeA 73, p. 295b-297a (Supplement I).

sented only three days (on September 8, 1692)[27] after the protest of
the Jewish leaders had been delivered to the Municipal Council. The
merchants denied the Jewish claim that the ban would occasion grievous harm to the commercial interests of Breslau. Their real motive
was to force their Jewish competitors—the brokers engaging in commercial affairs in Breslau throughout the year—to leave the city. It
was this, rather than the specific ban on worship, which concerned
them. They were not in the least interested in imposing restrictions
on the non-resident Jewish merchants, travelling to and fro, in whose
hands lay almost all Polish, Lithuanian, Russian and even Bohemian-
Moravian trade. To these they would grant all rights: of prayer (albeit
not in "synagogues"), freedom of travel and shipping of goods,
accommodation in hostelries and inns as long as their business kept
them in Breslau, and the like. They thereby created the possibility
for the Municipal Council to formulate a compromise proposal. This
gave precise expression to the attitude of the merchants regarding the
Jews, namely, that they were a necessary evil. At the same time, it
relieved the city of taking further steps against the rented rooms in
which services were held, since they were not formally synagogues
and were primarily used by non-resident Jews. This meant that they
did not come within the scope of the ban against "synagogues."

5

In March 1694 His Majesty's *Oberfiskal* (Deputy of the Ex-
chequer) Christian Ferdinand Frantz, in a report to the Crown
Chamber,[28] attested to the importance of the Jews in trade with Poland. Referring to the decree of March 20, 1694,[29] aimed at a complete expulsion of Jews from Breslau, he insisted that there were no
grounds for this action. He pointed out that the *Jus Judaeos non
tolerandi* was invalid, since it had never been put into force there. He
noted that "over 50 families of Jews as well as various synagogues
were quite knowingly tolerated in the city." On September 28, 1694,

---

[27] *Ibid.,* p. 297a-298b (Supplement II).
[28] *Ibid.,* p. 432a-439a. The quoted lines below are taken from p. 434, which
also contains the oft-quoted sentence in which Frantz himself admits that at least
two-thirds of the trade with Poland was in Jewish hands, a fact which could easily
be substantiated by reference to the border customs office.
[29] BoeA 73, p. 430b-432a. This decree of the Municipal Council provided for
the expulsion of all Jews from Breslau. Only merchants could receive special permission to remain in the city for several days. The same decree prohibits physical
assaults on Jews, which apparently occurred then.

Frantz was authorized by the Breslau bishop, Franz Ludwig, Palsgrave of Rhine, to close all synagogues in Silesia.[30] It is uncertain whether this authorization was ever put into force.[31] From other sources, however, it is known that Frantz was well-disposed toward Jews, for strictly financial reasons.[32]

Jewish religious worship continued to be the target of agitation. The campaign gained the support of the Church Consistory and the Bishop of the Breslau Episcopate. The latter had learned from the depositions of two Christians that the Jews had observed their "great New Year," i.e., Yom Kippur, in seven synagogues on Monday, September 19, 1695.[33] These depositions contain accounts of the conditions of these synagogues. This is our first source of information about the seven synagogues in Breslau existing as early as 1695. Most of them were located on Antonienstrasse (or, as it was then called, Hundegasse[34]) and behind the "Hundhäuser" (the houses between the horsemarket and Reuschenstrasse).[35] The following synagogues are mentioned there:[36]

(1) The synagogue of the Jews of Kalisz, in which "about 200 Jews" prayed, located behind the Hundhäuser; (2) the synagogue of the Jews of Glogau, on the same street. Two synagogues were located in the Fechtschule, in the homes of (3) Jacob Viktor, *shamash*, and (4) Hirschel the butcher, both of Krotoszyn; (5) the synagogue in the Pokoyhof, where the Prague and Moravian provincial *shamash* lived, called the "Landschul"; (6) the synagogue in the rear building of Das Goldene Rad, in Antonienstrasse; (7) a private synagogue, that of the minter Herz (Hartig) Moses of Hamburg. This was largely frequented, it is known, by Jews from Prague. This synagogue is reported to have been in a building "specially rented for the purpose" on Antonienstrasse.

The synagogue of Jews of Lissa (Leszno), founded in 1685,

---

[30] *Ibid.*, 75, p. 318b-319b.

[31] In BoeA 75, p. 318b-319b the following note is found: This order of the bishop "was found on September 28, 1699, among *Oberfiskal* Frantz's papers." Evidently the order was unknown prior to that time.

[32] And this was frequently brought up. See, for example, BoeA 72f, p. 442a.

[33] NNN 449c. Yom Kippur was referred to by the Christians as "the great New Year" to distinguish it from Rosh Hashana.

[34] Markgraf, *op. cit.*, p. 9.

[35] *Ibid.*, p. 7. These two streets were referred to as "Jewish streets" in 1687 (BoeA 72, p. 10a).

[36] On the history of the Breslau synagogues and a detailed account of those mentioned here, see Heppner, A. and Brilling, B., in the *Breslauer jüdisches Gemeindeblatt* (1932) nos. 5, 7; (1934) no. 12.

whose "annals" were recorded as early as 1692, was certainly one of these seven. The other synagogues, however, were probably as old as, if not older than, the Lissa synagogue.

6

The Jews, unaware of the impending storm and secure under the protection of the Jewish *Veadim,* continued to engage in their "Religions-Exercitia," as it was termed in official parlance. They were, however, not to remain undisturbed for long. The clergy and the merchants, religious hatred and commercial interests joined in a pact against Jewish "superstition," as the one party termed it, and against Jewish competition, as the other thought. On March 11, 1696, the merchant leaders again presented a memorandum to the Municipal Council,[37] in which they attributed the decline in Breslau trade as well as the growing inflation to the Jews.[38] The petition—written in a highly aggressive tone—does not fail to mention that Jews even dared to conduct their own religious services in Breslau.[39] The charge naturally culminated in the time-worn and oft-repeated request that all the Jews be banished from the city. Exception was made for Polish Jewish traders, who were to be permitted to remain for a specified time upon payment of a "Zoll-Legitimation."[40] A second proposal involved the closing of the synagogues.[41] The merchants had evidently assured themselves of the support of the Consistory, which wrote to the *Oberamt* (Crown Commission) on May 3, 1696, in this connection,[42] remonstrating against Jewish religious worship, "a public ridicule of Christianity," and demanding its prohibition. On May 7, the *Oberamt* asked the Municipal Council of Breslau for a complete report.[43] The Council, prepared by the deposition of the merchants, replied on May 18. It stated that even prior to the inquiry of the *Oberamt,* it had (evidently acting on the aforementioned petition of the merchants) ordered all the Jewish residents of the city to leave. It had, in this connection, assembled the *shamashim,*[44] i.e., the official Breslau representatives of the foreign Jewish communities of Poland and of the crown provinces of Bohemia, Moravia and Silesia, as well as the Christian proprietors of the inns which Jews frequented. The

[37] BoeA 74, p. 276-287.
[38] *Ibid.,* p. 280b.
[39] *Ibid.,* p. 285b.
[40] *Ibid.,* p. 286b.
[41] *Ibid.,* p. 286a.
[42] NNN 449b.
[43] NNN 449a.
[44] See fn. 18.

shamashim had been forbidden, under severe penalty, to conduct Jewish religious services either on the fair grounds or elsewhere. The innkeepers had been instructed to report immediately all violations of this order to the Council.[45] This report of the Municipal Council resulted in the prohibition by the *Oberamt* of "synagogues," that is, of all Jewish worship.

Thus for the second time Jews were forced to defend themselves in this matter. Several fairs coincided with the Jewish holidays. The Crucifixion-Market Fair, for example, held in September, often occurred at the same time as the High Holy Days. Unable to travel home, Jews were compelled to conduct their holiday services in Breslau. The *Oberamt*'s edict had applied to all Jews without exception. The Breslau Jewish representatives of the Polish Jews (i.e., of the *Vaad Arba Arazot*) and of the three crown provinces (Bohemia, Moravia and Silesia) issued a joint protest[46] against this edict. Their petition to the *Oberamt*[47] argued that in actuality the edict did not apply to those whom they represented. Since there had been no synagogues—that is, public buildings specially constructed for worship—in Breslau, obviously none could be ordered closed. They had merely conducted their usual services. They were fully cognizant, however, that this argument would not suffice to have the edict set aside. As in 1692, they seized upon the one means which could succeed (it had succeeded previously): the threat of a boycott. They pointed out to the *Oberamt* which, as His Majesty's representative, had a keen interest in maximal tax income, that if the ban on their services continued, they would boycott Breslau, "thereby not only causing an immense decline in the great trade which our people conduct, but resulting in a most serious decrease in the tax and other forms of annual income of His Imperial Majesty." It is evident that the Jews were fully aware of the important role they played in Breslau commerce, which *Oberfiskal* Frantz had already noted in 1694, when he attributed two-thirds of the total trade with Poland to them.[48]

The warning seemingly had the desired effect on the *Oberamt*. On July 4, 1696, it transmitted the Jewish petition to the Breslau Muni-

[45] Hs.F.8, 29, p. 227a-228a (Stadtarchiv Breslau).
[46] On joint actions of Polish and Bohemian-Moravian Jewries as early as the 17th century see Brilling, B., in *ZGJT*, vol. v (1938) p. 59-62; Halpern, Israel, *Pinkas vaad arba arazot*, introduction to no. 6, p. xxiii.
[47] NNN 449d 1. See Supplement VI.
[48] See fn. 28. Cf., Wendt, H., *Schlesien und der Orient* (Breslau 1915) p. 123, and Brann, "Geschichte des Landrabbinats . . .," p. 225.

cipal Council, requesting detailed information on the accuracy of the Jewish denial of the existence of "synagogues" in Breslau.[49] It evidently required no confirmation of the substantiality of the Jewish threat of economic boycott, for no reference was made to it.

Once again the Municipal Council assembled the Jewish elders and the innkeepers. The latter were asked how the Jews went about conducting religious services. They replied that they had noticed the Jews "mumbling" out of books several times, and, taking it for a "synagogue," had forbidden them to do so. The elders were then asked to describe the rituals which made up their prayers. They replied—in full truth—that what the innkeepers had observed was not identical with "observance" (i.e., the celebration of religious worship) in a synagogue. The latter required special equipment (presumably referring to the Ark and the cantor's lectern). In the observed cases, all that went on was that some ten or twelve Jews gathered for a half or at most a full hour in a room in which someone lived, and quietly recited their prayers.

The Municipal Council, likewise aware of the economic implications of the Jewish boycott threat, was basically relieved to perceive a way out of the problematic situation. On July 21, 1696, it reported on the interviews with the Jewish elders and the innkeepers to the *Oberamt*. The Council left it to the *Oberamt* to decide whether to permit the Jews to pray in the manner indicated by their elders, thus revoking the ban again. At the end of its communication it nevertheless added that it would prefer to see the ban continue in full force.[50]

This state of affairs remained. The long-sought resolution had been found: the Jews were forbidden to maintain "synagogues," as the merchants and clergy had demanded; on the other hand, considering the economic role of the Jews, their desire to be allowed to continue "to pray" was granted. Thus the second round of the struggle against Jewish worship also ended in a partial victory for the Jews.

7

The Jews could well be content. In other cases, too, their opponents were only able to achieve a partial victory.[51] The Jews con-

---

[49] NNN 449d.

[50] Hs. F.8. 29 f., p. 244b-245b.

[51] Thus, for example, the Jews of Lissa, who were to be found in great number even after fair time in Breslau, were expelled. At the complaint of Count Leszynsky,

tinued their religious observances and ceremonies. Thus, for example, a circumcision was celebrated in Breslau in December 1696.[52] For over three years they remained undisturbed. In 1699 the Municipal Council itself admitted that only with the greatest of effort, and then with limited efficacy, could they check Jewish daily religious services.[53]

The third and final attack on the Jewish "synagogues" was made in 1700. This clash followed the pattern of that of 1696. Disregarding the ban, the Jews once again began to establish real "synagogues" —if rooms containing Holy Arks can be called synagogues. These were denounced by baptized Jews[54] to the Consistory. Evidently this body had no more pressing preoccupation, for it quickly approached the *Oberamt*, on December 7, 1700, proposing a ban on these synagogues,[55] which the Jews, without any authorization, instituted in their rooms in place of the "silent prayers." The *Oberamt* transmitted this proposal to the Municipal Council on December 22, 1700, for further consideration.[56] On January 7, 1701, the latter body issued an order banning Jewish synagogues.[57]

Once again, the autonomous Jewish organizations were the only force which could offer any significant opposition to the ban. By a strange—or perhaps not so strange—coincidence, the elders of the *Vaad Arba Arazot* and of the *Veadim* of Bohemia and Moravia hap-

---

the *Oberamt* intervened on behalf of these Jews, albeit motivated by the desire to increase the income from taxes. BoeA 74, p. 328f.

[52] Mentioned in a letter (dealing with the elimination of Glogau Jews) from the silk merchants to the Municipal Council of December 18, 1696. BoeA 74, p. 395a.

[53] Hs. F. 8. 31 f., p. 25b. In a petition of May 2, 1699, from the Municipal Council to the crown, protesting the permanent residence permit granted to S. Wertheimer, the Council bolsters its opposition on the grounds that his home is a meeting place for Jews in business matters as well as for religious services, "which we have heretofore, at the annual fairs, hardly been able to prevent even with the greatest of effort."

[54] NNN 449f. In those days apostates were a source of great trouble for Breslau Jews in other respects as well. Thus Berl Maier of Kremsier was arrested in 1695, when two baptized Jews accused him of having blasphemed Christianity (Hs.F.8. 29f., p. 21b-23a). The Jewish book shop was searched in 1694 (*MGWJ*, vol. xl [1896] p. 560-561) on the denunciation of the converted Jew Michael Paul (Hs.F.8. 30, p. 152b-154b). Moses Abraham Kuh, whose descendants were themselves baptized, was the victim in 1698 of a denunciation by two apostates, the linguists Leon and Michael Hirsch, on a charge of rape (Landsberger, J., in Brann, M., *Jahrbücher zur Unterhaltung und Belehrung*, 46 Jahrgang [1899], p. 26, fn. 1).

[55] NNN 449h.

[56] NNN 449g.

[57] NNN 449f.

pened to be in Breslau at the time.[58] They once again joined in a united action. In a memorandum to the *Oberamt*[59] they contended that they had merely followed the sanctioned ways, namely, praying only in their own rooms, "and thus had not organized any public gatherings or maintained any synagogues." The false reports which stated otherwise were to be traced back to the slanderous gossip spread by apostates solely in their own interest. From their previous interventions, the Jewish elders, however, were fully aware of the Achilles' heel of the *Oberamt* and of the Municipal Council: the interests of imperial finance. Appropriate thereto was the threat of boycott, which they once again, quite undisguisedly, levelled. "His Imperial Majesty's interests," they declared, "would—particularly since we pay a double duty on our departure—be most grievously affected if we and our Jewish trade, which redounds to the profit of the entire Duchy of Silesia, should be compelled by such edicts to withdraw to other areas."[60]

As was to be expected, this had the desired effect. On January 17, only three days after the Jewish memorandum had been presented to the *Oberamt*, it was transmitted to the Municipal Council, requesting a report on the matter.[61] The Council, vacillating between the Consistory and the *Oberamt*, i.e., between the Judophobes and the interests of trade, could find no way out of its dilemma other than turning for information about the worship of the arriving and departing Jews to Daniel Springer, professor of Hebrew at the Elisabethgymnasium. They posed three questions: (1) Had Breslau Jews ever had synagogues, or had they always conducted services in rented rooms? (2) What was the content of the Jewish prayers, and was there any truth to the reports of the apostates that these prayers contain calumnies against Christians as well as lèse-majesté? (3) What was the significance of the accouterments of Jewish daily worship—the phylacteries, prayer-shawl, and the Scroll of the Law? Daniel Springer's reply,

---

[58] The Jewish elders were generally at the fairs (in Bohemia and Moravia they were exempt from entry duties) both in connection with personal business matters as well as with Jewish communal affairs. *ZGJT*, vol. ii, p. 4-5 (on Moravian Jews). In the statutes of the Breslau Municipal Archives, lists of visitors to fairs in the 18th century are found in which the Jewish elders are mentioned as such.

[59] NNN 449f.

[60] Quoted by Brilling, B., in "Die Bedeutung des jüdischen Handels für den Fiscus im 17ten Jahrhundert," *Schlesische Geschichteblätter* (Breslau 1933) no. 2, p. 33, fn. 4. The source is used by Weinryb, *op. cit.*, p. 34.

[61] NNN 449e.

delivered on March 9, was a thoroughly objective statement, and fully substantiated the explanations of the Jews.[62]

He answered the first query in the negative. Defining synagogues as buildings specially constructed and designated for the purpose of religious worship, he stated that Jews had never had synagogues in Breslau, such as they maintained in Bohemia, Moravia, Frankfurt am Main, Amsterdam, Great and Little Poland, Lithuania, Rome and Italy. (Non-Christian Turkey was, naturally, omitted from the list.) In Breslau, Jews held services only in rented rooms. His reply to the second question was also favorable to the Jews: he had never found anything hostile to Christianity or to the authorities in any of the prayerbooks printed in Amsterdam, Prague or Dyhernfurt (Brzeg Dolny) or in manuscript prayerbooks. On the contrary, he reported that, much to his own surprise, he had discovered a specially composed Hebrew prayer for the well-being of His Majesty and of the authorities.[63] He gave the text of this prayer in German translation in his deposition. The third question was naturally easily answered: the phylacteries, he wrote, served Jews as "a reminder of God's commandments"; the *tallis* was a prayer shawl; and the Scroll of the Law contained the Pentateuch in Hebrew.

While Professor Springer, however, was occupied with drawing up his expert's testimony, the struggle against the Jewish synagogues was carried on. For the Consistory, the back-and-forth bureaucratic procedure of the *Oberamt* and Municipal Council was too protracted. It conducted inquiries on its own initiative and ascertained the existence of ten Jewish synagogues in Breslau. On March 10 it presented the *Oberamt* with a list of the ten synagogues. It requested that, since the annual Mid-Lenten-Market was close at hand, the *Oberamt* order an investigation of these places and punish the Jews for violation of the ban.[64]

On March 14 the *Oberamt* acceded to this request. The Municipal Council was instructed to look into these places, close the synagogues,

---

[62] NNN 4491, published in *Breslauer jüdisches Gemeindeblatt*, vol. viii (1931) p. 119-120. On Professor D. Springer see Zedler, in *Universallexikon* (1744) vol. xxxix, p. 507.

[63] The 17th century statutes of Moravian Jewry (the so-called "311 Statutes," published by G. Wolf as *Die alten Statuten der jüdischen Gemeinden in Mähren* [Vienna 1880]) contains the following: "Prayers are to be said in each synagogue every Saturday in honor of His Imperial Majesty" (§300, p. 77).

[64] NNN 449h, 449i.

and forbid their continued existence on pain of punishment.[65] Professor Springer's interim deposition notwithstanding, the Council gladly complied with the *Oberamt*'s instructions. It had the designated premises searched, uncovering various religious articles which, in the Council's opinion, were of little necessity in Jewish religious worship. This led it to assemble the Jewish elders, who were reproved and ordered to remove immediately from the city the articles, such as the Holy Ark, lamps, candelabras, and the like. However, they were not forbidden to conduct services, a result presumably to be attributed to the implicit threat of boycott as much as to the expert testimony of Professor Springer. The elders' reply covered several points: The religious articles were employed "only in prayer." Their presence in the rooms used for prayers was no indication that these were synagogues, and hence did not violate the agreement with the Municipal Council. Finally, they pointed out, their prayerbooks contained nothing antagonistic to Christianity or temporal authority. (Evidently they had some knowledge of Springer's communication.) The Council insisted on the retention of the ban on "Jewish synagogues." It went so far, however, as to acquiesce to the right of individual Jews, or of as many Jews as a room could contain, to pray silently and to omit all "Jewish ceremonies." This meant that the Jewish synagogues, which were located in rented rooms, were to all intents and purposes sanctioned, for they could, in any case, hold no more people than a room could contain.

This decision was contained in a report of the Municipal Council to the *Oberamt* of April 5, 1701,[66] conveying the results of its investigation and negotiations. The report contains a sally implicitly critical of the *Oberamt*: were it up to the Council alone, it states, no Jews would be allowed to remain in Breslau at all.

8

Thus the struggle concluded with a "victory" for the Jews. The threat of a boycott had disarmed even their greatest opponents. Jewish worship within the walls of Breslau thereafter continued undisturbed. The gains thus made were never again seriously threatened, despite occasional minor complaints and charges.

The account of the struggle of the last decade of the 17th century

[65] NNN 449g.
[66] Hs. F.8. 32 f., p. 50b-52a.

for the right of Jewish religious worship in Breslau reveals that the establishment and maintenance of the synagogues of Breslau is to be attributed solely to the protection and influence of the large Jewish associations of Poland (particularly the *Vaad Arba Arazot*), Bohemia and Moravia. The respect in which these Jewish "national associations" were held by the Breslau authorities was so great that not only were they considered worthy of commercial credit,[67] but their threat of boycott was taken most seriously.

THE JEWS IN THE CITIES OF THE REPUBLIC OF POLAND

By Jacob Lestchinsky

Originally published in the *Yivo Bleter*, XX (1942) and XXI (1943)

The growth of the population and its distribution according to regions and peoples were processes that had a direct bearing on the situation of the Jews in the Republic of Poland. However, since more than three-fourths of the Jews were city dwellers, the processes that occurred in the urban sector of the population affected the Jews more profoundly and more widely.

The Republic of Poland was little urbanized and the tempo of urbanization was very slow. According to the census of 1931, the urban population of Poland comprised only 27.2% of the total population. Taking Poland with its geographic boundaries of 1931, the urban population comprised:

1870	16.0%	of the total population
1900	19.6%	" " " "
1921	24.6%	" " " "
1931	27.2%	" " " "

In the 60 years that are considered the period of most intensive capitalist development, the percentage of the urban population in Poland did not even double.

Much to our regret, we cannot directly compare the urban population of Poland with that of other countries, for the definition of "urban" varies greatly in different countries. We shall, therefore, compare given types of cities, such as furnish a very clear conception of the degree of urbanization in various countries. We shall take cities of over 100,000 inhabitants, to indicate the development of the large city in various countries, and cities of over 10,000 inhabitants, to serve as a criterion of urbanity in general.

The percentage of the population was:

103

Countries	Year of Census	In Cities of Over 100,000 Inhabitants	In Cities of Over 10,000 Inhabitants
England	1931	39.8	77.3
Germany	1933	30.2	49.6
U. S. A.	1930	29.6	47.5
France	1936	16.0	39.4
Hungary	1930	14.5	42.5
U. S. S. R.	1933	12.1	16.6
Poland	1931	10.8	20.9

Among the seven cited countries, Poland is last both in respect to dwellers in large cities and in respect to urbanity in general. We have no information on cities of over 10,000 inhabitants in the U. S. S. R. but it is clear that if cities of over 20,000 inhabitants comprise 16.6% of the total population, the percentage of cities of over 10,000 inhabitants is much larger.

The table includes highly industrialized countries, such as England, the United States, and Germany, and also countries with a predominantly agricultural population, such as Russia and Hungary. Poland differs from both of these types of countries. The percentage of the population of the large cities—and this is most important—in Poland is only about one-fourth the percentage of England, about one-third the percentage of Germany and of the United States. It is also smaller than in Hungary and the U. S. S. R.

Till now we have dealt with the population of Poland as a whole. If our study is resolved into ethnic groups, the picture changes considerably.

We have seen that only about 10% of the entire population of Poland lived in large cities of over 100,000 inhabitants. If we divide all the inhabitants of the country into two groups—Jews and non-Jews—we obtain the following results: 27.4% of all Polish Jews and only 8.5% of non-Jews lived in 1931 in cities of over 100,000 inhabitants; that is, the percentage of the non-Jews was less than one-third that of the Jews. The conclusion is that even in Poland the Jews are dwellers of large cities and in this respect are not behind the populations of the most advanced countries.

The tempo of increase of the metropolitan population was somewhat more intensive among non-Jews than among Jews.

The percentage of inhabitants in cities of over 100,000 population was:

Year	Jews	Non-Jews
1897	16.0	4.4
1921	22.4	6.0
1931	27.4	8.5

In the first period the tempo of increase in the metropolitan population was alike in both groups. In the last ten years, 1921-31, the increase in the percentage of the metropolitan population among non-Jews was twice that of the Jews.

In 1931 the urban population of Poland was 8,731,047, which comprised 27.2% of the total population. However, not all cities were alike; some counted a million inhabitants; others, but a few thousand. Let us now analyze the Jewish and non-Jewish population according to the various types of city. The official statistics, in so far as they have analyzed the census of 1931, divided the cities into four categories: (1) over 100,000 inhabitants, (2) 50,000-100,000, (3) 20,000-50,000, (4) below 20,000. We shall follow these divisions. The distribution of the percentages of the Jewish and non-Jewish population according to type of city is:

Size of City	Jews		Non-Jews	
	1921	1931	1921	1931
Over 100,000	29.9	36.3	33.2	40.5
50,000 - 100,000	7.6	7.0	9.5	7.0
20,000 - 50,000	17.5	17.6	14.4	16.3
Up to 20,000	45.0	39.1	42.9	36.2
Total	100.0	100.0	100.0	100.0

If we take the urban population as an entity we find in the metropolitan cities of over 100,000 population a higher percentage of non-Jews than Jews. These metropolitan cities comprised only somewhat over 36.0% of the urban Jewish population and over 40% of the urban non-Jewish population. Both groups showed in the period 1921-31 a nearly similar increase in the percentage of metropolitan inhabitants. In cities of less than 20,000 inhabitants the Jews comprise a larger percentage of their total urban popula-

tion than the non-Jews. Both groups showed a relatively proportionate decline in the percentage of inhabitants in the smaller cities
in the period 1921-31.

Of greater significance is the percentage of the urban population
in the entire population—the degree of urbanization. In this respect,
the Jews occupy first place.

In 1931, 2,380,075 Jews of a total of 3,113,933 were urban
comprising 76.4% of all the Jews in Poland. Of the 28,801,867 non-
Jews only 6,350,972 were urban, comprising 22.0%. The percentage
of the urban population among Jews was, therefore, three and a half
times that of the non-Jews.

It is unfair, however, to consider all non-Jews in one group, for
the difference between Poles on the one hand, and Ukrainians and
White Russians on the other, would be no less than the difference
between Jews and Poles. We shall, therefore, have to differentiate
among the ethnic groups and not lump them under the category
of non-Jews.

Of every hundred persons in each ethnic group the following percentages were urban:

Year	Jews	Poles	Germans	Ukrainians and White Russians
1921	75.0	22.5	26.6	6.8
1931	76.4	27.0	29.1	7.2

Taking the year 1931, we find that the percentage of the urban
Jewish population was almost thrice that of the Polish or German
urban population, and ten times that of the Ukrainian or White Russian urban population.

Urbanity, metropolitanism, the percentage of Jews in a given
place—these were certainly factors that determined to the largest
degree the economic, political, and national fate of the Jewish people.
But they embrace the aspects of Jewish life depending on the vicinage.
On the other hand, the Jews of Poland were not only a part of the
surrounding world, they were also a world in themselves, a distinct
national world, depending not only upon its strength with reference
to the outside world, but also upon its absolute strength in general.
Compactness, the degree of concentration, plays an immense role in
the national life of the Jews, possibly an even greater role than among

sovereign peoples. Social institutions play an enormous role in Jewish life, particularly in modern days, when the cohesive effect of religion has largely weakened. The existence, however, of such institutions is largely dependent upon the density of the Jewish population. A large, compact mass, even if not large in comparison with the neighboring population, bears nevertheless a greater amount of national energy than a small group of Jews comprising a high percentage in the surrounding world.

Let us examine the compactness of the Jewish population. The following table, based on the census of 1931, will indicate the distribution of Polish Jewry according to the size of the Jewish community.

Cities	Jews	
	Number	Percentage
In all of Poland	3,113,933	100.0
2 Cities of over 100,000 Jews	555,156	17.8
3 Cities of 50,000 - 100,000 Jews	211,116	6.8
11 Cities of 20,000 - 50,000 Jews	281,658	9.1
19 Cities of 10,000 - 20,000 Jews	256,639	8.2
Total in 35 Cities of over 10,000 Jews ..	1,304,569	41.9
In all other places	1,809,364	58.1

Over one-sixth of all Polish Jews, in 1931, lived in two communities. About one-fourth of them lived in five communities of over 50,000 Jews each. Communities of over 10,000 Jews, thirty-five of them in all, accounted for more than two-fifths of the Polish Jews.

Tables 1 and 2 indicate the growth of communities of over 10,000 Jews. The first table includes 25 communities in the former Russian provinces, and the second table counts 10 communities in former Galicia. From these tables we can see that within the boundaries of the Republic of Poland (there was no Jewish community of over 10,000 in the former German parts) there were the following communities of over 10,000 Jews.

1855-1860	8
1897-1900	20
1921	32
1931	35

Five of the 10 Galician communities had, even in 1855-60, over 10,000 Jews, whereas only 3 of the 25 Russian Polish communities had at that time over 10,000 Jews.

TABLE 1

The Growth of Jewish Communities in Poland in Cities of over
10,000 Jews in 1931

	Cities	Jewish Population			
		1856/57	1897	1921	1931
1.	Warsaw	41,062	219,141	310,322	352,659
2.	Łódź	2,775	98,677	156,155	202,497
3.	Vilna	23,050	63,996	56,163	55,006
4.	Białystok	6,714	41,905	39,602	39,165
5.	Lublin	8,588	24,280	37,337	38,937
6.	Częstochowa	2,976	11,980	22,663	25,588
7.	Radom	1,495	11,277	24,565	25,159
8.	Rowne - Woł.	3,788	13,780	21,702	22,737
9.	Będzin	2,440	10,839	17,892	21,625
10.	Brześć n/B.	8,136	30,100	15,630	21,440
11.	Grodno	10,300	22,684	18,697	21,159
12.	Sosnowiec	--	2,921	13,646	20,805
13.	Pińsk	5,050	21,065	17,513	20,220
14.	Kielce	101	6,399	15,530	18,083
15.	Łuck	5,010	9,468	14,860	17,366
16.	Kalisz	4,353	7,597	15,566	16,220
17.	Siedlce	4,804	11,440	14,685	14,793
18.	Chełm	2,370	7,615	12,064	13,537
19.	Kowel	2,647	8,521	12,758	12,842
20.	Piotrków	4,151	9,543	11,630	11,400
21.	Tomaszów Maz.	1,863	9,386	10,070	11,310
22.	Włodzimierz woł.	--	5,854	5,917	10,665
23.	Zamość	2,490	7,034	9,383	10,265
24.	Włocławek	719[1]	4,201	9,595	10,209
25.	Ostrowiec	2,236	6,146	10,095	9,934
	Total	146,118[2]	554,849	883,040	1,023,621

[1] Jewish population in 1841.
[2] Total not including Sosnowiec and Włodzimierz.

In 1897-1900 there were already 20 communities with over
10,000 Jews: 13 in Russian Poland and 7 in Galicia. In 1921 their
number rises to 32; 22 in Russian Poland, and 10 in Galicia. In the
last 10 years three more communities have come into this category,
making a total of 35 communities of over 10,000 Jews; 25 in former
Russian Poland, and 10 in Galicia.

TABLE 2

The Growth of Jewish Communities in Galicia in Cities of
over 10,000 Jews in 1931

Cities	Jewish Population			
	1855/60	1900	1921	1931
1. Lwów	26,694	44,258	76,854	99,595
2. Cracow	17,971	31,852	45,192	56,515
3. Stanisławów	8,088	13,826	23,248	24,823
4. Tarnów	11,153	12,484	15,608	19,330
5. Przemyśl	5,962	13,319	18,360	17,326
6. Kołomyja	9,019	16,417	18,246	14,332
7. Tarnopol	10,848	13,330	13,768	13,999
8. Drohobycz	15,711	8,674	11,833	12,931
9. Rzeszów	5,801	6,144	11,361	11,228
10. Stryj	4,405	8,554	10,988	10,869
Total	115,652	168,858	245,458	280,948

Let us now see what percentage of the Jewish population lived in communities of over 10,000 Jews in the periods covered by the above two tables. It is quite possible that here and there a community may have dropped out of that category because of the decline in its Jewish population. But we believe that such cases can be confined to one or two communities at the most.

The number of Jews living in communities of over 10,000 Jews was:

Years	Number	Percentage of the Jewish Population
1855-1860	156,789	11.2
1897-1900	715,210	24.3
1921	1,124,533	39.5
1931	1,304,569	41.9

The number of Jews living in communities of 10,000 Jews has multiplied more than eight-fold in the period of 1855-1931. The general Jewish population in Poland, however, has only slightly more than doubled in that period. Hence, the concentration of Jewish population in Poland was four times as intensive as the general rate of growth of the Jewish population. In 1855-60 slightly over one-tenth (11.2%) of all the Jews in Poland lived in communities of over 10,000 Jews; at the turn of the century this type of community accounted for almost one-fourth of the total Jewish population, and in 1921 for nearly two-fifths of the total. For the last ten years of which we possess data, 1921-31, both the absolute number of the concentrated Jewish population and the percentage of such population has increased considerably less than in previous years.

The rate of concentration in large communities differed in various periods. It was most rapid in the period 1900-21. In those years the percentage of the Jewish population living in large communities increased over 50%.

We have hitherto worked on the assumption that a community of 10,000 Jews may be considered a large one. Let us examine, nevertheless, the concentration of Jews in communities of over 20,000 Jews.

Communities of over 20,000 Jews were:

1885-1880	3
1897-1900	10
1921	11
1931	16

The number of communities of over 20,000 Jews has multiplied more than five-fold in the period 1855-1931. Particularly striking is the increase of the last 10 years, from 11 communities of over 20,000 Jews in 1921 to 16 in 1931. It suffices, however, to cast a glance at the tables to be convinced that this increase is not in every case the result of an organic development; in some instances it is rather the filling of a vacuum created in the years of World War I. The five cities that advanced, in the period 1921-31, from less than 20,000 inhabitants to the category of more than 20,000 inhabitants were all in the former Russian Poland. Only two of the five, Będzin and Sosnowiec, had an organic increase in their Jewish population springing from the development of these localities and their attraction of new settlers. The other three, Pinsk, Brest, and Grodno, had a larger Jewish population in 1900 than even in 1931. They had lost a large part of their Jewish population in World War I. In 1921 the loss was very considerable and in 1931 it was compensated to some extent, but not altogether.

Let us see what percentage of the Jewish population lived in cities of over 20,000 Jews in various periods.

Years	Number	Percentage of the Jewish Population
1855-1860	90,806	6.5
1897-1900	597,958	20.3
1921	813,803	28.6
1931	1,047,930	33.4

Here the concentration of the Jews in larger communities is much more evident than in the case of cities of over 10,000 Jews. The absolute number of Jews in cities of over 20,000 Jews has multiplied almost twelve-fold in the period of 1855(69)-1931. Furthermore, this tempo of concentration was maintained steadily. The percentage of Jews living in such large communities was in 1855(60) some 6½ and in 1931 over 33. Exactly one-third of all the Polish Jews, in 1931, lived in cities of over 20,000 Jews—totaling 16 such cities.

Of the 35 Jewish communities of over 10,000 people in 1931, 25 located in predominantly Polish districts, where the Jews faced a homogeneous majority; ten were in districts with a Ukrainian majority and 5 in districts with a White Russian majority.

Having determined a fairly intensive concentration of Jews in large communities, let us consider the vicinage in which these compact Jewish masses lived. We mean vicinage in the sense of strength with reference to the environment and also in the sense of the national uniformity of the non-Jewish population. The compactness of the Jewish settlement undoubtedly plays an important part, but no less important is the role of the surrounding world with which it is necessary to struggle not only for economic existence, but also for national survival.

Tables 3, 4 and 5 list 50 localities of a total population of 20,000 each. They include the 35 large Jewish communities with over 10,000 Jews. The other 15 cities have fewer than 10,000 Jews. Four of these 15 have even fewer than 5,000 Jews each. Two of these four cities have a total population of over 100,000. These two cities are Poznań and Chorzów.

Poznań is one of the oldest Jewish communities and had in 1840 a Jewish population of 6,763. It was then the largest Jewish community in Prussia. In 1871 the Jewish community had attained the number of 7,255. Then the decline set in. In 1905 it numbered no more than 5,761; in 1921 only 2,088, and in 1931, 1,604. Poznań is an example of a declining old Jewish community amidst a growing non-Jewish community.

The second city of a total population of over 100,000 and less than 5,000 Jews is an excellent example of a type of rapidly developed settlement that remained practically closed to the Jews. Chorzów was the center of the Polish chemical industry, which was almost entirely in the hands of the government.

TABLE 3
The Jewish Population in Eleven Cities of over 10,000 Inhabitants

	Cities	Total	1 9 3 1				1921		1897 or 1900	
			Jews		Poles		Jews	Poles	Jews	Poles
			Number	Per-centage	Number	Per-centage	Per-centage	Per-centage	Per-centage	Per-centage
1.	Warsaw	1,171,898	352,659	30.1	783,933	66.9	33.1	63.8	33.9	59.8
2.	Łódź	604,629	202,497¹	33.5	340,179	56.3	34.5	53.5	31.8	49.0
3.	Lwów	312,231	99,595	31.9	157,490	50.5	35.0	51.0	29.0	52.5
4.	Poznań	246,467	1,604	0.6	236,829	96.1	1.2	93.3	5.1	62.7
5.	Cracow	219,286	56,515	25.8	159,372	72.7	24.6	74.2	24.1	74.7
6.	Vilna	195,071	55,006	28.2	125,999	64.6	36.1	58.4	45.4	40.3
7.	Katowice	126,058	5,716	4.5	113,209	89.8	3.1	83.2	7.8	73.5
8.	Częstochowa	117,179	25,588	21.9	90,343	77.1	28.2	70.5	28.9	68.5
9.	Lublin	112,285	38,937	34.7	71,542	63.7	39.6	60.0	51.3	41.5
10.	Sosnowiec	108,959	20,805	19.1	86,605	79.5	15.8	76.9	--	--
11.	Chorzów	101,977	2,811	2.7	94,010	92.2	1.2	91.3	1.6	84.9
	Total	3,316,040	861,733	25.9	2,259,511	68.1	28.5	65.3	30.1	56.7

TABLE 4
The Jewish Population in Eight Cities of 50,000—100,000 Inhabitants

	Cities	Total	1 9 3 1				1921		1897 or 1900	
			Jews		Poles		Jews	Poles	Jews	Poles
			Number	Per-centage	Number	Per-centage	Per-centage	Per-centage	Per-centage	Per-centage
1.	Białystok	91,101	39,165	43.0	41,493	45.6	51.6	38.6	63.5	19.7
2.	Radom	77,902	25,159	32.3	51,811	66.5	39.7	59.2	41.5	52.6
3.	Stanisławów	59,960	24,823	41.4	22,312	37.2	45.2	37.7	51.2	30.8
4.	Kielce	58,236	18,083	31.0	39,524	67.9	37.6	61.8	30.4	63.4
5.	Włocławek	55,966	10,209	18.3	43,671	78.0	23.8	72.0	19.7	72.1
6.	Kalisz	55,007	19,248	35.0	33,746	61.3	34.9	61.3	31.1	56.8
7.	Piotrków	51,349	11,400	22.2	38,311	74.6	28.4	68.6	33.1	61.3
8.	Przemyśl	51,038	17,326	34.0	25,154	49.3	38.3	45.8	35.3	44.7
	Total	500,559	165,413	33.1	296,022	59.1	39.9	52.8	44.6	43.5

TABLE 5
The Jewish Population in Cities of 20,000—50,000 Inhabitants

Cities		Total	1931				1921		1897 or 1900	
			Jews		Poles		Jews	Poles	Jews	Poles
		Total	Number	Per-centage	Number	Per-centage	Per-centage	Per-centage	Per-centage	Per-centage
1.	Grodno	49,669	21,159	42.6	21,555	43.4	53.9	34.7	59.5	21.8
2.	Brześć n/B.	48,385	21,440	44.3	17,797	36.8	53.1	29.4	75.4	8.5
3.	Będzin	47,597	21,625	45.4	25,790	54.2	62.1	37.5	45.8	52.8
4.	Pabianice	45,670	8,357	18.3	32,354	70.8	24.4	65.8	18.8	42.7
5.	Tarnów	44,927	19,330	43.0	25,305	56.3	44.1	54.3	42.7	50.9
6.	Borysław	41,496	11,996	28.9	19,669	47.4	44.5	41.3	55.7	26.7
7.	Równe - Woł.	40,612	22,737	56.0	10,418	25.6	71.2	11.2	69.4	8.1
8.	Tomaszów Maz.	38,020	11,310	29.8	22,749	59.8	35.6	52.8	46.6	34.1
9.	Siedlce	36,931	14,793	40.1	21,559	58.4	47.9	51.2	53.2	38.0
10.	Tarnopol	35,644	13,999	39.3	14,611	41.0	44.6	29.9	46.5	25.9
11.	Łuck	35,554	17,366	48.9	10,669	38.0	70.2	15.7	72.1	9.8
12.	Kołomyja	33,788	14,332	42.4	12,450	36.8	44.4	35.8	50.8	28.1
13.	Płock	32,998	6,571	19.9	25,153	76.2	28.5	67.1	29.2	58.4
14.	Drohobycz	32,261	12,931	40.1	10,629	32.9	44.3	30.9	44.7	25.8
15.	Pińsk	31,912	20,220	63.4	6,324	19.8	74.7	10.9	74.2	7.5
16.	Stryj	30,491	10,869	35.7	10,311	33.8	40.2	32.8	37.9	33.1
17.	Chełm	29,074	13,537	46.5	13,232	45.5	52.0	40.9	57.8	18.8
18.	Kowel	27,677	12,842	46.4	9,638	34.8	61.3	19.2	58.9	10.7
19.	Rzeszów	26,902	11,228	28.7	15,410	57.3	45.5	53.5	48.3	50.6
20.	Zgierz	26,618	4,547	17.1	18,358	69.0	18.1	63.2	18.6	59.8
21.	Ostrowiec	25,908	9,934	38.4	15,812	61.0	51.2	48.5	63.0	36.2
22.	Łomza	25,022	8,912	35.6	15,707	62.8	41.5	56.8	46.3	45.3
23.	Włodzimierz Wol.	24,591	10,665	43.4	8,813	35.9	50.9	26.6	66.6	10.3
24.	Zamość	24,241	10,265	42.3	13,207	54.5	49.3	49.0	64.2	24.4
25.	Kutno	23,368	6,440	27.5	16,576	70.9	42.5	56.2	51.1	46.6
26.	Zdunska Wola	22,939	8,819	38.5	12,292	53.6	41.7	49.5	46.1	39.9
27.	Bielsko	22,332	4,430	19.8	12,645	56.6	20.1	54.2	15.0	56.3
28.	Jarosław	22,195	6,272	28.3	12,594	56.7	32.9	52.6	30.1	50.2
29.	Sambor	21,923	6,274	28.6	11,853	54.1	31.3	55.1	29.5	53.1
30.	Suwałki	21,826	5,811	26.6	14,715	67.4	34.2	60.2	41.0	48.5
31.	Skierniewice	20,143	4,445	22.1	15,480	76.8	28.4	70.7	32.7	54.4
	Total	990,714	373,456	37.6	493,676	49.8	45.3	42.3	48.5	33.3

Both Poznań and Chorzów are in the former German part of Poland.

Before proceeding to a detailed analysis of the respective tables, let us have a comprehensive view of the entire material. We shall juxtapose the percentage of Jews and Poles in the three types of cities in the beginning of the given period and its close.

Type of City	Jews			Poles		
	Percentage 1897 (1900)	Percentage 1931	±	Percentage 1897 (1900)	Percentage 1931	±
Over 100,000	30.1	25.9	— 13.9	56.7	68.1	+ 20.1
50,000 - 100,000	44.6	33.1	— 25.8	43.5	59.1	+ 35.8
20,000 - 50,000	48.5	37.6	— 22.5	33.3	49.8	+ 49.5

We see that the percentage of the Jews has declined in all the three types. The greatest decline was in the middle type of city, of a population of 50,000-100,000. Their strength, in that type of city, was reduced one-fourth. Second in decline were the small cities, of 20,000-50,000. There, Jews lost nearly one-fourth of their percentage. The smallest losses were sustained precisely in the largest cities; there, the decline in percentage was only one-seventh.

The percentage of the Poles, on the other hand, has increased in all types of cities, in the smaller ones, over one-third and in the cities with over 100,000, one-fifth.

Of the three types of cities, the Jews had the largest percentage in the small cities of 20,000-50,000, and the smallest in the large cities of over 100,000. In 1897 (1900) the Jews constituted, in the large cities, less than one-third, but in the small and middle cities they had a relative majority.

In 1931 the situation has radically changed. Jews had no longer even a relative majority in any of the groups.

The Poles had in 1897 (1900) an absolute majority only in the first group, of over 100,000. But in 1931 they attained a majority in all the three types of cities—an absolute majority in the large and middle types, and an approximate absolute majority (49.8%) in the small cities.

The above three types of cities, totaling 50, contain the core of the urban population of Poland, not only qualitatively (for they include the largest cities with the largest industrial and commercial establishments as well as administrative and educational institutions), but even quantitatively. In these 50 localities, 4,750,000 people lived in 1931, that is, over one-half of the total urban population of Poland and over 60% of the urban Jewish population.

Let us examine the individual tables. Table 3 shows 11 cities with a population of over 100,000 each. The constituency of these cities was such:

Nationality	1897 (1900)	1921	1931
Jews	30.1	28.5	25.9
Poles	56.7	65.3	68.1

The Polish majority had increased considerably, from 56.7% in 1897 (1900) to 68.1% in 1931, while the percentage of Jews declined from 30.1% to 25.9% during that period.

A striking point in this table is the fact that precisely in the largest cities the Jews have either gained slightly (Lodz) or lost very little (Warsaw), whereas in the middle cities they sustained considerable losses (Vilna and Lublin). Let us juxtapose the first two cities, the industrial and commercial centers of Poland, and the last two cities that were primarily administrative centers.

City	Jews		Poles	
	Percentage in 1897	Percentage in 1931	Percentage in 1897	Percentage in 1931
Warsaw	33.9	30.1	59.8	66.9
Łódź	31.8	33.5	49.0	56.3
Vilna	45.4	28.2	40.3	64.6
Lublin	51.3	34.7	41.5	63.7

The Jews sustained losses in three cities—Warsaw, Vilna, and Lublin. But whereas in the former the loss is negligible, in the latter two it is considerable. In Lodz the Jews even showed a slight increase. On the whole it can be said that in the two largest cities the Jews maintained their positions, but in Vilna their percentage declined 37.9% and in Lublin one-third.

The gains of the Poles were higher than the losses of the Jews, for the Poles also took the place of evacuated Russian and German officials.

The reason for the retention of the Jewish economic position in Warsaw and Lodz and its loss in Vilna and Lublin can be explained in the following manner. The economic gains of the Poles were greatest in commerce, the civil service, and the liberal professions.

In Lodz and Warsaw the Jews succeeded in industry, and that compensated for their losses in the other three branches of economy. In the provincial cities, where industry was relatively little developed, the Jews showed a decline in their numerical strength and the Poles a considerable gain.

Let us consider in somewhat greater detail the two largest cities of Poland, which contained on the eve of World War II fully 600,000 Jews, almost one-fifth of the Jewish population. The development of the Jewish population in these two cities reflects the process of growth of Polish Jewry as a whole, their constant rise in the course of the 19th century and up to World War I, and the crisis brought about by that war, which, as it were, interrupted the organic process of continuous growth.

The rise of the Jews in Warsaw:

Year	Jews	
	Number	Percentage of the Total Population
1781	3,532	4.5
1810	14,061	18.1
1856	44,149	24.3
1882	127,917	33.4
1897	219,141	33.9
1914	337,074	38.1
1917	343,263	41.0
1921	310,322	33.1
1931	352,659	30.1
1939 (est.)	375,000	29.0

Let us at once include the figures on Lodz, which are even more interesting and striking:

Year	Jews	
	Number	Percentage of the Total Population
1793	11	5.7
1856	2,775	12.2
1897	98,677	31.8
1910	166,628	40.7
1921	156,155	34.5
1931	202,497	33.5
1936	219,612	34.4
1939 (est.)	222,000	34.5

In the 160 years under consideration, the number of Jews in Warsaw has increased more than a hundred-fold, whereas the non-Jewish population has increased in the same period only twelve-fold. The percentage of Jews in the city has increased 6½ times. The line of development, of course, was not even; it was closely interrelated with the development of the non-Jewish population.

The Jews of Warsaw have had an absolute numerical increase practically all the time. The interruption in the period 1917-21 was due to specific war conditions and not to organic causes. In 1917 there were in Warsaw large numbers of refugees from the provinces. The high percentage of Jews in Warsaw in 1917 is attributable to the fact that a large part of the non-Jewish population left for the villages, where living conditions were more favorable. The small number of Jews who left for the interior of Russia on the eve of the German occupation in 1915 was more than counterbalanced by an influx of Jewish refugees. The decline in the number of Jews in 1921, in comparison with 1914, was most likely also a result of war conditions. Between 1917 and 1921 many refugees from the provinces returned to their homes, whereas the evacuees to Russia, or those drafted for compulsory labor to Germany, returned in but small numbers.

Let us, therefore, leave out the war period and analyze the growth of the Jewish population in normal years.

Up to 1882 we see an intensive rise in the absolute number of Jews. Their percentual increase is even greater. Between 1856 and 1882 their number rises by 80,000 and their proportional strength rises from 24.3% to 33.4%. This was the first stage in the development of the city, when Warsaw assumed the economic functions of Berdichev, the commercial and industrial center of the Ukraine in the first half of the 19th century. From a center of the fancy goods industry, Warsaw soon rose to a leading position in the general commerce of Russian Poland. This development attracted to the city more Jews than non-Jews.

From 1882 to 1897 the number of Jews in Warsaw rises by 91,000. The percentage of Jews, however, remains practically the same. The influx of non-Jews has approximated the influx of Jews. Those were the years of the rise and development of large industry, particularly heavy industry, which attracted large numbers of non-Jewish workers.

The first decade of the 20th century sees the rise of the Jewish small industry as a result of the expansion of the Russian market. The relative influx of Jews then exceeds that of the non-Jews. From 1897 to 1914 the number of Jews in Warsaw rises by 118,000 and their percentage exceeds 38.

At this point the war and its resultant crisis set in.

With the return of normality in 1921, the number of Jews continues growing, but to a much lesser degree than before the war. Far more significant is the fact that the Jewish percentage began to decline. True, at a slow rate, but decline it did, and a constant decline is symptomatic. The relative numerical strength of the Jews in Warsaw in 1939 fell considerably below that in 1882. The rise in the absolute number of Jews in Warsaw is to be explained by the fact that in the Republic of Poland, too, the city remained a great industrial center, and particularly a center of the almost exclusively Jewish fancy goods industry. The influx of Jewish workers and small entrepreneurs did not cease. But in the Republic of Poland Warsaw also became a far greater administrative and educational center. These last two branches of activity brought in Polish elements virtually exclusively.

Lodz was mainly an industrial city. Its industry, as far as ownership and management are concerned, was almost entirely in the hands of Jews and Germans. The Jews and the Germans have played a particularly prominent role in the textile industry, in which the majority of Jewish workers concentrated. For Lodz, too, World War I marked a crisis in the growth of the Jewish population. In 1910 the Jews constituted over 40% of the population, a percentage which they never attained thereafter.

In general, the growth of that city was remarkable. From a village of less than 300 inhabitants at the end of the 18th century Lodz attained a population of nearly 700,000 on the eve of World War II. But the growth of the Jewish population was even more phenomenal: from 11 people at the end of the 18th century to more than 200,000 on the eve of World War II. This rise was constant, with the exception of the period 1910-21. But the decline then was due to the war conditions, from which Lodz suffered more than Warsaw. Lodz was particularly affected economically. The Germans had removed the machinery of the textile mills to Germany, and the workers left the city. Furthermore, the number of Russian Jews in Lodz was larger than in Warsaw, so that the voluntary evacuation to the interior assumed greater proportions there.

The most intensive growth of the Jewish population in Lodz was in the 54 years between 1856 and 1910, from 2,755 to 166,628, from 12.2% to 40.7%. Under the Republic of Poland the absolute growth of the Jewish population continued. From 1921 to 1931 the Jewish population increased by 66,000, an increase as large as that of the Jewish population in Warsaw, which at the outset (1921) was twice as large as the Jewish population of Lodz. Nevertheless, the percentage of Jews in Lodz in 1939 was the same as in 1921.

Table 4 has 8 cities with a population of 50,000-100,000. Let us submit Bialystok to a closer consideration. In 1897 the Jews there comprised two-thirds of the population; in 1931, only 43%. True, this decline was not entirely the result of organic conditions. The Polish municipal administration had incorporated in the city a number of suburban sections with an exclusively non-Jewish population. In addition, the municipality lavished attention upon these newly embodied sections and opened a park there. All educational and recreational institutions were transferred there and a number of modern homes constructed. Soon this section supplanted the older sections, where a Jewish majority remained, as the municipal center. Owing to this mechanical manipulation as well as to their organic influx, the numerical strength of the Poles rose considerably in that city: from 19.7% in 1897, they attained 45.6% in 1931, that is, nearly a majority.

The decline of the Jewish community in Bialystok becomes more marked when we take into consideration the number of Jews in a period prior to 1897. We know the number of Jews in 1887 and their percentage.

Year	Total Population	Jews	
		Number	Percentage
1887*	50,726	42,798	84.4
1897	66,032	41,905	63.5
1931	91,101	39,165	43.0

* *Памятная книга гродненской губернiи*, 1897, 10-11.

The total population nearly doubled in the given period, whereas the Jewish population lost over 3,000 people. The percentage of Jews has been reduced to nearly one-half.

Table 5 gives the Jewish population and its percentage in 31 cities of 20,000-50,000. In 1897, Jews in these cities comprised 48.5%, which constituted a considerable relative majority, since the Poles comprised only 33.3% and all others 18.2%. In 1931, the Jews in these cities comprised only 37.6% and the Poles 49.8%.

The Jews comprised more than a half of the population in these 31 cities:

1897 (1900) .... in 14 cities
1921 .... " 10 "
1931 .... " 2 "

We have till now considered cities with no less than 20,000 inhabitants. Such cities, in all of Poland, totaled 50. These 50 cities had in 1931 more than a half of the total urban population and some 60% of the Jewish urban population. But even in 1931, the cities with less than 20,000 inhabitants still accounted for some 40% of the urban Jewish population. In the 19th century the percentage of Jews in the small cities was considerably higher. It will, therefore, be of great interest to consider the Jewish percentage in all urban places over a comparatively lengthy period.

TABLE 6

The Percentage of the Jewish Population in the Cities of Russian Poland

Percentage	1827		1857		1897*		1921	
of Jews	Number	Percentage	Number	Percentage	Number	Percentage	Number	Percentage
Below 10%	20	11.1	13	7.2	0	-	6	3.1
10% - 20%	24	13.3	11	6.1	5	4.6	14	7.1
20% - 30%	23	12.7	19	10.5	3	2.7	27	13.8
30% - 40%	35	19.5	18	9.9	21	19.1	50	25.5
40% - 50%	18	10.0	32	17.7	24	21.8	41	20.9
50% - 75%	55	30.6	76	41.9	54	49.1	55	28.1
Over 75%	5	2.8	12	6.7	3	2.7	3	1.5
Total	180	100.0	181	100.0	110	100.0	196	100.0

* Data for that year are incomplete.

Table 6 shows the percentual distribution of Jews in nearly 200 urban places for close to a hundred years. This table covers the former Russian Poland. The data for 1897 are not complete; we have included them for the sake of the relative figures, which are not without some interest.

This table shows that in former Russian Poland there were urban places with a Jewish majority:

1827 .... 33.4%
1857 .... 48.6%
1897 .... 51.8%
1921 .... 29.6%

The growth of urban places with a Jewish majority continued to the end of the 19th century.

Places with a Jewish population of 30-50%, that is a considerable Jewish minority, were:

1827 .... 29.5%
1857 .... 27.6%
1921 .... 46.4%

The number of these places has risen, at the expense of the places with a Jewish majority.

TABLE 7

The Percentage of the Jewish Population in the Cities of Galicia

Percentage of Jews	1880		1900		1921	
	Number	Percentage	Number	Percentage	Number	Percentage
Below 10%	3	2.4	3	2.4	2	1.6
10% - 20%	3	2.4	4	3.2	11	8.8
20% - 30%	15	12.0	17	13.6	22	17.6
30% - 40%	22	17.6	30	24.0	33	26.4
40% - 50%	27	21.6	37	29.6	30	24.0
50% - 75%	47	37.6	29	23.2	25	20.0
Over 75%	8	6.4	5	4.0	2	1.6
Total	125	100.0	125	100.0	125	100.0

Table 7 furnishes similar data for 125 urban places in Galicia. Unfortunately, our data go back no farther than 1880, a period in which the influx of the non-Jewish population into the cities exceeds the Jewish influx, so that the percentage of the Jews is on the decline.

Places with a Jewish majority in Galicia were:

1880 ....44%   of the 125 urban localities
1900 ....27.2% "   "   "   "   "
1921 ....21.6% "   "   "   "   "

In general, the following conclusion is warranted: the number of urban places with a Jewish majority was on the constant decline.

TABLE 8

The Percentage of the Jewish Population in Nine Cities in Volhynia in 1921, 1931 and 1937 *

City	1921				1931				Index:1921=100		1937				Index:1931=100	
	Jews		Non-Jews		Jews		Non-Jews				Jews		Non-Jews			
	Number	Per-centage	Number	Per-centage	Number	Per-centage	Number	Per-centage	Jews	Non-Jews	Number	Per-centage	Number	Per-centage	Jews	Non-Jews
1. Łuck	14,860	70.2	6,297	29.8	17,366	48.9	18,188	51.1	116.9	288.8	15,850	39.0	24,835	61.0	91.4	136.5
2. Kowel	12,758	61.3	8,060	32.7	12,842	46.4	14,835	53.6	100.7	184.1	13,200	40.0	19,800	60.0	102.8	133.5
3. Włodzimierz Woł.	5,917	50.9	5,706	49.1	10,665	43.4	13,926	56.6	180.2	244.1	11,550	39.0	18,060	61.0	108.3	129.7
4. Dubno	5,315	58.1	3,831	41.9	7,364	58.0	5,332	42.0	138.6	139.2	7,000	46.7	8,000	53.3	95.1	150.0
5. Krzemieniec	6,616	41.2	9,452	58.8	7,256	36.5	12,621	63.5	109.7	133.5	6,240	26.0	17,760	74.0	86.0	140.7
6. Sarny	2,808	47.3	3,123	52.7	3,414	45.0	4,173	65.0	118.5	133.6	4,950	45.0	6,050	65.0	145.0	145.0
7. Dąbrowica	2,536	94.1	158	5.9	2,536	90.0	378	10.0	100.0	239.2	3,225	43.0	4,275	57.0	127.2	1,131.0
8. Lubewno	3,141	94.4	187	5.6	3,807	91.3	362	8.7	121.2	193.6	3,160	62.0	1,940	38.0	88.0	535.9
9. Horochów	2,377	53.8	2,044	46.2	2,806	46.0	3,198	54.0	118.0	156.5	3,120	40.0	4,680	60.0	111.2	146.3
Total	56,328	59.2	38,858	40.8	68,056	48.2	73,013	51.8	120.8	187.9	68,325	39.3	105,400	60.7	100.4	144.4

* Uwagi i dane o możliwościach ekspansji gospodarczej kupiectwa i rzemiosła polskiego na Wołyniu. Opracował Władysław Pawlino. Warszawa, 1938.

TABLE 9

The National Structure of the Population of Six Cities of Volhynia in 1921 and 1937 *

City		1 9 2 1			1 9 3 7					
		Jews	Poles	Others	Number			Index: 1921=100		
					Jews	Poles	Others	Jews	Poles	Other
1.	Łuck	14,860	3,331	2,966	15,880	16,690	8,145	106.9	501.1	274.6
2.	Włodzimierz Woł.	5,917	3,087	2,619	11,550	12,730	5,330	195.2	412.4	203.5
3.	Dubno	5,315	1,065	2,766	7,000	4,000	4,000	131.7	375.6	144.7
4.	Krzemieniec	6,616	1,433	8,019	6,240	7,200	10,560	94.3	502.4	131.7
5.	Lubewno	3,141	58	129	3,160	665	1,275	100.6	1146.6	988.4
6.	Radziwiłłów	2,036	318	1,886	3,120	1,020	1,860	153.2	320.8	98.6
	Total	37,885	9,292	18,385	46,950	42,305	31,170	123.9	455.3	169.5

* *Uwagi i dane . . . .*

We have hitherto operated mainly with data that do not go beyond 1931—the last national census in Poland. But precisely in the last years of the Polish Republic the percentage of the Poles in the urban population has risen rapidly, particularly in the peripheral regions. The data for the years after 1931 are incomplete, but the few submitted in tables 8 and 9, on a small number of places in the district of Volhynia, furnish a picture that is certainly no exception.

Table 8 shows that in the given 9 places the Jewish percentage was:

1921 . . . . 59.2
1931 . . . . 48.2
1937 . . . . 39.3

This rapid decline in the percentage of the Jews was due to the very large influx of non-Jews, which completely annulled whatever Jewish influx there was.

Let us take 1921 as 100, then the situation in 1931 was:

Jews 120.8
Non-Jews 187.9

That is, the influx of non-Jews was over four times higher than that of Jews. If we take 1931 as 100, the situation in 1937 was:

Jews 100.4
Non-Jews 144.4

That is, the Jewish increase has ceased, while the non-Jewish continued at the previous rate.

BIBLIOGRAPHY

Jacob Lestchinsky, *Dos Yidishe Folk in Tsifern* ("The Jewish People in Figures"), Berlin, 1922.

Jacob Lestchinsky, *Di Antviklung fun Yidishn Folk far di Letste 100 Yor* ("The Growth of the Jewish People for the Last 100 Years"), *Shriftn far Ekonomik un Statistik,* Yidisher Visnshaftlekher Institut—Yivo, Vol. I, Berlin, 1928.

Menakhem Linder, *Di Natsyonale Struktur fun di Shtet in Poyln* ("The National Structure of the Cities in Poland"). *Yidishe Ekonomik,* Yivo, 1938, Nos. 1-2.

Bentsion Rubshtein, *Galitsye un ir Bafelkerung* ("Galicia and Its Population"), Warsaw, 1923.

Max Rosenfeld, *Die polnische Judenfrage,* Wien-Berlin, 1918.

Józef Buzek, *Pogląd na wzrost ludności ziem polskich w wieku 19-tym,* Cracow, 1915.

Alfons Krysinśki, *Ludność polska a mniejszości w Polsce w świetle spisów ludności 1921 i 1931,* Warsaw, 1933.

Bohdan Wasiutyński, *Ludność żydowska w Polsce w wiekach XIX i XX.* Warsaw, 1930.

Concise Statistical Yearbook of Poland, 1938, Warsaw, 1938.

Skorowidz gmin Rzeczpospolitej Polskiej. Statystyka Polski, Seria B: Zeszyt 8, Warsaw, 1933.

Statystyka Polski: Spis ludności Rzeczpospolitej Polskiej, Warsaw, 1926-28.

Первая всеобщая перепись населенія Россійской Имперіи, СПБ., 2, I.

THE ECONOMIC BACKGROUND OF JEWISH EMIGRATION FROM GALICIA TO THE UNITED STATES

By RAPHAEL MAHLER

Originally published in *Geshikhte fun der yidisher arbeter-bavegung in di fareynikte shtatn,* vol. i (1943)

The emigration of Galician Jews to the United States was inspired chiefly by causes of an economic character. In contrast to Russia, where pogroms and civil disabilities, in addition to poverty, were important factors in stimulating Jewish mass emigration, Jewish emigration from Galicia was entirely motivated by poverty, by the economic depression in the country which affected particularly the Jews. The tempo of emigration depended to a large degree on economic conditions in the United States. The depressions of 1893 and 1897 led to a decline in the number of Jewish emigrants from Galicia, as well as in the general emigration stream. Generally, however, there were no wide variations in the number of Jewish emigrants from Galicia from year to year. Jewish emigration from Galicia showed no sharp curves upward as did the emigration from Russia in years like 1882, 1891, 1904 and 1906.

Emigration of non-Jews (Poles and Ruthenians) from Galicia was proportionately smaller than the Jewish emigration. But the non-Jewish emigration from Galicia was also proportionately larger than the emigration of the same ethnic groups from tsarist Russia. Thus in the years 1901-1910, the number of Poles who emigrated to the United States from the Russian empire was 433,315 as compared to 398,347 from Galicia, even though there were twice as many Poles in Russia as there were in Galicia.[1] This indicates the presence of specific social and economic conditions in Galicia that caused mass emigration of both Jews and non-Jews.

[1] Hersch, L., *Di yidishe emigratsye* (Vilna 1914) p. 12, Table III.

Poverty in Galicia, notorious since the end of the 18th century, became especially pronounced during the last decades of the 19th century. Whereas neighboring countries and other provinces in Austria, as well as the adjacent Russian Poland, participated in the general process of capitalist development, with the resulting increase in industry and in standard of living, Galicia was barely touched by these economic developments. The progress of industrialization in Galicia was only about one-fifth of that of Austria as a whole.[2] In 1900 more than 80 percent of the Galician population was still engaged in agriculture.

The industrial backwardness of the country was not due to the absence of natural resources, but was mainly the result of social relations in the agrarian economy. The concentration of land in the hands of wealthy landowners was greater here than in any other of the former provinces of Poland. About 40 percent of all the land in Galicia was held by landowners possessing more than 50 hectares (approximately 125 acres) and 37 percent of this land was in the hands of owners of more than 100 hectares. On the other hand, 71 percent of all the peasants in Galicia in 1902 had holdings of less than 5 hectares (about 13 acres) and 44 percent had holdings of less than two hectares.[3]

The very low purchasing power of the largest part of the population, which was the result of the feudal conditions in the village, was the main obstacle in the industrial development of the province. Economic stagnation in Galicia was also aggravated by the policy of the Austrian government. Austria deliberately and consistently promoted a system of "colonial policy." Galicia was set aside as a market for the products—chiefly the so-called "inferior" goods for the "use of Galicia"—that the industrial areas in the monarchy produced. In this respect the interests of the Austrian government coincided with those of the large Polish landowners. The landowners developed only those branches of industry that served to increase the profits from their vast estates. About one-third of the mechanized industry in Galicia at the end of the 19th century consisted of beer breweries, distilleries and mills.[4]

---

[2] Kempner, St. A., *Dzieje gospodarcze Polski Pozbiorowej* (Warsaw 1920) vol. i, p. 344.

[3] Bujak, Franciszek, *O naprawie ustroju rolnego w Polsce* (Warsaw 1919) p. 17.

[4] Feldman, Wilhelm, *Stan ekonomiczny Galicji* (Lwów 1900) p. 18.

Under such circumstances it is no wonder that the misery of the Galician population increased sharply. The consumption in Galicia of such staples as grain, meat and potatoes was one-half of that in western Europe.[5] According to income-tax figures the per capita income of the population in Galicia was one-tenth that of the rest of Austria. The Polish economist Stanisław Szczepanowski pointed out the tragic results of this situation: 55,000 people died of starvation in Galicia annually.[6]

In addition to these general social and economic conditions Jewish misery was aggravated by other specific conditions. In 1900 the Jewish population in Galicia numbered 811,371, constituting about 11 percent of the total population. According to the census of 1900, the relatively largest occupational group consisted of merchants, dealers, shopkeepers and brokers, comprising 29.4 percent of all gainfully employed Jews. To this group should be added the tavern and inn-keepers who, according to the Austrian census, were listed under "industry and trade," thus making a total of over 37 percent of Galician Jews who earned their living from trade.

Poverty-stricken Galicia thus had proportionately twice as many tradespeople as the rich industrial provinces of Austria. According to unofficial but trustworthy figures derived from a private economic inquiry, there was in some districts one merchant or broker to every eight or ten families. Even in the villages the ratio was not much lower: in a village of 80 peasants there were generally six or seven dealers and shopkeepers.[7] About 88 percent of Galician trade in 1900 was in Jewish hands. This plethora of petty trade in such a poor land reflects the misery of the largest occupational group among the Jewish population in the country. According to reports from the end of the 19th century, the stock of the average Jewish shop in Galicia was worth about $20,[8] and frequently no more than four dollars.[9]

Even more abnormal was another, almost exclusively, Jewish occupation in Galicia, namely tavern keeping. According to official statistics, over 70,000 Jews in Galicia derived their living in 1900 from tavern keeping, and 22,981 Jews were actively engaged in this

[5] Szczepanowski, Stanisław, *Nędza Galicji*, cited by Kempner, *op. cit.*, p. 339.
[6] *Loc. cit.*
[7] Fleischer, Siegfried, "Enquete über die Lage der jüdischen Bevölkerung Galiziens," in *Jüdische Statistik* (Berlin 1903) 218.
[8] Landau, S. R., "Unter jüdischen Proletariern," in *Die Welt* (1897) no. 26.
[9] Pappenheim, Bertha, and Rabinowitsch, Sara, *Zur Lage der jüdischen Bevölkerung in Galizien* (Frankfurt 1904) p. 29.

occupation. Jewish tavern keepers and liquor dealers comprised four-fifths of the more than 88,000 people that made their living in Galicia by selling alcoholic beverages.[10] They constituted nearly 9 percent of the entire Jewish population in the country. The exceptionally large number of taverns and saloons, reflecting the frightful extent of alcoholism in the country, could nevertheless not provide a livelihood for the considerable number of Jews in the villages and towns who were engaged in this deplorable occupation, because of the terrific competition existing in the field.

In Jewish industry we also find the same atomization as in Jewish trade. Because of the low level of capitalist development in the provinces, the small artisan's shop prevailed in Galician industry. Nearly two-thirds of all the people engaged in industry worked in such shops. Nearly 38 percent of these shops employed from two to five persons. Jewish industry in particular was of this small-scale character. Whereas the number of independent enterprises for Galicia as a whole numbered 38 percent of the total, among Jews it comprised nearly 52 percent (according to the figures of 1900). The number of workers among Jews was less than one-third of all the Jews employed in industry, whereas among non-Jews that number was more than one-half. If we include helpers (members of the family) among the independently employed, some two-thirds of the Jews in industry would be in this category, whereas in the general industry of the country this category constituted only 45 percent of the total employed in industry.[11]

According to official statistics,[12] 28 percent of all Galician Jews gainfully employed in industry were in the clothing industry. If tavern keeping is not included under the heading of industry the figure for those gainfully employed in the clothing industry would be more than 40 percent. (The number of Jews in the entire clothing industry of the country amounted to more than 50 percent.) The second largest Jewish industrial branch was the food industry, in which one-fifth of the number of Jews gainfully employed in industry, exclusive of the tavern keepers, was engaged. (The Jews numbered 45 percent of the entire food industry in the country.) The Jews were also prominently represented in the leather and paper industries (43 percent), the

---

[10] Thon, Jakob, *Die Juden in Österreich* (Berlin 1907) p. 121.
[11] Bujak, *op. cit.*, vol. i, p. 203, 134.
[12] The following figures are taken from the Tables of J. Buzek, cited by J. Thon, *op. cit.*

chemical industry (38 percent), printing (21 percent), quarrying (21 percent) and woodworking (carpentry and the like—18 percent). Jewish participation in communication and transportation amounted to only about 2 percent of all gainfully employed Jews in 1900 (of the general population only 0.7 percent) but these constituted nearly 18 percent of all those gainfully employed—both Jews and non-Jews—in this field. In the cities and towns of eastern Galicia most of the coachmen were Jews.

The very slow but systematic penetration of capitalism into the Galician economy during the last quarter and particularly during the last decade of the 19th century aggravated still further, both directly and indirectly, the poverty of the Jewish population in the country. It affected adversely the most important occupations in which Jews were engaged. Capitalist concentration of trade, which was accelerated by the expansion of railroad communication, cut into the business of the Jewish shopkeepers in the small towns. Larger purchases were no longer made in the small towns but in the larger district cities or in the capital, Lemberg. The growth of modern forms of business organization also reduced greatly the economic opportunities of a large number of Jewish brokers and middlemen.[13] This same process which brought the consumer in direct contact with the larger city also reduced the economic importance of the fairs and market days in the small towns, and thousands of Jewish families were thus deprived of their livelihood.[14]

In a similar manner, the beginnings of capitalism and the development of modern communications led to the great impoverishment of Jewish artisans, particulraly tailors. The more prosperous townspeople and the landed gentry now had their clothes made in the larger cities instead of by the small town tailor.[15] Furthermore, Austrian, especially Viennese, firms opened branches in Galician cities and flooded the market with ready-made clothes. Viennese shoe manufacturers, furniture makers, and tinware manufacturers likewise opened branches in the larger cities of Galicia and thus deprived the Jewish artisans of their livelihood.[16] The expansion of the railroad

[13] Fleischer, *op. cit.*, p. 218-19.

[14] *Cf.* the report of Dr. Leon Horowitz, president of the Cracow Jewish community, in *Menorah*, vol. xxvii (1899) 364.

[15] *Die Welt* (1897) no. 3, interview with deputy Dr. Roman Jaroszewicz.

[16] Feldman, *op. cit.*, p. 20.

system also rendered superfluous the large number of Jewish coach-men and drivers.[17]

The development of modern banking, mortgage banks, and sav-ings and loan associations practically did away with private money-lending, which had become particularly widespread among Galician Jews, especially among the village shopkeepers, after the abolition of serfdom in 1848.[18] The most powerful competitors of the Jewish moneylenders in the villages were the rural co-operative plan asso-ciations. In 1901 these associations numbered 720.[19] With the cul-tural development of the Galician village during the last quarter of the 19th century also came the development of the co-operative move-ment. In 1882 the "Association of Agricultural Circles" (Towa-rzystwo Kółek Rolniczych) was established and in 1890 it operated 607 country stores. Six years later that number was increased to 1,220. These co-operative stores sold goods and agricultural implements, and also bought up the agricultural products from the peasants. This resulted in the elimination, in many sections, of the Jewish country shopkeepers, the village peddlers, and the Jewish grain and cattle dealers. Jewish trade in agricultural products in the cities also suffered greatly.[20]

The activity of these *kulkes* (circles), as they were generally called, was not limited to economic affairs. They launched a nationalist antisemitic propaganda with the slogan of "Polonization of trade" by boycotting the Jewish shopkeepers. Autonomous provincial adminis-tration in Galicia aided these agricultural *kulkes* by providing them with free subsidies and low credit rates. Other means were also used by the autonomous administration to take the trade out of Jewish hands. The Wydział Krajowy of Galicia utilized the monopoly on the sale of salt to turn over the trade in this important commodity almost exclusively to non-Jewish stores, both co-operative and private. Purchase orders made by the administration were given to Poles only. To appease the "dominant" Polish group in Galicia, the central admin-istration of the country also sought to limit Jewish trade. Jewish store-keepers had to pay a higher income tax than their Polish competitors;

---

[17] The cited interview with Dr. Jaroszewicz.

[18] Bujak, *op. cit.,* vol. i, p. 102.

[19] *Ibid.,* p. 537.

[20] The Ukrainian trade co-operatives of the "Narodna Torhovlia," established in 1885, were then still very few in number.

the sale of tobacco, a state monopoly, was systematically taken away from Jewish stores and given to Christians.[21]

The condition of the thousands of Jewish tavern keepers also deteriorated greatly during the last quarter of the 19th century. The right to distill and sell liquor ("propination"), which had formerly belonged to the nobility, was purchased in 1889 by the state for the huge sum of 124 million kronen. This transaction brought economic hardship to the Jewish tavern keepers. The same nobles now leased from the state the "propination" rights for entire districts and the Jewish tavern keeper became a sub-lessee, frequently from the same noble as before, but at a much higher rental.[22]

The weak beginnings of capitalist development in Galicia did not bring to the Jewish masses the economic compensations that usually come with capitalist expansion. The new factories that were established were inadequate to absorb any considerable number of the pauperized Jewish artisans and tradesmen. Jewish workers as a rule could find employment only in Jewish industrial enterprises, and these were limited both in size and in scope.

Jewish workers in the last quarter of the 19th century were employed, in addition to the aforementioned occupations, such as tailoring, shoemaking, baking, carpentry, printing, also in the manufacturing of men's and women's ready-made garments, in water-and steam-mills, distilleries, sawmills, tanneries, brushmaking, chemical industries, oil wells and oil refineries.[23] In the match factories of eastern Galicia, in Kołomyja, Stanisławów, Stryj, Skała, and Bolechów, most of the workers at the end of the 19th century were Jews.[24] In 1897 there were still 6,000 Jewish workers, out of a total of some 9,000, employed in the oil wells in the district of Borysław.[25]

In the last decade of the 19th century the process of eliminating Jewish workers from certain industries began. This process came as a result of the concentration of industry and its increasing dependence upon finance capital. Since the victims of this process of concentration were the smaller enterprises—and Jewish enterprises were exclusively in that category—Jewish workers and employees lost their jobs in increasing numbers. This was the case, for instance, in the distilleries,

---

[21] Cf. the cited article by Dr. S. Fleischer and the report of Dr. L. Horowitz.
[22] Cf. Fleischer, op. cit., p. 216 and Horowitz, p. 362.
[23] Cf. Thon, op. cit.
[24] Landau, op. cit.
[25] Loc. cit.

beer breweries, brick-yards and similar industries. The Galizischer Creditbank and the Wiener Länderbank purchased most of the oil wells and ozocerite mines in Borysław.[26] As a result a large number of Jewish workers and foremen lost their jobs in the shafts and in the paraffin refineries. The antisemitic administration paid no attention to the fact that many of these Jews had worked in the oil wells for over 20 years, and some even longer.[27] As a result of this systematic elimination of Jewish workers from the oil wells in Borysław Jewish participation in the industry declined in the course of 15 years from over two-thirds to an insignificant percentage.

Information regarding the wages of Jewish factory workers in Galicia at the end of the 19th century is found in scattered sources. In the Kołomyja match factory adults working $12\frac{1}{2}$ hours a day were paid from 4-5 gulden per week; girl helpers received 1.50-1.80 gulden a week; in the oil refinery and candle factory in Kołomyja the 70 workers, of whom 50 were Jews, were paid 3.50 gulden per week; in the *talith* factory in the same town, young helpers were paid about 1.20 gulden per week. In the tannery in Stanisławow (250 workers, of whom 175 were Jews) the wages were 6-9 gulden per week; in the Borysław oil wells, 4.20-6.50 gulden per week (for stone carriers and washers).[28] According to a newspaper report of 1902, the weekly wages of a Jewish male worker in Galicia were 4-5 gulden and of a female worker 3-4 gulden.[29] The bakery workers in Cracow in 1894 earned 8 gulden per week.[30] The Jewish artisan did not earn much more than the worker. A cabinetmaker in Stanisławów in 1897 earned 6-7 gulden per week; a tailor's apprentice got 6-8 gulden; a vestmaker earned considerably less—about 2 gulden a week; a tailor-repairer earned 1.50 gulden. The seamstresses in Tarnów and in other cities earned 0.80-2 gulden per week.[31] The net earnings of a coach-man in Kołomyja were 5-7 gulden per week; of a porter in Stanisławów 2-3 gulden per week; of a woman poultry dealer 1.20-1.80 gulden; of a Hebrew teacher 150 gulden for a term, which meant 6

[26] Feldman, *op. cit.*

[27] Landau, in *Die Welt* (1897) no. i, p. 31.

[28] *Ibid.*, no. i, p. 23, 26, 28, 31.

[29] "Die Juden in Galizien," in *Jüdische Volkszeitung* of Cracow (1902) no. 7.

[30] Bross, Jacob, "Der onheyb fun der yidisher arbeter-bavegung in galitsye," in the Yivo *Historishe shriftn*, vol. iii, p. 502. (The article by Bross appears in English trans. in *Yivo Annual*, vol. v, p. 55-84.—*Ed.*)

[31] Pappenheim-Rabinowitsch, *op. cit.*, p. 10.

gulden per week; of a *belfer* (assistant teacher) an average of 1 gulden per week.[32]

In most instances the wages of the better categories of Jewish workers were lower than the earnings of the well-paid Jewish artisans, such as skilled tailors, cabinetmakers and bakers. But factory wages were higher than the average earnings of the lower categories of artisans (tailor-repairers, vestmakers), unskilled laborers and traders. The factory workers were also less subject to seasonal unemployment. The inadequacy of these earnings—considering even the low cost of living in Galicia—becomes even more pronounced when it is borne in mind that the lowest rent (that of a woman poultry dealer, for instance) was 30 gulden per year, while better living quarters (of a *melamed,* for instance) rented for 120 gulden per year, *i.e.* more than 2 gulden per week.[33]

The position of the Jewish worker was worse than that of the Polish and Ukrainian workers. The industries in which most of the Jewish workers were concentrated were overcrowded, the competition severe, the earnings of the masters and the wages of the employees minimal. The Jewish worker, moreover, was not in a position to supplement his wages from other resources such as a house of his own or a plot of land or garden, as was the case with the non-Jewish worker. The latter often continued to live in a village or suburb and his work in the factory or shop was secondary to the income he derived from agriculture. The especially sorry condition of the Jewish workers was noted by both Jewish and Polish labor leaders. The organ of the Jewish Social-Democrats in Lemberg, *Der Arbeter* (1894, no. 18) described the Jewish proletarian as "the poorest of the poor, the most oppressed of the oppressed."[34] The organ of the Polish Social-Democrats, *Naprzód,* reported to the congress of the Galician Social-Democratic Party in Lemberg (August 1894) that the movement was most ineffective among Jewish workers (and among women) because their misery was so great that it made the task of organizing them very difficult.[35]

The upper strata of Galician Jewry—the big merchants, bankers, manufacturers—were not affected by the economic backwardness of the country. Jewish big business in the large cities was established on

[32] Landau, *op. cit.*
[33] *Loc. cit.*
[34] Cited by Bross, *op. cit.*, p. 506.
[35] *Ibid.*, p. 504.

the ruins of the petty trade in the small towns. The masses of Jews were progressively suffocating in want and misery. The poverty of the Jewish population was noticeable even against the general background of poverty in the country at large. Jews in Galicia suffered doubly: from the general poverty and from the specific Jewish penury. In 1897 some 1,200 Jewish families in Stanisławów applied to the Jewish community to supply them with their Passover needs.[36] This amounted to about 6,000 individuals, which means that almost one half of the Jewish population in Stanisławów had to depend on charity. The Galician deputy in the Austrian parliament, Roman Jaroszewicz, a physician, said in an interview in 1897: "When I am called to a Jewish patient the prescription is almost invariably the same: food. The answer to this prescription is a silent gesture. This tells all...."[37]

Pogroms in the Russian manner did not take place in Galicia but antisemitism found fertile soil here. In 1893 an antisemitic Peasant Party, patterned after the Austrian and German Christian-Social Party, was established under the leadership of the ex-Jesuit Father Stojałowski. Antisemitic agitation in Galicia was able to operate very easily with demagogic slogans because of the frightful poverty of the peasantry and the economic role of Jewish traders and tavern keepers. The activities of Stojałowski's party were not merely limited to agitation calling for a boycott of Jewish stores. In June 1898, organized mobs of peasants attacked the Jewish quarters in the towns and villages of central and western Galicia and hundreds of Jewish taverns and stores were plundered and destroyed. Only when the movement assumed a social character and when the peasants advanced upon the estates of the nobles and the homes of the Christian townspeople, were troops dispatched to the affected regions. A state of emergency was proclaimed in 33 districts of Galicia and in several of them martial law; a number of peasants were killed and several hundreds were imprisoned.

These events of 1898, which came to be known in the Jewish tradition of Galicia as the tragic experiences of "plunder," illuminated in their flames the tragedy of the Galician population at the end of the past century: the frightful poverty of the peasants and the even more frightful poverty of the Jews, caught in a social and economic vise.

[36] Landau, in *Die Welt* (1897) no. 26.
[37] *Die Welt* (1897) no. 3.

Up to the middle of the 19th century the emigration of Galician Jews to America was small; only a few individuals came to this country. This emigration was much smaller than that of the Russian and Polish Jews, which was also only sporadic at that time. The year 1848 was a critical date for the Galician Jews also in respect to emigration. The revolution also stirred the spirits of the Jewish population. Political emancipation gave impetus to the initiative of Jewish communal leaders, and projects for emigration were formulated. A proclamation appeared in Lemberg which began with the words: "Capitalists! Thousands of Jews yearn to go to the land of freedom and happiness, to America." An article was sent from Brody to the Viennese German-Jewish publication *Österreichisches Central Organ für Glaubensfreiheit, Cultur, Geschichte und Literatur der Juden* (published by Isidor Busch and Meir Letteris), advocating emigration to America. Jewish committees to organize emigration were established in Lemberg after the manner of those set up in Vienna and Budapest. The well-known German Jewish novelist Leopold Kompert also participated in the discussion regarding emigration. His articles on that question in the *Central Organ* were titled "Up, and to America!"* The young German Jewish poet Sigmund Herzl published in the same journal an enthusiastic poem, in which he sang the praises of freedom in America.[38]

The extent of the influence of this propaganda is not known. All we know is that in the entire Austrian empire 27 Jews expressed their readiness to go to America at their own expense. This group consisted of artisans, shopkeepers and one engineer.[39] Greater interest in emigration to the United States was occasioned by the California gold rush of 1848. Simon Berman of Cracow, author of the memoirs, *Masoes shimen,* relates that when he arrived in New York in 1852 he found over 100 Jews from Cracow. Many of these Jews had arrived not long before him—in 1851-52. Several settled together with him in Cincinnati. Some engaged in peddling, others found work in factories (cigar factories in New York). Some became suc-

---

* An English translation of these three articles is published in *Yivo Annual of Jewish Social Science,* vol. vi, p. 97-103.—*Ed.*

[38] Friedmann, Filip, *Die Galizischen Juden im Kampfe um ihre Gleichberechtigung (1848-1868)* (Frankfurt 1929) p. 65; A. M. F. (Albert M. Friedenberg), "An Austrian-Hungarian Movement to Encourage the Migration of Jews to America," in *Publications of the American Jewish Hist. Society,* vol. xxiii (1915) 187-89.

Isidor Busch, editor of the *Central Organ,* emigrated to America toward the end of 1848 and came to play a considerable role in political and economic life.

[39] A. M. F., *op. cit.*

cessful and opened their own stores. Others saved some money and returned home to Cracow.[40]

The emigration of Galician Jews to America did not assume wide proportions up to the 1880's. According to certain estimates, emigration from Galicia between 1857 and 1869 was minimal. Immigration to Galicia exceeded emigration by 67,415 persons. In the decade of 1870-80 this excess of immigration over emigration declined to less than 2,000.[41] The real immigration of Galician Jews, just as of Galician Poles, began only in the 1880's.

In the decade of 1881-90 Jewish immigration to America from all of Austria-Hungary numbered 44,619.[42] What proportion of these immigrants were from Galicia is not known, but we may assume it did not amount to more than two-thirds, which means about 30,000. It must be borne in mind that the total emigration of Galician Jews in that decade numbered 36,660 (the difference between the natural and the actual increase of the Jewish population)[43] and that in those days Galician Jews emigrated also to other European countries, and especially to the other provinces of the Austro-Hungarian monarchy, such as Silesia (Teschen), Moravia (Brünn), Bohemia (Prague), Lower Austria (Vienna), and Hungary.

In the last decade of the 19th century, 1891-1900, Jewish immigration to America from all of Austria-Hungary numbered 83,720,[44] i.e. almost twice the number of the previous decade. Of this number Galicia contributed no less than four-fifths, i.e. about 67,000. (To the general Austro-Hungarian immigration to America in 1891-1900 Galicia also contributed four-fifths.)[45] Even this estimate, however, is too low. Galician Jewish emigration to all countries in 1891-1900 (the difference between the natural and the actual increase of the Jewish population) numbered about 120,000.[46]

[40] Berman, Simon, *Masoes shimen* (Cracow 1879) p. 16-19, 23-24.

[41] Buzek, Joseph, "Das Auswanderungsproblem und die Regelung des Auswanderungswesens," in *Zeitschrift für Volkswirtschaft, Sozialpolitik und Verwaltung* (1901) 444.

[42] Joseph, Samuel, *Jewish Immigration to the United States* (New York 1914) p. 110. The figures are for all of Austria-Hungary. The predominant majority of the immigrants, however, came from Galicia, as will be seen in the following paragraphs. Hungarian Jewish immigration was insignificant at that time. Even in 1911-12 Hungarian Jewish immigrants constituted no more than one-fifth of the total of Jewish immigrants from Austria-Hungary.

[43] Rosenfeld, Max, *Die polnische Judenfrage* (Berlin 1918) p. 81.

[44] Joseph, *op. cit.*, p. 110.

[45] Bujak, *op. cit.*, p. 465.

[46] *Ibid.*, p. 469.

No matter how conservative our estimate is of the number of Galician Jewish immigrants to America, in the last decade of the 19th century that immigration was at least twice as great as in the 1880's. To be sure this increase in immigration may also be explained by such movements as the rise in the cultural state of Galician Jews, the spread of general education and the resultant weakening of religious orthodoxy, which had frequently deterred the hasidic masses from emigrating to free America. That this consideration was a serious hindrance may be seen from the fact that even the more enlightened rabbis of Bohemia in 1848 strongly opposed the propaganda for emigration to America on religious grounds. The Bohemian rabbis Adolf Schmiedl and Friedrich Mannheimer declared in the columns of Busch's *Central Organ* that they were categorically opposed to Jewish emigration to America because it was difficult to be an observant Jew in America.[47] The difference in the state of culture between those two decades was at any rate less than the difference in economic conditions, which deteriorated progressively toward the end of the 19th century. Because of these economic conditions the immigration of Galician Jews to America in the last two years of the 19th century (1899-1900) numbered almost as much (27,991) as the immigration in the preceding four years (28,917 in 1895-98). In 1901-1910 the average annual emigration of Austro-Hungarian Jews to America was 15,000.[48]

We have no special figures on the occupational and social structure of the Galician Jewish immigrants. Some reports in the press indicate that the Galician Jewish immigrants were mostly artisans and workers. In a report of 1897 we read of Jewish brushmakers (pig hair sorters) of Kołomyja who emigrated to America and later returned home.[49] The aforementioned deputy Jaroszewicz tells that in the same year most of the Jewish tailors of Borszczów (district of Lemberg) left for America, for they were deprived of their livelihood by the competition of the clothing factories in the large cities.[50] In 1900 the Committee for the Relief of Unemployed Jewish Workers in the Oil Wells of Borysław arranged to aid some of them to emigrate to America.[51]

[47] A. M. F., *op. cit.*, 187-89.
[48] Joseph, *op. cit.*, p. 93.
[49] Landau, in *Die Welt* (1897) no. 23.
[50] *Ibid.*, no. 3.
[51] See the appeal of Kornhaber, mayor of Borysław, in the biweekly, *Der yud* (Cracow 1900) no. 18, May 3.

JEWISH AND NON-JEWISH CRIMINALITY IN POLAND, 1932-1937

By LIEBMAN HERSCH

Originally published in the *Yivo Bleter*, XX (1942)

In 1937 the Yivo published the author's study *Farbrekherishkeyt fun Yidn un nit-Yidn in Poyln* ("Delinquency among Jews and Non-Jews in Poland"), which was an elaboration of a paper read at the world conference of the Yivo in Vilna in 1935. The study, subsequently translated into English (*Journal of Criminal Law and Criminology*), French, and Polish, was based on Polish official statistics for 1924-1925. The present work is an analysis of the problem a decade later.

1. THE PROBLEM STATED

World War II has brought to an abrupt end a highly important chapter in the history of Poland, and with it a characteristic period in the Jewish history of that country. A page has turned in the history of mankind, and as usual—perhaps to an even greater degree than usual—also a page in Jewish history, that tells of great strivings and superhuman endurance, crushing blows and indestructible achievements. Time and again we shall have occasion to refer to this *interbellum* period, to ascertain facts, to analyze and appraise them, to draw conclusions and to judge personalities and groups, social movements and political regimes, states and peoples.

In certain respects it will be impossible to summarize the period under discussion until some future date. In other respects we are at present in a position to determine the factual aspect of the situation, to the extent that later information will not effect any substantial changes in the data now available. Included in this last category would be a study of the extent and character of Jewish criminality in Poland, in comparison with non-Jewish criminality. Seemingly, no more surprises are possible here. Undoubtedly, there will be no other materials from the period under consideration than those published to date, and the picture of this phase of the epoch, based upon the materials available at present, will remain final.

The most important materials on Jewish criminality in the postwar Republic of Poland, both in extent and thoroughness, are the two volumes of the official *Statystyka Kryminalna* ("Statistics of

Crime") for the years 1924 and 1925.[1] In addition there are the previously published but less detailed official Polish reports for the years 1923 and 1926-28.[2]

On the basis of these data, it was established that despite the fact that the Jews in Poland are a predominantly urban population, while the non-Jews are chiefly rural dwellers, and that the urban population in Poland has a far larger criminality than the rural, Jewish criminality in Poland is less in extent and degree of severity than non-Jewish criminality. The Jewish criminality as compared with the non-Jewish was particularly slight in the capital, the only place that offered a possibility of comparing an urban Jewish population with a similarly urban non-Jewish population.

The conclusions reached were little short of startling. The validity of those conclusions was recognized by such eminent specialists in the field of criminology as Professor Bonger of Amsterdam and Professor Sheldon Glueck of Harvard. Some critics, however, presumably basing their views on the summary figures of the *Mały Rocznik Statystyczny* ("Little Annual of Statistics") for the last years, countered with the statement that in the years immediately before the present war Polish statistics showed a higher criminality among Jews than among non-Jews.

Were these critics justified in their opinion? Did Jewish criminality in the years immediately before the present war actually exceed non-Jewish criminality? The answer to this question is interesting, regardless of the political conclusions that may possibly be drawn from it. It is a question of the spiritual physiognomy of the Jewish population in a given period. Did this physiognomy, in a given moment of the period under consideration, suddenly undergo radical changes as a result of certain circumstances, or did the Jewish population in Poland maintain in regard to criminality the characteristics previously noted?

To the elucidation of this question the present article is dedicated.

2. A Distorted Image

First, what statistical material is available concerning Jewish criminality for the years subsequent to the period previously analyzed?

---

[1] *Statystyka Kryminalna,* 1930 (published in Polish and in French).
[2] L. Hersch, *Ekonomishe Shriftn,* Yivo ("Yivo Studies in Economics"), II, pp. 174-200; L. Hersch, *Farbrekherishkeyt fun Yidn un nit-Yidn in Poyln* ("Delinquency among Jews and Non-Jews in Poland"), Vilna, Yivo, 1937, 49 pp.

No information concerning Jewish criminality was published in the years 1929-31. For the years 1932 and 1933 the *Mały Rocznik Statystyczny* (of 1934 and 1935) published with reference to the Jews (as in general with reference to the religious affiliation of the offenders) only the total number of convicted in the three main regions of Poland, without any information as to the nature of the offense. The annals of 1936-38 furnish for the convicted of the various denominations in the years 1934-36 half a page of information about certain types of crime. Only for the year 1937 does the *Mały Rocznik Statystyczny*—M. R. S. (of the year 1939, pp. 365-366) furnish more detailed information concerning the types of crimes and the religious affiliation of the convicted in Poland. This is the sum total of information that we possess on criminality among Jews and members of other faiths in Poland published subsequently to the previously mentioned *Statystyka Kryminalna.*

It should be especially emphasized here that the scope of the offenses taken into consideration by the Polish statistics in the last years differed vastly from the scope of previous years. The M. R. S. (1934, p. 194, and following years) states explicitly that the new statistical information "is not at all comparable to that previously published," since the earlier statistics referred to those convicted for *crimes* only; whereas the later figures included all who were sentenced in court, regardless of the penalty meted out, i.e., also those convicted for offenses against the various administrative regulations. It should be noted that such simple offenses[a] far exceed in number the actual crimes. If the crimes and offenses are lumped together, the result is a grossly inflated figure, representing criminality as in a distorting mirror. If one place (or group of the population) has one half the number of actual crimes, but twice as many simple offenses as another place (or other group of the population) it will seem as if the criminality were much greater in the first instance than in the second. The picture would naturally be different if we possessed numerical information about actual crimes and offenses separately. In the summary information of the M. R. S. about criminality in recent years, however, both types are lumped and counted together.

The extent to which the actual crimes are thereby lost in the vast mass of "transgressions" becomes obvious when we compare the number of convicted in the central and eastern *Województwos* (i.e.,

---

[a] The official Polish term is *przekroczenia.*

in the former Russian provinces) on the basis of the statistics of 1923-28 with the number in the statistics of 1932. According to the former (when only actual crimes were taken into consideration) the number of the convicted (Jews and non-Jews) fluctuated between 49,000 and 60,000 annually, with an average of 54,000 yearly. In 1932, when offenses too were included in the figure, the number rose suddenly to 473,000, that is, a nine-fold increase over the previoius figures. In reality, no such rise in criminality has taken place. We are plainly dealing here with incomparable figures. In the figures of 1932, criminality is practically lost in the vast mass of offenses.

How perverted a picture of the Polish population is obtained through the distorting mirror of such inflated figures can be clearly seen in the following. According to the census of September, 1931, there were in the *Województwos* (provinces) of former Russia a total of 14,082,000 inhabitants ten years old and over. In 1932, as stated before, these districts had 473,000 convicted, i.e., in one year 336 convicted for each 10,000 of the above-indicated age. According to the Polish mortality table of 1931-32, we can put the average life expectancy of the population ten years and over at $34\frac{1}{4}$ years. Hence, according to the criminality record of 1932, each 10,000 inhabitants ten years old and over would furnish for the rest of their lives 11,500 ($336 \times 34\frac{1}{4}$) convicted, i.e., the entire population would consist of former or potential "criminals," and in addition 15% would have to be recidivists!

Apparently, the Chief Bureau of Polish Statistics itself (or the Minister of Justice) was struck by the senselessness of including such colossal numbers of minor offenses in the figure of criminality. In subsequent years, the figures decline progressively, undoubtedly through the omission of very minor offenses. The M. R. S. (1939, p. 363) explicitly indicates that the figures for the years 1932-37 are not quite comparable to each other.

Thus the Polish statistics of the convicted in the years 1932-37 give no adequate idea of the state of criminality in the individual years, nor of any change that took place since the period of 1923-28, nor of the developments within these very years.

This, however, does not mean that the figures regarding the last years, and especially the very last year (1937, published in 1939) are altogether valueless. It indicates merely how easy it is to draw false conclusions on the basis of these figures, particularly if one is unmindful of the fact that they include a much larger number of offenses than actual crimes.

With reference to Jewish criminality in particular, the question arises: What effect does the inclusion of the enormous number of "offenses" have on the extent of the Jewish criminality in comparison with the non-Jewish?

On the basis of the detailed information of the Polish *Statystyka Kryminalna* which we had analyzed in our previous works, we came to the conclusion, among others, that, in general, the more serious the kind or degree of crime, the lesser the rate of Jewish criminality in comparison with the non-Jewish. Jewish criminality is particularly small in comparison with the non-Jewish in the category of serious crimes, while conversely, in the matter of minor offenses it approaches, and at times exceeds, the non-Jewish criminality. We can, therefore, conclude in advance that Jews would make out a larger percentage among those convicted for simple offenses than among those convicted for actual crimes. Hence, if those convicted for offenses are included in the total, the figures for Jewish criminality will be much higher in comparison with non-Jewish criminality than if actual crimes only were taken into consideration. The more (and the less serious) the offenses that are included in the statistical totals, the greater the Jewish criminality would *appear* in comparison with the non-Jewish. Conversely, the more narrowly limited the criminal statistics are to actual crimes, the smaller the Jewish criminality in comparison with the non-Jewish. It could have been anticipated in advance that even without any change in the degrees of criminality, under the new method of counting the convicted, the Jewish criminality would appear much higher in comparison with the non-Jewish than in previous years.

The actual state of Jewish criminality, according to the Polish statistics, we shall now observe.

3. TOTAL CRIMINALITY

The total figure of convicted for crimes and offenses among Jews and non-Jews in the Polish Republic in each of the years 1932-37 is given in Table 1. For the purpose of orientation, the average number of convicted for actual crimes in the year 1923-28 is also indicated. Let us further add that Jews constituted 10.5% of the population of the Polish Republic in the census of 1921, and 9.8% in the census of 1931.

TABLE 1

Total of Convicted per Year in the Republic of Poland in the Years 1932-1938

Year	Number Convicted for Actual Crimes			Percentage of Jews among the Convicted	Convicted per 10,000 Inhabitants* (Criminality)		Jewish Criminality in Ratio to Non-Jewish Criminality
	Jews	Non-Jews	Total		Jews	Non-Jews	
1923--1928	8,981	171,056	180,037	5.0	31.6	70.3	45.0
	For Crimes and Transgressions						
1932	95,578	654,708	750,286	12.7	306.9	227.3	135.0
1933	65,515	577,176	642,691	10.2	210.4	200.4	105.0
1934	63,266	605,051	668,317	9.5	203.2	210.1	96.7
1935	56,557	565,494	622,051	9.1	181.6	196.3	92.5
1936	42,473	483,603	526,076	8.1	136.4	167.9	81.2
1937	23,131	334,905	358,036	6.5	74.3	116.3	63.9

* For the years 1923-28, our figures on the population are based on the census of 1921, for the years 1932-1937, on the census of 1931.

As already stated, one need not infer from the above table that in the year 1932 criminality in Poland suddenly showed an enormous rise in general and among the Jews in particular, and that subsequently there was a continuous decline. The figures simply do not admit comparison, because of the varying number of offenses included in the various years. This, however, we can establish (especially on the basis of the last column):

1) In the years 1932-37, when the actual crimes were, in a manner of speaking, dissolved in the mass of offenses, the Jewish (inflated) criminality appeared indeed greater in comparison with the non-Jewish than in the previous years (1923-28), when only actual crimes were taken into consideration.

2) The more inflated the number of convicted, through inclusion of minor offenses (e.g., in 1932), the greater the Jewish criminality appears in comparison with the non-Jewish; the less inflated—insofar as the number of convicted refers to actual criminals (e.g., in 1936 and 1937)—the smaller the Jewish criminality appears in comparison with the non-Jewish. The figures for the years 1932-37 corroborate in this manner what could have been predicted in a general way on the basis of the established facts for the previous years.

3) In the last year for which official Polish statistical information is available (1937), when the number of convicted was still

almost twice as large as the average for the years 1923-28, *thus including some 160,000-180,000 (Jews and non-Jews) convicted for simple offenses, the total Jewish criminality proved nevertheless to be one-third less than the non-Jewish* (64% of the non-Jewish for a similar number of the population).

For that same year, the last issue of the M. R. S. (1939, p. 365) also computed the total criminality (convicted for each 10,000 population) among the various denominations in Poland, and found: 113 for the Roman Catholics, 127 for the Greek Catholics, and only 72 for the Jews. And that, as already stated, is with the inclusion of a high number of offenses.

4. THE THREE MAIN CRIMINAL CATEGORIES

As previously noted, the last M. R. S. furnished somewhat more detailed information on the religious affiliation of the convicted (1937). We thus have an opportunity for a more intimate examination of the Jewish criminality, toward the end of the period that has now terminated. Let us look at those figures. In this process we shall adhere as far as possible to the same classification of the material as we have pursued in our previous works. We shall, in the first place, distinguish three main categories of crime. First, crimes against the state and the social order (political crimes, ill-usage of the government organs, bribery, forgery, etc.). Second, crimes against the person (against life, health, personal liberty, family and sex morality). Third, crimes against property (theft, receiving and trading in stolen goods, fraud, robbery, etc.). The detailed content of these three categories of crime we shall see in the next paragraphs, where each of them is discussed separately.

TABLE 2

The Convicted in 1937 Classified according to the Three Main Categories of Crime

Crimes and Transgressions	Number			Percentage of Jews among the Convicted	Convicted per 10,000 Inhabitants (Criminality)		Jewish Criminality in Ratio to Non-Jewish Criminality	Distribution Categories per 100 Convicted	
	Jews	Non-Jews	Total		Jews	Non-Jews		Jews	Non-Jews
1	2	3	4	5	6	7	8	9	10
Against the state and the social order...	10,099	81,605	91,704	11.0	32.4	28.3	114	43.6	24.4
Against the person....	1,705	47,975	49,680	3.4	5.5	16.7	33	7.4	14.3
Against property......	11,327	205,325	216,652	5.2	36.4	71.3	51	49.0	61.3
Total.............	23,131	334,905	358,036	6.5	74.3	116.3	64	100.0	100.0

In Table 2, column 8, we find among the Jews a slightly higher criminality (14%) than among non-Jews, only in the category of crimes against the state and the social order, a category of crime that (as we have pointed out in our previous works) is especially prevalent in the city and is little known in the village. On the other hand, the percentage of crime against the person and property remained much lower among the Jews than among the non-Jews. The Jewish criminality against property was one-half, and against the person only one-third, of the non-Jewish. The Jews in Poland, constituting exactly 10% of the population, furnished 11% of those convicted for crimes and offenses against the state and the social order, but only 5% of those convicted for crimes against property, and only 3% for crimes and offenses against the person (column 5).

The composition of the mass of the convicted among Jews is therefore quite different from that among non-Jews. True, among Jews and non-Jews the highest percentage of convicted is for crimes against property, to be followed in the case of both groups by those convicted for crimes against the state and the social order. The lowest percentage for both groups constitute those convicted for crimes against the person. Nevertheless, one could establish (on the basis of columns 9 and 10) the fact that among the Jews the convicted for offenses against the state and the social order accounted for almost one-half (44% of all the convicted, whereas among the non-Jews they accounted only for one-fourth. Conversely, while crimes against property composed almost two-thirds (61%) of all the convicted among the non-Jews, Jews furnished less than one-half (49%) of this category; among the non-Jews every seventh convicted (14%) was guilty of a crime or offense against the person, among the Jews only every fourteenth (7%).

Since 1923-28 the absolute and relative numbers of the convicted have changed both among Jews and among non-Jews. Notwithstanding this and regardless also of the large number of transgressions included, we find among the Jewish and non-Jewish convicted in the three chief categories of crime, in the main, the same similarities and characteristics as in the previous years.

5. Various Types of Crime

Each of the main categories of crime, however, embraces offenses of varying type. Insofar as the extant statistical material will permit, we shall examine these offenses more closely. Since comparatively detailed statistics are available for only one year (1937), we shall not be able to dwell upon individual sorts of offenses and transgressions which embrace only a small number of convicted, or differ but slightly from other sorts of offense of the same kind. Nevertheless, the more important kinds we can consider separately. Let us begin with that category of offense in which Jewish criminality, according to official statistics, was higher than non-Jewish.

Offenses against the State and the Social Order

The data of the M. R. S. (1939) afford us an opportunity to differentiate the following more important offenses and transgressions against the state and the social order: political offenses (treason, offenses against public institutions, against religious sentiments, participation in rioting and illegal assembly, resistance to the authorities, insulting the authorities, other offenses against the state and the authorities), venality and abuse of public power (offenses of public officials, venality, usurpation of power, perjury, false accusation and other offenses in the domain of the court), counterfeiting (documents, money, bills, weights), offenses against regulations governing foreign exchange, offenses constituting a public danger (incendiarism, arson, causing explosions, etc.) and other not clearly defined offenses "against the public order."

The criminality of all these kinds for the last year is indicated in Table 3.

TABLE 3

The Convicted in 1937 for Crimes and Transgressions against the State and the Social Order
Classified according to Type of Offense

Crimes and Transgressions	Number			Percentage of Jews among the Convicted	Convicted per 10,000 Inhabitants (Criminality)		Jewish Criminality in Ratio to Non-Jewish Criminality
	Jews	Non-Jews	Total		Jews	Non-Jews	
1	2	3	4	5	6	7	8
Political offenses..........	3,130	37,556	40,686	7.7	100	130	77
Ill-usage of the government organs.............	682	8,808	9,490	7.2	22	31	71
Forgery of documents, money, notes............	1,042	6,759	7,801	13.4	33	23	143
Violations of the valuta regulations.............	1,395	3,112	4,507	31.0	45	11	409
Crimes against the public...	46	4,812	4,858	0.9	1.5	17	9
Other offenses against the public order........	3,804	20,558	24,362	15.6	122	71	172
Total...................	10,099	81,605	91,704	11.0	324	283	114

The last, not clearly defined group of offenses and transgressions "against the public order" is a veritable hodge-podge of the most diversified offenses. In it are included violations of the press laws, mendicity, residence without personal identification documents, arranging prohibited games, smuggling, dealing in gold and silver without grade marking, and a whole series of various other offenses and transgressions. We can, therefore, hardly say anything definite about this group. The other two groups in which the Jewish criminality is higher (and indeed considerably higher) than the non-Jewish—counterfeiting of documents, money and bills, and violation of the regulations governing foreign exchange—comprise, incidentally, offenses mainly committed by tradespeople. Now according to the last census (1931) the relative number of Jewish tradespeople in Poland was thirteen times that of non-Jewish (2.8% of the non-Jewish population and 36.6% of the Jewish). Therefore, taking into consideration the relative numbers engaged in trade, even these crimes are found to be less frequent among Jews than among non-Jews. For, although the Jews comprised according to the last census not quite two-thirds (59%) of the entire trades population of Poland, they constituted less than one-third (31%) of those convicted for violating regulations governing foreign exchange, and less than one-seventh (13.4%) of those convicted for counterfeiting money, bills, documents, weights, etc.

The other kinds of offenses against the state and the social order, enumerated in our Table 3, are generally less prevalent among Jews than among non-Jews. Particularly striking here is the difference between the Jewish and non-Jewish population with reference to offenses constituting a public danger (arson, blowing up, etc.). This type of offense is relatively one-eleventh as frequent among Jews as among non-Jews. Among the condemned for this type of crime in Poland, Jews constituted less than 1%.

It is interesting to note that in the last year (as we had established for the previous years, too) political criminality proved to be considerably lower (23%) among Jews than among non-Jews. And just as in previous years, this time, too, the following significant fact can be established: the criminality of Jews in respect of treason to the state—a crime which in Poland included membership in the Communist Party—is considerably higher than that of non-Jews (primarily a rural population): 15 convicted per 100,000 population among Jews, and 9 among non-Jews. Conversely, for resistance to the authorities the number of convicted was 36 per 100,000 population among the non-Jews, and 27 among Jews; for insulting the state and its representatives, 45 among non-Jews and 23 among Jews; for participation in disorders, 6 among non-Jews and 1 among Jews.

In spite of differing figures, we thus find for the last year, too, the same characteristic of Jewish criminality as was established by us on the basis of the statistics of the previous years.

Offenses against Property

As we see in Table 2, the criminality among Jews, in regard to offenses against property, is in general one-half that of non-Jews. Nevertheless there are certain types of crime in that category that occur more frequently among Jews. A clearer idea of this will be gained from Table 4.

TABLE 4

The Convicted in 1937 for Crimes and Transgressions against Property Classified according to Type of Offense

Crimes and Transgressions	Number			Percentage of Jews among the Convicted	Convicted per 10,000 Inhabitants (Criminality)		Jewish Criminality in Ratio to Non-Jewish Criminality
	Jews	Non-Jews	Total		Jews	Non-Jews	
1	2	3	4	5	6	7	8
Trade and credit dealings....	1,747	11,394	13,141	13.3	56	40	140
Fraudulent practices.........	3,811	25,590	29,401	13.0	122	89	137
Betrayal of confidence.......	626	6,164	6,790	9.2	20	21	95
Receiving and trading in stolen goods............	1,746	19,552	21,298	8.2	56	68	82
Embezzlement................	174	2,580	2,754	6.3	6	9	67
Theft......................	2,719	124,852	127,571	2.1	87	433	20
Brigandage.................	25	1,459	1,484	1.7	0.8	5.1	16
Other offenses against property.................	479	13,734	14,213	3.4	15	48	31
Total..................	11,327	205,325	216,652	5.2	364	713	51

A higher rate of convicted among Jews than among non-Jews is found only in the field of trade and credit and in acts of fraudulence. Since these offenses appertain primarily to people engaged in trade, it is obvious that the higher criminality among Jews in this respect is due to the higher percentage of tradespeople among Jews, and not to the fact that the Jewish tradesman is presumably more inclined to crime than the non-Jewish. Conversely, if we recall here again what we stated previously (in regard to perjury of bills, and offenses against regulations governing foreign exchange) about the percentage of Jews among the tradespeople and the convicted, we can establish the fact that although the Jews comprised almost 60% of the tradespeople of Poland, they comprised only 13% of the convicted for the offenses under consideration, which are primarily those of tradespeople (col. 5). We can, therefore, conclude that the Jewish tradesman is considerably less criminal than the non-Jewish. Of particular interest in this respect is the fact that another offense appertaining almost exclusively to tradespeople, receiving and trading in stolen goods, was in general even numerically less frequent among Jews than non-Jews, in spite of the fact that there were 13 times as many Jewish tradespeople as non-Jewish, in ratio to the population.

It is worth while noting that whereas among non-Jews theft occupies by far the most prominent place (over 60%) among those convicted for offenses against property, and those convicted for acts of fraudulence constitute only one-fourth or one-fifth of that number, among Jews, on the contrary, the defrauders occupy the first place, and the thieves the second. Such a great difference could not be established on the basis of the figures of the previous years, although even then more defrauders and considerably fewer thieves were found among Jews than among non-Jews. Through inclusion of smaller transgressions, the number of Jews convicted for minor acts of fraudulence rose markedly, as well as the number of non-Jews convicted for petty thefts. The difference between Jews and non-Jews with regard to theft, on the basis of the figures of the last year, is therefore slightly greater. Those convicted for theft among Jews were five times as rare as those convicted among non-Jews: the ratio of Jewish convicted for theft in ratio to the non-Jewish convicted is one-fifth.

A great rarity is the proverbial "Jewish brigand." Brigandage, the most brutal type of offense against property, which is frequently associated with acts of violence against the person, was naturally among non-Jews, too, comparatively rare (80 times rarer than theft); among Jews, however, six times as rare as among non-Jews (100 times as rare as theft among Jews).

Criminality against the Person

Criminality against the person was and remained much lower among Jews than among non-Jews. That is true in general, and also with regard to the more important types of offense in this category, as evidenced in Table 5.

TABLE 5

The Convicted in 1937 for Crimes and Transgressions against the Person Classified according to Type of Offense

Crimes and Transgressions	Number			Percentage of Jews among the Convicted	Convicted per 10,000 Inhabitants (Criminality)		Jewish Criminality in Ratio to Non-Jewish Criminality
	Jews	Non-Jews	Total	Convicted	Jews	Non-Jews	
Manslaughter.................	22	1,308	1,330	1.7	0.7	4.5	16
Other offenses against life and health.........	454	26,479	26,933	1.7	15	92	16
Offenses against personal freedom................	988	17,768	18,756	5.3	32	62	52
Offenses against morality.	241	2,420	2,661	9.1	7.7	8.4	92
Total..................	1,705	47,975	49,680	3.4	55	167	33

The difference between Jewish and non-Jewish criminality was, in the last year, smallest in respect to offenses against sexual and family morality. In this respect the Jewish criminality almost equalled that of the non-Jewish. According to the figures of previous years, this criminality was much lower among Jews than among non-Jews (twice as low in Galicia, and almost four times as low in the former Russian Poland). And although the figures for the last years, as stated above, are indeed not comparable to those of the previous years, it is nonetheless hard to conceive that such a great change in the Jewish criminality in comparison with the non-Jewish should stem only from the inclusion of the minor transgressions. It is highly possible that the criminality of the Jews in respect of sexual and family morality has actually risen to a certain extent lately and approached that of the non-Jews. Most prevalent relatively among the individual types of offense in this sphere last year, as in previous years, was that connected with traffic; least prevalent, that associated with acts of violence. For white slave traffic (souteneurs and procurers) there were convicted among Jews in 1937, 25 per million inhabitants, a rate four times as high as that among non-Jews; for rape the number of convicted among Jews was 4 per million, a rate about one-fourth that of non-Jews.

As in previous years, the difference between Jewish and non-Jewish criminality remained most pronounced in the field of offenses against life and health: six or seven times lower among Jews than among non-Jews: 7 cases per million inhabitants (45 among non-Jews). Also very rare among Jews are those convicted for very serious bodily injuries: 8 per million inhabitants among Jews, and 25 among

non-Jews. For serious bodily injuries, the number of Jewish condemned per million inhabitants was 44; and 213 among non-Jews.

Women, Juveniles, and Recidivists among the Convicted

Women have generally a lower and lighter criminality than men.
The criminality among Jewish women in Poland was, according to
the earlier detailed *Statystyka Kryminalna* much lower (less than
one-half) than that among non-Jewish women. If the number of
serious offenses is particularly small among the Jewish women and
the number of minor offenses relatively high, we should then expect
that with the inclusion of the convicted for simple transgressions
the percentage of Jewish women among the convicted would rise;
that is, the criminality of the Jewish women in comparison with the
non-Jewish would seem higher than before. Such was actually the
case. The M. R. S. for 1939 again furnishes data on the sex of the
convicted for the last years. In 1937 a total of 59,671 women were
convicted in Poland for offenses and transgressions, 4,936 Jewish
and 54,735 non-Jewish. The Jewish women thus constituted 8.3%
of all convicted women. There were 30 Jewish women convicts per
100,000 Jews; and 37 non-Jewish per 100,000 non-Jews. The Jewish
female criminality thus constituted five-sixths of the non-Jewish, which
is considerably higher than formerly, when transgressions were not
included; but even inclusive of transgressions, it was one-sixth lower
than the non-Jewish.

The M. R. S., however, furnishes no data on the various kinds
of offenses of the women and the juveniles. We must, therefore, be
content with the comparison of the total Jewish and non-Jewish
criminality.

The data on juvenile delinquency according to religions, which the
last M. R. S. furnishes, respect generally a new departure in Polish
(and not only Polish) criminal statistics. According to this information, the total of juvenile (up to and including 17 years) delinquents
of both sexes convicted in the year 1937 was 8,380; of these 462 were
Jewish and 7,918 non-Jewish. The Jewish juveniles convicted, therefore, constituted 5½% of the juveniles convicted (as against 10½%
of the population). Among non-Jews were 44 convicted per 100,000
juvenile inhabitants, and among Jews, only 22. Jewish juvenile delinquency was thus only half of the non-Jewish. In addition, it is
worth noting that among Jews as well as non-Jews, female juvenile
delinquency was about one-tenth that of the male (among Jews,

TABLE 6

Recidivists among Adults * Convicted in 1937

Adult Recidivists	Number			Percentage of Jews among the Adult Recidivists (Recidivism among the Convicted)	Recidivists per 100 Adult Convicted (Recidivism among)		Jewish Recidivism among the Convicted in Ratio to Non-Jewish Recidivism	Recidivists per 10,000 Inhabitants (Recidivism among the Population)		Jewish Recidivism Ratio to Population in Non-Jewish Recidivism
	Jews	Non-Jews	Total		Jews	Non-Jews		Jews	Non-Jews	
Convicted only once previously.........	2,398	45,676	48,074	5.0	10.6	14.0	76	23.5	42.8	55
Convicted more than twice previously...	2,306	57,898	60,204	3.8	10.2	17.7	58	22.6	54.3	42
Total...............	4,704	103,574	108,278	4.3	20.8	31.7	66	46.2	97.0	48
Among them, women										
Convicted only once previously.........	352	4,547	4,899	7.2	7.2	8.4	86	7.0	8.6	81
Convicted more than twice previously...	197	4,540	4,737	4.2	4.0	8.4	48	3.9	8.6	45
Total...............	549	9,087	9,636	5.7	11.2	16.8	67	10.9	17.2	63

* Aged 17 and over

4.4 convicted girls against 42 boys per 100,000 juvenile inhabitants of the respective sex).

Another new feature in the last M. R. S. is the information—howbeit brief—about the number of adult recidivists among the convicted, according to their religion. Comparing these figures with the figures of the convicted and of the population, we obtain Table 6.

We thus come to the following conclusions:

(1) Among both Jews and non-Jews, recidivism is much rarer among women than among men.

(2) Among Jewish convicted, both male and female, recidivists are considerably rarer than among the non-Jewish. In 1937 the percentage of Jewish recidivists among the convicted, both men and women, was only two-thirds (66.6%) of the percentage among non-Jewish convicts.

(3) A still rarer phenomenon among the Jewish convicted, in comparison with the non-Jewish, is recurrent recidivism. The percentage of recidivists previously convicted twice or more times among the Jewish convicts was just over one-half that of the non-Jewish. The Jews, comprising 9.8% of the population, comprised in 1937 6.5% of the first-time recidivists, and 3.8% of the recurrent recidivists.

(4) Inasmuch as the Jewish criminality *per se* is considerably smaller than the non-Jewish, and recidivists among the convicted are rarer among Jews than among non-Jews, the difference between the Jewish population and the non-Jewish in respect of recidivism is consequently even greater than the difference in the number of Jewish and non-Jewish convicted. The recidivism of the population (recidivists per 10,000 adult inhabitants) in the last year was, among Jews, only 48% that of the non-Jews; and the recurrent recidivism among Jews, only 42% that of the non-Jews.

In respect of recidivism, too, we thus recognize the fact that Jewish criminality in Poland was lower, not only quantitatively but also qualitatively, than non-Jewish.

The official Polish criminal statistics, published on the very eve of the present war, under constantly deteriorating conditions of the Jewish masses and with a changed standard of offenses taken into consideration, thus confirms and complements in certain respects the more important conclusions, which we reached on the basis of statistical data of the previous years. The considerably lower and lighter Jewish criminality, in comparison with the non-Jewish, thus remains a definitely established characteristic of the Jewish population in the Republic of Poland.

Religious, Educational and Cultural Problems in the Eastern European Ghettos under German Occupation

By Isaiah Trunk

The pre-war *kehillas* in Poland did not engage in cultural activities in the strict sense of the word. The law governing the *kehillas* of 1927 confined their activities to religious matters (including religious education) and welfare. This applied particularly to the smaller *kehillas*, where the Agudath Israel was an important, frequently a decisive, factor. In the field of education their activity was limited to maintaining Talmud Torahs for poor Jewish children. At the most they would assign on the basis of compromises among the various *kehilla* parties small subventions to the cultural institutions established by the social groupings outside the *kehilla*.

In the occupied areas of pre-war Soviet Russia there existed no organized *kehillas* altogether. In the areas occupied on the basis of the Molotov–Ribbentrop pact of August 1939 (the former Polish areas of Western White Russia and the Western Ukraine and the Baltic countries) the *kehillas* were formally disbanded in the first weeks of the occupation. However, in the religious domain (ritual slaughtering, ritual food, public worship) the *kehillas* continued their activity.

So soon as the *Judenraete* became the only government recognized organs for the internal affairs of the Jewish population cultural affairs in the ghetto automatically assumed their stamp. On the basis of a special decree only the *Judenraete* had the right to open

155

schools. The same applied to courses, public artistic programs and the like. (Warsaw was in this respect the exception; there the social element concentrating in the "Jewish Culture Organization" was the moving spirit of all cultural activity in the Ghetto.)

RELIGIOUS CONDITIONS

Because of the overt hostile attitude to the Jewish religion on the part of the occupants—one of the first anti-Jewish decrees was the ban on *shehita*[1]—the care for the religious needs of the Jewish population by the *Judenraete* encountered great obstacles. In conformity with the Nazi conception of Jews as a race the *Judenraete*, in contrast to the former *kehillas,* could not have a religious character. This conception found expression in the order of September 1939 to change the name of the Cracow *kehilla* from "Jüdische Kultusgemeinde" to "Jüdische Gemeinde,"[2] for as far as the Nazis were concerned it had to represent all racially pure or mixed Jews regardless of religious affiliation.

A semi-official commentary to the decree of November 28, 1939, governing the *Judenraete* in the *Gazeta Żydowska* (no. 30, Nov. 1, 1940) reads: "In consonance with this decree the *kehilla* should be designated as a Jewish fellowship living within the boundaries of a political community. The decree of July 24, 1940, on the definition of the concept 'Jew' determines who as a Jew belongs to the Jewish community. The *kehilla* no longer forms a religious association but a national or racial fellowship, hence the satisfaction of the religious needs of its members is no longer its exclusive task." On the assumption that the law of October 14, 1927, had not been formally rescinded, the *Judenraete* maintained that the satisfaction of the religious needs was also within their domain.

Because of this attitude to the Jewish religion, the *Judenraete,* especially those in the smaller ghettos, apparently deemed it advisable not to create a special division for religion in the administrative apparatus. To date only two large ghettos (Warsaw and Lodz) are known in which rabbinical boards functioned officially. In Lwow such a board existed under the guise of a division of the *Judenrat*

1 *Verordnungsblatt für das General Gouvernment,* no. 1, Oct. 26, 1939.
2 *Die jüdische Gemeinde in Krakau in der Zeit vom 13 Sept. 1939 bis 30 Sept. 1940 und ihre Tätigkeit* (Cracow 1940), p. 3. (Hereafter called *Bericht Krakau.*)

called "Culture Bureau." The only religious activity that pleased greatly the supervising power was that of the Holy Burial Association.

In many ghettos the occupation authorities compelled the *Judenraete* from the very beginning to summon the Jewish population to work on the Sabbath and holidays and even the High Holidays. In Lodz the authorities compelled the opening of all Jewish stores and offices on Yom Kippur in 1939.[3] The Cracow *Judenrat* was compelled on the first day of Rosh Hashana 1940 to issue a call to the Jewish population to report to work on the second day of Rosh Hashana and on the following Yom Kippur and to keep open all stores and shops under threats of severe penalties.[4] Apparently, pious Jews ignored these threats and failed to report to work on these holiest of days, or left work in the middle of the day to attend a religious service. On September 20, 1940, the Lublin *Judenrat* issues a warning (Announcement no. 184) against arbitrarily leaving work on both days of Rosh Hashana and Yom Kippur.[5] Similarly, the *Aeltestenrat* of Siauliai had to issue a summons on the very day of Yom Kippur (Sept. 4, 1942) to the Jewish compulsory laborers to report to work on that day.[6]

In this respect the Lodz Ghetto had it somewhat easier. On the eve of Yom Kippur in 1940 Rumkowski announced (Announcement no. 134) that the following day, which occurred that year on the Sabbath, as well as all following Sabbaths, would be observed as official days of rest in the Ghetto.[7] Two circulars of the Ghetto Administration, of September 30 and October 15, 1941, proclaimed also Rosh Hashana and Sukkot as days of rest in the offices and shops.[8] But this tolerant attitude toward the Jewish religion on the part of the authorities was of short duration. In the following years Rosh Hashana and Yom Kippur were regular working days. Similarly, the Sabbath as a weekly day of rest was under the pressure of the "Ghetto Administration" virtually abolished. On October 17, 1941, Amtsleiter Biebow applied to the Gestapo for the abolition of the Sabbath as a day of rest in the Ghetto and its substitutions by

[3] Gersht, J. L., *Min hamezar* (Jerusalem 5709), pp. 39-41.
[4] *Gazeta Żydowska*, Oct. 7, 1940.
[5] Archive of Bet Lohame Hagetaot, doc. 1884/32.
[6] Yerushalmi, E., *Pinkas shavli* (Jerusalem 5718), p. 113 microfilm.
[7] Zonabend Collection, doc. 185.
[8] *Ibid.*, docs. 542, 548.

Sunday. In support of his application he pointed to the difficulty created for him and the supervising authorities in the discharge of their control functions by the double set of rest days. On account of this German officials were sometimes compelled to work on Sunday, he argued, and there was delay in unloading goods arriving in the Ghetto on the Sabbath.[9] Needless to say the Gestapo acted favorably on his application. To some extent up to September 1942 the determination of the rest day depended upon the shop managers, and some factories did not work on the Sabbath. Rumkowski permitted observant Jews to transfer to such factories.[10] In effect, this choice of the rest day by the manager created a situation that for quite a while the Ghetto worked both Saturdays and Sundays. Only on January 29, 1943, Sunday was declared as the official rest day in the Ghetto, which, however, was not observed too strictly.[11]

After the establishment of the Ghetto in Warsaw the *Judenrat* applied to the authorities to declare the Sabbath as the rest day there since all contacts with the Aryan part of the city had been severed. (Up to that time the *Judenrat* bureaus and the public institutions were closed both Saturdays and Sundays.) The authorities agreed to this request. Under the date line of April 15, 1941, the *Gazeta Żydowska* published Cherniakov's decree declaring the Sabbath, Rosh Hashana, Yom Kippur, Sukkot (4 days), Passover (4 days) and Shavuot as official rest days in the Ghetto. In addition New Year and other Catholic holidays were also declared rest days. This decree, the notice specified, did not apply to those works carried out by order of the Transferstelle of the district chief as well as to those tasks that because of circumstances had to be executed also on the Sabbath.[12]

The attitude of the authorities toward public worship too varied with place and underwent changes both for better and worse. In Ghetto Lodz the change was for the worse. In the High Holydays of 1940 public worship was conducted with the permission of the city authorities and German officers even attended a Kol Nidre service. Services were conducted in many places and even outdoors.[13] To

9 Archives of the Gettoverwaltung, no. 144, JM/828, Yad Washem.
10 Zonabend Collection, docs. 304, 569.
11 *Ibid.*, doc. 1616; A. Eisenbach, *Getto Łódzkie* (Lodz 1947), p. 245.
12 *Biuletyn Wydziału Statystycznego Rady Żydowskiej w Warszawie*, p. 126; *Gaz. Żydowska*, April 29, 1941.
13 Trunk, I., *Lodzher geto* (New York 1962), p. 403.

establish a synagogue or even a conventicle the permission of Rumkowski was required.[14] Later on public worship had to be conducted
in great secrecy and guarded against undesirable visitors.[15] Also in
Sosnowiec the authorities permitted public worship on Rosh Hashana 1940 in the Home for the Aged.[16]

In Warsaw public worship was prohibited by the authorities
on January 26, 1940, under the pretext of danger of epidemics.[17]
However, over a month earlier, on December 19, 1939, Cherniakov
had noted in his diary that all public worship places had been
closed. A following notation, of December 20, 1939, mentions the
order he had received to close all synagogues and houses of prayer.
The last notation on this subject, of January 5, 1940, includes the
closing of the ritual bath.[18] In effect, many houses of prayer and
conventicles had been converted earlier into shelters for the large
number of refugees.

Only by the decree of the Government General of March 4,
1941, were the Jews permitted to conduct services in private homes,
synagogues and Houses of Study on Passover (4 days), Shavuot
(2 days), Rosh Hashana (2 days), Yom Kippur and Sukkot (4
days). On this basis the supervising authorities permitted the
Judenrat on March 17, 1941, to open three synagogues. On Shavuot
1941 services were conducted in the renovated "Great Synagogue"
on Tlomackie Street.[19] Prior to the decree of March 4, 1941, public
worship was conducted secretly in private conventicles.

In many cities where the synagogues were burned by the Germans in the first months of the occupation,[20] or where they were
located outside the ghetto, services were conducted in private conventicles under constant threat of discovery and attendant punishment. Even after the decree of March 4, 1941, the Jews hesitated
to gather in large numbers for services for fear of being taken to
compulsory labor or of visits from the S.S. who delighted in mocking
the religious sentiments of the Jewish population.[21] Observant Jews

14 Zonabend Collection, doc. 160.
15 Trunk, I., *op. cit.*, p. 404.
16 *Gazeta Żydowska*, Oct. 10, 1940.
17 *Ibid.*, Nov. 8, 1940.
18 Cherniakov's Diary.
19 *Gazeta Żyd.* Apr. 29, May 27, 1941.
20 Huberband, Shimon, "Memoryal vegn oprateven di reshtlekh fun yidishe
kultur-oytsres in poyln," *Bleter far geshikhte*, vol. I, no. 2, 1948, pp. 105-110.
21 *The Persecution of Jews in German-Occupied Poland* (London), p. 18.

therefore preferred services at small private conventicles or prayed at home.

Concerning the other occupied areas, such as Ostland, it is note-worthy that the German Jews brought to the Riga Ghetto had their synagogue (the Cologne Synagogue) where services were conducted on the Sabbath and holidays, whereas the local Jews were not per-mitted to attend services and they worshipped in private conventicles (in the home of Rabbi Zak.) [22]

After the incorporation of the District of Galicia in the Govern-ment public worship was prohibited in Lwow. Services were con-ducted in secret conventicles. When one such conventicle was dis-covered as a result of the work of an informer the worshippers were taken to prison, whence none returned.

The *Judenraete* also attempted to provide a minimum quantity of matzos for Passover. For Passover 1941 the Jews of Lodz received on their ration cards two and a half kilos of matzos per person. (In the previous year ration cards had not yet been introduced and peo-ple could obtain matzos on their own initiative.)

For Passover 1940 the *Judenrat* in Lublin upon its intercession with the authorities received 100,000 kilos of wheat flour (in Lodz the matzos were made from rye flour) for 100,000 zlotys. A Matzo Commission of 11 councilmen was appointed, which fixed the price of matzo at three zlotys a kilo. There was a slight surcharge for the more affluent, which made it possible to distribute matzos to the poor at reduced prices or even gratis. The latter category numbered 13,000 people. A total of 90,347 kilos of matzos were sold or dis-tributed and the report of the Matzo Commission proudly declared that no Jew in Lublin was without matzos that year. The Commis-sion's deficit in the amount of 12,000 zlotys was covered by the treasury of the *Judenrat*.[23]

The supplying of matzos and other Passover provisions in 1940 and in part in 1941 was made possible through JDC help which provided over half a million kilo of matzos, distributed among 344 communities.

On Passover 1941 in the Warsaw Ghetto matzos were obtainable on the appropriate ration cards.[24] Similarly in other ghettos too the

22 Kaufmann, M., *Khurbn letland* (Munich 1947), pp. 89, 167, 169.
23 *Sprawozdanie Rady Żydowskiej w Lublinie* . . . , pp. 71-72.
24 *Gaz. Żyd.*, Apr. 11, 1941.

Judenraete succeeded in the first year of the occupation to provide a small amount of matzos more as a symbol than for the satisfaction of hunger.[25]

In many ghettos the *Judenraete* established at their own initiative or at the initiative of the Orthodox circles special kosher kitchens within the framework of the free kitchens.[26]

In the Lodz Ghetto religious life was regulated by the Rabbinical College, consisting at first of 15 rabbis and from December 1941 of 19 (four rabbis were coopted from among the German deportees). These rabbis were considered employees of the Ghetto administration and their salary was at the end of 1941 250 mk. a month. They could perform marriages only on authorization of the Jewish Standes-Amt. In other religious matters they were autonomous. They could render decisions in ritual matters, arbitrate in litigations and the like. The Ghetto had one *mohel* and an assistant. Other religious functionaries, such as cantors, shohetim and sextons were assigned to the Ghetto shops to avoid the status of unemployed. Many of them worked in the Cemetery Division.[27] After the 1942 "September action" against children (up to 10), old people and the ailing, when most of the rabbis were deported, Rumkowski abolished the Rabbinical College and performed marriages himself.[28]

The German authorities did not recognize formally marriages in the Ghetto and the female spouse retained her maiden name. The only concession made was that the children bore the father's name. Divorces were administered by the Scheidungs Kollegium of the Standes-Amt, which consisted of a judge and two rabbis. The couple had to appear before an open or closed court session.[29]

In the beginning of February 1941 the entire Warsaw Ghetto area was divided into 28 rabbinical districts under the jurisdiction of 16 rabbis, members of the Warsaw rabbinate. Besides religious matters these rabbis had also to keep the vital statistical records for the *Judenrat*, which issued on the basis of these records the pertinent

---

[25] *Kobrin,* Zamlbukh (Buenos Aires 1951), p. 260; Feigenbaum, M. I., *Podlashe in umkum* (Munich 1948), p. 179; Kurz, I., *Sefer Edut;* Yerushalmi, *op. cit.,* p. 181.

[26] Trunk, *op. cit.,* p. 409, n. 254; Brener, L., *Vidershtand un umkum in tshenstokhover geto* (Warsaw 1951), p. 43; Gaz. Żyd., April 11, 1941.

[27] Trunk, *op. cit.,* pp. 410–411.

[28] *Ibid.,* p. 408.

[29] Zonabend Coll., no. 44, p. 2, no. 845.

documents.[30] Following the "deportation" of the summer of 1942, in which the majority of the rabbis perished and the Jewish population was reduced to almost one-tenth of its former number, the rabbinical college went out of existence. Three or four rabbis remained who, with the exception of one, perished in the actions of 1943.

The rabbinate in Lwow officially ceased functioning under Soviet occupation in 1940-41. Chief rabbi Dr. Louis Freund died in April 1940 and his associate, Dr. Lewin, was murdered in prison on July 2, 1941. The first chairman of the *Judenrat* reorganized the rabbinate, which consisted of rabbis and assistant rabbis (*dayanim*) of Lwow and vicinity and refugees of other communities, such as Dr. Kalman Chameides, rabbi of Katowice, and others. But the reorganization did not bring about a revival of religious life. The ban on *shehita* effective in the four parts of the Government General was extended to the newly incorporated district of Galicia. The rabbinate conducted its activity in constant fear. The rabbis were afraid to issue marriage certificates for that could have betrayed the existence of the rabbinate, which had no official sanction of the authorities. Tragic was the problem of divorce, which mostly involved "Aryan" women who had embraced the faith of their Jewish husbands. Through divorce they and their children would be exempt from ghetto liabilities. As a rule, it was the husbands who urged them to this step to save them and their children from a forlorn fate. Following the great "deportation" of June-July 1943, in which nearly all rabbis perished, the office of the rabbinate went out of existence.[31]

Under the specific ghetto conditions observance of the Jewish law—the Sabbath, dietary laws, Passover—was virtually impossible. The rabbis were fully aware of this and ready for compromise. Thus the Board of Rabbis of the Lodz Ghetto permitted non-kosher meats to the sick, women in confinement and all those "who were growing weak" and were under physician's orders. This permission, granted February 27, 1941, was signed by all 15 rabbis.[32] For Passover 1941 the Warsaw rabbinate "permitted all kinds of peas and lentils for

30 *Gaz. Żyd.*, February 2, 1941. Information by Dr. Hillel Seidman, an employee of the Community Archives in Warsaw.
31 Testimony of Rabbi David Kahane.
32 Zonabend Coll., doc. 1268.

fear of insufficiency of matzos."[33] Similarly in the Kaunas Ghetto the rabbis were lenient in their interpretation of the law in the specific conditions. They permitted the cooking of meals on the Sabbath for compulsory laborers, the performance of abortion on women who were under the threat of death penalty (conception was punishable with death), and the like.

The traditional Jewish garb and the beard and *peot* similarly fell victim to the ghetto conditions. In the Lodz Ghetto Rumkowski, undoubtedly by order of the supervising authorities, launched a campaign against the long gaberdine and the beards and *peot*. In an item in the *Geto-tsaytung* he announced the ban on the gaberdine for all below 50 years, with the exception of rabbis and possessors of rabbinical degrees. In exceptional cases he granted special permits to wear a gaberdine.[34] In an address delivered on June 1, 1942, he announced that beards too must disappear from the Ghetto within eight days under penalty of loss of job.[35] On June 13, 1942, the Jewish *Ordnungsdienst* conducted raids on bearded in the streets of the Ghetto; the victims were dragged into barber shops where their beards were cut.[36] In several other ghettos too the authorities ordered the *Judenraete* to exercise care that the Jewish workers report to work cleanly shaved.[37]

A specially complicated religious problem was created for the *Judenraete* by the converts forced into the ghettos. Thus in 1941 with the transports of German Jews there arrived in Lodz some 250 Protestants and Catholics, converts and their children, who had long since severed all links with the Jewish people. They organized in the Ghetto a Christian Association and conducted public services.[38] Also in the Warsaw Ghetto the Jewish Christians had their priest and church, where public services were conducted.[39]

In the Riga Reichsghetto the German Jews of the Catholic faith

33 Ringelblum, E., *Notitsn fun varshever geto* (Warsaw 1952), p. 112.

34 *Geto-tsaytung*, July 15, 1941.

35 Zonabend Coll., doc. 29, p. 1.

36 *Ibid.*, doc. 29a, bulletins of the daily ghetto chronicle of June 14 and 18, 1942.

37 See nn. 35 and 36; *Seyfer borshtchev* (Tel Aviv 1960), p. 197; Oshri, Efraim, *Sheelot uteshuvot mimaamakim* pp. 115–116; *Pinkes zamoshtsh* (Buenos Aires 1957), p. 1005.

38 Zonabend Coll., doc. 1192, p. 9.

39 Ringelblum, *op. cit.* p. 107.

gathered in the dwelling of their *Aelteste*, also a Catholic, who read the mass and functioned as a priest.[40]

Consistent with the German plans to reduce the Polish areas to a kind of colonial hinterland for the Reich, the German educational policy in the occupied areas aimed at a reduction of public education to the most elementary level. The goal was to train workers, artisans and trained farmers. Hence only elementary and trade schools were permitted; secondary and higher education was expressly prohibited. The same policy applied to the Jewish population only in a much more drastic form.

The war broke out on the day of the opening of the school year 1939/1940 and the schools did not open. On October 8, 1939, there appeared an announcement of the Commander-in-Chief of the Army of Occupation permitting the opening of all educational institutions in Warsaw operating before the war. Several Jewish schools opened. Toward the end of November the civilian authorities ordered the closing of the Jewish schools under the pretext of epidemics, and on December 4 the last Jewish elementary school closed.[41] The general elementary schools were permitted to remain open by the authorities, but they were ordered to bar Jewish teachers and pupils. These tactics were employed in practically all occupied areas.[42]

The unemployed teachers appealed continually to the *Judenrat*, CENTOS and other Jewish organizations to begin a camouflaged schooling program under the guise of child protection. A memorandum to the *Judenrat* by the teachers' representation stated that there were in Warsaw 50,000-60,000 Jewish children aged five to twelve, among them thousands who were left without adult supervision and exposed to the demoralizing influence of the street.[43] In the meantime, in many of the children's kitchens opened at the initiative of the former school organizations and CENTOS a program of

---

40 Kaufmann, *op. cit.*, p. 169.

41 Natanblut, Anna, "Di shuln in varshever geto," *YIVO-bleter*, vol. XXX, no. 2, p. 173.

42 By decree of Governor General Hans Frank, of March 10, 1940, special permission was required for the opening of a private school.

43 Neshamit, S., "Lefarshat hahinukh hameurgan begeto varsha," *Yediot bet lohame hagetaot*, no. 21, May 1951, p. 113.

unofficial education was arranged for several hours daily. Thousands of children took advantage of this program.

On September 11, 1940, there appeared Governor General Hans Frank's decree, dated August 31, 1940, on "The Jewish School System in the Government General," granting the *Judenraete* permission to open elementary and trade schools with the status of private schools. Supervision of the schools was vested in the German authorities and the *Judenrat* had to obtain permission for the opening of a school from the local authorities. This opened a door to all kinds of chicaneries and even outright denial of permission.[44] Moreover the publication of the decree eleven days after the opening of the other schools was deliberate: the Jewish and non-Jewish schools should not open in the same day. The *Judenrat* began to make preparations for the implementation of the decree, establishing a school commission consisting of representatives of former Jewish school organizations. The German Sanitation Department issued a warning that the opening of the Jewish schools might spread the typhus epidemic and the preparations were discontinued.[45]

But precisely in the summer and fall of 1940 the incidence of typhus and spotted fever which had broken out in the fall of 1939 markedly declined. Thus in December 1939 there were among the Jews 540 cases of typhus and in the summer of 1940 the rate declined to about 10 per month. Similarly the cases of spotted fever declined from 407 in April 1940 to 18 in August.[46] Patently, the "danger of epidemic" was a mere pretext for sabotaging a decree— albeit a German—if the Jews stood to gain by it.

In January 1941 the *Judenrat* renewed its efforts along these lines—without results. Only in April 1941 was permission granted for the opening of a number of elementary schools, initially, for 5,000 children. The school commission was reactivated and the general framework of a school system comprising six types of schools (TsYShO, Tarbut, Shulkult, Yavne, Horeb, Bet Yaakov) was worked out. Also lists of teachers and principals were submitted,[47] but no action was taken by the authorities.

---

[44] *Verordnungsblatt für das General Gouvernment*, I, no. 51, Sept. 11, 1940.
[45] *Biuletyn Wydziału Statystycznego* . . . , no. 12 c, p. 2; *Gaz. Żyd.*, Jan. 24, 1941.
[46] Trunk, I., "Milkhome kegn yidn durkh farshpreytn krankeytn, *YIVO-bleter*, vol. XXXVII, p. 61.
[47] Wasser Coll. (YIVO Archives), doc. 36 a/1.

Finally in September-October 1941, sixteen schools opened under the following auspices: TsYShO—3, Tarbut—3, Shulkult—1, religious schools (Bet Yaakov, Horev, Yavne)—5, schools with Polish as the language of instruction—4.[48] These schools had three grades, in some there was also a fourth and even a fifth grade. They imparted instruction to some 10,000 children, that is one-fifth of all children of lower elementary school age.

A measure of formal instruction was also given to the children in the homes maintained by CENTOS. On December 1, 1941, CENTOS had under its care 25,648 children, and on February 5, 1942, it had a staff of 319, including 85 teachers.[49]

The frightful material conditions of the Ghetto made it well-nigh impossible to conduct a halfway normal program of education. Following is the report of a supervisor for January 1942:

> ... The poor attendance is due to the cold weather, lack of clothing and shoes, the unheated or insufficiently heated rooms . . . The program of studies concentrates on the cycle of the year. There is no art work, such as drawing or work in clay.[50]

Despite these conditions the attainments were considerable. Children in the ghettos matured at an early age and their yearning for knowledge was great. Moreover, the school constituted the only bright spot in their otherwise dreary life.

Secondary education, which was forbidden, was conducted clandestinely, mainly in the form of "students' contingents," organized by teachers and consisting of six to twenty students. Instruction was given in the homes of the students or the teachers and the program was that of the state secondary school, with the exception of some technical subjects. According to a statistic compiled by a group of teachers some 20 percent of the former secondary school students were enrolled in these "contingents," which numbered several hundred in 1941. "Contingents" were also established by political and educational groups (Hashomer Hatzair, ORT, Mizrachi and others).[51] For a while two clandestine gymnasiums were operative. The Tarbut gymnasium, with three grades and six teachers and several

---

48 Natanblut, Anna, op. cit., pp. 175-176.
49 Wasser Coll., file 49; Berman, A., "O losie dzieci w getcie warszawskim," Biuletyn Żydowskiego Instytutu Historycznego, no. 28, 1958, pp. 67–68.
50 Wasser Coll., file 49.
51 Neshamit, S., op. cit., pp. 106–107.

score students existed to June 1942 and the graduates were given certificates.[52] The Dror gymnasium, opened in August 1940 with 7 students, had in 1941 120 students and 13 teachers.[53]

The permission granted in August 1940 to open trade schools was utilized to teach also general subjects and even advanced theoretical studies. The responsibility for these trade courses was vested in the Commission for Trade Education, consisting of representatives of ORT and the *Judenrat*. On June 30, 1941, there existed 24 courses with 832 boys, another 24 with 818 girls and 16 coeducational courses with 681 students—a total of 2,331 students. Up to April 1941 there were also 4 advanced courses. Because of the precarious conditions attendance at these courses was irregular and constantly declining.

In time trade courses on a college and even university level, with a broad theoretical curriculum, were established, such as the School of Nursing, with 250 students, who were employed in the Ghetto hospitals and the School of Nursing of the Jewish Hospital, with a two-year curriculum; the Pharmaceutical Course, with 50 students; the Course in Applied Chemistry, with 50 students and a Course in the Graphic Arts.[54] Also two clandestine courses on a university level were established: a medical and technological. A course in education on the same level was legal. The teachers of these courses were Jews or converts, former professors in Warsaw's higher institutions of learning. The medical courses, headed by the renowned epidemiologist, Professor Ludwig Hirschfeld, enjoyed a high reputation. Some 250 students attended these courses.[55]

Permission for the course in education was granted in the aforementioned decree of August 31, 1940, providing for the training of teachers for the Jewish schools. The decree stipulated that no humanistic studies be included in these courses, except Judaic studies. Like the other courses this one too was expanded to include philosophy, psychology and general educational theory. The teachers were former professors at the Judaic Institute and the State Seminary for Jewish Teachers of Religion.[56]

[52] Eck, Nathan, "Shnayim shesardu," *Davar*, Apr. 28, 1957.

[53] "Korespondenzia pnimit, mispar 4, Dror," *Dapim leheker hashoa vehamered*, vol. I, 1951, pp. 155–156.

[54] Goldhar-Mark, Ester, "Dos yidishe fakh un hekhere shulvezn in varshe in der tsayt fun der daytsher okupatsye," *Bleter far geshikhte*, vol. II, 1949, pp. 195-202; *Gaz. Żyd.*, Feb. 11, Apr. 22, 1941.

[55] Hirszfeld, Ludwik, *Historia jednego życia* (Warsaw 1947), pp. 207–215.

[56] Goldhar-Mark, E., *op. cit.*, p. 201; Natanblut, A., *op. cit.*, p. 138.

There were also courses of immediate practical utility: gardening and farming. These were arranged by the pre-war Society for the Promotion of Agriculture (ToPoRol) and ORT, and included the study of botany, chemistry and related sciences. A report on ToPoRol's activities for the semester, dated June 30, 1941, states that 324 students attended the agricultural course and that 267 people attended the shorter course in the same subject.

The same tactic of delay and slow motion was also characteristic of other cities. Thus the *Gazeta Żydowska* reported that toward the end of March 1941 all preparations for the opening of the school in Radom, in which some 2,000 children had registered, had been completed. All that was lacking was the official authorization for opening the school. A correspondence from the same city, dated August 18, 1941, hints that "the school situation is still in the planning stage."[57] Presumably, the required authorization had not been granted. An article in the *Gazeta Żydowska* of January 7, 1941, notes that "owing to local conditions the authorities have postponed the opening of Jewish schools in various localities."

Similarly in Zamosc and in Lwow the *Judenraete* failed to obtain permission to open schools.[58] At the initiative of a group of teachers in Lublin, shortly after the occupation a four-grade school with over a hundred children was opened. Similarly the Tarbut school, with a greatly reduced staff and student body, and a private elementary school opened. In the middle of November, 1939, on the occasion of the closing of the Polish secondary schools, the above schools were closed. All attempts to reopen the Jewish schools after August 1940 met with great obstacles. In March 1941, when permission had finally been received to open the school the great deportation began. Later on, when conditions became somewhat "stabilized," it was impossible to find accommodations for a school because of the abnormal crowding in the Ghetto. The courses in Yiddish and Hebrew offered by the *Judenrat* were but a sorry substitute for a school. Greater significance attaches to the clandestine "contingents" organized by the teachers, with about 10 pupils in each group. A teacher of such a "contingent" tells in his memoirs: "With beating hearts we conducted the lessons, simultaneously on the alert for the

---

57 *Gaz. Żyd.*, Aug. 18, 1941.
58 *Pinkes zamoshtsh*, p. 1156; Friedman, P. "Hurban yehude levov," *Enziklopedia shel galuyot* (Jerusalem-Tel Aviv 1956), vol. IV, p. 683.

barking voices of the S.S., who frequently raided Jewish homes. In such a case all incriminating traces immediately disappeared. Gone were books and notebooks. The pupils began to play and the teacher became a customer: in a tailor's house he began to try on clothes and in a shoemaker's house—shoes."[59]

In Rzeszow the *Judenrat* opened schools on October 27, 1940.[60] After prolonged endeavors the *Judenrat* of Cracow was permitted toward the end of September 1940 to reactivate the Jewish school system, which numbered 6,400 pupils when the war broke out.[61] In Jaslo a seven-grade school was opened in December 1940;[62] in Kazimierz—a four-grade school on December 1, 1940;[63] in Opatow—a four-grade school with 302 pupils.[64] Similarly, the *Judenrat* opened schools in Gorlice and in Miedzyrzec.[65] The schools that opened in the summer or early autumn of 1940 completed the year in the summer of 1941 with formal closing exercises (Cracow, Jaslo), which were linked with Herzl-Bialik memorial programs.[66] On July 18-20, 1941, an exhibit of children's arts and crafts was shown in Cracow.

In several places the opened schools were soon ordered closed. Thus in Gorlice the school was closed in January 1942 "because of epidemics."[67] In Kaunas the two elementary schools established at the initiative of the teachers in December 1941 were ordered closed toward the end of August 1942.[68] In addition there functioned in the Ghetto up to that time a private Hebrew kindergarten, private *hadarim* and a yeshivah.[69]

One of the greatest problems of the schools in the ghetto was finding suitable accommodations. Jewish schools as a rule had been located in the main streets, which were excluded from the ghetto areas. Thus in Kazimierz the school was housed in the old synagogue, the only large building in the Ghetto. In Radom three rooms were

[59] Korn, N., "Dertsiungs-problemen und kinder-elnt in geto," *Dos bukh fun lublin* (Paris 1952), pp. 503–506.
[60] Gaz. Żyd., Nov. 8, 1940.
[61] *Bericht Krakau*, pp. 113–114; Gaz. Żyd., July 27, 1941.
[62] *Ibid.*, Dec. 13, 1940.
[63] *Ibid.*, Dec. 17, 1940.
[64] *Ibid.*, July 16, 1941.
[65] Weichert, M., *Milkhome*, p. 318; Gaz. Żyd., Dec. 12, 1940.
[66] Gaz. Żyd., July 27, 1941.
[67] Weichert, *op. cit.*, p. 318.
[68] Garfunkel, L., *Kovno hayehudit behurbana* (Jerusalem 1959), pp. 113–114; Kaplan, Y. "Kovner shul un lerershaft in umkum," *Fun letstn khurbn*, no. 9, Sept. 1948.
[69] Garfunkel, *op. cit.*, p. 236.

renovated in the old Talmud Torah for the planned school, which would have to operate in three shifts. In the Kutno "death camp" (thus the Germans referred to the Kutno Ghetto) a new school building was erected but an outbreak of typhus compelled its conversion into a hospital.[70]

The second major difficulty was the problem of language of instruction, textbooks and teachers. Although the original decree had left the problem of the language of instruction open, the local authorities insisted upon Yiddish or Hebrew. In Radom the authorities demanded Yiddish exclusively. Before the war only a small percentage of the Jewish children attended the TsYShO or Tarbut schools; the majority attended the state elementary schools for Jewish children. For the latter the transition from Polish to Yiddish or Hebrew created a serious educational problem. The classes consisted of children with different linguistic backgrounds and it was no easy task to find a common language. Some schools (Cracow, Jaslo) began with Polish as the language of instruction but were ordered by the authorities to change to Hebrew. In some schools certain subjects were taught in Hebrew, others in Yiddish.

Many Jewish book stores were destroyed in the war; others were closed and their stock confiscated. Special permission was necessary for the purchase of textbooks. By and large, the textbooks were collected from among the pupils themselves.

The teacher shortage was acute, particularly in the smaller towns. A large number of teachers, mainly those who had been politically and communally active, fled eastward. Of the remaining, some found it impossible or extremely difficult to teach in Hebrew or in Yiddish. To alleviate the situation, teachers courses were opened in Warsaw, Radom, Lodz and several other places. The curriculum in Lodz consisted of Yiddish language and literature, folklore, music and the history of the Jewish school (presumably a camouflage for Jewish history).[71]

In some places where the *Judenrat* was denied permission or unable to open a school partial instruction was given under the auspices of child care organizations, such as CENTOS, TOZ and similar

---

70 Testimony no. 303 in the Archive of the Jewish Historical Institute in Warsaw.
71 *Gaz. Żyd.*, March 21, 1941; Gersht, Y. L. "Lererkursn far yidish in lodzher geto," *YIVO-bleter*, XXX, no. 1, pp. 152–155.

organizations. In Czestochowa, for instance, TOZ converted its refectories into children's clubs where some instruction was provided for about 2,000 children by a staff of professional teachers. (Over 200 Jewish teachers remained in the city.) Periodically, clandestine dramatic presentations were given by the children, "which brought in a measure of festivity into their dreary life."[72]

Permissions for trade schools were granted more liberally, for it meant training a "Jewish labor force" for the Germans. Accordingly, several such schools opened in a number of cities under the auspices of the *Judenraete* or local relief committees affiliated with the Jewish Social Self-Help in Cracow. Prior to the war there had existed in Poland several Jewish trade schools (Piotrkow, Czestochowa and others). These were destroyed in the war; their machinery looted or confiscated. The problem of equipment for the new schools now came up. In Czestochowa, for instance, it was solved by employing the trade school pupils as apprentices in the Ghetto shops. This makeshift solution was hardly satisfactory, and several machines were obtained with great difficulty. In early December 1940 permission was granted to open courses for carpenters, locksmiths and seamstresses. The first two courses opened on May 16, 1941, with 46 pupils; the last in the first half of May, with 37 pupils. These courses went on for about 4 months and closed for unknown reasons.[73]

Trade and continuation schools for boys and girls aged 14-16 were operative in Rzeszow in December 1940, which trained carpenters, electricians, printers and designers. The practical work was done in the shops. There was also a course for nurses.[74] Such trade courses were offered in a number of places.[75]

Frequently, the trade courses served as a cover for general studies, the demarcation line between practical and theoretical studies being very thin. They also created a spiritual climate preserving the morale of the young people. Illustrative is the trade school in the Kaunas Ghetto, which opened on Purim 1942 with a course for locksmiths, with 40 pupils. It was opened at the initiative of a group of ORT teachers with the aid of the *Judenrat*. A considerable part of the equipment was smuggled into the Ghetto by the instructors,

[72] Brener, L., *op. cit.*, pp. 51–53.
[73] *Ibid.*, p. 56.
[74] *Gaz. Żyd.*, Dec. 20, 1940.
[75] *Ibid.*, passim; Dvorzhetski, M., *Yerusholaim delite in kamf un umkum* (Paris 1948), pp. 235–236; Trunk, *op. cit.*, 53–54.

at the risk of life and limb. On August 26, 1942, the school was ordered closed. In November 1942 the *Judenrat* succeeded in convincing the new Ghetto chief that the school was indispensable to the growing industry there and permission for its reopening was granted. It operated three courses for boys, training them as locksmiths, tinsmiths and carpenters; two for girls, training them as seamstresses and embroiderers. In addition there was a course in gardening, with practical work in the hot-house and in the Ghetto gardens. Later on, a course in arts and crafts for the most promising girls was added, with the study of art history, theory of colors and the like.

The school became the hub of the cultural life in the Ghetto. Lectures on art and literature were given there. A choir of over 100 students and a dramatic circle were organized and a library was opened. In July 1943 the school arranged an exhibit of arts and crafts and a dramatic presentation of Peretz' "Cabalists," which was repeated several times. Toward the end of March 1944 the school was incorporated, as a cover, in the Ghetto shops and continued up to the liquidation of the Ghetto in July 1944.[76]

In two large ghettos, Lodz and Vilna, the educational program of the *Judenrat* met with few obstacles on the part of the authorities. In Lodz, which was in early October 1939 incorporated in the Reich, the administration sought to restore life to its normal course. On October 25, 1939, the City Commissar authorized the Judenaelteste Rumkowski to take over the Jewish schools and maintain them by a tax on the Jewish population. At the outbreak of the war there were in Lodz 21 Jewish elementary schools, with 17,902 pupils; 12 *hadarim*, with 1,452 pupils; 10 gymnasiums, with 1,861 pupils and 10 preparatory schools at the gymnasiums, with 1,112 pupils—a total of 63 schools with 22,327 pupils.[77]

Rumkowski was ordered to dismiss all Polish teachers in the state schools for Jewish children with suitable compensation. (The order was executed by decree of October 18, 1939.) The Jewish teachers were dismissed from the general schools without compensation.[78]

Beginning with October 1939 the schools were in charge of a

76 Oleyski, Y., "Di fakhshul in kovner geto," *Fun letstn khurbn* (Munich), no. 9, Sept. 1948; Kaplan, *op. cit.*
77 Zonabend Coll., doc. 1464.
78 *Ibid.*, doc. 931/1.

School Commission of six, later transformed into a School Council. In September 1941 it consisted of a chairman and two members (inspectors). Two superintendents visited the schools.

The schools in Lodz opened on September 11, 1939. Eight large school buildings, mainly the gymnasiums, had been requisitioned by the Germans, a large number of teachers had left the city, others were seized for compulsory labor—all these together with the general precarious situation interfered with the normal functioning of the schools. On December 15, 1939, studies ceased and were resumed only after the entry into the Ghetto (in the beginning of March 1940). Moreover, because of overcrowding (of the 31 elementary schools only 8 were in the Ghetto area) classes were conducted in two or even three shifts and at that there were far too many students in a class (in the gymnasium—90). Because of the long interruption the school year was extended to September and the vacation made to coincide with the High Holidays.

In the first year the elementary schools had 10,462 pupils, the two gymnasiums—508, the two lyceum classes—125 and the trade school—56,[79] a total of 11,151 and a decline of over 50 percent. Attendance, however, was poor and in May 1940 declined to 7,366. In the second year, which began on October 29, 1940, the attendance improved considerably, with an average of 10,300 and in January 1941 it rose to 14,944.[80] These schools employed 482 teachers—295 women and 187 men.[81]

Hitherto the curriculum was similar to that of the previous Polish schools. Under pressure of the authorities Rumkowski discarded this curriculum and replaced it with a rich program of Jewish studies, with Yiddish as the language of instruction. In the previous year the teachers had taught in the language of their preference. Now a new problem arose. The teachers, most of whom had previously taught in the state schools for Jewish children (319 out of a total of 482) were not prepared to teach in Yiddish and special courses had to be opened for them. One such course, in four sessions, opened in May 1941 and continued through September 1941.[82]

Instruction was also given to the inmates of the childrens' homes

79 *Ibid.*, doc. 1464.
80 *Loc. cit.*, p. 73; doc. 933.
81 *Ibid.*, 1464, p. 5.
82 Gersht, *op. cit.*, pp. 152–153.

in the Marysin district of the Ghetto, which on July 31, 1941, had 1,250 pupils. To Marysin were also transferred the two secondary schools and the trade school which had been closed by order of Rumkowski in January 1941. (The authorities apparently began to look askance at the imparting of secondary instruction to Jews and the schools were moved as far as possible from the Ghetto center.) When the authorities reduced the Ghetto area in February 1941, several schools had to close.[83]

In August 1940 "higher lyceum courses" were established, which were to provide the nucleus of a university, with 10 departments and some 30 professors. Three hundred and eighteen students, secondary school graduates and some with university training, registered for these courses. Up to September 20, 1940, 27 lectures were delivered, with an average audience of 250.

Rumkowski had given oral permission for these courses. Soon afterward he ordered their closing. Apparently in the hope of a quick reopening, a second registration opened and 116 additional students registered.

In addition to the aforementioned difficulties that handicapped the Jewish school program there was the serious encroachment of the shop on the school population. Economic misery compelled many children, even at the tender age of ten or eight to leave school and enter the factory. In August 1942, 13,861 youngsters, some of them no older than eight, were employed in the Ghetto shops.[84]

In some of the shops in addition to the specific skills the employed youngsters were also taught general subjects, such as mathematics, Yiddish.[85] Some opened "day shelters" for the children of their employees, where they were given instruction by former teachers employed as shop workers.

For a short time after the closing of the schools some instruction was given in the childrens' homes in Marysin. Toward the end of 1942, Rumkowski, by order of the authorities, requested to discontinue all such instruction, even the informal talks to the children.[86]

Three days after the establishment of the Vilna Ghetto a group of teachers decided to open a school. The school buildings were

---

[83] Zonabend Coll., doc. 1213.
[84] *Ibid.*, doc. 940.
[85] *Ibid.*, doc. 30; bulletin of the daily ghetto chronicle, July 31, 1942.
[86] *Loc. cit.*

badly damaged and required considerable repairs. These were undertaken jointly by teachers and prospective students. The unanimity of this enterprise is thus described in the memoirs of participants: "Teachers and pupils became one family. Together they cleared the rubble . . . brought together from one ruin a door, from the other a window frame, a board, to create a semblance of a room. Together they chopped wood to heat the freezing rooms . . . In the first few weeks there were no chairs and the children sat huddled on the floor . . . or stood leaning against the wall, supporting their notebooks on their fellows' shoulders.[87]

In the first school year (1941/1942) three elementary schools were opened and some gymnasium courses. Outside the Ghetto, in the workmen's blocks of "Kaylis," another school was opened, with an attendance of 50-80. (A census taken in the Ghetto showed that there were at that time 2,700 children, aged 5-14.) [88] The progress of these schools can best be gauged from the following figures: From January to December 1942 the number of classes rose from 9 to 40; number of teachers—from 23 to 72 and average daily attendance from 590 to 1405. Also overcrowding was somewhat lessened. In the first half-year the average number of students in a classroom was 50-70, in the second—40.[89] Toward the end of the year 1,800 children received instruction, that is two-thirds of the total number of school age.

To the elementary schools were attached kindergartens. Some instruction was also given in the two children's homes, numbering 103 inmates and in the Children's Transport Brigade (some 80 adolescents and children engaged in porter service in the Ghetto).[90] Nevertheless, hundreds of children of school age remained without schooling. These were exempted because they "fulfill important economic functions in the family" or they were orphans who had to provide for themselves.[91]

In March 1943 the schools were dealt a severe blow. Some of the school buildings had to be assigned for housing of the arrivals from

[87] Dvorzhetski, op. cit., pp. 226–227; Leykin, S., "Strashun gas 12 in vilner geto," YIVO-bleter, vol. XXX, no. 2, 1947, pp. 317–318.
[88] Sutskever-Kaczerginski Coll. (YIVO), doc. 291 and 384; Dvorzhetski, op. cit., pp. 227–228.
[89] Sutskever-Kaczerginski Coll., doc. 288.
[90] Dvorzhetski, op. cit., p. 228; Sutskever-Kaczerginski Coll., doc. 383.
[91] Ibid., doc. 385; Dvorzhetski, op. cit., p. 223.

the liquidated ghettos in the vicinity. A number of classes had to be rescheduled for the afternoon hours.[92]

The program of studies was in the best traditions of the former celebrated school system and comprised the following subjects: Yiddish (the language of instruction), Hebrew, arithmetic, natural sciences, geography, Jewish and general history. The gymnasium courses offered in addition physics, Latin and German (the last subject—beginning with July 1942).[93] In August 1942, following a petition by the rabbis to the Ghetto chief, religion was introduced as an elective. The Culture Department, which was in charge of education, was thoroughly secularist in spirit. In December the head of the department petitioned, unsuccessfully, the Ghetto chief to remove religion from the curriculum.[94]

In addition to the formal studies, there was an ongoing and ramified program of extra-curricular activities. The pupils had literary, dramatic, arts and crafts and similar clubs.[95] For the older pupils there was a young people's club (from July 18, 1942) with dramatic, literary, historical, philosophical and folklore sections. A number of literary programs were arranged, such as the "Josephus Flavius Trial," a Yehoash soiree in conjunction with an exhibition. The club also published a wall-bulletin.[96]

The teachers were organized in a professional association, engaging in cultural activity. Occasionally, they had to do charity work —help a needy colleague, intervene with the Ghetto chief on behalf of a member in distress.

In addition to the general school system the Ghetto also maintained a net of religious schools, established at the initiative of the Orthodox. This included two elementary schools, an elementary yeshiva (authorized by the Ghetto chief in December 1942) and a yeshiva in the name of Rabbi Khayim Oyzer Grodzenski. They were all housed in the *kloyzn*.[97] Essentially, the elementary religious schools were supplementary, meeting in the afternoon, so that their pupils could also attend the general schools. They had some 200

92 Sutskever-Kaczerginski Coll., doc. 352.
93 *Ibid.*, doc. 385; Dvorzhetski, *op. cit.*, p. 225.
94 Sutskever-Kaczerginski Coll., docs. 348, 350, 353.
95 *Ibid.*, doc. 346.
96 *Ibid.*, doc. 352.
97 *Ibid.*, doc. 533.

students. These schools would arrange periodically public examinations followed by refreshments.[98]

The Ghetto technical school had to limit its sights to the needs of the day and confine its work to the training of electro-technicians and locksmiths. Its trainees were absorbed in the Ghetto industry.

The Jewish schools functioned practically to the last days of the Ghetto (end of September 1943). Following the deportations to Estonia (September 1943) the number of pupils was reduced from 1500 to 900 and of teachers from 60 to 35.[99] The Siauliai Ghetto opened its school rather late, on June 15, 1943. It was housed in two *kloyzn* and had an initial registration of 200 in 7 classes. Toward the end of the month the number rose to 360 and 7 teachers. There were two shifts—one in the morning and the other in the late afternoon. In the beginning of October 1943 the school was ordered closed.

In August 1941 the *Judenrat* in Bialystok received permission to open schools. A School Commission was appointed and a registration of pupils and teachers was conducted.[100] In the beginning of October 1941 the first two grades opened and in the course of four months five more grades were added. In this school some 1,600 pupils were taught in 39 classes in three shifts. A second school was opened on November 10, 1941, with a registration of some 500. The first school was secularist in orientation and co-educational; the second was traditionally oriented, with separate classes for boys and girls.[101] On September 6, 1942, the second school year began. In the beginning of November the Bialystok district was engulfed by a wave of destruction and the school came to an end.

Summing up the educational experience of the Ghetto, we may say that:

(1) The sharp culture differentiation so characteristic of pre-war Jewish life in Eastern Europe, and particularly in Poland, was with few exceptions attenuated in those ghettos where the Judenrat assumed the leadership of the culture sector, such as Vilna, Lodz, Bialystok. In these ghettos a more or less uniform school system

---

[98] Dvorzhetski, *op. cit.* p. 233.
[99] Sutskever-Kaczerginski Coll., Doc. 281.
[100] Mersik-Tamaroff Coll., announcements of the Judenrat of Aug. 29 and Sept. 5, 1941.
[101] *Ibid.*; announcement of Nov. 9, 1941; Blumental, N. *Darko shel yudenrat* (Jerusalem 1962), p. 375, n. 195.

with a uniform program was established in which various elements of a cultural-political nature (Yiddish, Hebrew, religion, Palestine) may have been differently accentuated depending upon the affiliation of the given principal or teacher. The prescribed list of courses was obligatory for all schools. Of the large ghettos studied only the Warsaw school system remained divided along ideological lines.

(2) Jewish studies occupied the center of the curriculum. In Ghetto Lodz Yiddish was in theory (in practice concessions had to be made to such inexorable facts as the lack of textbooks in that language or lack of familiarity with it on the part of the teachers) the language of instruction in the unified school system. In Vilna, Kaunas and Bialystok, with an old tradition of Yiddish and Hebrew schools, Yiddish as the language of instruction was axiomatic.

(3) The main achievement of the schools was not so much in the communication of knowledge as such, to which conditions were anything but conducive, but in the spiritual support they provided for the pupil exposed to the demoralizing influence of ghetto life, the emotional relief and even joy brought into an otherwise frightful existence, and in their ability to involve large segments of the population.[102]

CULTURE ACTIVITY

The cultural life in the ghettos was outside the direct interests of the occupation authorities, who as a rule did not prohibit Jewish cultural activity except secondary and higher education. Some are of the opinion that similar to their culture policy in other occupied countries their interest was in promoting the vulgar amusement culture providing an outlet for their disaffection for wide sectors of the population and demoralizing them. Thus it is well known that the German Ministry of Propaganda promoted the dissemination of pornographic "art" on the screen and in illustrated journals in Poland as a means of demoralizing the population and numbing their sense of resistance. In the case of the Jews there may have been the added factor of creating the illusion of the duration of the ghetto where Jews may live their cultural life undisturbed.

---

[102] Wasser Collection, doc. 1; Natanblut, A., *op. cit.*, p. 183; Dvorzhetski, *op. cit.*, pp. 231–232; Kruk, H., *Togbukh fun vilner geto* (New York 1961).

Besides, this was an area of Jewish "autonomous" life that the authorities most likely considered safe from interfering with their plans. More than that it brought calm and a sense of relaxation into the ghetto and distracted attention from actual danger. A memorandum of the Rassenpolitisches Amt of the NSDAP on "The Treatment of the Population of the Former Polish Areas from the Racial-Political Point of View" of November 25, 1939, says the following: "Jewish political groupings must be banned together with the Polish. On the other hand, Jewish culture associations could be tolerated more freely than the Polish. Greater latitude should be given to the Jews in this respect than to the Poles, for politically they do not possess such real power as the Poles . . ."[103]

In practice the German policy governing Jewish cultural life was not uniform. In consonance with the principle of "local leadership" it depended upon the attitude of the individual commander. Thus in the Warsaw Ghetto Jewish schools with Polish as the language of instruction were permitted or at any rate tolerated, whereas the chief of the Sochaczew district in the Warsaw region, in a letter dated January 14, 1941, declared that in the Jewish elementary school the language of instruction must be Yiddish or Hebrew, citing a decree of the Warsaw district chief of December 27, 1940. In Jaslo the Jewish school was compelled to change from Polish to Yiddish as the language of instruction, with Polish only as an aid in instruction.[104] In Lodz two Jewish secondary schools were permitted, whereas elsewhere—except Vilna—they were prohibited. While the sale and reading of German and Polish newspapers were forbidden in the Government General and in Warteland, the library in the Vilna Ghetto officially subscribed in 1943 to a German and a Polish newspaper.[105] In contrast to Warsaw, Lodz and Vilna, where the Yiddish theater was tolerated, the chief of Czestochowa rejected a petition by the *Judenrat* for the opening of a Yiddish theater, dated July 5, 1941.[106] In Warsaw the Jewish orchestra was not allowed to play the works of "Aryan" composers, whereas no such ban existed in Lodz or in Vilna.

In sum, Jewish cultural life in the Ghetto was in a large meas-

[103] *Documenta Occupationis Theutonicae* (Poznan 1952), vol. V, p. 35.
[104] *Gaz. Żyd.*, Apr. 4, 1941; Ringelblum Archive I, 998.
[105] Sutskever-Kaczerginski Coll., doc. 378 and 379.
[106] Brener, *op. cit.*, p. 56.

ure determined by external and internal local conditions. Nevertheless a general and typical pattern can be distinguished. In many ghettos, mainly the larger ones, there comes to the fore an intensive yearning for cultural esthetical experience in general and a renewed interest in Jewish cultural values in particular on the one hand and a strengthening of assimilationist tendencies, on the other. The "yearning for a Jewish book," Jewish music and the theatre is fully recorded in the contemporary sources on the Warsaw, Vilna and other ghettos.[107] This was a phenomenon of "psychological escapism" from the dreadful ghetto existence, a "book intoxication," and also a desire for compensation for the inferiority feeling and dehumanization that the Germans attempted to impose upon the ghetto Jew. It was also an honest attempt to become acquainted with the literature and martyrdom of the Jewish people and draw comfort in the agony of the hour. Especially was this the case among the self-conscious and socially minded young people.

The assimilationist tendencies were strengthened by the presence in the ghetto of large numbers of the assimilated intelligentsia and a number of converts. In some places, in Warsaw, for instance, they exerted considerable influence on ghetto life thanks to the leading positions they came to occupy in the *Judenrat* and its institutions. The negative aspects of ghetto life they took to be characteristics of Jewish life in general and the former indifference turned to contempt and hatred of the Jewish masses and their culture.

The hand of fate lay more heavily on the less religious or less nationally minded and prompted them to seek escape. Conditions were favorable for "national mimicry," and the widespread dream of escaping to "the other side," where survival was possible only as a non-Jew, also pointed in the direction of assimilation. It is significant that prominent writers and intellectuals in the Warsaw Ghetto expressed the fear of large-scale apostasy after the war to escape a precarious future.[108] In the ghettos of Warsaw and Lwow there were a not inconsiderable number of conversions from ma-

---

107 Sutskever-Kaczerginski Coll., doc. 291; Ringelblum, *op. cit.*, p. 244; Zonabend Coll., doc. 29; bulletin of the daily ghetto chronicle, June 9, 1942.

108 Replies to a questionnaire of the Ringelblum Archive, *Bleter far geshikhte*, vol. I, no. 2, 1948, pp. 118–122; no. 3–4, p. 199.

terial motives: The converts were cared for by the Catholic organization Caritas.[109]

Among the intellectuals there were some who up to a certain period believed in the possibility and effectiveness of Jewish cultural activity in the ghetto. These included Hillel Zeitlin in Warsaw and Zelig Kalmanovitch in Vilna.[110] On the other hand, the writer Aaron Einhorn and the chairman of the Health Department of the Warsaw *Judenrat*, Dr. Y. Milikowski were of the opinion that cultural creativity in the ghetto was an utter impossibility.[111] Without taking sides, let it be stated that at the time such activity played an important role in the life of the ghetto. It attempted to immunize the population, mainly the young people, against the inescapable demoralizing effects of ghetto life, providing a spiritual support in an atmosphere of crass materialism which prevailed in many ghettos. It bore the indelible stamp of a spiritual resistance.

The cultural life of the ghettos sprang from the social-cultural institutions and the political groupings with many years of experience in Jewish cultural activity. For legal reasons it bore as a rule the official stamp of the *Judenrat*. In the Warsaw Ghetto there existed for a short while a kind of antagonism between the Jewish Cultural Organization (YIKOR) and the *Judenrat*. The social services and cultural activity formed an area in which the efforts of groups and individuals could have found expression outside the framework of the *Judenrat*. The cultural activities were closely linked with the campaigns of the "Social Self-Help" and also served to raise funds for the social service committees.

The cultural life in a given ghetto depended in a large measure upon the intensity and vitality of that life generations before the war. Ghetto Vilna is a good illustration. There Jewish cultural activity manifested itself at its best, embraced wide segments of the population and was an official and important function of the *Judenrat*. A historian of the Vilna Ghetto states: "If the Vilna Jewish community for years bore the name of Jerusalem of Lithuania, Ghetto Vilna is worthy . . . of the name of the Jerusalem of the

109 Ringelblum, *op. cit.*, p. 184.
110 See n. 108, pp. 111–122; Kalmanovitch, Zelig, "Der gayst fun geto," *YIVO-bleter*, vol. XXX. no. 2, p. 172.
111 See n. 108, vol, I, no. 3–4, 1948, pp. 189–190.

ghettos, as a symbol of Jewish spiritual resistance under Nazi regime."[112]

In reading the comparatively rich material on the cultural life in Ghetto Vilna, one frequently hesitates to believe that it was the product of a ghetto housing the remnants of a decimated community over which the sword of Damocles was suspended all the time. Activities were in charge of the Culture Division at the *Judenrat*, comprising the Sections on Schools, Library, Theatre, Archives, Statistics, Folklore Museum, Sports, School of Music and the Book Store. The Division also published the "News of the Ghetto."[113]

Vilna was blessed with a large folk intelligentsia. To this were added in the fall of 1939 and the summer of 1941 numerous writers, teachers and cultural leaders who fled to Vilna. These assumed their responsibilities in their new domicile. Some of the key positions in the Culture Department were occupied by Warsaw and Kaunas refugees.[114]

There is a paucity of materials on *Judenrat* activities in the field of culture. Clearly, the *Judenraete* were far too much absorbed in current and urgent affairs to have time and energy for matters cultural. This applies particularly to the smaller ghettos where the number of those who fled eastward was considerable. Many Jewish towns and townships in Western and Central Poland were deserted by their teachers and cultural activists, leaving a cultural void.[115] The description of the ghetto in Leczyce, a community of some 3,000 Jews in Wartheland, characterizes all the others. It reads: "We cannot even think of a school or cultural undertakings. Some mothers teach their children, but there is no communal endeavor."[116]

LIBRARIES

Shortly after the occupation of Poland the Germans closed Jewish book stores and libraries (the celebrated library of the Warsaw Synagogue on Tlomackie, the Vilna Strashun and YIVO libraries) and confiscated their books. The Warsaw *Judenrat* peti-

---

[112] Dvorzhetski, *op. cit.* p. 222.
[113] Sutskever-Kaczerginski Coll., docs. 291 and 341.
[114] Dvorzhetski, *op. cit.,* p. 265, 268 and 270.
[115] YIVO Archive, file on Refugees in Vilna.
[116] Ringelblum Archives, I, no. 1172, p. 8.

tioned successfully for permission to open a circulating library and book stores in the Ghetto. The official in charge of the confiscated collections consented to the transfer of Yiddish and Hebrew books to the Ghetto.[117] Also several private libraries and book stores were opened. By order of the authorities these were closed in January 1942.[118] However, several mobile libraries operated clandestinely. CENTOS maintained a mobile library for the children in its institutions.[119]

Four days after the establishment of the Vilna Ghetto the doors of the popular Mefize Haskalah Library were opened to the public. In September 1941 the *Judenrat* decided to turn over to this library all books in Jewish homes outside the Ghetto and the superintendents were requested to deliver them to the authorized persons. In March 1943 Ghetto Chief Jacob Gens ordered the delivery of all books in private possession (with the exception of textbooks and prayerbooks) to the library.[120] The Jewish employees of the Einsatzstab Rosenberg, who worked in the YIVO building at sorting the collections brought there from all over the city and vicinity, smuggled in considerable quantities of books to the Ghetto.[121] Upon the outbreak of the war a resolution was adopted to merge the Strashun library with the YIVO.

In the beginning of January 1942 the library had 93,463 volumes and in August 1942, 3,864 subscribers out of a total Jewish population of some 17,000.[122] It also established small collections in the neighboring labor camps (Osmiany and others), which were under the jurisdiction of the Vilna Ghetto chief.[123] The library maintained a reading room, which between July 1942 and March 1943 served on the average 150 people daily.[124] At the initiative of the librarian a book store was opened which, according to a report of the Culture Division for August 1942, sold that month 198 books and had a stock of 7,281 books.[125]

117 *Gaz. Żyd.*, June 10 and July 30, 1941.
118 Ringelbllm, *op. cit.*, p. 203.
119 *Ibid.*, p. 100; Berman, *op. cit.*, p. 69.
120 Sutskever-Kaczerginski Coll., doc. 352 and 380.
121 *Ibid.*, doc. 353; Pupko-Krinsky, R., "Mayn arbet unter di daytshn," *YIVO-bleter*, V. XXX, no. 2, pp. 317–320.
122 Sutskever-Kaczerginski Coll., doc. 476; Dvorzhetski, *op. cit.*, p. 241.
123 Sutskever-Kaczerginski Coll., doc. 382.
124 *Ibid.*, docs. 346, 352 and 353.
125 *Ibid.*, docs. 375 and 376.

In Lodz only one private circulating library remained, which had in the beginning of 1944 7,500 volumes and some 4,000 subscribers. All other Jewish libraries and collections had been confiscated in the winter of 1939/1940 by the Lodz Nebenstelle of the Hauptpropagandaamt. However, a number of small circulating libraries operated in private homes, with the connivance of the authorities. These could not circulate German war literature or books banned in the Reich. The political parties maintained clandestine libraries.[126] When the deportations began piles of books were left in the vacated homes, which were sold as wastepaper. At the initiative of the chief of the Evidence Division, the superintendents of the houses were ordered to go through the vacated premises, gather all the books and deliver them to the office of the division. Some 30,000 books were thus accumulated in the course of 1942 and the first half of 1943, including the large collection of Rabbi Treistman, which were sorted and catalogued. From this vast store of books several hundred were selected and set aside as mobile collections for young people and children in the various institutions.[127]

Theatre and Music

The war caused severe unemployment among the hundreds of Jewish actors, musicians, artists, book illustrators in the larger Jewish centers. To these were added the "non-Aryan" Polish artists who were forced into the ghettos. Their economic situation was desperate. In Warsaw some actors would appear at private gatherings in artistic presentations, at the end of which a collection would be made for their benefit. Gradually through bribe or influence permits were obtained for the opening of amusement halls and theatres in the ghetto, which proved very popular. An item in the press reads: "There is a great demand for artists. . . . Every cafe, bar and restaurant advertises its artistic attractions. . . . A number of such spots recently opened in the Ghetto, such as "The Idyll," "Bagatelle" and others. According to Ringelblum, there were in April 1941 61 amusement halls in the Warsaw Ghetto.[128]

---

[126] Trunk, *op. cit.*, p. 400.
[127] *Ibid.*, p. 401.
[128] Ringelblum, *op. cit.*, pp. 93 and 112; *Gaz. Żyd.*, June 17, 1941.

The artistic level of these amusement halls and "theatres" was low. To raise standards and to protect the professional interests of the artists a Central Programs Commission at the Self-Help was formed in the beginning of September 1940. Up to the end of September 1941 the commission registered 267 professional artists and 150 musicians, giving them the right to public appearance. In the course of one year the Central Programs Commission arranged 1,814 artistic programs, including 8 symphony concerts.[129] In addition, a string quartet and a chamber music group were giving concerts, as well as several choirs, including the synagogue and the children's choirs.[130] A number of musicians remained in the employ of the private amusement halls or organized in court bands. A number of artists were employed in the CENTOS institutions. It is in a large measure their merit that the children's presentations attained such a high level of excellence. "The program was distinguished in its acting, music, dance and picturesqueness," noted the inspector of the Ghetto schools.[131]

In the Warsaw Ghetto there were five permanent theatres—two Yiddish and three Polish. Since they obtained their permits through contact with "the others," they were not subject to the jurisdiction of the Central Programs Commission. In the ghetto arose a new high income class—smugglers, con men and the like,—who sought cheap amusement, and they became the mainstay of the theatre, which played down to their taste. A notable exception in this respect was the Polish theatre, whose repertory remained on a high level.[132] Also a marionette theatre, organized by a group of Lodz artists, was active in the Ghetto. A second marionette group was established to play for the children in the CENTOS institutions. Moreover, several ballet studios and schools for rhythmic art were operating in the Ghetto.[133]

Undoubtedly at the request of the authorities, the *Judenrat* attempted through its Art and Culture Department, which showed no signs of life, and later (after April 1942) through its Programs

[129] *Gaz. Żyd.*, Nov. 6, 1941.
[130] Turkov, J. *Azoy iz es geven. Khurbn varshe* (Buenos Aires 1948), pp. 195–204. Turkov was chairman of the Program Commission of the Jewish Social Self-Help.
[131] Natanblut, *op. cit.*, p. 181.
[132] Turkov, *op. cit.*, pp. 206–210 and 212–213.
[133] *Ibid.*, pp. 207–230.

Referee to gain control of the theatre and entertainment area. An announcement in the *Gazeta Żydowska* in April 1942 declares that the aim of the referee is to raise the level of artistic programs and henceforth all places where such programs are presented must be registered with the *Judenrat* and the programs submitted to the referee for approval. Since the Central Programs Commission at the Self-Help was in an unofficial way competing with the Programs Referee, the head of the *Judenrat* Cherniakov, after an unsuccessful attempt to incorporate it in the *Judenrat* apparatus, resolved upon its dissolution. The commission did not yield and continued its work autonomously up to the deportation at the end of July 1942.[134] This deportation put an end to the ramified cultural activity in the Warsaw Ghetto and to the rivalry between the communal sector and the *Judenrat* for its control.

Just as in the Warsaw and Czestochowa Ghettos, and in others, in the Lodz Ghetto too Jewish cultural life had its impulse in communal initiative. In October 1940 a Jewish Culture Association was founded for the purpose of organizing a library, a people's university, a dramatic circle, Yiddish courses for teachers and adults, concerts and the like. The Hazamir Society renewed its activity, a symphony orchestra and choirs were organized. Rumkowski who rightly realized that his power in the Ghetto would not be complete without control of the cultural life, resolved to liquidate these independent institutions. Opinion has it that he was prompted thereunto by the supervising authorities, who through him possessed full control of the Ghetto and refused to tolerate a Jewish activity not under the supervision of Rumkowski and his administration.

On March 1, 1941, the House of Culture opened, in charge of the chief of the Labor Bureau. Two types of programs were presented: symphony concerts with soloists and revues by the theatre studio Avant-Garde.

There was considerable artistic talent left in the Ghetto. This was augmented after the "importation" of the West European Jews by a group of highly qualified musicians, actors and singers. By order of Rumkowski, the House of Culture registered the artists among the new arrivals, who by December 6, 1941, numbered 60

---

[134] *Ibid.*, pp. 236–238.

musicians, singers and actors and 10 painters and sculptors. A large part of them was integrated in the cultural life of the Ghetto.

In 1941 the symphony orchestra gave on the average 10 concerts a month, in 1942 only 4 (on Wednesdays). The revues were given twice and thrice a week. In 1941 (beginning with March) these presentations drew an attendance of nearly 70,000. In addition, special programs were presented for the workers in the Ghetto shops. The choir of the gymnasium students, who were under the strict supervision of Rumkowski, also presented their programs in the House of Culture. These occasions Rumkowski frequently utilized for speeching.

The painters and sculptors were employed in providing the scenery for the revues in the graphic division of the Statistical Bureau and in the "Scientific" Division (whose purpose was to make plastic figures of Jewish types and scenes of the Jewish mode of life for the museum of the German Ghetto Verwaltung). A special room was assigned to the painters and sculptors in the House of Culture. The artists working there were promised free food coupons.

In January 1944 the Germans confiscated all musical instruments and the concerts stopped. Simultaneously the revues were discontinued.[135]

In the first executions at Ponary 20 actors and 7 members of the technical staff of the Yiddish theatre in Vilna perished.[136] The survivors decided to open a theatre in the Ghetto. The decision met with a storm of protest and indignation: the theatre would constitute a desecration of the sorrow for the thousands of victims. Organized labor decided to boycott the performances and there were suggestions for noisy interruptions of them.

The Culture Division too was opposed to the theatre, as was also the case in Kaunas.[137] Its only support came from the Ghetto police and its chief. As late as April 17, 1942, the chief pleaded with the Culture Division to withdraw its opposition.[138] On the premiere day black-bordered leaflets were distributed in the Ghetto, bearing the message: "On a cemetery no theatrical performances are given."

---

135 Trunk, *op. cit.*, 393–398.
136 Sutskever-Kaczerginski Coll., doc. 424.
137 Garfunkel, *op. cit.*, pp. 250–251.
138 Sutskever-Kaczerginski Coll., doc. 529.

The first performance, on January 18, 1942, was given in a mood of deep seriousness and received in the same spirit. The audience consisted mainly of members of the police force and their families, members of the *Judenrat* and other Ghetto functionaries. To the second concert, one week later, there also came German and Lithuanian officials who were directly involved in the executions. A contemporary chronicler gives expression to his indignation: "Thus the chief murderer . . . and one of the greatest sadists . . . was properly entertained."[139] Gradually, the psychological inhibitions to the theatre in the Ghetto broke down and attendance improved. Profits went to the Social Self-Help.

The theatre section at the Culture Division comprised actors, musicians, singers, a Yiddish and a Hebrew choir. The dramatic ensemble numbered twenty-odd people, the orchestra—30, the Yiddish choir—80 and the Hebrew—75. Three orchestras gave concerts, including a jazz band.[140] The dramatic performances were mostly revues; occasionally a full play was given.

The dramatic programs were generally a blend of serious classical pieces with dramatization of current events in the specific humorous vein of the Ghetto—a kind of laughter through tears. The function of the theatre was to provide an escape—for a few hours at least—from the unbearable reality of the Ghetto. This function the theatre fulfilled admirably. "People literally fought for tickets" to some performances.[141]

In certain months theatrical performances were given daily or every other day. In October 1942 22 programs were offered—16 theatricals, 3 concerts of the choir, 2 symphony concerts and a concert by the students of the Music School, which in August 1942 numbered 95 students. In December the number declined to 18 programs and in January 1943 it rose again to 25.[142] In the course of 1942 the theatre gave 120 peformances, with an attendance of 38,000. On Sundays in March 1943 6-7 performances were given, with a total attendance of 2,000.[143]

139 *Ibid.,* doc. 479; Dvorzhetski, *op. cit.,* pp. 248–249; Kruk, *op. cit.,* pp. 136, 138 and 146–147.
140 Sutskever-Kaczerginski Coll., docs. 349, 406, 459 and 460.
141 *Ibid.,* doc. 350.
142 *Ibid.,* docs. 348, 350 and 351.
143 *Ibid.,* doc. 352; Dvorzhetski, *op. cit.,* p. 250.

The symphony orchestra gave 2-3 concerts a month, playing among others Beethoven, Mozart and Schubert without interference (in Warsaw and other ghettos "Aryan" music was barred). In addition there were given concerts of chamber music, recitals of singers and soloists.[144]

In addition to the two aforementioned choirs there was also a religious choir. Its first public appearance was in a Hanukah concert in December 1942.[145]

Special "workers programs" were arranged for those who were employed outside the ghetto on Sundays. These consisted generally of a lecture on a literary or communal subject, recitals and songs of the ghetto artists and the youth clubs.[146]

The *Judenrat* also subsidized the Writers and Artists Association, which attracted the creative elite of the Ghetto and was the moving spirit in its cultural life. The association frequently arranged literary-artistic programs, concerts, literary discussions and the like.[147] As a form of moral—but also material—support for writers and artists, the association would conduct literary and artistic contests. These took place under the aegis of the Ghetto Chief. He appointed, nominated or approved judges and provided the prizes.[148]

Museums, Archives and Publications

The Culture Division also helped organize the Ghetto Museum in Vilna, which gathered art works, ceremonial objects, scrolls of the Torah "found in the deserted and ruined homes in the Ghetto." Included in this category were materials of the Zionist Archives in Vilna, Rabbi Khayim Oyzer Grodzenski's archive, minute-books of societies and *kloyzn*. Objects smuggled in by the Jewish employees of Einsatzstab Rosenberg were hidden in the Museum cellar.[149]

The Ghetto Archives, under the auspices of the Culture Division aimed at concentrating under its roof all documentation of and pertaining to the Ghetto: decrees of the *Judenrat*, the Ghetto

---

[144] Sutskever-Kaczerginski Coll., docs. 481, 482 and 485.
[145] *Ibid.*, doc. 488.
[146] *Ibid.*, docs. 519 and 522.
[147] *Ibid.*, docs. 45a, 361, 496–502, 619, 623–625.
[148] *Ibid.*, docs. 40–44.
[149] *Ibid.*, docs. 65–67.

police, reports of the various divisions, the Statistical Bureau, shops and factories, eyewitness testimony of escapees from Ponary and the liquidated ghettos and the like. The Archives also kept manuscripts of writers, scholars, memoirists and the like. Its activities were legal and open. The materials were concealed in tin cans and buried in bunkers. Some of them were found after the war and brought to the YIVO Archives.

The major achievement with respect to the establishment of a documentation center for the history of Polish Jewry under Nazi occupation was the so-called Oneg Shabat, a cryptonym for the clandestine Ghetto archive, or as it was named after the war the Ringelblum Archive (for its founder, the historian Dr. Emanuel Ringelblum). Designed and launched in the first days of the occupation, under strictly conspiratorial conditions, to record the most tragic period in the history of Polish Jewry, the Ringelblum Archive continued activity under the direst conditions. In its extraordinary wealth of material accumulated on practically every aspect of Jewish life under the Nazis, it is a national monument to the three and a half million Jews of Poland and above all to the largest Jewish community in Europe.

In Ghetto Lodz the Archives fulfilled the functions of a registry, but also those of a documentation center of the Ghetto. The staff, including several intellectuals deported from Vienna and Prague, wrote monographs and reportages on various aspects of Ghetto life and in the beginning of 1944 compiled an Encyclopedia of the Lodz Ghetto. Beginning with January 12, 1941, the Archives published semi-official daily, weekly and monthly information bulletins in Polish and in German (from 1943 only in German), which continued to July 1944. These are now among the most important sources of the internal history of the Ghetto.[150]

The Lodz *Geto-tsaytung*, which appeared under the editorship and control of Rumkowski and the Gestapo from March to September 1941 (18 issues), contained announcements of the Ghetto administration, reports on the various divisions, verdicts of the Ghetto Court and mainly Rumkowski's accomplishments for the Ghetto. Each number had four pages, sixteen by ten.

The Agriculture Division published for the benefit of those

---

[150] Trunk, *op. cit.*, pp. 42–43.

who leased from the division small parcels in the Ghetto a "Handbook for the Small Gardener," with professional information for the new ghetto "farmers" utterly inexperienced in gardening. From June 5 to June 19, 1942, three issues appeared (hectographed) ; an issue appeared also on July 2, 1943.[151]

The *Mitteilungen des Judenrates in Lemberg* contained communiques, instructions of the various divisions, the Ghetto Police, the *Judenrat*, the Jewish Social Self-Help, legal advice, as well as decrees by the supervising authorities. The editor was Stanislaw Matfus. In the course of January-March, 1942, three issues appeared, each eight pages, twelve by eight. Apparently, the third number was also the last.[152]

At the request of the authorities the Cracow *Judenrat* formed a Division for Construction and Conservation for the care and preservation of historical monuments, such as synagogues, cemeteries, ceremonial objects. There was even a proposal to establish a Museum of Jewish Religious Art.[153] After the final liquidation of the Cracow Ghetto in March 1943 the old synagogues and the cemetery remained derelict.[154] This was also the fate—with few exceptions—of the other Jewish historical monuments in the other communities in Eastern Europe.[155]

[151] Zonabend Collection, docs. 21, 888–890.
[152] Zaderecki, Prof. M., ms. 0–6/2 in the Archives of Yad Washem.
[153] *Gaz. Żyd.*, Dec. 10, 1940, Jan. 3 and 14, 1941.
[154] Bernstein, Tatiana and Rutkowski, Adam, "Prześladowania ludności żydowskiej . . . ," *Biuletyn Żydowskiego Instytutu Historycznego*, no. 38, 1961.
[155] Starr, J., "Jewish Cultural Property under Nazi Control," *Jewish Social Studies*, vol. XII, pp. 27–48.

WAS THERE AN "OTHER GERMANY" DURING THE NAZI PERIOD?

By Philip Friedman

The period of Nazi barbarism has, as it were, relegated to the dim, distant past the years in which Lessing wrote *Nathan der Weise* and *Die Juden,* the epoch in which German scholars, poets and diplomats found inspiration in the Jewish salons of Berlin and Vienna and in correspondence with prominent Jewish men and women. The twenty odd years in which Hitlerism cast its shadow over world history have been subjected to intensive research. Nonetheless, there are some aspects of this dreadful period which remain relatively neglected. Moreover, the approach to the subject is at times burdened by subjectivity and partisan motivations.

Among the most neglected questions is that of the attitude of the German people—of its cultural and religious leadership as well as of the masses—toward Jewish persecution. Were their sympathies with the Nazis or with their victims? If the latter, was their opposition to Nazi barbarism limited to moral sentiments, or extended to open protest and a readiness to aid the victims? What were the attempted or actual achievements of anti-Nazi Germans on behalf of the Jews?

Despite the paucity of research in this area, much has been written bearing directly or indirectly on the subject, particularly in German. This ranges from expressions of regret and repentance to attempts at a whitewash. The literature of the former type contains forthright, unequivocal statements of individuals and organizations, particularly Protestant groups. The resolution adopted by the Protestant Synod in Berlin in April, 1950, and the comments made by Pastor Martin Niemoeller, one of the Synod's leaders, in proposing the resolution, are striking expressions of contrition. The text of the resolution reads as follows:

> Wir sprechen es aus, dass wir durch Unterlassung und Schweigen vor dem Gott der Barmherzigkeit mitschuldig geworden sind an

dem Frevel, der durch Menschen unseres Volkes an den Juden begangen worden ist.

"Ich bekenne mich schuldig als mancher SS-Mann . . ," Niemoeller added. "Zehn Jahre liessen wir Gott warten. Wir müssen aber unsere Schuld nicht nur vor Ihm, sondern auch vor dem Menschen bekennen."[1] Other church leaders,[2] writers and scholars, such as Rudolph Pechel[3] and Karl Jaspers,[4] have spoken in the same vein.

[1] Taken from the detailed report given in *Rundbrief zur Förderung der Freundschaft zwischen dem Alten und dem Neuen Gottesvolk im Geiste der beiden Testamente* (Freiburg) vol. ii, no. 8-9 (1950) p. 18. (Hereafter cited as *Rundbrief.*)
The intensity of feeling of the repentance-literature in certain circles is also seen in the dramatic declaration of the chairman of the Synod: "Und auf der Gesamtsynode in Berlin-Weissensee traf es uns ins Herz, als Präses *Kreyssig* uns unsere Schuld so verdeutlichte: In jedem Zug, der Juden in die Todeslager im Osten deportierte, hätte wenigstens ein Christ freiwillig mitfahren müssen!—Wir haben es nicht getan; wir sind dem Leiden ausgewichen, und Israel musste für uns leiden. *Darum* sind wir den Juden gegenüber jetzt auf den Mund geschlagen. . . ." Küppers, Erica, "Kirche und Israel," in *Bekennende Kirche. Martin Niemöller zum 60. Geburtstag,* Supplement (Munich 1952) p. 16.
Niemoeller had been even more outspoken on other occasions. In an address to leaders of the Confessional Church in Frankfurt am Main on January 6, 1946, he said: "The guilt exists, there is no doubt about it. Even if there were no other guilt than that of the six million clay urns, containing the ashes of burnt Jews from all over Europe. And this guilt weighs heavily on the German people and on the German name and on all Christendom. For these things happened in our world and in our name. . . . Can we say it is not our fault? The persecution of the Jews, the manner in which we treated the invaded countries. . . . We cannot get out of it with the excuse: I might have had to pay with my life had I spoken out." In Niemoeller, Martin, *Of Guilt and Hope* (New York, n. d.) p. 13-15. In the original: *Über deutsche Schuld, Not und Hoffnung* (Zurich 1946).
[2] Schmidt, Heinz, *Die Judenfrage und die Christliche Kirche in Deutschland* (Stuttgart 1947) p. 57-58: "Im besonderen wird die christliche Kirche in Deutschland in Beugung und Busse Gottes Gerichte sehen und bejahen müssen. An ihr wäre es gewesen, Deutschland zu warnen und zu retten. Wir haben der Überhebung unseres Volkes, dem Hass gegen die Juden kaum widersprochen. Viele Christen haben dabei sogar mitgetan. . . . So werden wir gerade als Christen in Deutschland unsere Schuld gegen Israel bekennen müssen. . . . Es ist nötig so klar von unser Schuld als Prediger und Glieder der Gemeinde Jesus Christi zu reden wie dies die kirchliche Theologische Sozietät in Württemberg am 9 April 1946 getan hat: 'Wir sind mutlos und tatenlos zurückgewichen als die Glieder des Volkes Israel unter uns entehrt, beraubt, gepeinigt und getötet worden sind. . . .'"
[3] Pechel, Rudolf, "Judentum, Christentum, Abendland," *Deutsche Saat,* vol. lxxiii, no. 2-3 (1950) p. 65-66: "Über jedem Gespräch zwischen Juden und Deutschen, besonders den christlichen Deutschen, liegt der schwere Schatten einer beispiellosen Schuld. . . . Denn die Behandlung der Judenfrage durch Hitler und seine Henker ist der Punkt, an dem wir Deutsche als Nation unsere Ehre verloren haben. Es sind Verbrechen begangen worden, die jedes Mass übersteigen und die Grenzen des menschlichen Vorstellungsvermögens, ja selbst einer ausschweifenden Phantasie, überschritten haben."
[4] Speaking at the reopening of Heidelberg University on August 15, 1945, Jaspers said: ". . . Es war möglich, in der Würdelosigkeit den Tod zu suchen,— 1933, als nach dem Verfassungsbruch durch eine Scheinlegalität die Diktatur errichtet und, was sich widersetzte, im Rausche eines grossen Teiles unserer Bevölkerung hinweggeschwemmt wurde. Wir konnten den Tod suchen, als die Ver-

The problems touched upon in this repentance literature are symptomatic of certain post-war spiritual trends in Germany and are not quite pertinent to our present inquiry. The literature, however, contains ample material on the Nazi period. These books, pamphlets and articles, as well as the literature of the resistance, constitute an important source for the study of the attitudes and behavior of organized and unorganized anti-Nazism with respect to Jews and Nazi persecution of Jews. Some writers use the phrase "the other Germany" to refer to an allegedly organized anti-Nazi movement. This is not a precise phrase. To some it denotes organized anti-Nazi resistance; to others, all manifestations of anti-Nazi sentiment or behavior on the part of the people at large. In the present study, we have used the term in the second, more inclusive sense.[5] We have also included materials on the anti-Nazi opposition in Austria after the Anschluss in 1938.[6]

The present article is part of a larger work on "The 'Other Germany' and the Jews," which consists of the following sections: (1) Religious Opposition; (2) Political Resistance Groups and Movements; (3) Opposition within the Wehrmacht; (4) The Anti-Nazi Elements in the Administration; (5) Attitudes of the German Populace; and (6) Literary Opposition. This paper is based on the first two sections of the larger study.[7]

Finally, we would like to note that research in this difficult, complex area is subject to the intense pressures of various ideological and emotional elements. It is the responsibility of the historian to assemble all relevant materials, to present them as objectively as possible, and thus to aid the reader in finding a solution to the

---

brechen des Regimes öffentlich in Erscheinung traten am 30. Juni 1934 oder mit den Plünderungen, Deportationen und Ermordungen unserer jüdischen Freunde und Mitbürger, als zu unserer untilgbaren Schmach und Schande 1938 in ganz Deutschland die Synagogen, Gotteshäuser brannten. . . . Wir sind nicht, als unsere jüdischen Freunde abgeführt wurden, auf die Strasse gegangen, haben nicht geschrien, bis man auch uns vernichtete. Wir haben es vorgezogen, am Leben zu bleiben mit dem schwachen, wenn auch richtigen Grund, unser Tod hätte doch nichts helfen können. Dass wir leben, ist unsere Schuld. Wir wissen vor Gott, was uns tief demütigt." Jaspers, Karl, *Die Schuldfrage. Ein Beitrag zur deutschen Frage* (Zurich 1946) p. 49.

[5] Cf., Fraenkel, Heinrich, *The Other Germany* (London 1942); Hassel, Ulrich von, *Vom Anderen Deutschland* (Zurich 1946).

[6] The anti-Nazi struggle in pre-Anschluss Austria, such as the movement of Irene Harand, is, however, excluded from the study.

[7] We wish to express our appreciation to Mrs. Sophie C. Fryde for assistance in assembling the materials upon which this study is based.

perplexing questions of our generation on the basis of the soundest evidence available.

I. CHURCH OPPOSITION AND THE JEWISH QUESTION

1. *The Clash between Christianity and Nazism*

The conflict between the Christian churches and the Nazis was both political and ideological. The political factor was predominant in Nazi-Catholic relations, whereas the conflict with the Protestant Church and with smaller sects was primarily ideological. Ideological friction had been manifested as early as the beginning of the 1920's. It did not become pronounced until 1933, after the Nazis had come into power.

The struggle was waged orally, from the pulpit, and in writing. There is a rich polemical literature on the subject: books, pamphlets, periodicals, pastoral letters, documents, miscellanies, sermons, memoranda, and the like.[8]

The Nazis accused the church—particularly the Catholic Church— of having political ambitions, of being universalistic and cosmopolitan, and of opening its ranks to Jews and to other alien elements, thereby harming the ideal of the racial purity of the German nation. Alfred Rosenberg (in his "Myth of the 20th Century" and elsewhere) went further, accusing the Catholic Church of betraying Germany. Subsequently, Hitler made it quite clear that the Nazi attack was not directed against this or that one of "the hundred and one different kinds of Christianity," but against Christianity in general.[9] In conversation with his associates, Hitler allegedly said:

> [Italian] Fascism, if it likes, may come to terms with the Church. So shall I. Why not? That will not prevent me from tearing up Christianity root and branch, and annihilating it in Germany. . . .
>
> Whether it's the Old Testament or the New . . . it's all the same old Jewish swindle. . . . A German Church, a German Christianity,

---

[8] A bibliography on this subject cannot be presented here. The references cited in this article are those which were of immediate relevance to our study. Some notion of the extensive literature on the subject can be obtained by reference to the following bibliographies published in the *Bulletin* of the Wiener Library of London: "The German Churches under Nazi Rule," vol. ii, no. 5 (1948) p. 29; "Good Will toward Men. A Bibliography on Christian-Jewish Relations," *ibid.*, p. 28; "The Story of Rosenberg's *Mythos*," vol. vii, no. 5-6 (1953) p. 33-34; Lakebrink, Bernhard, "Catholic Action against Rosenberg," *ibid.*, p. 34; A Student of German History, "Anti-Christian Literature, the Need for a Bibliography," vol. i, no. 5 (1947) p. 29.

[9] *The Nazi War against the Catholic Church* (Washington, D. C., U. S. National Catholic Welfare Conference, n. d.) p. 27.

is distortion. One is either a German or a Christian. You cannot be both.[10]

The Nazi war against the church was conducted on several fronts. Most important was the fight over the education of the young. Shortly after the assumption of power, the Nazis—through the State and the Party—monopolized the entire educational system, taking over both schools and youth organizations from the church. Nazi education was strongly anti-Christian and anti-Jewish. Thus children were taught songs mocking Christianity.[11] A secret guide for leaders in Nazi youth camps in Austria, issued on Easter, 1938, reads:[12]

> Point 2. Christianity is Communism. They are one and the same. . . .
> Point 4. The New Testament is a Jewish invention. . . .
> Point 20. Christianity derives from Judaism and was brought into being by Jews. . . .
> Point 26. Jesus is a Jew.

Not long after Hitler's rise to power, arrests and persecution of clerics began. Many were sent to concentration camps, there to undergo torture and ridicule of their clerical garb as well as of their faith.[13]

How did the Christian churches meet the Nazi attack? There is a sizable literature, both Catholic and Protestant, which attempts to show the intensity with which the church fought the Nazis. On the other hand, there are those who admit that the struggle might well have been greater than it was. This is particularly the case with respect to resistance to anti-Jewish persecution. An official Protestant publication grants that "the conduct of Christians, including members of the Confessional Church, with respect to the National-Socialist

---

[10] Rauschning, Hermann, *The Voice of Destruction* (New York 1940) p. 49.

[11] For examples of such songs, see: Macardle, Dorothy, *Children of Europe* (Boston 1951) p. 33; Harcourt, Robert d', "National Socialism and the Catholic Church in Germany," in M. Baumont, J. H. Fried, and E. Vermeil, eds., *The Third Reich* (New York 1955) p. 803-804.

[12] Oesterreicher, John M., *Racisme—Antisemitisme—Antichristianisme* (New York 1943) p. 140-144.

[13] The wealth of concentration camp literature—particularly about Dachau—provides much evidence for this. One typical anthology of verse describes the suffering of an Austrian Catholic priest in Dachau, and contains many striking examples of the vilification of Christianity in the camps by SS-men. See Huppert, Hugo, *Der Heiland von Dachau* (Vienna 1945). Cf., the material on the Protestant pastor Paul Schneider's experiences in Buchenwald, in *Der Prediger von Buchenwald. Das Martyrium Paul Schneiders* (Berlin 1953) and Steinwender, Leonhard, *Christus im Konzentrationslager* (Salzburg 1946).

persecution of Jews, presents a picture of great weakness and uncertainty."[14]

How can we account for this weak, equivocal attitude? It must be remembered that the masses of Germans, Catholic and Protestant alike, looked on in passive apathy as the Nazi terror engulfed Germany in 1933, and subsequently allowed themselves to be harnessed to the Nazi chariot of victory. Evidently the Christian churches felt too weak to oppose the Nazi wave. At first, both Churches strongly desired to reach a compromise and to avoid a break with the new regime.

We shall consider later the substantial differences, in this respect, between the Protestant and the Catholic Churches. On the whole, it would seem that part of the clergy, and the lower ranks in particular, were sympathetic to the Nazis at first, and some of them even joined the Party.[15] From the very beginning, however, there was a minority, including in its ranks many of the leading figures of both Churches, which opposed Nazism. Their protests against the Nazis grew ever louder. These were the only voices of protest which were not always silenced by the totalitarian terror of Nazi Germany. It was only rarely that the Nazis dared arrest high church dignitaries, though the number of lower clergy arrested reached into the thousands.[16] Their calculation was simple: they had no desire to increase the popularity of leading church figures by lending them an aura of martyrdom.[17]

---

[14] *Die Evangelische Kirche Deutschlands und die Judenfrage. Ausgewählte Dokumente aus den Jahren des Kirchenkampfes 1933 bis 1943,* prepared and published for the Flüchtlingsdienst des Oekumenischen Rates der Kirchen (Geneva 1945) p. 6. On the Confessional Church, see below, part 3.

[15] See Rodnick, David, *Postwar Germans* (New Haven 1948) p. 202. The author, an American anthropologist, quotes a speaker at a Social Democratic convention in 1946 as saying that "a large part of the [German] clergy joined the Nazi party" and "helped persecute the Jews and turned their backs to the cruelty inflicted on concentration camp inmates."

In 1933, the pro-Nazi elements scored an important victory in the elections to the National Synod of the Protestant Church, their list receiving the support of a majority of pastors (see part 3 below).

[16] According to the U. S. Federal Council of the Churches of Christ, about 9,000 Catholic and Protestant clergymen were arrested prior to March 1938. See Lande, Adolf, ed., *Chronology of Adolf Hitler's Life* (Washington, U. S. Office of War Information, 1944) p. 125. According to a statement of Hans Kerrl, Nazi Minister for Church Affairs, an additional 8,000 Catholic monks and lay brothers were arrested prior to December 1937. *Ibid.,* p. 108.

[17] This is explicitly acknowledged in Alfred Rosenberg's diaries. On December 13 and 14, 1941, a gathering of Nazi leaders in Hitler's home discussed the strong anti-Nazi utterances of the Catholic Bishop von Galen. Rosenberg reports: "The

During the first phase of the Nazi-Christian conflict, the Jewish question was raised only within the realm of theoretical, theological discussion. After 1933, however, more concrete issues came to the fore. On April 7, 1933, the Nazi government issued a decree removing all "non-Aryans" from government positions.[18] It was followed by pressure to introduce the "Aryan paragraph" into the churches, to which the Protestant denominations quickly yielded. Overriding the energetic opposition of a bold minority, the synods of the various Protestant churches decided to exclude non-Aryans and spouses of non-Aryans from appointment to the clergy or church offices. Non-Aryans occupying church positions were to be dismissed.[19] The Catholic Church, thanks to its legal and organizational status, which differed from that of the Protestant churches (see parts 2 and 3 below), was able to avoid a total capitulation to the "Aryan paragraph."

On the heels of their first important triumph, the Nazis began to demand that converts be isolated into special "Jewish-Christian congregations." This demand ceased to be actual with the introduction of the Nuremberg Laws in 1935. Converts and baptized children of mixed marriages were thenceforth considered Jews and subject to all anti-Jewish decrees, such as compulsory membership in the Jewish community, residential limitations, wearing the Star-of-David, deportations and similar measures.

The number of Christians of Jewish descent affected by the Nuremberg Laws was great. The noted statistician Friedrich Burgdörfer estimated it at 340,000 in 1933 in Germany: 50,000 converts; 210,000 "half-Jews" (children of mixed marriages); and 80,000 "quarter-Jews" (those with one Jewish grandparent). To this total

---

Führer declared that these gentlemen wish to become 'marytrs,' expecting to be accorded an 'arrest of honor'." See Kempner, Robert M. W., ed., "Der Kampf gegen die Kirche. Aus unveröffentlichten Tagebüchern Alfred Rosenbergs," *Der Monat*, vol. i, no. 10 (July 1949) p. 37; Auerbach, Philip, *Wesen und Formen des Widerstandes im Dritten Reich*, unpublished doctoral dissertation, University of Erlangen, 1949, p. 76 (mimeographed copy in the YIVO Library). Another source reports that Hitler overruled Himmler's proposal to execute Bishop von Galen. See Smith, Patrick, transl. and ed., *The Bishop of Münster and the Nazis. The Documents in the Case* (London 1943) p. 52.

[18] *Reichsgesetzblatt*, i, no. 34, p. 175f., reprinted in Blau, Bruno, *Das Ausnahmerecht für die Juden in den europäischen Ländern, 1933-1945, I. Teil, Deutschland* (New York 1952) p. 15-19.

[19] *Die Evangelische Kirche* . . ., p. 35-113, contains the text of the decree and a review of the subsequent discussions which took place in Protestant circles in Germany.

should be added many tens of thousands of converts and *Mischlinge* (half- or quarter-Jews) in Austria.[20]

With the progressive deterioration of the legal and economic position of non-Aryan Christians, the churches began to organize special relief activities for their benefit. The first organization set up in this field was the Reichsbund Christlicher Deutscher Staatsbürger nicht-arischer oder nicht-rein-arischer Abstammung, in 1933, which became the Protestant Paulsbund Vereinigter nicht-arischer Christen in 1937. It was followed by the formation of other Protestant groups with the same purpose in mind (see part 3 below). A parallel Catholic organization was the St. Raphael Verein, headed by Bishop Berning of Osnabrück, which was instrumental in the escape from Germany of many non-Aryans. In Berlin, Catholic relief was centered in the diocesan office and was headed by a highly courageous woman, Dr. Sommer. The German Quakers engaged in relief activities for the benefit of non-Aryan Christians not belonging to the Catholic or Protestant Churches, but to various sects, and also aided some Jews. By and large, cooperation among the various relief organizations was quite common. At critical moments, requiring emergency relief and instant decisions, rigid division of rescue work along confessional lines was impossible. Most Christian organizations also cooperated with Jewish groups and, under certain circumstances, aided Jews directly, particularly Jewish children.[21] Jewish organizations would, likewise, assist non-Aryan Christians at the request of Christian relief administrators.

[20] Burgdörfer, Friedrich, "Die Juden in Deutschland und in der Welt," *Forschungen zur Judenfrage*, vol. iii (Hamburg 1938) p. 152. The preliminary results of an Austrian census conducted on May 17, 1939 showed that there were 18,106 "part Jews of Grade I" (having two Jewish grandparents) and 8,479 "part Jews of Grade II" (having one Jewish grandparent). The number of converts is not given. It is to be presumed that they were included among the 94,553 "full Jews." *Nazi Conspiracy and Aggression*, vol. iv, Document PS-1949 (Washington 1946) p. 587, 591. The number of Jews reported by the census is only slightly more than half the number of Jews in Austria prior to the Anschluss. From this we can deduce that the number of converts and *Mischlinge* was also substantially higher prior to March 1938 than in May 1939. One authority estimates their number at 100,000 in 1938. See Karbach, Oskar, "The Liquidation of the Jewish Community of Vienna," *Jewish Social Studies*, vol. ii, no. 3 (1940) p. 259.

[21] Further details on these relief organizations are to be found in Auerbach, *op. cit., p.* 77; Weltlinger, Siegmund, *Hast Du es schon vergessen? Erlebnisbericht aus der Zeit der Verfolgung* (Frankfurt a/M 1954) p. 19; Lamm, Hans, *Über die innere und äussere Entwicklung des deutschen Judentums im Dritten Reich*, unpublished doctoral dissertation, University of Erlangen, 1951, p. 90 (mimeographed copy in the YIVO Library); Neuhäusler, J., *Kreuz und Hakenkreuz*, vol. ii (Munich 1946) p. 377 f.

The problem of mixed marriages was closely related to that of non-Aryan Christians. Though most often the Jewish partner had converted to Christianity, it was not infrequent to find Jewish members of mixed marriages who had not relinquished their religion. The Aryan partners were subjected to various legal restrictions and administrative discrimination.[22] The Nazis were intent upon breaking up mixed marriages, but met with strong opposition on the part of the Christian churches on this issue and were forced to retreat. Until the very end of the regime, the Nazis respected these marriages, and treated the Jewish partners much more leniently than they did other Jews. As a result, many of the Jews married to Christians managed to survive.

The firm stand of the churches on this issue is attributable to a number of factors. For Catholics, the opposition to divorce as a fundamental Church dogma was crucial. No less unequivocal was the stand of the Protestant Confessional Church. On its behalf, Bishop Wurm addressed the Nazi government on July 16, 1943 as follows:

> Insbesondere erheben wir eindringlichen Widerspruch gegen solche Massnahmen die die eheliche Gemeinschaft in rechtlich unantastbaren Familien und die aus diesen Ehen hervorgegangenen Kinder bedrohen.[23]

A second significant factor was the fact that the churches sensed the moral support of the German population on this issue. As noted above, the number of children of mixed marriages in Germany and Austria was very large. There is evidence that in many cases the German partner in mixed marriages stood up to the Nazi terror and remained loyal to the Jewish spouse. Reporting the results of a survey conducted on this question in 1945, an American anthropologist writes:

> We were very much struck by the large number of German men who refused to divorce their Jewish wives and did all they could to protect them under the Nazis. In one case we knew of, a husband whose Jewish wife was gassed in a concentration camp committed suicide. In another instance the Jewish wife of a former naval captain was hidden by her husband in their home for eight years.

---

[22] A survey of such laws, decrees and discriminations is to be found in Blau, Bruno, "Die Verfolgung von Nichtjuden im Dritten Reich—wegen Juden," *Rundbrief* . . ., vol. iv, no. 16 (April 1952) p. 34-36.

[23] *Die Evangelische Kirche* . . ., p. 190.

. . . We encountered a number of German women who had been forbidden to marry Jews or half-Jews under the Nazis; all of them remained single waiting for a change in the government which would permit them to marry their lovers.[24] One physician's wife had waited 13 years to marry him. . . . Another woman . . . waited 12 years. . . . In all our contacts we came across only one case of betrayal . . . but we heard many stories of loyalty involving great sacrifice.[25]

One hears of cases of German women, married to Jews who had been imprisoned in the *Judenhaus* in Munich, visiting their husbands in disregard of the SS commandant's wrath.[26] Similar cases of loyalty of Germans to their Jewish spouses are described elsewhere in the literature.[27] The story is told of a German doctor who voluntarily followed his deported Jewish wife to the Warsaw Ghetto and perished in the Ghetto revolt of 1943.[28] So strong were the sympathies of the populace with couples who had intermarried, that the Nazi regime was compelled to take this into account even in cases where its prestige was at stake. On February 27, 1943, the Nazis conducted mass arrests of Jews in Berlin (the so-called "factory action").

On the same day [writes Bruno Blau] Jews who had non-Jewish wives were arrested and placed in the administrative building of the Jewish community. The wives of the arrested persons gathered in front of the building every morning to demand the release of their husbands. Despite the police who harassed them they persisted in their demonstrations until the men were released.[29]

There were, however, no demonstrations protesting the deportation of other Jews from Berlin.

During 1943, Christian circles became increasingly fearful that "the danger was imminent that about 400,000 'half-Aryans' would

[24] In 1937 the German Reichsgericht annulled several marriages between Jews and Germans, thereby setting a precedent which acted to prevent mixed marriages. Evidently there were frequent cases of such marriages until that time. See Blau, *op. cit.*, p. 133. In the summer of 1935, the *Essener National Zeitung*, Goering's organ, complained that in Berlin alone 667 mixed marriages had occurred. See the collection *The Yellow Spot: The Outlawing of Half a Million Human Beings* (London 1936) p. 273.

[25] Rodnick, *op. cit.*, p. 121-122.

[26] Behrend-Rosenfeld, Else R., *Ich stand nicht allein. Erlebnisse einer Jüdin in Deutschland 1933-1944* (Hamburg 1945) p. 188-189.

[27] Cf., Paepke, Lotte, *Unter einem fremden Stern* (Frankfurt a/M 1952); Hoffman, Ruth, *Meine Freunde aus Davids Geschlecht* (Berlin 1947) p. 127-133; Holtzman, Anna, "Iberlebungen als aryerin fun yidishn gloybn," *Fun letstn khurbn*, no. 7 (May 1948) p. 87-88.

[28] Poliakov, Léon, *Bréviaire de la haine* (Paris 1951) p. 324.

[29] Blau, Bruno, "The Last Days of German Jewry in the Third Reich," *Yivo Annual of Jewish Social Science*, vol. viii (1953) p. 202.

follow the Jews to their death."[30] The Protestant Church began to protest sharply against the Nazi policy of extermination, and proposed to the Catholic Church that it take similar steps.

By and large, it may be said that during the first years of the Hitler regime, the church opposition spoke up on the Jewish question only in so far as it involved its own ideological fundamentals or the interests of converts. It was not until the last years of the regime that direct protests against the persecution of Jews were voiced by the central church organizations. It is, however, true that protests by individuals had been heard earlier. The pogroms of November, 1938, in particular, had led a number of Christians to assist Jews in hiding from the murderous SS bands. There were clergymen who referred from the pulpit to the persecution of Jews, albeit in veiled language. This led to the arrest of a number of them. Generally, the Nazi regime, and most particularly the Gestapo, portrayed "the church as the agent of Jewish world politics," and accused "certain clergymen of defending the Old Testament" or of "recommending more and more that children be given at baptism 'Judaeo-Christian' [i.e., Biblical] names."[31]

The various aspects of the church-Nazi conflict over the Jewish question can best be clarified by considering each of the confessions separately.

2. The Catholic Church

The Catholic Church was not only an ideological opponent of the Nazis, but a political one as well. The Catholic Center Party was one of the strongest political parties in Germany. After the Social-Democratic and Communist Parties had been crushed, the Center Party was one of the most serious obstacles to a Nazi monopoly of political power. The Catholic Church, moreover, had the support of a powerful world political force totally independent of the Nazis—the Vatican. It was, therefore, constantly attacked as "the politicizing church," the "Romanists" (i.e., Vatican subjects), "pacifist traitors," "birds befouling their own nests," and the like. In a speech in March,

---

[30] Schütz, William W., *Pens Under the Swastika* (London 1946) p. 42. Presumably Schütz's figure of 400,000 also includes those non-Aryan Christians in the territory then considered part of the Reich: Austria, Bohemia and Moravia, and parts of occupied Poland and France.

[31] Steward, John S., comp., *Sieg des Glaubens. Authentische Gestapoberichte über den kirchlichen Widerstand in Deutschland* (Zurich 1946) p. 90, 91, 115-116. These reports, marked *"Streng vertraulich,"* are mostly from 1942-43.

1933, Goering said that the Weimar Republic's tricolor symbolized the triumvirate of Germany's international enemies: the black (Catholic), the red (Communist) and the yellow (Jewish) internationals. No sooner had the Nazis taken power than they proceeded to arrest a number of Catholic priests (June 20-28, 1933). Within a few days thereafter, an edict was issued liquidating all the larger Catholic youth organizations.[32]

It was, therefore, with considerable amazement that the world learned on July 8, 1933, of the signing of a Nazi Germany-Vatican Concordat. This made the Vatican the first political power in the world to acknowledge the stability of Hitler's regime. The Concordat heightened the regime's prestige outside Germany and solidified its rule within. The Concordat was subjected to strong criticism. One scholar later referred to it as the "Roman Catholics' Munich." The view was expressed that the Concordat thwarted any potential Catholic opposition to Hitler.[33] It was only after years of bitter disillusionment brought about by the Concordat that the Vatican, in 1945, justified it on the grounds that it had "at least prevented worse evils."[34] There is no doubt that the Concordat weakened the fighting spirit of the Catholic Church. Some politically naive members of the lower ranks of the Church hierarchy accepted the Nazi propaganda. One priest, with avowed Nazi sympathies from 1929 to 1938, justified his attitude as follows:

> I must admit that I was glad to see the Nazis come into power, because at that time I felt that Hitler as a Catholic was a God-fearing individual who would battle Communism for the church. . . . The antisemitism of the Nazis, as well as their anti-Marxism, appealed to the church in Germany as a counterpoise to the paganism which had developed after 1920. . . . It was not until after 1938 that I saw that Hitler and the Nazis hated Catholicism as much as they did Communism.[35]

[32] A brief review of the relations between the Nazis and the Catholic Church until about 1940 is to be found in Harcourt, *op. cit.*, p. 797-810.

[33] Micklem, N., *National Socialism and Christianity* (New York, Pamphlets on World Affairs no. 18, 1938) p. 13-14. Cf., A. E. Kerr's review of Monsignor Ronald Knox's book, *Nazi and Nazarene*, in *Dalhousie Review*, vol. xxi, no. 3 (October 1941) p. 381; Jansen, Jon B. and Weyl, Stefan, *Silent War, The Underground Movement in Germany* (Philadelphia 1943) p. 243. Karl Jaspers describes his reaction as follows: "Es war die erste grosse Bestätigung des Hitlerregimes, ein gewaltiger Prestigegewinn für Hitler. Es schien zunächst unmöglich. Aber es war Tatsache. Uns befiel ein Grauen." Jaspers, *op. cit.*, p. 69-70.

[34] Weizsäcker, Ernst von, *The Memoirs of E. von Weizsäcker* (London 1951) p. 269.

[35] Rodnick, *op. cit.*, p. 189. Similar sentiments were expressed in an official

Yet despite the facts that a number of Catholic figures had positive attitudes to Hitler and that there were several official as well as individual peace overtures on the part of leading Catholic dignitaries,[36] the Nazi Party and regime continued to persecute Catholic priests and to conduct anti-Catholic propaganda.[37] German church leaders, as well as the Vatican itself, often protested that the German government was failing to live up to its responsibilities as detailed in the Concordat. Finally, Pope Pius XI issued his famous encyclical of March 14, 1937, *Mit brennender Sorge,* in which he openly condemned Nazi racist principles:

> Whoever transposes Race or People . . . from the scale of earthy [*sic*] values and makes them the ultimate norm of all things . . . perverts and falsifies the divinely created and appointed order of things. . . . Only blindness and self-will can close men's eyes to the treasure of instruction for salvation hidden in the Old Testament. He who wishes to see Bible history and the wisdom of the Old Testament banished from church and school blasphemes the word of God, blasphemes the Almighty's plan of salvation and sets up narrow and limited human thought as the judge of God's plans.[38]

The encyclical was read aloud from all German Catholic pulpits, despite the efforts of the Gestapo to prevent it. It is noteworthy that certain German Catholic leaders played a part in the issuance of the encyclical. This is above all true of Joseph Wirth, former German Reichskanzler and leader of the Catholic Center Party. Wirth was active during the 1930's in fighting anti-Semitism in various European and American lands, and was in contact with various Jewish figures.[39]

At first, the protests of the leading Catholic dignitaries referred only to the persecution of Catholics and the vilification of Catholic dogma and doctrine. The ideological aspect of the conflict inevitably drew the Church into a defense of the Bible and of "Biblical Jewry" against the onslaught of Nazi propaganda. This is particularly man-

---

publication of the Archbishop of Freiburg, Konrad Grüber: *Handbuch der religiösen Gegenwartsfragen* (1937) p. 149.

[36] A number of such acts are described in Lande, *op. cit.,* p. 95-96; Child, Clifton J., "Germany—1939-45," in A. and V. Toynbee, eds., *International Affairs. Survey of 1939-1946: Hitler's Europe* (New York 1954) p. 35.

[37] The following contain much factual material on such persecutions: Lande, *op. cit.,* p. 108, 95-96; Oesterreicher, *op. cit.,* p. 136-137; *The Nazi War against the Catholic Church,* passim: Pinson, Koppel S., *Modern Germany* (New York 1954) p. 512f.

[38] *The Nazi War against the Catholic Church,* p. 34-47; Steward, *op. cit.,* p. 9.

[39] Details on Wirth's activities against anti-Semitism are to be found in Waldman, Morris D., *Nor by Power* (New York 1953) p. 81-88, 91-100.

ifest in the anti-Nazi struggle conducted by the "Lion of Munich," Cardinal Faulhaber. In December, 1933, the Cardinal delivered a series of three sermons, from the pulpit of Munich's St. Michael's Cathedral, on the subject of the religious and moral values of the Old Testament.[40] Faulhaber's sermons created a stir. He defended boldly and unequivocally the moral, ethical and religious value of the Bible and of "Biblical Jewry" and affirmed the chosenness of the (Biblical) people of Israel. Neither then nor at any time subsequent to it did he have anything to say in defense of contemporary Jewry, for, as he put it, his scholarly competence was limited to the period of the Old and the New Testaments.[41] Though Faulhaber, as far as is known, had nothing more to say about the Jewish question in his official statements, he personally assisted a number of converts as well as Jews, as reported by his secretary, Msgr. Joseph Weissthanner,[42] and by several German Jews.[43] In October, 1938, Faulhaber despatched a truck to the Chief Rabbi of Bavaria to rescue the Scrolls of the Law and other religious articles from the Great Synagogue which were in danger and had them brought to his palace for safekeeping. In November, after another powerful sermon attacking the totalitarian regime, an enraged mob stormed the palace of "Faulhaber, the friend of the Jews."[44] In November, 1941, when deporta-

[40] Published in English as *Judaism, Christianity and Germany* (New York 1935).

[41] Faulhaber's views are brought out clearly in his series of three sermons. Cf., Stummer, Friedrich, "Kardinal Michael von Faulhaber und das Judentum," *Rundbrief . . .*, no. 21-24, p. 21-23. The well-known Basle paper, the *National Zeitung*, August 18, 1934, reprinted the text of a courageous, uncompromising statement by Faulhaber. The paper reported that the text was confiscated in Germany. It reported Faulhaber as saying: "History teaches that God had always punished the tormentors of his Chosen People, the Jews. No Roman Catholic approved of the persecution of Jews in Germany. When God made June 30 the judgment day for some of the tormentors of the Jews, the punishment was well deserved. . . . Racial hatred is a wild poisonous weed in our life. Root out the terrible inhuman prejudice against the forever suffering people." Quoted in the *Wiener Library Bulletin*, vol. vi., no. 3-4 (May-August 1952) p. 19.

[42] Weissthanner, Josef, "Liebe und Recht," in K. C. Knudsen, ed., *Welt ohne Hass* (Berlin, 2nd ed., 1950) p. 154-155.

[43] Cf. a number of articles which appeared in Israeli papers after Faulhaber's death: Ben-Horin, Shalom, in *Yediot hadashot* (Jerusalem) June 20, 1952; *Mitteilungsblatt Irgun Oley Merkaz Europa* (Tel Aviv) no. 25, June 27, 1952.

[44] Martin, Hugh, et al., *Christian Counter-Attack. Europe's Churches against Nazism* (London 1943) p. 24; Lande, *op. cit.*, p. 125. The Nazi press occasionally published inflammatory articles directed against Faulhaber, e.g., Seitz, Karl, "Nochmals Kardinal Faulhaber und das Alte Testament," *Der Weltkampf* (Munich, May 1934) p. 138-141.

tions to Eastern Europe began, Faulhaber again aided a number of Jews and non-Aryan Christians.[45]

In Western Germany, the Bishop of Münster (later Cardinal), Count Klemens August von Galen, headed the Catholic opposition. He was thus characterized in a confidential Gestapo report of January, 1942: He has had a "Jewish and Jesuit education" and "he continues to correspond, to this very day, with leading Jewish figures . . . As late as 1939 he consistently voiced the opinion that the Jewish people was God's Chosen People."[46]

Bishop von Galen's three strong speeches in 1941 and a declaration the following year made a great impression. About that time a pastoral letter was circulated by the German bishops, adopted at a conference in Fulda on July 29, 1941, which explicitly declared that "it is impermissible to destroy human life, except in the event of a just war."[47] Nonetheless, these were all only indirect allusions. This lack of forthrightness was criticized in a rather interesting Polish pamphlet (presumably put out by an underground organization of Polish slave labor in Germany). The pamphlet reports the slaughter of 500 Jews in Oshmyany (Vilna district) by the German police shortly after the Germans had occupied the area. Further details are given about massacres of Jews and Poles, and the German Catholics are bitterly criticized because of their silence in the face of such crimes. The pamphlet then describes the courageous anti-Nazi struggle of Bishop von Galen, and the persecution of German Catholics, and concludes: "No matter how great our sympathies with the German Catholics . . . we do not believe that they can be absolved of this terrible responsibility [of remaining passive to the Nazi persecution of Jews and Poles]."[48]

On December 13, 1942, Cardinal Conrad Count von Preysing, Bishop of Berlin, issued a forthright pastoral letter, which reads, in part:

---

[45] *Rundbrief. . .*, no. 17-18 (August 1952) p. 36.

[46] Steward, *op. cit.*, p. 104. Alfred Rosenberg speaks of Bishop von Galen with great bitterness. See *Memoirs of Alfred Rosenberg,* with commentaries by Serge Land and Ernst von Schenck, tr. from the German by Eric Possett (Chicago 1949) p. 97-98.

[47] Rothfels, Hans, *German Opposition to Hitler* (Hinsdale, Ill., 1948) p. 44; *The Nazi War against the Catholic Church,* p. 117, 120-121; Schütz, *op. cit.,* p. 35; Portmann, Heinrich, *Dokumente um den Bischof von Münster* (Münster 1948) p. 154-155.

[48] Portmann, *op. cit.*, p. 153-155. Cf., Portmann's second book, *Kardinal von Galen. Ein Gottesman seiner Zeit* (Münster 1948).

> Every human being has rights of which no earthly power can deprive him . . . the right to live, not to be hurt, to be free, to own property, to have a family life. These rights cannot be infringed upon by the government. . . . No one can be deprived of them because he is not of our blood or does not speak our language. . . . We must understand that taking away these rights or acting cruelly against our fellowmen is an injustice, not only to the stranger, but also to our own people.[49]

The sharper the conflict between the Nazis and the Catholic Church became, the more forthright were the latter's protests against the persecution of Jews. In a joint pastoral letter in 1943 the German bishops declared:

> The extermination of human beings is *per se* wrong, even if it is purportedly done in the interests of society; but it is particularly evil if it is carried out against the innocent and defenseless people of alien races or alien descent.[50]

In 1944, a Gestapo report complains: "From various places we hear that priests have recently begun to praise Jewry very highly in their sermons." In general, a second report notes, "the Catholic Church wishes to know nothing of a war against Judaism and Bolshevism. Her 'faithful' embrace both sides of the battlefield, praying not for a German victory, but for peace."[51]

In contrast to the aforementioned Nazi policy of not arresting high church dignitaries lest they become martyrs was the frequent arrest of clergy of middle and lower rank. The detention of one such priest, Monsignor Bernhard Lichtenberg of the St. Hedwig Cathedral, in Berlin, received widespread attention. Lichtenberg, a man of profound religiosity and moral stature, was head of the Bishop's relief program in the German capital for many years. Throughout the worst years of Nazi persecution, he called daily upon the faithful in his church to pray for the "poor persecuted Jews," for those imprisoned and for "our non-Aryan coreligionists." In a sermon on August 29, 1941, he declared that, unable to bear Nazi vandalism any longer, he would thenceforth include the Jews in his daily prayers, "since the synagogues had been set aflame and Jewish businesses had been closed."

---

[49] The full text of the letter is given in *Rundbrief. . .*, no. 8-9 (August 1950) p. 14. Preysing's anti-Nazi utterances are reprinted in *Dokumente aus dem Kampf der Katholischen Kirche in Bistum Berlin gegen den Nationalsozialismus* (Berlin, Bischöfliches Ordinariat, 1946).

[50] Schütz, *op. cit.*, p. 35; Auerbach, *op. cit.*, p. 78.

[51] Steward, *op. cit.*, p. 74, 81.

An American writer who visited St. Hedwig's (presumably before the war, or, at the latest, in 1940; no date is given), describes the strong impression made by Lichtenberg's sermons, the words "that came out of the depth of his heart, beautifully spoken, moving, stirring."[52]

Lichtenberg was arrested by the Gestapo on October 23, 1941, and sentenced to jail. After serving his term, he was consigned to a concentration camp for "reeducation." He asked to be sent to the Jewish Ghetto in Lodz, but instead was shipped to Dachau. The ailing priest, however, did not live to complete the journey. On November 3, 1943, on the way to the concentration camp, he died in the city of Hof.[53]

Jews as well as non-Aryan Christians received considerable assistance, particularly during the period of deportations, from the Catholic society Caritas. In the spring of 1943, the Gestapo learned of these activities and arrested the leaders, among them Dr. Gertrud Luckner and Grete Wünsch. After two years in a concentration camp, liberation found the former "in bad physical shape but spiritually unbroken." Dr. Luckner returned to her home in Freiburg, where she founded the journal *Rundbrief*, which she has been editing to this day. A member of the Bonn Parliament, she visited England at the invitation of Dr. Leo Baeck in 1950, and was warmly received by the German-Jewish refugees, who knew her relief work quite well. Dr. Luckner received a similar reception on her visit to Israel in 1951.[54]

3. *The Protestant Church*

It might have been anticipated that the Protestant opposition to Nazism would have been greater than the Catholic, for, in 1938, 64 per cent (45,000,000) of the German population of 70,000,000 were Protestants. Their power, however, was not proportionate to their numbers. Protestants were divided into 29 independent regional organizations and denominations, among which there had been sec-

---

[52] Jordan, Max, *Beyond All Fronts* (Milwaukee 1944) p. 132-133.

[53] Leber, A., Brandt W., and Bracher, K. D., eds., *Das Gewissen steht auf. 64 Lebensbilder aus dem deutschen Widerstand 1933-1945* (Berlin 1954) p. 180; Erb, Alfons, *Bernhard Lichtenberg* (Berlin 1946); *Rundbrief. . .*, vol. iii-iv, no. 12-15 (December 1951) p. 5; Blau, *Rundbrief . . .*, no. 21-24 (February 1954) p. 36.

[54] *Rundbrief. . .*, vol. ii, no. 7 (April 1950) p. 24; vol. iii-iv, no. 12-15 (December 1951) p. 56; Boehm, Erich, ed., *We Survived* (New Haven 1949) p. 232.

tarian strife for many years. Moreover, they had no international body upon which they could rely, such as the Catholic Church had. A further source of weakness lay in the institutional structure of Protestantism. According to Lutheran tradition, the relationship between "altar and throne" was one of subordination of the church to secular authority. This disciplined attitude of deference was so deeply rooted that it paralyzed large numbers of Protestants even under the anti-Christian regime of the Nazis. Finally, many Protestants were ensnared by point 24 in the Nazi program, which spoke of a "positive Christianity."

Possessed of no political ambitions, the Protestants hoped that they would be accorded freedom in religious affairs by the new government. They were, therefore, at first disposed to be loyal to the Nazi regime. This led the 29 Protestant groups to unite voluntarily in a Deutsche Evangelische Kirche. Dr. Friedrich von Bodelschwingh was elected the first German Protestant Reichsbischof. The Nazis, however, were not appeased. The pro-Nazi Protestant elements, who had organized themselves into the Glaubensbewegung Deutscher Christen in March, 1932, urged the formation of a "German Church of Christians of the Aryan race." Their activities finally compelled Dr. Bodelschwingh to resign. In the church elections of July, 1933, the National Socialists received a majority, and the Nazi military chaplain Dr. Ludwig Müller was elected Reichsbischof. In short order, the Protestant Synod introduced the "Aryan paragraph" into the church.[55]

The rapid victory of the National Socialist elements, in part a result of government pressure, wrought widespread confusion in Protestant ranks. Several outstanding theologians, such as Professor Karl Thieme, turned to Catholicism in protest.[56] A substantial number of Protestant pastors, however, opposed to Müller and to the "Aryan paragraph," resolved to fight. Some 2,000 pastors left the official Protestant Church to form the Pfarrer Notbund, which later became the Confessional Church, led by a Vorläufige Kirchenleitung der deutschen Evangelischen Kirche (VKL). The Confessional Church never received official recognition by the Nazi regime. Nazi persecution notwithstanding, the Church grew steadily. One of the early

---

[55] These developments are discussed in many works. See, for example, Forell, Birger, "National Socialism and the Protestant Church in Germany," *The Third Reich. . .*, p. 812-825; Child, Clifton, *op. cit.*, p. 35-36.

[56] See Thieme's letter to Martin Buber, reprinted in *Rundbrief. . .*, no. 5-6 (December 1949) p. 21.

public demonstrations of the Pfarrer Notbund in Berlin, held on November 27, 1933, attracted 10,000 people. The number of pastors enrolled in the organization doubled within a short time. By February, 1936, the Confessional Church was reported to number 9,000 pastors. According to an estimate made in December, 1938, about 40 per cent of German Protestants were sympathetic to the Confessional Church, 10 per cent supported the official Protestant German Church, and half remained indifferent.[57]

One of the founders and outstanding leaders of the Confessional Church was Martin Niemoeller. Captain of a U-boat in World War I, Niemoeller had the aura of a military hero, a fact of some import to the Germans. This was, however, not his only qualification for leadership. One writer refers to the following aspects of his character: "Courage . . . resolution . . . wisdom . . . dynamism . . . a gift of word . . . kindness . . . and simplicity."[58] He also proved to be nimble and flexible in politics. His talent for political maneuvering was particularly displayed in the years following World War II.[59] Politically, Niemoeller was a German nationalist and, at first, his attitude to Hitler and the Nazis was not entirely negative. In this, he agreed with other leaders of the Protestant opposition, such as the leader of the Altona circle of Protestant theologians, Hans Christian Asmussen, or the noted religious philosopher, Karl Barth. At first, these men were not opposed to the National Socialist regime, but to the religious innovations of the "German Christians."[60] Niemoeller, it would seem, at first accepted Hitler's declarations and promises about the creation of a "positive Christian church." It was not until

[57] *Die Evangelische Kirche* . . ., p. 38-39; Lande, *op. cit.*, p. 96-97, 125; cf., Kerr, *op. cit.*, p. 381. In Berlin in 1937, about 160 of the 400 Protestant pastors belonged to the Confessional Church, 40 to the German Church and the rest were "neutral." Rothfels, *op. cit.*, p. 42.

[58] Niemoller is the subject of many biographical and polemical accounts. His own writing also contains much biographical and historical material. The present quotations are taken from Bartning, Ludwig, "Martin Niemöllers Berufung," in *Bekennende Kirche* . . ., p. 133-134.

[59] After World War II, Niemoeller became president of the Hessian regional Protestant Church and head of the foreign affairs office of the Protestant Church. In 1952 he journeyed to Moscow to negotiate, as he himself puts it, with the Soviet government, the release of the remaining German prisoners of war in Russian camps. Niemoeller was severely criticized by a number of German writers and church leaders for making this trip, and he was even accused of political careerism. For example, see Hein, Herbert, "Pastor Niemoeller und Moskau," *Aktion* (Frankfurt a/M) no. 12 (1952) p. 17-20.

[60] Jansen and Weyl, *op. cit.*, p. 243; *Der Kirchenstreit in Deutschland. Bibel und Rasse* (London, n.d. [1935?]) p. 21; Roy, James A., "Pastor Niemoeller," *Dalhousie Review*, vol. xxi, no. 1 (April 1941) p. 88.

he was convinced that they were deceptive that he became the driving force in organizing the Protestant opposition. Its struggle was oriented to a defense of the Bible against the attacks of the Nazis and to opposition to the "Aryan paragraph."[61] The Jewish issue, in the early period, was of no concern. Much as various Catholic leaders, Niemoeller defended "Biblical Judaism" and the Old Testament, while disregarding the fate of contemporary Jewry in Nazi Germany. After the war, when he was reproached that he had failed to protest the Nazi persecutions of Jews, Niemoeller is reported to have replied that his struggle had been ideological-ecclesiastic, and that he had kept out of politics.[62]

Niemoeller issued a statement opposing the "Aryan paragraph" in principle, but with qualifications:

> In the [church] community we must recognize converted Jews ... as full-fledged members, whether we like it or not. ... A church edict which excludes non-Aryans or those not wholly Aryan ... from church offices is contrary to religion [bekenntniswidrig]. ... Such a stand requires great self-sacrifice from us, a people that has suffered severely from the Jewish influence. ... It is, indeed, unfortunate that, in days such as these, a pastor of non-Aryan descent should occupy a position in church leadership ... but we cannot permit the introduction of such an edict.[63]

Further developments, however, led Niemoeller and his colleagues to adopt bolder steps and formulations both in the general ideological struggle as well as in the Jewish question.

Evidently Hitler had not anticipated such strong Protestant resistance. He regarded with disdain the "insignificant people, submissive as dogs," who "will betray anything for the sake of their little incomes."[64] He was, therefore, surprised at the extent of the Protestant opposition. Opposition to the "Aryan paragraph" was so great that even Reichsbischof Müller's resignation was demanded.[65]

---

[61] Miller, Basil, *Martin Niemoeller, Hero of the Concentration Camp* (Grand Rapids, Mich. 1942) p. 81, 84; Roy, *op. cit.*, p. 88.

[62] See Z. B. Kamaika's report of a meeting with Niemoeller in Chicago, in the *Morgn-zhurnal* of January 22, 1947, p. 3. In this connection, the complaints of an American rabbi against Niemoeller, voiced in 1938, are of some interest. See Fram, Leon, *The Story of the Conflict between Hitler and the Christian Church* (Detroit [1938]) p. 8.

[63] The complete text of Niemoeller's statement in 1933 appeared in Schmidt, Kurt D., *Die Bekenntnisse des Jahres 1933, 1934, 1935*, vol. i (1933) (Göttingen 1934-36) p. 96f.

[64] Duncan-Jones, A. S., Dean of Chichester, *The Crooked Cross* (London 1940) p. 2.

[65] Gerstenmaier, Eugen, "The Church Conspiratorial," in Boehm, *op. cit.*,

In March, 1935, the opposition pastors issued a manifesto stating that Nazi doctrine based on a "racist and nationalist world outlook," constitutes a "deathly danger" for the German people. To prevent the reading of this manifesto from the pulpit, some 700 pastors were subjected by the government to home arrest for a brief time.

The struggle grew more and more intense, and gradually was transformed from a Biblical-theological controversy to a conflict over problems of race and over the Jewish question. Speaking to a large audience in March, 1935, Niemoeller defiantly pointed out that "The Jews are not the only ones who crucified Christ."[66] On May 27, 1936, a memorandum was submitted to Hitler by the leaders of the Confessional Church, dealing, among other things, with the Jewish question:

> When blood, race, nationality, and honor are regarded as eternal values, the first Commandment obliges the Christian to refuse this valuation.... While the Christian is compelled by the Nazi *Weltanschauung* to hate the Jews, he is on the contrary bidden by the Christian commandment to love his neighbor.[67]

Nevertheless, none of these manifestoes or declarations make explicit reference to the bitter fate of the Jews of Nazi Germany. None other than Niemoeller himself has confirmed this. In a public speech delivered before a student audience at Göttingen on January 17, 1946, he said: "I am guilty. . . . I kept silent! I only began to speak up when the Church was affected. I feel that I am guilty!"[68]

On June 23, 1937, the Gestapo arrested most members of the Vorläufige Kirchenleitung, and closed its Berlin offices. Niemoeller

---

p. 173. Gerstenmaier, at present writing president of the Bonn Bundestag, was one of the most active members of an opposition group (the so-called Kreisau Group) which conducted negotiations with groups abroad and which aided a number of Jews.

[66] Albus, Harry, *Concentration Camp Hero* (Grand Rapids, Mich. 1946) p. 64; Miller, *op. cit.*, p. 85.

[67] *Die Evangelische Kirche* . . . p. 152; Rothfels, *op. cit.*, p. 41-42; Schütz, *op. cit.*, p. 65.

[68] Niemoeller, Wilhelm, *Macht geht vor Recht. Der Prozess Niemoellers* (Munich 1952) p. 110. The author is Martin's brother. Other writers have likewise criticized the absence of reference to Jewish persecution in the declarations of the Confessional Church. Cf., Beyer, Franz, *Menschen warten. Aus dem politischen Wirken Martin Niemoellers* (Siegen 1952) p. 118; Stewart, Herman W., *The Rebirth of the German Church* (New York 1946) p. 48. This view is disputed by Wilhelm Jannasch in *Deutsche Kirchendokumente. Die Haltung der Bekennenden Kirche im Dritten Reich* (Zurich 1946) p. 11: "Kann man einer Kirche, in der einzelne und Gemeinschaften von Anfang an, privat und öffentlich in der Judenfrage vorstellig geworden sind und ihre Meinung gesagt haben vorwerfen, dass sie inmitten des Dritten Reiches eine schweigende Kirche gewesen sei?"

was arrested on July 1, 1937. When asked after the war to account for his arrest, he replied: "I think the concrete and final motive was provided by the Memorandum at the end of 1936. . . ."[69] The Nazi regime preferred to avoid a public trial of Niemoeller, lest it enhance his popularity. The special court which tried him in closed session ruled that the seven months of internment which he had completed constituted sufficient sentence. On "medical advice," however, he was transferred for convalescence to the Sachsenhausen concentration camp.[70]

Until the date of his arrest, Niemoeller had been pastor of the Protestant congregation in Dahlem, a suburb of Berlin. This congregation was one of the strongholds of the Confessional Church, and remained so even after its spiritual leader had been arrested. A German painter, Miss Valerie Wolffenstein, a Protestant of Jewish descent, thus describes her visit to the Dahlem church at the beginning of 1943:

> As I entered the church, the congregation was reciting the 126th Psalm: "When Jehovah brought back those that returned to Zion, we were like unto them that dream." This was January 30, the tenth anniversary of Hitler's accession to power. At the end of the service, at which point the prescribed prayer for the Fuehrer is recited, Pastor Dehnstedt, Niemoeller's successor, said: "O Lord, perform what seems impossible to us mortals, perform a miracle—turn the obdurate heart of our Fuehrer." . . . He then read the names of those pastors who had been sent to prisons or concentration camps. Members of this congregation did much to hide Jews and faced many risks in aiding them.[71]

Once again, we see the same state of affairs as of the Catholics: an open, official declaration against the Nazi persecution of the Jews is avoided, but help is extended to persecuted individuals.

Toward the end of the 1930's and the beginning of the 1940's, the Jewish lot grew so critical that the Protestant Church could no longer very well continue its policy of "staying out of politics." After the pogroms of November, 1938 (the *Kristallnacht*), an "atonement service," which filled the church completely, was held in Dahlem. At its conference of December 10-12, 1938, the Synod of the Con-

[69] Niemoeller, Martin, *op. cit.*, p. 72.

[70] Niemoeller's trial and sentence are a complicated issue. It is discussed in: Gisevius, Hans B. *To the Bitter End* (Boston 1947) p. 261-264; Lande, *op. cit.*, p. 124-125; *Die Evangelische Kirche . . .*, p. 157. See also fn. 68.

[71] Wolffenstein, Valerie, "Shadow of a Star," in Boehm, *op. cit.*, p. 86.

fessional Church circulated a call to its member congregations with
clear reference to the pogroms: "We remind our congregants to care
for the physical and spiritual needs of their Christian brethern and
sisters of Jewish descent and to pray to God on their behalf." A second statement issued by the Synod referred to the Protestant pastors
who, "on seeing the treatment meted out to the Jews, ardently
preached the Ten Commandments, for which act not a few were
persecuted."[72]

The dangers confronting opposition pastors were not limited to
official acts—arrests, concentration camps, compulsory military service, or being sent to the front.[73] The following is typical of what
happened to some. After the November progroms, Pastor von Jan
of Oberlenningen, Württemberg, said the following prayer, in which
the word "Jew" was not even mentioned:

> . . . Openly and in secret much evil has been done . . . men's lives
> and livelihoods have been damaged and destroyed . . . property has
> been robbed and the honor of neighbors assailed. Lord God we con-
> fess before Thee these our sins and our nation's sins. Forgive us and
> spare us from Thy punishment. Amen.

The pastor was shortly thereafter dragged out of a Bible class by a
band of Nazi hooligans bearing placards with the word "Jew-lackey,"
beaten brutally, and thrown into the local jail. At the same time, his
vicarage was wrecked. In the town of Ludwigsburg, a mob demonstrated against Deacon Dörrfuss, carrying similar posters. The
pastor of Böckingen, near Heilbronn, was fired upon and had the
windows of his home broken.[74]

Despite the double pressure of the government and of the mob,
Protestant opposition and courage grew steadily. Reference to the
Jewish question was made more and more openly. The story of
Theophil Wurm, Regional Bishop of Württemberg, is a good exam-
ple of the progression from a Biblical-theological controversy to poli-
tical opposition. During the early 1930's, he and Hans Lilje, Bishop
of Hanover, were regarded as leaders of the moderate wing of the
Confessional Church, in contrast to Niemoeller, who led the radical

---

[72] Rothfels, *op. cit.*, p. 32; *Die Evangelische Kirche* . . ., p. 163-164; Jannasch,
op. cit., p. 80.

[73] By April 1942, about 7,000 Protestant pastors and other church officials
were mobilized and many of them were sent to the front. Of these, 698 were
killed. Rothfels, *op. cit.*, p. 44.

[74] Fraenkel, Heinrich, *The German People versus Hitler* (London 1940)
p. 131-132.

wing.[75] Wurm was, nonetheless, the first bishop to be arrested by the Nazis. This happened in September, 1933, as a consequence of his vigorous protest against Nazi efforts to create a "Nordic-Christian hybrid religion." His arrest was followed by that of the Bavarian bishop, Hans Meiser. His followers staged protest demonstrations in the streets of Munich, and both bishops were freed in October, 1933. On December 3, 1938, Bishop Wurm addressed a plea to the Minister of Justice to "do all within your power to restore authority, law and the sense of justice."[76] Though this plea was an explicit reaction to the November pogroms, the word "Jew" is not mentioned therein. In various memoranda and declarations issued up till the end of 1942, Wurm protested against the persecution of non-Aryan Christians.

It would seem that a significant departure was made, at least by a number of members of the Protestant opposition, from the policy of caution with respect to Jewish persecution by the beginning of 1943. During Easter, 1943, Bishop Meiser of Munich received an anonymous memorandum from two members of the Protestant Church. He could not prevail upon them to sign their names. After the war, it was learned that the author was Pastor Diem, chairman of the Württemberg "Theological Society." The anonymous message did not mince words:

> As Christians, we can no longer tolerate the silence of the Church in Germany about the persecutions of the Jews. In the Protestant Church, all congregants are equally responsible for the failure of the clergy to fulfil its duties. Hence we, too, feel guilty of the fact that we have failed in our duty in this matter. . . . Every non-Aryan in Germany today, be he Jew or Christian, is as one who has fallen among murderers. We must ask ourselves whether we are to meet him as did the priest and the Levite, or the Samaritan? No talk of a "Jewish question" can absolve us from facing these alternatives. . . . The Church must bear witness against the regime, testifying to the significance of the people of Israel for the idea of redemption, and must oppose with all its might the attempt to "resolve" the Jewish question according to an artificially conceived gospel, that is, the attempt to exterminate Jewry.[77]

Bishop Meiser transmitted the memorandum to Bishop Wurm in Württemberg, who had just then begun his own protest campaign

---

[75] Forell, *op. cit.*, p. 820.

[76] Hermelink, Heinrich, ed., *Kirche im Kampf. Dokumente des Widerstands und des Aufbaus der Evangelischen Kirche Deutschlands von 1933 bis 1945* (Tübingen 1950) p. 648-649.

[77] *Die Evangelische Kirche* . . ., p. 196-197; Hermelink, *op. cit.*, p. 650.

against the extermination of Jewry. In the spring of 1943, the latter addressed the German government as follows:

> There must be an end to all these measures of putting to death members of other nations and races, without either civil or military trial, solely on the basis of membership in a certain nation or race. One hears more and more about such deeds from [military] personnel on leave, and this weighs heavily on the consciences of all Christian fellow-citizens, for such deeds are a direct controversion of God's commandment. . . . For this, our people will some day be subjected to a terrible retaliation.

An even more dire warning was issued by Wurm to the government at the end of December, 1943:

> From the depths of my religious and moral feelings, and in agreement with the thoughts of all true Christians in Germany, I must declare that we Christians consider the policy of extermination of Jews to be a grave wrong, which will have fatal consequences for the German people. To kill beyond the necessities of war and without a trial...is against the commandments of God....Our nation widely regards the suffering wrought by enemy fliers as a just retribution for what has been done to the Jews. The houses and churches aflame, the walls crashing during air raids, the flight from destroyed homes with the remnants of one's belongings, the helpless wandering in search of a refuge—these are agonizing reminders of the sufferings the Jews have undergone.

That the destruction wrought in Germany by enemy planes was an act of God in retribution for the extermination of the Jews was a charge for which the Nazis could not forgive the Bishop. In the spring of 1944, they threatened him again with arrest, but did not carry out the threat.

Finally, an official body of the Confessional Church had its say openly on the extermination of Jews. In the fall of 1943, the Confessional Synod of the Old-Prussian Union, the Church's largest group, issued the following declaration:

> Such conceptions as "extermination," "liquidation," "worthless lives" are unknown to Divine Providence. . . . God has not granted the right to the government to destroy people because they belong to an alien race. . . . The lives of men—and those of the people of Israel as well—are in the hands of God alone and sacred to Him.[78]

In addition to the Paulsbund, the Confessional Church set up a second central organization to assist Protestants of Jewish descent,

---

[78] *Die Evangelische Kirche* . . ., p. 190-196; Hermelink, *op. cit.,* p. 650-656; Schütz, *op. cit.,* p. 43-44; *Bekennende Kirche* . . ., p. 175; Auerbach, *op. cit.,* p. 77.

which later included Jews among those it aided. After an unsuccessful attempt in 1934-36, the Confessional Church, at the session of the fourth Synod in February, 1936, set up an "Office for Christians of Jewish Descent." This was headed by Pastor Martin Albertz of Berlin-Spandau. Among his colleagues were Pastor Hermann Maas and his secretary, Miss Charlotte Friedenthal, herself non-Aryan. This relief organization really began to expand in September, 1938, when a central office was set up in Berlin headed by Pastor Heinrich Grüber of Berlin-Kaulsdorf. This became known as the Grüber Bureau. It had a permanent council, which included Albertz, Maas, and other important Protestant figures. In addition to the Berlin office, it had branches in Heidelberg (Maas), Breslau (the wife of the vicar Staritz), Kassel and other cities.

One of the Bureau's leading tasks was to assist converts and Jews in emigrating from Germany. Until 1940, the Gestapo favored a rapid emigration of Jews, and hence the Bureau's activities were tolerated by Nazi authorities. It also extended aid in various other ways: provision of jobs, material and legal aid, and, for converts, religious support. Since the children of converts and mixed marriages were, subsequent to August, 1939, not permitted to attend general schools, and since the alternative was the Jewish religious schools, the Bureau founded a Christian school for these children in Berlin.

Grüber went several times to Switzerland, Holland and England in efforts to obtain visas. The Bureau often worked closely with Catholic and Jewish relief organizations, and among those it assisted in emigrating, particularly children, was a substantial proportion of Jews.

In 1940, however, Nazi policy on Jewish emigration underwent a major change, and Grüber's activities came into disfavor. On December 19, 1940, he was arrested and sent to Sachsenhausen, later to be transferred to Dachau. The Berlin office of the Bureau was closed, though the local offices were permitted to operate for some time thereafter.[79] Grüber relates a moving story about his arrival in the concentration camp:

[79] *Die Evangelische Kirche . . .*, p. 150-151, 180-182; Albertz, Martin, "Die Vorläufige Leitung der Evangelischen Kirche," in *Bekennende Kirche . . .*, p. 168-171; *Schuld und Verantwortung, Zehn Jahre nach dem Kristallnacht, Nov. 8, 1938* (Hanover 1948) p. 3-5. Dr. Grüber today holds a high position in the Protestant Church in Berlin. In 1947, he was chairman of the "Association of Nazi Victims" (VVN) in Berlin. His rescue work is described in a special report. *An der Stechbahn. Erlebnisse und Berichte aus dem Büro Grüber in den Jahren der*

On my arrival in Sachsenhausen Camp shortly before Christmas, I was approached by one of the long-suffering, tortured Jews, who had known me from Berlin. It was in the evening that he stole out of the Jewish barracks and came to me, saying: "Herr Pastor, your having been brought to the camp is the most wonderful holiday gift for us Jews." Throughout the years [of camp imprisonment], this child-like, simple sentence was gospel and mission to me.[80]

The close of the Grüber Bureau bore heavily on the Protestant converts, for they could receive little aid from either the Catholic or the overwhelmed Jewish relief organizations. Grüber's successor, Pastor Werner Sylten, continued its activities in semi-clandestine ways until he too was arrested in 1941 and deported to Dachau, where he died in 1942. His work was carried on to the extent possible by Martin Albertz and his three non-Aryan secretaries, aided by a number of Protestant pastors. The rescue activities of this group, too, were uncovered, and Albertz and some 25 of his assistants were arrested and sentenced to various prison terms. Several months later, Mrs. Staritz, head of the Breslau office, was also arrested.[81]

The Heidelberg division of the organization was headed by Pastor Hermann Maas. An ardent Zionist (in his own words, "a quiet Lover of Zion since 1903, since the fifth Zionist Congress"), Maas visited Palestine in 1933. His daughter Brigitta lived in Palestine for many years, where she and Ahuva Yellin, daughter of the Hebrew educator David Yellin, founded a weaving school for Jerusalem Jewish youth. Maas' rescue activities on behalf of Jews and non-Aryan Christians began immediately after Hitler's assumption of power. He was particularly active in arranging the emigration of Jewish children, which work took him to England a number of times. When the Nazis learned of his activities, he was deposed from his post as pastor of Heidelberg's largest church, the Church of the Holy Spirit. This was a heavy blow to Maas, who came from a family with a clerical tradition going back to 1625. He continued his illegal work, suffered

---

Verfolgung (Berlin 1951). Unfortunately, a copy of this work was unavailable in New York at the time of writing.

[80] Grüber, Heinrich (Häftling 27832), "Gottes Liebe schenkt die Bruderschaft, die zum Lobpreis Gottes führt," in *Bekennende Kirche* . . ., p. 186.

[81] *Die Evangelische Kirche* . . ., p. 181-184. The management of the Breslau office was not the only reason for Mrs. Staritz' arrest. When the Nazis introduced the wearing of the "Yellow Badge" in the fall of 1941, Mrs. Staritz circulated an open letter protesting the new decree. After her arrest, she was the subject of a sharp attack in the December 8, 1941, issue of the official organ of the SS, *Das schwarze Korps.*

arrests a number of times, was sent to France for forced labor, and, several days before the end of the war, was sentenced to death. After the liberation, Maas wrote letters to his Jewish friends, which are marked by a great warmth and affection for the Jews.[82]

Maas was the first German to receive a formal invitation from the Israeli government. The Jewish National Fund honored him on his 75th birthday by planting a forest in his name.[83] Maas published the impressions of his trips to Israel in 1950 and 1953 in two books.[84] On his return from the first of these, he addressed a meeting of the "German Parliamentary Society in Bonn." In this talk, he dwelt on the problem of "our guilt toward Jews"—using "our" rather than "Nazi." He said:

> Every man is judged in two courts. He defends himself in the first, in the earthly court, in order to receive a lighter punishment. We—even those who were not directly guilty, but who were, and even today remain, thoughtless, silent or forgetful—have deserved the death sentence even from an earthly judge. How much greater, then, is our guilt in the sight of the Eternal Court.

Maas also urged his listeners to understand Jewish feelings of disgust, hatred and mistrust toward Germany. His address made a strong impression on his audience, which included the President of the Bonn Republic, Dr. Theodor Heuss, the Vice Chancellor, many professors, government officials and members of Parliament.[85]

Another philo-Semite who was active in aiding Jews during the Nazi period was Pastor Albrecht Goes, a student and follower of Martin Buber and of his philosophy of Hasidism. Goes writes:

> When in 1933-34 Nazi tyranny was capturing one position after the other before our very eyes, we had one consolation: the certainty that Martin Buber was still at his home on the Bergstrasse in Heppenheim, and that we could still come to him for help and advice, much as the Hasidim would come to the Great Magid or to Reb Shmelke of Nikolsburg.

---

[82] See Supplement I.

[83] Hermann Maas is the subject of a number of articles in the New York *Aufbau*: Belzner, Emil, "Der Brückenwächter der Menschlichkeit," May 5, 1950; "Ein Deutscher in Israel," April 21, 1950; "Brief von Pastor H. Maas," February 22, 1946. Cf., Wolman-Sheratshek, Miriam, "Vos hot mir dertseylt der daytsher pastor doktor Hermann Maas," *Yidishe tsaytung* (Buenos Aires) November 10, 1953.

[84] Mass, Hermann, *Skizzen von einer Fahrt nach Israel* (Karlsruhe 1950); *idem, —und will Rachels Kinder wieder bringen in das land. Reiseeindrücke aus heutigem Israel* (Heilbronn 1955).

[85] The excerpt from Maas' talk is taken from an article by Marian Gid in the Buenos Aires *Yidishe tsaytung*, March 14, 1952, p. 5f. Unfortunately, we have not yet been able to obtain a copy of the original text.

Soon thereafter, however, Goes continues, Buber left Germany for Palestine, and his followers were left leaderless. Goes has recently published a tale describing Jewish suffering in Nazi Germany and the action of a simple German woman in helping the persecuted.[86]

Further examples of aid rendered to Jews by Protestants could be cited. Thus, before emigration became impossible in February, 1940, Pastor Zwanziger of Munich aided 65 people to flee the country.[87] Several members of the Berlin Dahlem congregation saved the lives of a number of converts and Jews by providing them with false Aryan papers. Dr. Kaufman, himself a convert, headed this work. He was captured by the Gestapo and sentenced to death.[88] Most of the defendants in a large-scale trial of "defenders of the Jews" which took place in Berlin in January, 1944, were members of the Confessional Church.[89]

4. Other Christian Denominations

The fact that Jews received little aid from the various other denominations in Germany was due to a number of reasons. In the first place, their membership was quite small. Out of a total population of 70,000,000, only 150,000 belonged to these sects.[90] Secondly, most of these sects were themselves victims of political persecution. Thus, for example, almost all members of the Ernste Bibelforscher (Jehovah's Witnesses) were sent to prison or concentration camps. Thirdly, not all of these sects had a positive attitude toward Jews or toward aiding Jews.

One group which manifested great sympathy for Jews from the very onset of the Nazi persecution was the Quakers. They set up an organization to help non-Aryan victims of Nazism with food, clothing and secret shelters. This was known to the British consul-general in 1938. Various Jewish writers also refer to the assistance rendered by the small Quaker communities in Berlin, Munich and Isarthal (near Munich).[91]

---

[86] Goes, Albrecht, "Martin Buber, der Beistand" in *Jewish Travel Guide,* 1953-54, p. 97-104; *idem, Das Brandopfer* (Frankfurt a/M 1954).

[87] Auerbach, *op. cit.,* p. 77.

[88] Boehm, *op. cit.,* p. 82-84, 87.

[89] Jannasch, *op. cit.,* p. 6.

[90] Forell, *op. cit.,* p. 813-814.

[91] Great Britain, Foreign Office, *White Book. Germany,* vol. ii (London 1940); Behrend-Rosenfeld, *op. cit.,* p. 84; Weltlinger, *op. cit.,* p. 19. S. Dorfsohn, writing from London, published an account of 56 Jewish orphans who were brought to England by the Quakers from Germany and Austria. There was no thought of

The Baptists, too, were well-disposed toward the Jews. Emanuel Ringelblum wrote about a German Baptist occupying a high post in the administration of the Warsaw district who had a friendly attitude. In the Lodz area, too, even during the worst of Nazi persecutions, there were German Baptists who maintained a sympathetic attitude. One Pietrick, a German weaver, and his wife were sent to the concentration camp at Dora (near Buchenwald) and their property confiscated as a result of their aid to Jews and their open anti-Nazi talk.[92]

The story of Jehovah's Witnesses is a chapter all in itself. They were hated by the Nazis for a number of reasons. They were, in the first place, a sect which had originated abroad, with headquarters in New York.[93] The Nazis and their ideological predecessors had conducted an intense propaganda campaign against the sect since the early 1920's, accusing them of being "collaborators and servants of Judaism and of Jewish world imperialism."[94] Jehovah's Witnesses, particularly in America, openly proclaimed their opposition to totalitarianism. Shortly before his death in January, 1942, Judge Joseph Franklin Rutherford, leader of the sect, published a pamphlet predicting the downfall of the Axis powers.[95] In consequence of their opposition to military service, the sect underwent much hardship in many countries.[96] Their categorical refusal to use the "Heil Hitler" salutation, a grave offense in Nazi Germany, particularly enraged the Nazis. They

---

converting these children. Moreover, their hosts were concerned to give them a Jewish religious education, saw to it that they attended synagogue, and provided a strictly kosher kitchen. "Pleytim-kinder vos men hot ahergebrakht in milkhome-tsayt," *Morgn-zhurnal*, December 28, 1949, p. 7.

[92] Ringelblum, Emanuel, *Notitsn fun varshever geto* (Warsaw 1952) p. 99. An entry dated February, 1941, reads: "Legendary tales are told about Dr. Schubert from this district. He is a sponsor of Gancwajch. He puts on an armband and enters the ghetto. He is said to save Jewish property occasionally. He is a Baptist." The story of Pietrick is told in *Belkhatov, yizker-bukh* (Buenos Aires 1951) p. 421-422.

[93] The sect was founded in Pennsylvania in 1872.

[94] The following more important works convey the character and orientation of this propaganda: Rosenberg, Alfred, "Die 'Ernste Bibelforscher,'" in his *Kampf um die Macht* (Munich 1937) p. 328-332; Braeunlich, Paul, *Die "Ernste Bibel-forscher" als Opfer bolschewistischer Religionsspötter* (Leipzig 1926); Fritsch, Theodor, "Ernste Bibelforscher" in *Handbuch der Judenfrage*, 30-te völlig bearb. Auflage (Leipzig 1931) p. 263-268; Freyenwald, Hans Jonak von, *Die Zeugen Jehovas; Pioniere fuer ein juedisches Weltreich. Die politischen Ziele der inter-nationalen Vereinigung "Ernster Bibelforscher"* (Berlin 1936).

[95] Rutherford, J. F., *End of the Axis Powers. Comfort All That Mourn*, cited in Stroup, Herbert H., *The Jehovah's Witnesses* (New York 1945) p. 167.

[96] Stroup, *op. cit.*, p. 148-149; American Civil Liberties Union, *Jehovah's Witnesses and the War* (New York 1943).

were furthermore accused of conducting anti-Nazi propaganda and spreading defeatist prophecies about the coming downfall of "anti-Christ" (Hitler) and of the Day of Judgment for his regime.[97] According to Annedore Leber (widow of the murdered Socialist leader Julius Leber), there were 6,034 Witnesses in Germany from 1933 to 1945, of whom 5,911 were arrested.[98] In the concentration camps, the Witnesses were treated far more leniently than the Jews. Nevertheless, more than 2,000 were killed, often as a result of their refusal to compromise their beliefs. The literature of concentration camp memoirs contains many instances of individual Witnesses being tortured to death for their fearless behavior. The same sources report the existence of friendly relations among Jews and Witnesses in the camps.[99] Since so few members of the sect retained their freedom, there was no question of their rendering aid to the Jews. There are cases in which Witnesses at liberty—both German and others, e.g., Esthonians and Hungarians—did help Jews.[100] The sufferings of the

[97] The question of the anti-Nazi propaganda of the sect is discussed in detail in a memorandum of July 15, 1943, from Ernst Kaltenbrunner, head of the German Security Police, to Himmler. The text of the memorandum is in Friedman, Philip, *Oświęcim* (Warsaw 1946) p. 179-186. On their opposition to Nazism, cf., Pechel, Rudolf, *Deutscher Widerstand* (Zurich 1947) p. 106-107.

[98] Leber, Annedore, *op. cit.,* p. 20. These figures are almost identical with those given by Judge Rutherford. In his book *Armageddon* (1937), he writes that about 2,000 Witnesses were arrested in Germany. In a second publication, *Judge Rutherford Uncovers the Fifth Column* (1940, p. 20), he reported that over 6,000 Witnesses had been arrested, and that many of them had been executed. Cited in Stroup, *op. cit.,* p. 147-148.

[99] Zürcher, Franz, *Kreuzzug gegen das Christentum* (Zurich 1938); Friedman, *op. cit.,* p. 179-186, 210-218; Wormser, Olga and Michel, Henri, comps., *Tragédie de la déportation,* 1940-1945 (Paris 1954) p. 229, 262-264; Boehm, *op. cit.,* p. 27, 137, 208; Rothfels, *op. cit.,* p. 40; Cohen, Elie A., *Human Behavior in the Concentration Camp* (New York 1953) p. 27; Kogon, Eugen, *Der SS-Staat. Das System der deutschen Konzentrationslager* (Berlin 1946, 2nd. ed.) p. 51, 241-243; Buber, Margarete, *Under Two Dictators* (New York, n.d.) p. 186, 188, 204, 219f., 247f., 261, 265, 271, 274, 277, 280, 317-318, 233-235, 236-238, 222-223; Wiechert, Ernst, *Der Totenwald. Ein Bericht* (Munich, n.d.) p. 148-155.

[100] In Grossman, Khayke, *Anshe hamahteret* (Merhavia, Israel, 1950) p. 388-394, there is a description of a German, Busse, who headed an artist's studio in Bialystok. Originally from a wealthy East Prussian family, Busse had become a Bible and Talmud scholar. Although a member of the Nazi party, he was an opponent of Nazism. He had a great liking for Jews, and established contact with the Jewish underground organization, often providing a good deal of important information. He also was of great help to the Jewish workers employed under him. B. Mark, in *Der oyfshtand in bialistoker geto* (Warsaw 1950) p. 346, cites evidence to the effect that Busse was a member of Jehovah's Witnesses. In an article "Di oysderveylte," in the *Landsberger lager-tsaytung* of May 3, 1946, Isaac Nementchik writes about a Witness in Esthonia who regularly brought food for Jews in the concentration camp of Kuremaa, and otherwise aided them as much as possible. The *Morgn-zhurnal* of January 6, 1940, p. 1, reported a "Jehovah Organization" to aid

Jehovah's Witnesses did not end with the war. In Eastern Germany they were tried in 1950 for "systematic boycott, incitement to war, espionage in the service of American imperialism and illegal activities." A number of their leaders were imprisoned, and the sect itself declared illegal.[101]

II.   The German Resistance Movement and the Jewish Question

The discussion about the historical significance of the German resistance movement is far from over. It has been the subject of innumerable books, pamphlets and articles, written in either critical, polemical or reminiscent vein. Among the critics, there are those who maintain that the chroniclers of the movement have, for various reasons, gone too far in exaggerating insignificant facts and personalities. These critics hold that a more objective approach would show that there were only a few, tiny isolated groups which were either limited to theoretical discussions about opposition, or invariably failed when they did actually formulate concrete plans, such as inciting the German people to revolt against Nazism or to unseat Hitler. It may be that these critics are too extreme and biased. Perhaps the most judicious approach is that of the historian Hans Rothfels, who suggests that the role of the historian today is primarily that of a finder, recorder and scientific analyst of relevant factual materials, leaving evaluation to a later date.[102] In our opinion, this approach is even more valid with respect to the Jewish aspect of the German anti-Nazi opposition.

The various scattered groups constituting the German opposition drew their members from all social strata of the German people— from the working class, professionals, aristocracy, military, and, to some extent, from the different religious groups.[103] Between 1933 and 1945, no fewer than three million Germans were sent to prison or concentration camps for political crimes. Of these, about 500,000 paid with their lives. Nevertheless, it cannot be inferred that German

---

Jews in Hungary, and that 36 of its members were arrested. Thus far, no more precise details in this matter have ben found.

[101] Kalikstein, M., " 'Yehoves eydes' geyen tsurik in tfise arayn . . .," *Yidisher kemfer* (November 17, 1950) p. 8-12; "Jehovah's Witnesses, Persecution Past and Present," *Wiener Library Bulletin*, vol. v, no. 1-2 (1951) p. 8.

[102] Rothfels, *op. cit.*, p. 158-159.

[103] *Ibid.*, p. 45, 47-48, 53, 141; Boehm, *op. cit.*, p. 193; Pechel, *op. cit.*, p. 71-113.

resistance was an active mass movement. Most of the arrests stemmed from the Nazi policy of "prophylaxis." This led the Nazis to try to imprison all potential enemies—the functionaries and activists of all other political parties, and, in general, all those upon whom any suspicion fell of being actually or potentially disloyal to the Nazi regime. It is estimated that 800,000 of the three million arrested were real anti-Nazis, and that the number of those who were compelled to live an underground existence because of their anti-Nazism amounted to no more than 150,000 (of whom about 10,000 were Jews).[104]

The backbone of any potential large-scale resistance movement was broken by the mass arrests. The German resistance movement was caught in a moral dilemma, particularly after the outbreak of the war in 1939. Resistance to the Nazis meant, in effect, working for Germany's defeat and seeking aid from its military and political enemies. The Nazis took advantage of the opportunity to label the resistance movement as unpatriotic and traitorous. It took great moral courage to make a declaration such as that of one of the leaders of the Protestant opposition, Pastor Dietrich Bonhoeffer. Asked for whom he prayed, Bonhoeffer answered: "Truth to tell, I pray for the defeat of my country, for this is the only possibility of atoning for all the suffering which my country has inflicted upon the world."[105]

Prior to the introduction of the Nuremberg laws in 1935, Jews participated in the resistance movement, particularly in the labor groups. Thereafter, however, their number constantly decreased. The greater the anti-Jewish terror became, the more Jews became liabilities to a conspiratorial group, for they were subject to special persecution (the yellow badge, limited mobility, deportation, arrest). Jews were placed under close surveillance by the German police and the Gestapo, which added to the dangers facing any illegal group.[106]

Thus there are few known cases of Jewish participants in the German opposition groups. One of the exceptions is that of Max Fleischmann, Professor of International Law at the University of Halle. He

104 Boehm, *op. cit.*, p. viii; "Buchenwald: Reverse Allied Atrocity Propaganda," *The Network*, vol. ii, no. 7-8 (1945, published by the American Association for a Democratic Germany) p. 13; *Inside Germany Report* (New York, November 20, 1944) p. 15.

105 Hooft, W. A. Visser 't, "Begegnung mit Dietrich Bonhoeffer," in *Das Zeugnis eines Boten. Zum Gedächtnis von Dietrich Bonhoeffer* (Geneva 1945) p. 7; Rothfels, *op. cit.*, p. 141-142; Minssen, Friedrich, "Der Widerstand gegen den Widerstand," *Frankfurter Hefte*, vol. iv, no. 10 (1949) p. 884-888.

106 Jansen and Weyl, *op. cit.*, p. 250.

was in close contact with the opposition leader Fabian von Schla-
brendorf and with the bitter enemy of Nazism, State Secretary Herbert
von Bismarck. Nevertheless, when in 1943 Fleischmann, like all other
Jews, received the order to be prepared for deportation to Poland, his
highly-placed friends could be of no assistance to him, and he committed suicide.[107] The young Jew Hans Dankner played an important
role in the Communist underground movement in Dresden. He was
responsible for all border activity in the Sudeten region until 1939.
(This involved smuggling people across the Czech border, and illegal
literature into Germany.) In March, 1939, he was imprisoned, and
in 1943 he was deported to Oswiecim, whence he did not return.[108]

The two leading figures of the most influential opposition group,
Colonel-General Ludwig Beck, chief of the German General Staff,
and Dr. Karl Friedrich Goerdeler, spoke out clearly on the Jewish
question on various occasions. General Beck prepared a manifesto
addressed to the German people which was to be published after the
Hitler regime had been overthrown. The manifesto sharply condemned the "blasphemous race theory" and the "frightful crimes"
of the Nazi regime, and declared that the Jews should be compensated for their suffering.[109]

As is well known, the submission of the Western powers to Nazi
Germany and Hitler's unanticipated victory in the matter of the
Sudeten question in 1938 frustrated the plans of the German opposition for an uprising against Hitler. The leaders of the opposition
made various attempts at the time to convince the Western powers
that appeasement of Hitler was a mistaken policy. They warned that
it would strengthen his prestige in Germany and make a revolution
impossible. Among the political figures approached was Chaim Weizmann. In September, 1938, shortly before the Munich conference,
Goerdeler transmitted a document to Weizmann in London which
described the political situation in Germany in detail, and called upon
Prime Minister Chamberlain not to be fooled by Hitler. Weizmann
immediately turned the document over to a high British official, but
Chamberlain did not even take the trouble to read Goerdeler's
missive.[110]

---

[107] Pechel, *op. cit.*, p. 74-75.
[108] Zimmering, Max, *Widerstandsgruppe "Vereinigte Kletter-Abteilungen"*
*(VKA). Ein Bericht von der Grenzarbeit der Dresdener Arbeitersteiger in der
Sächsischen Schweiz und dem östlichen Erzgebirge* (Berlin 1948) p. 28-29.
[109] Rothfels, *op. cit.*, p. 107; Pechel, *op. cit.*, p. 213.
[110] Weizmann, Chaim, *Trial and Error* (London 1950) p. 505.

Goerdeler was undoubtedly the leading figure among the civilian members of the resistance movement. In certain opposition circles, he was seen as the future Reichspräsident after the defeat of Hitler. He had been Bürgermeister of Koenigsberg since 1920, and Oberbürgermeister of Leipzig since 1930. In 1931, he also took on the responsible position of Reichskommisar for Price Control. The Nazis took the occasion of Goerdeler's absence from the city on vacation to remove the Mendelssohn memorial from the square in front of the "Gewandhaus." On his return, Goerdeler vigorously demanded the return of the statue. The Nazis refused, and in March, 1937, Goerdeler resigned his post as Oberbürgermeister in protest.[111]

Subsequently, Goerdeler played a leading role both in the preparations of the opposition within the country as well as in negotiations on behalf of the German opposition with various refugee organizations abroad. He maintained close contact with the Gentile banking family Wallenberg of Stockholm, and especially with Raoul Wallenberg, who was later to rescue thousands of Hungarian Jews (1944-45). He was arrested after the unsuccessful attempt on Hitler's life on July 20, 1944. Evidently Heinrich Himmler knew of Goerdeler's political contacts, for he proposed that Goerdeler, through Weizmann, Raoul Wallenberg and King Gustav of Sweden, try to contact Prime Minister Churchill and induce him to agree to early peace negotiations. The plan fell through when Goerdeler specified the condition that he be allowed to leave for Sweden to undertake the mission. Shortly thereafter, he was sentenced to death.[112]

A second opposition group which was sympathetic to the persecuted Jews was the Kreisau Circle. The group was named after the Silesian estate of one of its leaders, Count Helmuth James Moltke, a nephew of the famous German general of Bismarck's days. The Kreisau Circle included people from various walks of life—aristocrats, military men, Catholic and Protestant figures, Social Democrats, diplomats, intellectuals, and the like.[113] The Kreisau Circle was in-

---

[111] Krause, Friedrich, ed., *Goerdelers politisches Testament. Dokumente des Anderen Deutschlands* (New York 1945) p. 16; Rothfels, *op. cit.*, p. 85; Auerbach, *op. cit.*, p. 84; Schacht, Hjalmar, *76 Jahre meines Lebens* (Bad Wörishofen 1953) p. 548; Zeller, Eberhard, *Geist der Freiheit. Das zwanzigste Jahrhundert* (Munich 1952) p. 31.

[112] Ritter, Gerhard, *Karl Goerdeler und die deutsche Widerstandsbewegung* (Stuttgart 1954) p. 427-428.

[113] More precise details on the members of the Kreisau Circle are to be found in: *A German of the Resistance. The Last Letters of Count Helmuth James Moltke* (London 1946); Rothfels, *op. cit.*, p. 112-129; Pechel, R., *op. cit.*, p. 117-118;

strumental in aiding a number of Jews to flee Germany. Count Moltke was also connected with the noted rescue of Danish Jews. Through his friends in high government positions, Moltke had learned that the deportation of Danish Jews was scheduled for October, 1943. He transmitted this information to his friends in Copenhagen, who in turn informed the Danish government and the Jewish community administration.[114] Moltke and a number of his colleagues were arrested at the beginning of 1944, and executed shortly thereafter.

The Solf Circle was closely connected with the Kreisau Circle. Dr. Wilhelm Solf had been State Secretary in the German Colonial Office before World War I. From 1921 to 1928 he served as German Ambassador to Japan. He helped a number of persecuted academicians, among them some Jews, to leave Germany in the first years of the Nazi regime, and obtained posts for them in Japan. After his death in 1936, his wife Hanna and daughter, Lagi Countess Ballestrem-Solf, continued the rescue work for victims of Nazism. Among the members of the group was the former German consul-general in New York, Dr. Otto Karl Kiep. On Albert Einstein's arrival in New York, Kiep received an invitation to the banquet arranged in the physicist's honor. Despite the fact that he was a high-ranking German official (Kiep was also German chargé d'affaires in Washington at the time), he accepted the invitation. This was a sin the Nazis could not overlook, and he was soon relieved of his post.[115]

> As the persecution of Jews intensified [writes Countess Balles-trem-Solf] I made it my special task to aid them. . . . My mother and I did our best to get emigration affidavits for Jews and she visited innumerable embassies and consulates in quest of visas. . . . It became increasingly important to save Jewish families by getting them out of the country illegally or by hiding them. We sheltered some in our house and helped others to find hiding places. . . . One day we learned of a chance to smuggle some of our protégés into Switzerland

---

Auerbach, *op. cit.,* p. 88; Zeller, *op. cit.,* p. 73, 75-80; Boehm, *op cit.,* p. 182-183, 189; Homan, Helen Walker, *Letters to the Martyrs* (New York 1951) p. 187-206.

[114] *A German of the Resistance . . .,* p. 11; Boehm, *op. cit.,* p. 178. The German who transmitted the information to the Danish premier about the plan to deport the Jews was G. F. Duckwitz, a high official in the German administration in Copenhagen. See Bertelsen, Aage, *October '43* (New York 1954) p. 17.

[115] The Solf Circle's activities are discussed in the following: Ballestrem-Solf, Lagi, "Tea Party," in Boehm, *op. cit.,* p. 132-150; Paetel, Karl O., *Deutsche innere Emigration* (New York 1946) p. 19; Pechel, *op. cit.,* p. 88-93; Leber, *op. cit.,* p. 143; Rothfels, *op. cit.,* p. 32.

... [through] a small farm close to the border in Baden, from which a few field paths led to Switzerland.[116]

The Gestapo knew about the Solf Circle. In the first months of the war, the Countess was called in by the Gestapo and warned against being a "Jew-lackey." In January, 1944, both mother and daughter were arrested. They were sent to the Ravensbrueck concentration camp, where they managed to survive. They were fortunate ones, for most of the other members of the Solf Circle, arrested at the same time, were condemned to death. No less than 80 per cent of the members perished, among them Dr. Otto Kiep.[117]

Another opposition group, consisting of high officials in the German Foreign Office, was known as "The Red Orchestra," (possibly because its members favored cooperation with the Soviet Union in the overthrow of the Nazi regime). They aided Jews with food, money and shelter. In a German diary, we find reference to the activities of a group which went under the name of "Uncle Emil." This was presumably the same as "The Red Orchestra." One of the heroes of this book is called "Erich Tüch," easily identified as the noted German diplomat Dr. Erich Kordt (a member of Ribbentrop's staff).[118] A member of this group, Dr. Philipp Schaeffer, a distinguished Sinologue, attempted to save a Jewish couple who, in despair, turned on the gas. In the attempt, which proved futile, Schaeffer fractured his pelvis and thigh, and was caught by the Gestapo. He was sentenced to death.[119]

Another small, isolated group consisted of students and faculty at the University of Munich. It was known as the Scholl Circle, after its leaders, Hans Scholl and his sister Sophia. One of its members, Hans Karl Leipelt, was half-Jewish. He had gone through the war in Poland and in France, received an Iron Cross, but was discharged because of his "racial impurity." He, as well as the other

---

[116] Ballestrem-Solf, *op. cit.,* p. 133-134.

[117] Boehm, *op. cit.,* p. 142, 145, 149; Rothfels, *op. cit.,* p. 32; Gisevius, *op. cit.,* p. 433.

[118] Andreas-Friedrich, Ruth, *Der Schattenmann, Tagebuch-Aufzeichnungen 1938-1945* (Berlin 1947), Engl. ed., *Berlin Underground, 1938-1945* (New York 1947); Rothfels, *op. cit.,* p. 33, 56; Gisevius, *op. cit.,* p. 433; Weizssäcker, *op. cit.,* p. 145, 220. Erich Kordt himself published two books on his work in the Foreign Ministry and in the German opposition movement: *Wahn und Wirklichkeit. Die äussere Politik des Dritten Reiches* (Stuttgart 1947); and *Nicht aus den Akten. Die Wilhelmstrasse im Frieden und Krieg. Erlebnisse, Begegnungen und Eindrücke 1928-1945* (Stuttgart 1950).

[119] Weisenborn, Günther, "Reich Secret," in Boehm, *op. cit.,* p. 205.

members of the group, were caught by the Gestapo and sentenced to death.

Using the name *Die Weisse Rose*, the group distributed anti-Nazi circulars and leaflets. One of the leaflets (issued in the spring of 1942) dwelt at some length on the Jewish question:

> As an example, we wish to mention that 300,000 Jews have been murdered bestially in Poland since the German occupation. This is the most horrible of crimes, unparalleled in all human history. . . . Why is the German people so apathetic in the face of such revolting, inhuman crimes? Almost no one takes any note of it. The facts are known, but are set aside as mere documents. And the German people goes on in a stupor, giving these fascist criminals the courage and the opportunity to continue their berserk rampages, which they indeed do. . . . Will the German finally awaken from this stupor, protest as only he can against this clique of criminals, sympathize with the hundreds of thousands of victims, and sense his guilt? . . . For there are none free of guilt. Each [of us] is guilty, guilty, guilty![120]

Another illegal group which provided Jews with false documents and hid them was located in Berlin. A leading part in this group was taken by Kurt Christian Knudsen, now a book publisher and noted Protestant leader and writer.[121]

Annedore Leber's book tells of other anti-Nazis, presumably in

[120] Vossler, Karl, *Gedenkrede für die Opfer an der Universität München* (Munich 1947); Huch, Ricarda, "Die Aktion der Münchener Studenten gegen Hitler," *Neue Auslese*, vol. iv, no. 1 (1949) p. 12-18; *Rundbrief . . .*, no. 19-20 (1953) p. 8; Scholl, Inge, *Die Weisse Rose* (Frankfurt 1952) p. 91-93. In this book (p. 48) Inge Scholl, a sister of Sophia and Hans, cites an episode from her murdered brother's diary dating from the period of his service as a German soldier in Poland:

". . . Sie hatten während des Transportes an einer polnischen Station einige Minuten Aufenthalt gehabt. Am Bahndamm sah er [Hans Scholl] junge Frauen und Mädchen gebückt, die mit Eisenhacken in den Händen schwere Männerarbeit taten. Sie trugen den gelben Zionstern an der Brust. Hans schwang sich aus dem Fenster seines Wagens und ging auf die Frauen zu. Die erste in der Reihe war ein junges abgearbeitetes Mädchen, mit schmalen Händen und einem schönem intelligenten Gesicht, in dem eine unsägliche Trauer stand. Hatte er denn nichts bei sich was er ihr schenken konnte? Da fiel ihm seine 'Eiserne Ration' ein, ein Gemisch von Schokolade, und Nüssen und er steckte es ihr zu. Das Mädchen bückte sich blitzschnell und warf es ihm mit einer gehetzten aber unendlich stolzen Gebärde vor die Füsse. Er hob es auf, lächelte ihr ins Gesicht und sagte: 'Ich hätte Ihnen so gern eine kleine Freude gemacht.' Dann bückte er sich, pflückte eine Margerite und legte sie ihr samt Päckchen mit einer leichten Verneigung zu Füssen. Aber schon rollte der Zug an, und mit ein paar langen Sätzen sprang Hans auf. Vom Fenster aus sah er, dass das Mädchen dastand und dem Zug nachblickte, die weisse Margerite im Haar."

[121] Boehm, *op. cit.*, p. 68; Knudsen, Knud C., ed., *Welt ohne Hass. Aufsätze und Ansprache zum I. Kongress über bessere menschliche Beziehungen in München* (Berlin 1950).

Socialist circles. Among others, Dr. Lili Gloeder and her husband are mentioned. Both were sincere opponents of Nazism, who hid victims of anti-Jewish persecution and Nazi political terror. For this activity, husband, wife, and mother were sentenced to decapitation in November, 1944. The nurse Gertrud Seele was also sentenced to death for this type of activity.[122] Dr. Otto Heinrich Greve, a Social Democratic member of Parliament, aided Jews to flee Germany. Now a member of the Bonn Parliament, Greve visited Israel in 1955 at the invitation of the committee which observed the tenth anniversary of the liberation of Bergen-Belsen.[123]

At the first world congress of the reconstituted Socialist International, held in Frankfort-on-the-Main in July, 1951, a question arose concerning the extent to which the German Socialists aided Jews during the Nazi period. Professor Liebman Hersch, speaking in the name of the Jewish Socialist Bund, issued a declaration "On the German Question." Dr. Kurt Schumacher, leader of the German Social Democrats, replied to it in a lengthy address delivered to a mass meeting called in honor of the congress. Schumacher touched on the events and problems of the Nazi period, in a general way, devoting himself mainly to a sharp attack on the recent signs of "fascism, chauvinism and anti-Semitism," and calling for a struggle "against the danger of a new bestiality."[124]

The Communist underground organizations published a number of illegal pamphlets sharply castigating Nazi anti-Semitism.[125] Their relief activity was centered on the rescue of party comrades, among whom were undoubtedly a number of Jews. Since Communist pub-

---

[122] Leber, *op. cit.*, p. 76, 81.

[123] *Der Tog* (New York) April 18, 1955; *Allgemeine Wochenschrift der Juden in Deutschland* (Düsseldorf) May 20, 1955.

[124] Hersch, Liebman, "Tsu der frage daytshland," *Unzer tsayt* (September 1951) p. 12-15; Scherer, Emanuel, "Der nayer sotsialistisher internatsional," *ibid.*, p. 4-12, especially p. 7. On several other occasions, too, Schumacher touched on the question of Nazi persecution and anti-Semitism in Germany. In these talks, however, he is more concerned with the future of German Jewry than with the facts of past events. Likewise, he does not deal with the problem of aid rendered by Social-Democratic circles to Jews during the Nazi period. See Scholz, Arno, and Oschilewski, Walther G., eds., *Turmwächter der Demokratie. Ein Lebensbild von Kurt Schumacher*, vol. ii (Berlin 1952-54); *Reden und Schriften* (Berlin-Grunewald) p. 130, 104, 175.

[125] In a bibliography of illegal, anti-Nazi publications distributed in Germany during the Nazi period—most of them Communist organs—there are at least four pamphlets which are primarily devoted to Jewish persecution, particularly the pogroms of November, 1938. These rare pamphlets are to be found in the Alfred Wiener Library in London. See *Wiener Library Bulletin*, vol. v, no. 3-4 (1951) p. 21.

lications rarely mention "racial," religious or ethnic origin, it is difficult to obtain a clear picture of the Jewish aspect of their rescue
work.[126] In Communist literature occasional reference is made to
rescue acts on behalf of Jews as such, irrespective of party membership. One such case is told about the Oswiecim concentration camp.[127]
Assistance rendered to Jews by various unidentified underground
organizations is described by Ruth Andreas-Friedrich.[128]. The pogroms in November, 1938 had a particularly strong impact on opposition circles, and led many new people to participate in the illegal
activity on behalf of Jews. It was this series of events which catalyzed
the resolve of many to participate in this activity, or at least to see
to it that the Nazi crimes were recorded. Thus Ruth Andreas-Friedrich writes in the introduction to her book: "The burning of the
synagogues on November 10, 1938, moved me to resolve to write
[this book]."[129] Ulrich von Hassel, former German Ambassador to
Italy and one of the leading figures of the German opposition, entered the following in his diary on November 25, 1938:

> I am writing under crushing emotions evoked by the vile perse-
> cution of the Jews after the murder of vom Rath. Not since the
> World War have we lost so much credit in the world. But my chief
> concern is not with the effects abroad.... I am most deeply troubled
> about the effect on our national life, which is dominated ever more
> inexorably by a system capable of such things.[130]

[126] One Communist publication relates how a Communist resistance group in
Dresden, on Party orders, smuggled a number of "anti-fascists who were endangered" across the border into Czechoslovakia. The explicit comment is made that
"We didn't know the names of these [rescued] people, nor did we inquire." Zimmering, *op. cit.*, p. 14.

[127] A transport of 160 Hungarian Jewish orphans, aged 11 to 17, was sent
from the Carpathian Region to the coal-mining camp Yavishovitz (a division of
Oświęcim). The underground political organization managed to have a Communist
camp inmate appointed *Stubenältester* of the block in which the children were
quartered. In his memoirs, he writes that 158 of the 160 children were kept alive
until the day of liberation. See Hoffman, Erich, "Im Bereich der Hölle von
Auschwitz," *Dokumente des Widerstandes* (Hamburg 1947) p. 88-90.

[128] The following are quotes from her diary (Andreas-Friedrich, *op. cit.*):
"Juden besitzen keine Kleider-Karten . . . [Wir] haben sämtliche Restpunkte in der
Bekanntschaft gesammelt. Für vierzehn Onkel Heinrichs. Und für zwei und
zwanzig Tante Johannas..." (p. 81) "...Man muss die Kinder unterbringen.
Frank hat vier Schützlinge, Heike zwei. Fünf haben sich beim Andrick gemeldet,
und was bei Flamm in dieser Hinsicht gefällig ist, das kann von einen einzelnen
Menschen schon kaum noch bewältigt werden . . ." (p. 100). ". . . Für morgen
habe ich zwei Schlafgelegenheiten. Für übermorgen drei. Ab 15 Dezember [1942]
steht in Lankwitz eine sturmfreie Wohnung zur Verfügung." (p. 102)

[129] *Ibid.*, p. 7.

[130] *The von Hassel Diaries, 1938-1944* (Garden City, N. Y. 1947) p. 14. In
September, 1944, von Hassel was arrested and condemned to death. Sentence was
carried out within two hours.

Several German poets expressed their sense of sorrow and shame in poems which circulated illegally in thousands of copies throughout the land.[131]

The November pogroms also led a number of Germans to take more direct action. In the middle of November, 1938, a number of British Jews in London formed a rescue committee for German Jews. On its behalf, Sir Michael Bruce, a colorful figure with rich experience in special missions of various sorts, was sent to Berlin.[132] In his memoirs, Bruce writes that, on his arrival in Berlin, he approached, through arranged contacts, a secret German organization, whose members were jurists, doctors and military men. According to Bruce, this group did a wonderful job in assisting Jews. All the relief work was conducted in close contact with the leadership of the Berlin Jewish community.[133] Several months priors to this, in March, 1938, Bruce had carried out a similar rescue action on behalf of Viennese Jews, with the cooperation of Austrian anti-Nazis.

> [At the time, Bruce remarks] we therefore built up, with the aid of a group of Austrian anti-Nazis, an escape organization. . . . There were, in fact, a number of these organizations, of which ours was only one. How many people were concerned altogether I have no idea. I believe my own section contained eighty men and women. . . .[134]

It is noteworthy that a number of members of the anti-Nazi opposition, stationed in occupied territories, criticized the anti-Jewish Nazi extermination policy in their letters and even in their memoranda to their superiors. Thus, for example, one high-ranking officer, in a letter from Minsk of November 19, 1941, bitterly criticized the deportations of German Jews to Eastern Europe and the introduction of the yellow badge in Germany. He warned that just retribution would be meted out.[135] General Georg Thomas, chief of the War Produc-

---

[131] See Supplement II.

[132] Prior to his departure for Germany, Bruce conferred with the following British Jews: Lord Rothschild, Lord Samuel, Lionel Rothschild, Neville Laski, and Otto Schiff. See Bruce, Sir Michael, *Tramp Royal* (London 1954) p. 236-239.

[133] Bruce writes that he met with the proprietor of the noted Berlin department store Wilfred Israel, and with the following leaders of the Jewish community: Epstein, Stahl and Seigishon (presumably Seligsohn). *Ibid.*, p. 239.

[134] *Ibid.*, p. 230-231.

[135] "Ausgewählte Briefe von Generalmajor Hellmuth Sieff," *Vierteljahreshefte für Zeitgeschichte* (Munich) vol. ii, no. 3 (1954) p. 302-303: "Es gibt grosse Bahneinschränkungen . . . Aber dafür reicht die Bahn noch aus, jeden zweiten Tag einen Zug mit Juden aus dem Reich zu fahren und sie dann dort ihrem Schicksal preiszugeben. Das ist, ebenso wie der Judenstern in Berlin, wie ich ihn im September dort sah, eines angeblichen Kulturvolkes würdig! *Es muss* sich ja das alles mal

tion Office in the German Ministry of War, was also a staunch opponent of Nazism and member of the opposition. It is, therefore, plausible that it was upon his initiative that the memorandum of December 2, 1941, was prepared by Peter-Heinz Seraphim, German expert on Eastern European affairs. This memorandum pointed out the undesirable consequences of the mass executions of Jews in the Ukraine: in the first place, it weakened the economic potential, particularly that of military supply production; secondly, it had negative repercussions abroad; thirdly, it had a bad effect on German soldiers; and finally, it brutalized the German police responsible for carrying out the executions. At the same time, the memorandum smuggles in, as it were, indirect criticism of the extermination not only of men, but of "old men, women and children." "The great masses executed make this action more gigantic than any similar measure taken so far in the Soviet Union."[136]

In a second such case, an active member of the military opposition, stationed in White Russia, prepared a memorandum on the extermination of Jews. On October 19, 1941, an "extermination platoon" of Einsatzgruppe A celebrated a "festival of the German police," perpetrating a ghastly slaughter of Jews in Borisov, in which over 7,000 people were killed.[137] Both this memorandum and the aforementioned one on the Ukraine evidently went unanswered.

There were rare instances in which German officers and civilian officials not only protested, but aided Jews with actual deeds. In one case, a high-ranking German police officer in Warsaw took great interest in a farm operated by haluzim in Grochow, helping them as

---

an uns rächen, —und mit *Recht!*" General Sieff, a member of the organized opposition of high-ranking officers, was later condemned to death by the Nazis. See Zeller, *op. cit.*, p. 171-172.

[136] "An den Chef des Wi Rue Amtes im OKW, Herr General der Inf. Thomas," *Trial of the Major War Criminals before the International Military Tribunal*, vol. xxxii (Documents) (Nuremberg 1948) doc. PS-3257, p. 71-75; *ibid.*, vol. iii (1947) p. 563-565. In 1944, General Thomas was arrested and sent to the concentration camps of Flossenburg and Dachau. After the war, he published a brief account of his experiences and observations: "Gedanken und Ereignisse," *Schweizer Monatshefte* (December 1945) p. 537-559.

[137] Schlabrendorff, Fabian von, *They almost killed Hitler* (New York 1947) p. 37-38: "This report [on the Borisov massacre] raised such boundless indignation among the officers of our staff that several of them, with tears of rage, assailed Bock, the chief of our Army group, with the demand that he should interfere at once and put a stop to such atrocities. But Bock did not dare to use military force and indict the culprits. He merely ordered me to draft a memorandum to Hitler describing the appalling crime." Cf., Reitlinger, Gerald, *The Final Solution* (New York 1953) p. 196-197.

much as possible.[138] There is no way of knowing whether this German officer was aware that the farm was a base for a Jewish underground organization.

Though in this case there is uncertainty, there are at least some recorded cases of German anti-Nazis consciously and actively working with the Jewish underground. In Bialystok there was an entire group which cooperated. Among its members were: one Schade, director of a textile factory, who was a left Social Democrat; the aforementioned Jehovah's Witness, Busse; a Viennese Communist named Walter; several Sudeten Germans; and a German official whose Jewish wife and daughter had been murdered by the Nazis. This group provided the Jewish underground organization with every possible type of assistance. It saved Jews by providing jobs, false papers, and shelter. It gave arms to the underground and informed it of impending German moves. Two of these Germans were discovered by the Gestapo and sentenced to death.[139]

The case of Anton Schmidt in Vilna is perhaps the most interesting of this type. Schmidt had been pro-Zionist since his pre-war visit to Palestine, and was a thoroughgoing anti-Nazi. He rendered significant assistance to Jews in Vilna, where he was stationed, but was finally caught by the Nazis and sentenced to death by a courtmartial. His friend, the Jewish poet Herman Adler, relates that he was buried under a wooden cross in the German Army cemetery in Vilna.[140]

[138] This interesting story is related by Emanuel Ringelblum in his diary (*op. cit.*, p. 63). In an entry for October 20, 1940, he writes: "The *tsadik* among the Gentiles has berated the Polish commandant of Grochow for imprisoning the haluzim. He held him personally responsible for the safety of every last bit of farm property. He provided a Dutch cow for the farm. He is deeply moved by the fact of Jews [tilling] the soil."

[139] Mark, *op. cit.*, p. 347-348; Grossman, *op. cit.*, p. 388-400.

[140] Dvorshetzky, Mark, *Yerusholayim dlite in kamf un umkum* (Paris 1948) p. 332, 336, 340; Tennenbaum-Tamaroff, Mordecai, *Dapim min hadleka* (Tel Aviv 1948) p. 124. Tennenbaum, commander of the Bialystok resistance organization, refers to Schmidt in the following words: "May Anton Schmidt, a German sergeant from Vienna, be remembered for good. May his soul be bound up in the bundle of life, one of the pious among the nations, who endangered his life in saving hundreds of Jews in the Vilna Ghetto and was a devoted friend of the movement and of the writer. Killed by the gendarmerie because of his contacts with us."

A very detailed account of Schmidt's contacts with the Jewish underground and his aid to Jews is contained in a document preserved in the secret Jewish archives in Warsaw (Ringelblum Archives). It was printed in *Bleter far geshikhte* (Warsaw) vol. iv, no. 1 (1951) p. 96-101, but with many deletions and changes. For this reason, the complete text of the original document is reprinted as a supplement in the Yiddish original of this article, in *Yivo Bleter*, vol. xxxix.

THE BEARING OF EMANCIPATION ON JEWISH SURVIVAL*

By Horace M. Kallen

The theme of my talk this evening is not one I have chosen. It is one that your program committee has assigned to me, with the view of signalizing the one hundred and fiftieth anniversary of the meeting of the Great Sanhedrin which Napoleon I, Emperor of the French, directed the French Jews under his rule to convoke. Called for October 20, 1806, this Sanhedrin did not assemble until February 9, 1807, just about a century and a half ago. Your committee urged that this year's conference of Yivo could appropriately take note of the occasion by a discussion of the "emancipation," toward which that Sanhedrin is assumed to be a step, as "emancipation" bears on "Jewish survival."

This, then, is my theme. I am not sure that anything I can say, or anyone else can say, may in fact have any bearing on what is in the heart of any individual called Jew regarding his own struggle to survive as Jew. I address you without any confidence that my words can affect the inwardness of what you want or do not want to be, for yourselves and your children, the force and form of your Jewish being. I can only feel persuaded by your presence here and by the auspices under which you are present that you are concerned about Jewish survival; and that both are a testimony that emancipation does have a bearing on your concern.

Let me begin by inviting your attention to the terms of my theme. They are the three words: "emancipation," "Jewish," "survival." The nodal one is "survival." How shall we understand survival? What does it denote? The obvious answer is that we survive as we continue to exist, as we go on living, no matter how, or where. But the obvious answer is not the sufficient answer. To survive is not merely to keep living on; it is also to outlive other

* An address before the 31st Annual Conference of Yivo.

235

beings, living and non-living, with which we struggle to live on, with which we struggle for survival. It is a commonplace that "struggle for survival" denotes the human condition, always and everywhere. But precisely because the condition is universal, it discloses nothing of the actualities of the struggle, of its organs and instruments, its strategy, tactics and logistics, of the singularities of their configuration in any personal history or any society's record. These are what distinguish human survival from animal survival, and the survival of one configuration of the human struggle from another.

It is conceivable that one existence may survive another by sheer inertia, by persisting unchanged while the other changes, until death extinguishes it. I presume that Arnold Toynbee, a surrealist writing history, had some illusion of this sort in mind when he classified Judaism as a fossil religion. But this is illusory even in inanimate nature. Simply to exist is to change, to grow older and stronger or weaker and finally to become extinct. Extinct forms are fossil forms. The conditions of their struggle for survival have changed from the animate to the inanimate, and however slow the stretch, they change too, but in an incommensurable way and in an unrelated dimension.

Again, survival may mean that one form has changed more slowly or more rapidly than another, that it is assigned to a different time, that people call it anachronism. Customarily, "anachronism" refers to something that has outlived its own age; but in can just as readily refer to something that anticipates its own age. In experience, our present could consist of the contemporability of anachronisms. Whatever existence lacks functional relevancy to the changing world wherein it struggles to survive because it is either belated or premature is an anachronism. Its struggle for survival is a struggle either against or for changing itself and change of its surroundings. Change itself it must, whether animate or inanimate, functionally relevant or irrelevant. But all the living are also self-outliving things. They have each an individual history. They are born, they grow up, they grow old, they die. The phases of their existence make a consequential pattern of mutations, wherein the newer supervenes upon the older, contains and displaces it, until the process comes to a standstill and survival gives way to extinction. Egg, pupa, chrysalis, caterpillar, butterfly: egg, foetus, infant, child, adolescent, youth, adult. The later phases succeed the earlier and contain them like the phases of a melody or the words of a song.

The same holds for the psychological correlate of the biological succession. Personality creates itself as an ongoing absorption of experience in memory. Memory is the substance of personal identity and any individual who has lost his memory has been deprived of his identity as a person. He goes on as a biological organism, not as this human individual. For mind and body alike, every later formation compenetrates all the foregoing ones in a union which is the enduring individuality for whose survival the individual struggles; which is, indeed, the substance of the struggle itself. To struggle for survival is, first and last, to struggle to keep on struggling. These considerations channel, it seems to me, all the meanings which are given to the word Jew and its variants. What is a Jew? Who is a Jew? For the most part we take the answers as self-evident: Do we not perceive Jews every time we look in our mirrors to shave or to put on lipstick? Do we not for the most part recognize other Jews as we perceive them, in a perception as specific and singular as a thumbprint? Don't we just know that so-and-so is a Jew, and aren't we shocked and upset when we learn that he isn't, and that our intuition has played us false? And in instances when it has not played us false, when our perception who is a Jew is consequentially confirmed, we find our conclusions as to what makes any "who" a Jew involves so many, such diverse, such conflicting, such reciprocally tangent and even unrelated premises, that consensus regarding the conclusion is not to be had. We find that no unexceptionable definition of Jew is practicable, that the diversity of percepts somehow do not project a single concept on which opinions agree, that none applies equally to all individuals and groups everywhere in the world who either call themselves Jews, are so called by others or both. Even when an abstract definition is accepted by the head, the heart may doubt it, and that which is ineffable and irreducible in the personal life may refuse to accept the common denominator which the mind creates and acknowledges.

One such common denominator, perhaps the commonest, consists of a creed and a code; of certain beliefs, attitudes and ways of life enacting the attitudes and beliefs into a communion of conduct which is referred to shared ideals. All such communions survive in and by communication. It is communication that builds communion into community, and the what and how of communication take shape as a body of knowledge. The materials of this body are the artifacts we call symbols: weavings, carvings, paintings, mimes, and langague above all perhaps, language written, spoken, chanted. In the Jewish record, languages have been many and various: Hebrew, from the holy tongue of Scripture to the vernacular of Tel Aviv; Aramaic; Greek; Arabic; Ladino; Yiddish; English. The Hebrew of the Scriptures has sounded obbligato across them all, for most part recessive and marginal but even so outliving its more instantly relevant competitors. To the hearts of many Jews, Yiddish now no less recessive and marginal, has become an equally sacred tongue for whose survival its devotees passionately struggle, while during many years now English has become, among more and more of today's Jews, the dominant medium for the expression of their Jewishness. As once there was a Judeo-Greek version of the Hebrew Bible, so now there is a Judeo-English one; and as the generations had created Greek, Arabic, Ladino and Yiddish literatures uttering the culture and ideals of the Jews of their times, so now the generations are creating a Judeo-English one.

Shall we say that the Hebrew expressions contemporaneous with any of them are more authentically Jewish than these others, that Yiddish is more so than Judeo-Greek or Ladino, or English more so than Yiddish? Not in terms of the ongoing actualities. Not in the history of the Jewish spirit. They are all intrinsic to it, however, in their succession. One has superseded the others, whatever the form of the Hebrew that may have outlived them all. The later, the latest, nevertheless draws its own meaning and values from their succession, and the signification of Jew, Jewish, Jewishness contracts or expands as these figure in Jewry's living past; as they are forgotten or remembered forces and forms in Jewry's construction of its future as Jewish. Each carries a phase of the knowledge and the knowhow, the science and the art of the Jew's struggle for his Jewish survival. Each is in play with regard to the growth and preparation of food, with regard to the Jewish patterns of this essential to survival that is called *kashrut*. It is in play with regard to the clothing Jews may or may not

wear, such as *zizit* and *tefillin, yarmlkes* and *tallesim*. It is in play
with regard to the houses that shelter Jews: whether they fix
mezuzahs to their doorposts, images on their walls and make other
architectural modifications implied by creed and prescribed by
code. It is in play with regard to conceptions of the cause and
cure of disease, the treatment of the hair and beards of men and
the hair of women, the whole cosmetic economy of the person. It
is in play with the begetting and bringing-up of children, the
treatment of the sexes and the role of sexuality. It is in play with
regard to transactions with human beings not Jews, and with the
natural scene, from the man-made jungles of Williamsburg to
Jehovah's desert of Israel's Negev. Each language embodied for
its own users both a traditional and an innovative knowledge and
knowhow. Each still retains them to transmit to the generations
that have taken up other media of communication.

Now it must be obvious that it is the transmittal which holds
the vital role in the struggle for survival. A Jewish community
could take form, mature, age and die out, as it is feared, the community of the Second Aliyah in Israel might, if the elders did not,
in their struggle for Jewish survival, assign a paramount function
to informing the next generation with their Jewishness. Where
this function fails, extinction follows. The function is performed
by means of the records of events, the prescriptions of rites and
rotes graven, written, printed, passed on by word of mouth. Together these make up among Jews, the Bible, Hagadah, Halakhah,
Shulhan Arukh supplemented by the enormous mass of consequential comment, interpretation and reconstruction. Together
these are the directives of what is currently called "Jewish living"
and of worship and education among the diverse societies of Jews,
congregational, communal and others. Their vehicles are all the
languages such societies ever used. And within limits they all repeat certain conceptions which contemporary Jews are declared
to hold in common with their ancestors and to pass on to their
descendants. Such are the doctrines that there exists one and only
one God who is omniscient and omnipotent; that out of all the
families of Mankind, this God has chosen the Jews to be his people; that he has made a covenant with them, the Torah, wherein
he has revealed to them his will; that the Torah embodies a code
which the Jews have covenanted to obey; that in return for obe-

dience, Jehovah pledges them Palestine for their eternal possession; that because they broke the covenant by disobedience they
are in exile from their promised land, but that in the fullness of
time, the Lord will send Messiah son of David to restore them to
it; that a Jew is any one whose life is a discipline defined by these
doctrines. Struggle for Jewish survival would thus be struggle for
the upkeep of doctrine and discipline as the form of the personal
and group existence of human beings called Jews.

Now obviously it is no longer, if it ever was, the case that all
Jews are Jews because they believe and so conduct their lives.
There are many among you here, Jews ineluctably, who do not
believe that you are members of a chosen people, or that you live
in exile and look forward to being returned, either by a super-
naturalist Messiah, or a naturalist Zionism, to the land which the
God of your fathers promised them and their children for an ever-
lasting heritage. Some of you may question the existence of such
a God, the claimed validity of the Torah, and any other items
of the Judaist creed and code. You may give the word "God" various, even irreconcilable definitions. You may pick from Torah
some precepts and repudiate others. Or you may disregard them
all, and impattern the Jewish identity in a configuration of secular elements chosen from the total range of experience, present,
historic, personal and collective which the word "Jew" spans. Individuals agreeing on such selections and acting on them are united
thereby into societies of Jews. These either struggle with one another for the exclusive monopoly of the classification "Jew," shut-
ting out and cutting off, if they can, all who make different selections.

On occasion, confronting a foe to whom the differences of people they call Jews from one another make no difference, these
Jews unite for the common defense of their diverse self-identifi-
cations as Jews. The foe may be "pagan" and his warfare with
Jewry may have the motivation which all warfare has, whether
between alien or kindred peoples. In the long history of the Jewish societies since the rise of Christianity, the warfare is seminally
religious. It is signalized as the "anti-Semitism" of western culture, and is also postulated on belief in divine election and divine
rejection. This belief is not so singular to Jews as many of them
imagine. By and large it is an aspect of the attitude toward it-

self of any company of human beings comparing itself with other companies. It turns on an appraisal by an "in-group" of all outsiders. Let the in-group be a race, a nationality, a caste, a class, a profession or what have you. It makes up a closed society which assigns to itself a preferential status, and seeks to penalize outsiders simply because they are outsiders. The Greeks did it in characterizing non-Greeks as barbarians. The Christians do it in characterizing non-Christians as misbelievers and infidels, and especially the non-Christians who are Jews as a people once God-chosen now rejected by the God who chose them and replaced with another divine favorite, the Christians. The Moslems make similar distinctions. The Brahmans have their Sudras, and the "White" Citizens' councils of our Southland have their Negroes. For that matter, each such category of the Chosen splits up into sects and denominations and classes which in their turn treat each other as in- and out-groups. If the Judaists in the Jewish aggregate separate into Orthodox, Conservative, Reformed, Reconstructionist, Neture Karta, "Malochim" and the like, the Christians diversify as Catholics and Protestants, and these again into other denominations; the Muslims vary similarly, and so on everywhere among mankind.

But there is no other communion in the western world whose status is, like the Jews', reversed from the Chosen People to the Rejected People, as an article of religious faith. The Christian creed, whatever the denomination, declares the Jews to be an out-group to Christians wherever they dwell. The intellectual and democratic revolutions that got their start in the seventeenth century, with their new knowledge and new view of human relations, are altering this combination of faith and works, but it is still intrinsic to the Christian creed. This states that God as the Father had chosen the Jews in order that they should be the people of the sinless Virgin whom he had foreordained to become the human mother of God as the son assuming the flesh and form of man in order as such to suffer, be crucified and rise again, so that the original sin which no mere human can atone for, should nevertheless be atoned, and the children of Adam who accept this vicarious atonement thereby be saved from the wages of sin, which is death. But the people of Mary, mother of God, did not take her divine son for their Savior. They protested his claims and rejected his atonement. Whereupon God, the Father, rejected them. In their stead he chose those who did "believe on the Christ" and thus assured themselves of eternal salvation. He made with them a new covenant whereby the Jews were shut out and cut off from free communication with Christian mankind. They are permitted to live on, not as of right but on sufferance, as a testimony to the Faith until the son shall return to earth in glory as he had first walked it in humility. They live everywhere an out-group under penalty for their protest and dissent.

Jewry's reaction to this isolation and penalization was a mode of self-isolation, never entirely complete, but sufficient to create and sustain a hardly permeable boundary of Judaic creed and code within whose directives the institutions of their common life made up a ghetto. The Jewish denizen of this municipal configuration was widely believed, regardless of whether the believer ever met a Jew in fact, to be an evil, dirty, ugly, repulsive and disgusting alien, working at tasks forbidden to Christians, and without any rights a Christian was bound to respect. He could go on living his forfeit life only under protection, and at a ransom.

The Enlightenment, as it came to review and to criticize the creed and code on which this image of the Jew was postulated, found itself also reviewing the image, although reluctantly. England's "glorious Revolution" of 1688 was the social and political background of the critique and review. Its initiating faith gave rise to a movement whose next critical phase was the Democratic Revolution of 1776 in the British colonies of North America. The consequential spokesman of the "Glorious Revolution," the voice of its faith and vision, was the philosopher, John Locke. His conceptions of the human understanding, political organization, religious attitudes, and human relations in general figured seminally among the ideas of the Age of Reason or the Enlightenment. Many of its attitudes became largely extensions and adaptations of Locke's attitudes. Thus, what he had to say in his Letters of Toleration about the state or commonwealth and the role in it of sects and denominations, became in due course the view of the Age. The Commonwealth, Locke there wrote, is "a society of men constituted for the procuring, preserving and advancing their own civil interests" whereas "the care of every man's soul belongs unto himself and is to be left unto himself"; hence, since a creed is concerned with the soul, creeds cannot qualify commonwealths; "there is absolutely no such thing as a Christian commonwealth.... Neither the pagan, nor Mohammedan, nor Jew ought to be excluded from the civil rights of the Commonwealth because of his religion." Locke did make an exception to this rule of the Roman Catholics. He justified excluding Roman Catholics from civil rights on historic and personal grounds. The record showed the Roman Church to be an organization of political interests engaged in a conspiracy against the Commonwealth, "cloaked in the monkish hood of religion." As Locke saw the Papacy, it was a totalitarian international government aiming to conquer the world, thus a menace to government everywhere. Its priests, committed, not to the pursuit of truth but the propagation of church dogma, were not entitled to open and conduct schools or to serve on faculties. Their sole aim was the conspiratorial one to pervert youth "to the iniquitous ends of Papacy." The Lockeian combination of record and interpretation voiced a general sentiment which denied Roman Catholics in England equal civil rights until well into the nineteenth century, whereas in the United States they came with pagans, Mohammedans and Jews under the protection of the Lockeian principle of the separation of church and state.

His principle became in the course of time the consensus of the leading spirits of the Enlightenment. From his perspectives of human nature and human relations they drew an image of man and man's condition which they put in the place of the image postulated by the creeds and codes of the traditional religion. Man, they came to believe, is the child of nature and is endowed by nature with certain inherent and inalienable rights. All human beings participate in a common humanity and are, in spite of apparent differences, really the same and equal. But their identity and equality are overlaid by diversifications due to their association with one another in churches, states, economic endeavors, and other cultural deformations. It is these that generate the invidious social distinctions of birth, caste, class, faith, sex, occupations and possessions, imposing artificial differences not to be found in the state of nature, and requiring the inhumanities of man to man to maintain them. By the laws of nature and of nature's God, all men are created equal; all are brothers, equally children of God their Father, although the Enlightenment no longer thought that

God had made men in his own image, or that the visage of finite man could be the image of infinite God. The God of the Enlightenment was imaged prevailingly as *Deus,* not *Theos;* its conception of Deity like its conception of Humanity was more abstract, more impersonal, more generalized and mathematical than the traditional one. The belief that mankind are people whose differences from one another are by nature indifferent became a powerful shaper of the sequences which the Democratic Revolution consummated.

In the light of this belief, the dogmas and disciplines by which priests and princes rationalized their pretensions and validated their powers appeared de jure as well as de facto false and evil. To study them, to expose them alike as institutions and teachings, became intrinsic to the Age's intellectual enterprise. The undertakings which got to be called sciences of Man, "higher criticism" and its methods, were adopted from the methods that had proven so fruitful in the sciences of nature. Personages such as Voltaire, Diderot, the other contributors to Diderot's great Encyclopedia carried forward and diversified the initiatives of John Locke into fanes, the most secret and sacred, hitherto taboo to all profane inquiry and immune to every doubt. Their candid view of the figures and events of the Old Testament discovered a Jehovah who was a repulsive, cruel, vengeful and bloody tyrant, and a religion throughout its history superstitious, fanatical and intolerant, embodied in a Torah and Talmud whose teachers and teachings were enemies of all that the Illuminati meant by the human spirit. As for Jehovah's Chosen People—such Jews of their own day as they encountered in France, or Alsace, or Germany or Poland—what were they in actuality but dirty, lustful, prolific usurers exploiting peasants and nobles alike, clannishly keeping themselves strangers and apart everywhere, refusing to send down roots in the lands where they dwell, craving a Messiah to return them to Zion their Promised Land, and uttering attitudes and aspirations in a German-Hebrew rabbinical jargon. As you are, of course, aware, Jews themselves deprecated this language of theirs as jargon, and only a couple of generations or so ago began to reverence it as Yiddish.

Men with good will toward the Jews who championed their emancipation agreed with both secularist and sacerdotal anti-

Semites. Thus, the Abbe Gregoire, who is notable among the spirits arguing that the emancipation of Jews must be included in the more general emancipation of mankind, describes them (*Sur La Regeneration Physique, Morale et Politique des Juifs*, 1789) as "a state within a state" headed by "fanatic, narrow, ignorant rabbis" who, "instead of expanding the horizons of the human spirit... have consecrated its errors and declared as dogmas the false offspring of a delirious imagination." Voltaire, whose essay, *Tolerance*, carried the intent of English Locke's *A Letter Concerning Toleration* to all the freedom-seeking minds of Europe, wrote that he would sit and eat with "even a Jew, provided the Jew frees himself first of his hateful Jewish superstitions and prejudices."

The expressions I have quoted are representative. They convey a consensus on what the Jew looked like to those who favored his "emancipation" and those who opposed it. The latter held to the image of the Jew elaborated in Eisenmenger's *Entdecktes Judenthum*. However mistaken, it continued prevalent from 1700 and was honestly taken for true. Foes of emancipation invoked it as they argued that whatever emancipation might contribute toward improving the human nature of other enslaved peoples, it could contribute nothing toward improving the nature of the Jews. Some even doubted that Jewish nature was in fact human or could be. Proponents of emancipation were divided. Some held that it should be preceded by conversion, others held that it should supervene upon spontaneous self-reformation. Still others argued that both conversion and self-reformation are dependent on freedom, and that emancipation is, hence, the condition precedent to all desirable change in the Jewish nature; that it was the indispensable condition, as Herder urged, for "humanizing" the Jews.

To all groups alike, emancipation of Jew by Gentile was the same as the liberation of the Jews from their Judaism. It was to consist in liquidating the complex of attitudes, beliefs, memories, creeds, codes, works and ways whereby Jews altogether constituted Jews. As Clermont Tonnère advised the French National Assembly in 1791: "To the Jews as a people we owe nothing. To the Jews as human beings, everything." The price of equal liberty for any Jew was to be eradication of all in his individuality whereby he is a Jew. It was to be what has since come to be called "assimilation" with Judaism at most one of Locke's private perspectives upon some common faith. (The American Council for Judaism is a contemporary Judaist endeavor toward this end.) It discloses that the age of the Enlightenment used "emancipation" even as the ages of the theological darkness which it was struggling to dissipate, had used, and were using, isolation and degradation to shut out and cut off the Jew as Jew from the fellowship of mankind, and to cut off and shut out as such what is believed to be Jewish from the humane culture of the civilized world. "Humanizing" the Jew a la Herder was to destroy him as Jew, at most to reduce him to a Judaist. In effect the Enlightenment's toleration did not extend to the Jews, to their religion or to their culture and ideals.

Consequent to the Enlightenment, motivated by its vision of human nature and human relations, were the democratic revolutions of 1776 over here, and of 1789 in France, and more or less on the continent of Europe. In France, the drama of events turned liberation into terror and tyranny displaced the principles of Condorcet and Lafayette with the practices of Robespierre and Bonaparte. The latter, having made himself master of France and much of civilized Europe, and now considering the lusts and loyalties on which the security of his regime rested, gave some of his attention to the Jews and their condition. His image of them was that common to the men of the Enlightenment and their revolutionary epigons. A military statesman to whom religion signified, like all other human interests, only one more instrument of policy in the drive for power and dominion, Napoleon of course so viewed the Jews and their religion. If he advised the near-Eastern congregations that he intended to restore "Holy Jerusalem," he also threatened those of Alsace that he would "consider the Jews as a nation and not as a sect," thus intensifying their already extensive and penalizing isolation. In order that the assimilation of Jew into Frenchman might be sped, and that the commitment of the Jewries to the paramountcy over the Torah of the Code Napoleon be publicly and unreservedly promulgated by their leaders, he convoked an "Assembly of Jewish Notables." This was in 1806. Of this Assembly the Emperor asked twelve questions. He wanted statements of the Jewish position on marriage and divorce, on intermarriages, on dual allegiance, on the relations between religious and secular governments, on usury, and on the occupations wherewith Jews might earn their livings.

Of course the notables produced answers intended to satisfy their Emperor. They said what he wanted them to say. But they failed to provide him the certainty he required. He doubted if their authority was authentically authoritative. He required it to be validated by their religious authorities and validated for all times. So he had the Notables convoke a "Great Sanhedrin," to be composed of seventy-one spokesmen for all the Jewries of Napoleonic Europe, two-thirds of them to be rabbis. They defined themselves as Frenchmen of the Reformed Mosaic persuasion. They greeted Napoleon as their Messiah, and they arranged for the reorganization of the Jewish Congregation into "consistories." These were to be exclusively religious bodies, with hierarchies of rabbis and grand rabbis. One third of their membership was to be drawn from the lay communicants, none of whom had ever gone into bankruptcy or practiced usury. Consistorial government was to enforce decorum in worship and otherwise insure that the congregations produced their full quotas for Napoleon's armies and to supervise occupations. So reorganized and controlled, communities of Jews, the Emperor of the French believed, would be thinned down into congregations of Judaists, of Frenchmen of the Reformed Mosaic faith. Of course they also might consummate the assimilative purpose by conversion to Roman Catholicism or some other form of the Christian cultus. A different alternative, not envisaged, was secularization.

So much for the principle and program of "emancipation" as the Gentile, Christian and non-Christian, intended it. Among Jews it exercised a dual role. By and large, the restive and rebellious ones among them, the ones hungry for the obvious liberties enjoyed by Gentiles, tended to acquiesce in the Gentile image of the Jew, much as so many of their descendants, under Hitler, acknowledged the Nazi image, and referred to themselves as "non-Aryans." Hitler, you recall, had decreed that mankind consists of but two races, the "Aryan" or Nazi race, made up of him and his ilk, and the human race, making up the rest of mankind. He had decreed that the human race were soon to be living tools of the Nazi superhumanity, to be its servants and menials. But he excluded the Jews even from that category. He assigned them a sub-human status, and Hitlerite monstrosities like Himmler elaborated the assignment into a mad zoology with which he built his paranoiac rationalizations of his sadist obscenities toward people called Jews.

It is a significant phenomenon in intergroup relations—not by any means obtaining only among Jews—that the people thus devalued and despised, came to take the same attitude toward themselves and to seek every means to rid themselves of this outwardly suffered and inwardly felt dehumanization. To such self-oriented Jews, their "Judaism" was in Heine's oft-quoted words, not a religion but a misfortune. And how else can a man act toward a misfortune if not to put an end to it as he is able? Putting an end to the misfortune of Judaism, in the Christian culture which so instituted it, could be accomplished most simply and directly by means of "apostasy." Such Jews as Heinrich Heine, Ludwig Börne, Benjamin Disraeli, the descendants of Moses Mendelssohn looked to find in *shmad* an open sesame to the life more abundant and the things more excellent of the Christian culture. The emancipation they decided upon was an emancipation from Judaism, an excision of the totality of the Jewish being from their personal lives so far as they could achieve it. They decided upon suicide as Jews, that they might live on as something else. It is in these terms that Karl Marx made his communist version of the Enlightenment's version of the Christian principle for solving "the Jewish Question." But the subsequent attitudes toward their discarded Judaism of such worldly successes as Disraeli, and such literary successes as Heine point to a kind of zombie Judaism haunting the *vita nuova* of the emancipated. In whatever terms—racial, religious, cultural, ethical—they tend to exalt what they believed themselves to have discarded, while other converts manifested an analogous attitude via pathological exaggeration of the prevailing image of the Jew which they had hoped their conversion would eradicate. That it didn't was expressed by an anti-Semitism transcending any which non-Jews devised. Their hatred of the Jewish identity from whose disabilities conversion was to be the emancipation bound them all the closer to it, rendering their anti-Semitism almost a way of life. The case was different, somewhat, with those Jews whom the idea of conversion repelled and who sought emancipation in simply abandoning the ways and works of the Jewish communes, or by means of political action or else by identifying themselves as "socialists" instead of Jews, and digesting the singularities of being a Jew into the generality of being a worker, compelled by his needs and his separateness from the other workmen everywhere, to live the bondsman of whoever owned the tools with which he worked. "Workmen of the world unite, you have nothing to lose but your chains" was like the call to conversion, a call to liberation by means of assimilation, but not into Christianity. The emancipation envisaged was secular; the image of the emancipated was a political economist's, not a theologian's; revolutionary, not conformist.

I said that the idea of emancipation exercised a dual role. I turn now to the second of these roles. It differs from the first in that it does not call for the abandonment of Judaism but for its reformation. Its avatars concede much in the image of the Jew that the non-Jewish critics of the Jewish being dislike and condemn. But they do not conclude that these require suicide as Jew. They choose to preserve and perfect some traits, eradicate others, reshape still others. Their avatar is Moses Mendelssohn, a sage of the Enlightenment among the Illuminati, a prophet of the Enlightenment to the Jews. He agreed that Yiddish was a barbarous jargon and endeavored—not without initiating a kind of lettered snobdom in many of the *shtetls*—to replace it with German. He wanted to raze "the Ghetto of the mind," to translumine the substance of Scripture and the Talmud with the vision and the wisdom of the *Aufklärung;* he aspired to modernize them, but not to the point of abandoning the belief that the Jews were God's chosen people to whom he had revealed the moral law. In the spirit of the Enlightenment, Mendelssohn held that reason, with its dependence on equations expressing necessary connections of cause and effect, was somehow inadequate to the freedom and responsibility required by human existence and the sequences of human history. It is the latter which our action generates and sustains, and our action can be distinguished as right or wrong, good or bad only in the light of the revealed code. Judaism, for Mendelssohn, consists of such a code; he wrote in *Jerusalem* (1783) "I do not see how those who are born in the house of Jacob can at all conscientiously emancipate themselves from the Law." And the Law has an otherworldly dimension not subject or in conflict with the findings of reason about what the universe is and how

it got that way. For Judaism, the code of conduct needs no dogmas about God and the world to validate it.

Events did not confirm the Mendelssohnian reappraisal. The
Judaist Reformation did in fact so take shape as to "emancipate
from the Law," and to transpose the Jewish people, everywhere
even as in Napoleonic France, into such and such nationals of
"the Mosaic persuasion." The Reformation emancipated its aficionados from the notions of a Galut and of a Heaven-sent Messiah
who should restore the exiles from their Galut to the God-prom-
ised land of Israel. These the Judaist Reformation replaced with
an image of the Jews as a "priest-people," holy as the Lord their
God is holy, providentially dispersed among the nations to bear
witness to an "ethical monotheism" forever. The overall consequence was, more or less to separate the components of the Jewish culture-complex, to develop divergences which require the
student to distinguish as sharply between Jew and Judaist as he
distinguishes between American and Christian or Frenchman and
Moslem, or German and Catholic. It is in the enclaves of the Reformation, especially among the epigons of Mendelssohn in Germany, that Jews came to look at Judaism with the vision and in
the perspectives that the great English and French proponents of
the Enlightenment looked at Christianism and all religions. The
"Wissenschaft des Judenthums" lives in the application of these
attitudes to all that can be sought out, discerned and inquired
into, of the Jewish record.

The trend of the Judaist Reformation was centrifugal and
stayed so till long after the insurgence of that other consequence
of emancipation, Zionism. Before Zionism came the Jewish Renaissance, which followed the Reformation, whereas among the
Christian peoples—except the Germans—their Reformation followed their Renaissance. The Jewish Renaissance like the Judaist
Reformation was a consequence of Europe's Age of Reason, and
an effect of the Enlightenment. Its place was the *shtetl* of Eastern
and Slavic Europe. Although the armies of Napoleon carried something of the intention of the Revolution of 1789 right into the
heart of the Muscovite tyranny, its influence, if it had any, did
not become overt till generations later: neither democratism nor
socialism affected the *shtetl*'s climate of opinion save negatively
or tangently. The positive influence consisted in the constellation

of attitudes, beliefs, programs and the like for which the traditional term is Haskalah.

Haskalah brought the attitudes, understandings and values of
the Enlightenment into the *shtetl*. It was the paramount liberator
of the Jewish mind from its ghetto. It transvalued the "Jargon" of
the daily life into the Yiddish of literary excellence. It resurrected
Hebrew from the *loshon kodesh* of tradition into a contemporary
medium of communication regarding life and letters among a small
circle of modern-minded Jews and Jewesses. It gave "assimilation" a
reverse direction, for instead of dissolving Jewishness and Judaism
in the Gentile culture, it brought the liberating works and vision
of the Gentile world into the Jewish enclaves, there to be assimilated into, and by nourishing to enlarge and transvalue, the image
of the Jew.

With the Haskalah Emancipation became far less emancipation from, far more emancipation for, the survival of the Jewish
ethos in its diverse formations. Its intention was reenforced by
the nationalist ideal with which the peoples of Europe countered
the imperial oppression of Napoleonic France. The basic postulate
of that aggression was still the Enlightenment's conception of mankind as all natural men with inborn natural rights, each the same
as the others, each equal with the others, each different from the
others only because of society's force majeure which artificially
created and forcefully imposed the differences. By nature, free men
are equal men, interchangeable with one another. Emancipation
was to be the liberation of the individual from the social rule
with its false differentiations.

However, the peoples of Europe found that in practice this
emancipation consisted in but replacing a familiar and mitigated
native despotism by a strange, untempered foreign one. They
found that they felt freer under masters of their own familiar kind
that under alien soi-disant liberators. They found that the individual came into his own personal freedom far more readily and
surely in, through, and by the collectivity among whom he lived
and moved and had his being, than by abstracting himself, by separating from them and going it alone. They experienced a more
positive emancipation in their like-minded resistance to the Napoleonic aggression. The name of the rationale of this positive emancipation is prevailingly "nationalism." Variants of it are "racism,"

"culturism." Often "nationalism" comprehends them all, and then more. Its foremost spokesmen of the time have been the Germans Fichte and Hegel, and the Italian Mazzini. The Germans reinstated the in-group loyalties and out-group hatreds with their traditional relations. They presented the German-speaking peoples as the Chosen People, scions of the single Aryan master race, creators and missioners of a *Kultur* predestined to save the world from barbarism. The Italian reinstated the in-group and out-group in the perspectives of the Democratic Revolution. He saw mankind as a cooperative family of nations, each the equal of the others, each an organ of humanity endowed with its own singularity of vocation and culture, and each entitled to collective freedom as the ground and condition of the individual freedom of its members.

Both philosophies of nationalism affected the outlook and program of Jewish emancipation. With the German ones came anti-Semitism again, this time transposed into the racist and Kulturist conceptions which Hitler and his sadistocracy have put to such abominable uses. With the Italian one came a secularist confirmation of the persistent traditional nationalism of the world's Jewries. Both brought a certain disillusion regarding the Enlightenment's conception of emancipation as the liquidation of the Jew into, at most, a Judaist of such and such nation. It must be remembered that these new attitudes were long in penetrating the hard core of Jewry. This continued "orthodox" and built, against changes, defenses, sometimes even modernist ones, which brought changes of their own. Figures like Shneur Zalman, founder of the HaBaD, purported to stay unyielding of creed and code, and to fight against their violation or alteration even unto death. Such self-segregating groups as the Hassidim, Neture Karta, Agudath Israel, struggle for their own survival in terms of this image of themselves. Whether their intolerance could succeed without the toleration projected by the principle and effected in the program of Emancipation is hardly an open question.

In the nationalist climate of opinion, Jews who believed in the principle and program, who had pursued emancipation and struggled toward assimilation, found themselves, as individuals, confronting anti-Semite barriers anew, barriers bristling with the new conceptions of "Jew" and laid out by the new methods that

Europe's nationalism, racism and Marxism were projecting. These innovations were translating the chronic anti-Semitism of the Christian religion into acute secular forms requiring corresponding secular Jewish defenses. Many of the emancipated Jews were aware how little conversion could avail a convert against the racist denotation of the term "Jew." Indeed the Nazi doctrines of the twentieth century and the Stalinite and post-Stalinite Soviet applications of their Marxist ones brought many to recall how in the Spanish hands, Jewish converts to Roman Catholicism and their descendants, however devout, were kept segregated from their Gentile co-religionists from the times of Ferdinand and Isabella to those of Franco. It was, thus, not merely out of cowardice or conformities that emancipated Jews of the nineteenth century, whether Maskilim or religious modernists or utter assimilationists, suffused the traditional Jewish belief that they were a people or nation, and how and why they were such, with the new European nationalism. Certain of them transvalued the divine, messianic restoration of the Israel of God's promise into this-worldly recovery of their well-remembered ancient homeland by Jews returning to it and restoring it with the work of their hands. They identified and thus secularized the Judaist doctrine of Galut with the Gentile conception, "the Jewish Problem." They secularized the Judaist doctrine of ingathering and redemption of the exiles into the theory and practice of Zionism. Moses Hess, Leon Pinsker, Ahad Haam, Theodor Herzl, Max Nordau, and their kind were figures of the emancipation, disillusioned with emancipation, persuaded that the democratic ideal could not prevail against the nationalist and racist anti-Semitism of such freer societies as France, Germany, Austria, even England, to say nothing of the autocracies of Europe's eastern lands.

The same held for many Jews who had identified emancipation with socialism, whether democratic or Marxist. They also reverted to the traditional doctrine that Palestine is the land of the Jews, that they are in exile from it and will be neither free nor safe until they return to it. They also reshaped the belief by means of European nationalism, but a nationalism embodying socialist principles and programs. Nachman Syrkin may be said to have spoken for all denominations of them, when he declared "Zionism is a realization of socialism among the Jewish people."

Even Chaim Zhitlovsky came around to this view. A scion of the Lubavitcher *kloyz*, he very early became an apostle of the cult of the dehumanized, denationalized abstraction, the universal proletarian worker of the Marxist creed. However, events continually altered his perspectives. During much of his life, he figured as a prophet of "diaspora nationalism." In old age, he found a domicile of belief in Poale Zionism as well. Events had kept forcing upon him the recognition that the actualities of Jewish existence possessed certain positive differentiae, and his activities alternated between endeavors to defend and improve this angering life via his "socialist revolutionary" faith and his apostolic service to this faith in Europe and the United States. We find him restoring to his universal "workman" the secular singularities of the Jewish being, such especially as the Yiddish language. We find him challenging Zionism and proposing a socialist Yiddishism as an alternative. We find him urging upon the angry, sarcastic, irreligious Yiddish-speaking, anti-Jewish, anti-nationalist internationalist of the lower East Side's *yidishe gas* the synergic consistency of nationalism and socialism for his Yiddish people. We find him, with Y. L. Peretz and Nathan Birnbaum, persuading the Conference on the Yiddish Language which they convoked together at Czernowitz, to declare Yiddish the national language of the Jews. We find him urging Jews of the United States and Canada to establish secular Yiddish schools (now called *folkshuln* and in many places named for Sholom Aleichem). We find him at last a protagonist of the Congress movement in the American Jewish community, at once a Zionist and a diaspora-nationalist, who would set up, as the vital centre of this nationalism for Jews, a religion of Yiddishism and Socialism. What is known as the Bund makes the impression of a church confessing this faith. The turning point in Zhitlovsky's career of doctrine and discipline had been an argument widespread among his Gentile socialist-revolutionary comrades that pogroms against Jews were logically necessary steps toward the emancipation of all Russians. He could not stomach this conclusion from their dialectic of emancipation. He decided that Jewish emancipation had to be national wherever Jews lived, but in socialist modes. His first and last commitment was to a "diaspora nationalism" which included Zionism but gave it no preferential status.

Without socialism, without the Promised Land, Diaspora Nationalism becomes a nationalism of culture, the sort of nationalism Simon Dubnow professed. Such a nationalism follows from the intention of "emancipation" wherever the Jewish individual learns to recognize that he cannot abolish the Jewish components of his personal history; that his personal survival requires their perseveration and cultivation; that the latter are group activities, never to be effected in isolation, and that the groups involved are all such called Jews, always and everywhere. Simon Dubnow seems to have learned this in Poland. He came to argue that the Jewish psyche, the substance of which is the history of the attitudes, the faiths, the works and ways of *klal-yisroel*, is the same as the culture of the Jews, and that this is the same as their nationhood. It is a configuration of the spirit independent of place and developing through time. It is that in virtue of which Jews everywhere constitute one "cultural historical people." Palestine is no more essential to its survival than Poland, Poland than Australia or the United States. The collectivity which it organizes and defines can live on anywhere. But if it singles out any sole place it at once enters into a struggle with the political economy singular to the place and takes on the aggressive isolationism which having and holding the place necessitates. When the Jewish people lost Palestine, they became a landless people, with a developing pacific and truly ethical outlook. This is a creation of all Jews, generation by generation. It includes the excommunicated Spinoza even more than the communion which excommunicated him. Its secular components are as significant as its religious ones, and should not be subordinated to the latter. No item of Judaism is static; all evolve, and this means that the Yiddish and the socialism of Yiddishists are also passing phenomena in the total configuration that defines the Jews a "cultural-historical" nation figuring as one among others and needing to figure freely and equally with them in the multinational states of Europe. To Dubnow and his aficionados, emancipation for the individual Jew as Jew had to be secondary and derivative. It had to follow from the emancipation of the Jewish collectivities and their attainment of equality with the neighboring collectivities in freedom and rights. A Jew's freedom as Jew and for Judaism was to be attained by the emancipation of his in-group from the out-group bondage and disabilities imposed by other in-groups. Diaspora nationalism presumed this form of emancipation.

So much for the principles and programs of Jewish emancipation in Europe. In our United States Jews came to equal liberty and equal rights in quite other patterns of vision and action. Their source and sustenance are what has come to be called "the American Idea"—the creed and the code by virtue of which the American peoples are American. In the perspectives of the American Idea, the import of emancipation is not the suppression or liquidation of differences in sameness; it is not assimilation. It is the liberation of differences, their reciprocal protection and cultivation. Emancipation is the Democratic Revolution as the persistent struggle to remove penalty after penalty of all those which the traditional culture of the West—to say nothing of the rest of the world—had laid upon differences from the dominant classes and castes in "race," religion, sex, color, occupation, ancestry, possessions and so on, the absorption of privilege for some in equal opportunity and equal right for all. Underlying is a fighting faith that the right to be is nothing else than the right to be different; that this right inheres equally in all individuals struggling to preserve themselves, whatever their characters and roles; that law and government are devices to secure this right; that all associations and associations of associations are devised as means of assuring each individual associate equal conditions of freedom and safety in which to make his own different struggle to live on and be at home, not only in, but because of, the company of the other strugglers. The American Idea denotes a design for living which should convert men's feelings of exile into sentiments of freely belonging; it would emancipate their psyches from fear of the different and sense of aliency and homelessness among the different; it would generate and sustain in them the opposite sense of belonging together and being at home with one another as different. We may call this design, whose basic pattern is given in the Declaration of Independence and the Constitution, the plan of the peoples of America for their own Americanization.

There are many, in and out of our United States, who regard this grand design as utopian, and with good reason. They point to the persistence and power of old privilege, to the continual irruption of new. They point to the constant resurgence of penalties upon difference and the denials of freedom and safety to one sort of diversity or another in every state in the nation. Because the Idea of America is only spottily embodied in the fact of America, they belittle the event that the history of the United States is the history of an inveterate struggle completely to achieve this embodiment; that however diverse the lapses, however many the setbacks, the embodiment struggles forward, generation by loyal generation, reform by arduous reform.

This is why, whatever the resistances to the grand design of the Americanization of Americans have been and continue to be, emancipation according to the American Idea is emancipation *for* rather than *from,* creative rather than defensive. By intention, it releases the energies of men, elsewhere absorbed in preserving themselves against persecution, oppression, exploitation, for the free enterprises which diversely compose the human career. It secures to every individual alike the freedom at his own risk to think, to speak, to write, to invent, and to trade—by himself alone or in association with others—in the values of all fields of man's life and works: economic, political, religious, artistic, scientific, sporting. It enables a free trade between them in the spiritual, material and cultural diversities of their creation, a trade whereby each has his opportunity to contribute toward a life more abundant for all. Thus, the associations and movements which are known as the inter-faith, intercultural, interracial are of American origin and development. The United States began with the free, voluntary joining together of thirteen sovereign and independent states into a Federal Republic. They have made themselves one country, *e pluribus unum,* by means of their reciprocal commitment to the American Idea. Despite the resistance of tradition, recurrent disloyalties to the commitment, historically the Idea has been the shaping directive of the nation's development into a pluralistic society the union of whose diversities is the equal assurance to each by all of its rights freely and safely to be its different self. As against emancipation in Europe, this is what emancipation signifies in the United States.

For obvious reasons, it was harder for Jewish than for Gentile immigrants to appreciate this meaning of emancipation and to avail themselves of it. They found in due course that the anxieties and fears intrinsic to their trans-Atlantic value-systems received little sustaining nourishment in the United States. It did not take many generations, as history counts generations, to replace the prehension of emancipation as negation and flight by its prehension as diversified Yea-saying, development and cooperation. De Tocqueville had noted already in the 1840's that "in no country in the world has the principle of association been more successfully used or applied to a great multitude of objects than in America."

Thus, whereas "assimilation" continues to denote the self-liquidation of the Jewish psyche, the suicide of the Jew as Jew, this significance is being challenged and displaced by the realization that the Jew can as Jew be the assimilator instead of the assimilatee; that assimilation can consist in his nourishing his Jewishness by spiritual and cultural sustenance drawn as he participates in them from all the configurations the land diversely sustains. Assimilation of the Jew gets displaced with assimilation by the Jew.

Or an association of Jews may struggle on by endeavoring to nourish their Judaism exclusively on their Judaistic heritage: they may safely and freely refuse participation and exchange. The ways of the communions of Williamsburg or Brownsville are as unpenalized as those of the communions of Fifth Avenue. In terms of the Judaist tradition, there ranges between these two limits a diversified series of creeds and codes in virtue of which Judaism is as pluralistic as Protestantism. In this respect the Judaism of American Jews contrasts sharply with the much more infertile Judaisms of Europe and Israel. There, the alternative is either Jew or Judaist, either Judaist or infidel; in the United States none need shut the other out. All the diversities can, if they so choose, freely join together in order to assure to one another their diverse survivals. The same has held and holds for the Jewish as distinguished from the Judaist components of the Jewish culture-complex. If the Jewish communities of the United States have developed into the freest, the most diversified, the most prosperous, powerful and dynamic in the world, it is not because the tragedy of history has removed their most likely competitors in Europe, nor because the cultural economy of the State of Israel, however sanguine our view of its present and hopes for its future, is not yet able to go on its own resources. What the American Jewish communities have become, what they can grow into as configurations of Jewish culture and ideals, follows from the shaping influence of the American Idea taken as a fighting faith in the Jewish struggle for survival. Elsewhere, survival may contract to the repetition by diminishing generations of some form of the Judaist faith and the rites and rotes of this faith. It may, indeed become a hardening and fossilization. In the United States survival has consisted in an expanding struggle to go on struggling during which new beliefs, new ideas, new institutions, new ways of life and thought grow from the old, transform, absorb and use the old as a living past, presently creating a more diversely vital and abundant future.

Now in different degree, emancipation has brought to the Jewish being this heightened potential of self-development and self-enrichment in every land which has not blighted by anti-Semitism this release of the Jew's power to grow as Jew, or which has not starved and destroyed it by totalitarianism. Between the sittings of Napoleon's Sanhedrin and the totalitarian epidemic, red, black and brown, which poisoned Europe and still threatens all the world, the Jewish population of the West had increased from two and one half millions to fifteen or sixteen millions. In the *shtetls* of the Russian Pale, as well as in the free communities of American cities, the "jargon" of 1800 was transposed into the vital medium of literary expression of 1900 and beyond, while Hebrew was restored to a similar role, and English became a runner-up. The number and variety of professions and occupations by which Jews might earn their livings steadily multiplied, and their innovative role in the arts and sciences became so notable as to arouse anti-Semitic excommunication from the fields.

True, concurrently came pogroms, blood-accusations, the rest of the anti-Semite's armament against the Jews. Let us take full account of the Stalinist and Hitlerite mutations of traditional anti-Semitism and of the genocidal mania which aimed to destroy the object and to nullify the European credo of emancipation. Nevertheless it is of record that the credo has there served as a catalyzer and releaser both among non-Jews and Jews. Among non-Jews, notwithstanding the Toynbeean fantasies, the ideals of the Enlightenment have brought into being a humanistic understanding and appreciation of Judaism, of the Jewish culture-complex and of the people who by their participation in them are Jews. It is an understanding and appreciation sought and attained in the spirit of science and by the methods of science. It has enabled the discarding of the fantastic distinction between Jew as Jew and Jew as human being. It has brought about the acknowledgement of the right of the Jew to his Jewish difference, to live and labor as Jew without penalty, equally free and safe as all other societies of mankind.

Among Jews, the spirit of emancipation has transformed the conditions of Jewish survival. Even under the compulsory segregation of the Pale with its restriction upon movement, domicile and occupation, the idea of emancipation broke down the walls of the mind, shook up the ghetto of its habitation, opened the way to seeing, sharing, supplementing the Jewish culture-complex with others. Emancipation thus worked at the very roots of Jewish survival, affecting both its religious and secular principles and practices and the institutions which incarnate and channel them. Yet, in so far as it stayed an external condition its bearing upon them was neutral. As the record shows, emancipation, as proffered from without, could be only permissive. It provides opportunity, but neither moves the will nor produces the power and skill that seize and use opportunity. The source and seat of will, power and skill can be only the emancipated, not the emancipator. The emancipator can but open new channels to new chances, new roads to new experiences. But the emancipated do not in fact become such unless they have freely chosen between the alternatives which the emancipator opens up to their choice. For the Jews, the alternatives could be nothing if they were not the two modes of assimilation: assimilation as the suicidal extinction of the Jewish being and assimilation as the confirmation and enrichment of the Jewish power to survive, to grow, and to function in the freeing and enrichment of the spirit of the peoples.

This is the choice which actually the generations are continually making. It is manifest in the number and variety of societies of Jews, with their diverse Jewishnesses and Judaism, their different, conflicting creeds and codes. The societies together indicate to what degree and in what manner their aficionados regard being a Jew either a handicap or a penalty on personal survival, or else a value in whose configurations their own existence attains its meaning and survival-power. To those who experience emancipation as freedom *for* rather than freedom *from,* as opportunity for creation and not for suppression, withdrawal or flight, emancipation signifies auto-emancipation, and thus the one sure condition of Jewish survival and growth.

The Russian Roots of the American Jewish Labor Movement

By Ezra Mendelsohn

(Hebrew University)

The massive emigration of Russian Jews to America, in the wake of the pogroms of 1881–1882, was chiefly a movement of poor artisans, traders, and "people who lived on nothing" (*luftmentshn*) who came to the New World in search of an opportunity to work, to grow prosperous, and to live without fear. The emigration, however, was not homogeneous. Along with the Jewish "masses" there appeared on American soil in the 1880s a very different type, the Russian Jewish intellectual, whose condition and motivation for the voyage often had little in common with the typical Jewish immigrant. The gulf separating the two immigrant types was keenly felt by the intellectuals, who were quick to call attention to their unique status. Thus Alexander Harkavy, who reached New York in 1882, remarks in his memoirs: "The members of our society [the *Am Olam* group, which is discussed below] felt themselves to be on a higher level than the masses. They are not like us, we thought. We are not journeying to America for ordinary reasons; are we not idealists, who will demonstrate to the nations of the world that the children of Israel are capable of being farmers?" A decade later Leon Kobrin observed that his shipmates on the way to America were divided into "we" (the intellectuals) and "they" (everyone else). The relatively tiny number of intellectuals were prepared "to struggle and to die for the happiness of mankind" and earnestly discussed the great question—what is to be done in America to further this noble goal? The masses, on the other hand, "did not share our worries about what to do in America. They didn't think about such things. Each of them had already answered the question as follows: 'I have hands, I'll do allright.' " [1] In the end, the "we and they" dichotomy was resolved; the intellectuals, with their contempt for the materialistic Jewish immigrant masses, eventually came to involve themselves in the masses' struggle for a better life by organizing unions and preaching socialism to the Jewish proletariat. One of the aims of this essay is to investigate this process, which is of great significance in the history of organized Jewish labor in America.

What do we mean by the term "Russian Jewish intelligentsia?" At its most basic level, the word "intellectual" was employed to describe those Jews who, thanks to the Jewish "Enlightenment" (*Haskalah*) movement, to the russifying and relatively liberal policy of the Russian state during the reign of Alexander II, and to their own desire for education, had broken with the traditional Jewish way of life in the Pale of Settlement and had acquired a secular education. By the 1880s a considerable number of Jewish youths had attained the requisite secular education—by attending a Gymnasium, a Russian University, or a state-run Jewish institution of higher learning—to qualify formally as intellectuals.[2] The Jewish intellectual proudly wore his student uniform, striking evidence of his separation from the traditional Jewish world; above all, he spoke Russian rather than Yiddish. Indeed, when Abraham (Abe) Cahan, future editor of *Forverts* (*Forward*) and a graduate of the Vilna Jewish Teachers' Institute, sought out fellow-intellectuals in Brody on his way to America, he used a simple criterion: "I walked along the streets and listened to whether someone spoke Yiddish or Russian. If it was Russian that meant that he was an intellectual." [3]

The Russian Jewish intellectuals were therefore "russified"—a word which must be used cautiously, and should not be considered synonymous with "assimilated"—and one aspect of this russification was a disdain for the "jargon" (Yiddish) and traditional Jewish culture. The typical Jewish intellectual was alienated from the Jewish religion and from the world-outlook of the Jewish masses, who were regarded as still living in the "Middle Ages." Having discarded one identity the intellectual acquired a new one by identifying with the general Russian intelligentsia, which, as is well known, was the bearer of revolutionary ideologies within the Empire. Thus, along with our definition of the Russian Jewish intellectual as educated and russified, we should add that he was likely to be radical; in fact, owing to the all-pervasive nature of Czarist anti-Semitism he was even more likely to be radical than his Russian counterpart. We shall have occasion to examine in some detail the revolutionary baggage which the Jewish intelligentsia brought from Russia to America. Suffice it to say at this point that many Jewish intellectuals were convinced that the only life worth living was a life of service, and that the object of this service was commonly conceived to be the long-suffering Russian people. These views, of course, were transmitted to the Jewish students by Russian radicals who, despite the rising Marxist challenge, were largely of the Populist school.[4]

Given this dedication to serving the people, the true hallmark of the radical Russian intellectual, why did some Jewish intellectuals emigrate to America? The historian finds various motives. Some, like Louis Miller, who was to become an important labor leader in New York, and the famous anarchist Shoel Yanovsky, fled because their revolutionary activities attracted the attention of the police. And yet others left simply because in anti-Semitic Russia there was not much future. Y. Kopelov, who became an anarchist in America, recalls in his memoirs that ". . . to sit and wait for a wedding match with a dowry and then to become middlemen, storekeepers, or do nothing at all—for us, worldly, enlightened, socialist-minded youths this was impossible." [5]

Miller, Yanovsky, and Kopelov left Russia as individuals. There was, however, an organized emigration of Russian Jewish intellectuals to America in the early 1880s known as the *Am Olam* (*Eternal People*) movement. This movement, rather loosely organized but with a clear ideological position, developed as a result of the most important event in the history of Russian Jewry in the last quarter of the nineteenth century—the pogroms of 1881–1882. These pogroms had a devastating impact upon the Jewish intelligentsia, who were spared the actual physical torment of the victims only to suffer from acute psychological distress. For the pogroms seemed to demonstrate that the hopes of the russified intelligentsia had been dashed, that the longed-for rapprochement between the intelligentsia and the "people" was now an impossible dream, at least for Jews. Nothing in their world-outlook had prepared them for this upsurge of irrational hatred, hatred deriving from the very "people" in whom the intelligentsia had placed its trust. A young *Am Olam* participant who was in Odessa on the eve of the pogroms found that the Jewish students believed that "only peasants are people and [are] entitled to the attention of the intelligentsia." [6] These populist views were hard pressed by the peasants' participation in the pogroms, and many Jewish students found themselves shaken to the core. In Warsaw Yankev Milkh, a "one-half" intellectual who was to become a labor leader in New York, felt that "All my thoughts were overturned" and that his love for life had disappeared; an Odessa student informs us that, as a result of the pogrom in that city "people abandoned their studies and began to search for ways to escape from their miserable condition."[7]

What was to be done? The problem was to translate the general feeling of "bitterness" [8] into action, and there were various proposals. It was in the wake of the pogroms that Leo Pinsker wrote his famous pamphlet *Auto-Emancipation,* an affirmation of Jewish nationalism which nurtured the first generation of Russian Zionists. But those who were attracted to the idea of national rebirth on the ancestral soil were outnumbered by those who looked to America as a source of new life and new hope. In the major centers of Jewish life in Southern Russia (where the pogroms were concentrated)—in Odessa, Kiev, Kremenchug, Elizavetgrad, and Balta—circles of like-minded intellectuals and "one-half" intellectuals formed in order to promote the idea of organized emigration to the New World. [9] These students had come to the sorrowful conclusion that "emigration is the only way out." "We are far from idealizing America," one of them wrote, "we know that much suffering awaits us at first; but we are prepared to endure a hundred times as much material suffering than we endure at the present time, if only we can be freed from the Damoclean sword . . ." [10] They resolved, in the words of M. Bokal, one of the leaders of the movement, to ". . . disperse among the *free* nations in a new world. We shall be compelled to become agriculturalists and we shall be like other people—we will live like other people." [11]

If the *Am Olam* despaired of the future in Russia, it by no means abandoned the idealism of the intelligentsia. On the contrary, the movement fed on and lent new impetus to this idealism by presenting the migration to America as a migration of missionaries. The movement's ideologists advanced the notion that the Russian Jews, hitherto a race of unproductive middlemen, can redeem themselves only by adopting agriculture. This idea had long since been advocated by various would-be reformers of the Jewish condition, and was an integral part of the program of the Jewish "Enlightenment" movement in Russia. By adopting it the *Am Olam* signalled its acceptance of the accusation, usually associated with anti-Semitism, that the Jews were a parasitic people; like the Zionists, they felt that a return to the soil would guarantee a return to health. And, if the Jewish intelligentsia was barred from serving the Russian *muzhik*, it might nonetheless transform itself into a new class of Jewish peasants in a more favorable environment.

The idea of returning to the soil in the new world had great appeal to the intelligentsia. One member of *Am Olam* noted: ". . . it is a disgrace that a people should live off what others produce;" another wished ". . . to show the world that a Jew was able to become a productive worker if given the proper chance." [12] Shneyer Beyly was delighted with the opportunity ". . . to wipe away the stain that Jews were not agriculturists . . . ," and Moses Freeman, member of the Odessa *Am Olam*, defined the aims of his group as follows: "To settle on the land and to live from our own labor and to serve as an example to others. There in the colony, close to the tilled soil and in nature's bosom, the local storekeeper, middleman and 'luftmentsh' will be transformed into a useful member of society, for himself and for the world!" [13]

The *Am Olam* members, it should be noted, were interested not only in establishing colonies but in establishing these colonies on communal principles. They went off to America ". . . to demonstrate to the world that Jews are capable of being agriculturists; and as progressive, advanced and intelligent humans—live on communist principles." [14] The return to the soil would not take the form of private farming, but rather of sharing in the blessings of nature. It was in this sense, of course, that the colonists hoped to act as models; this would be their service to humanity.

The *Am Olam* groups began arriving in New York in 1882;

according to one source more than 1,000 intellectuals participated in the movement and set out to establish communal farms with such names as New Odessa and Bethlehem-Yehudah.[15] For various reasons—lack of funds, lack of experience, and the frailties of human nature—the colonies were largely unsuccessful. We need not go into the story of their collapse here; what is important is, first of all, that the movement brought to the new world a large contingent of Russian Jewish intellectuals and secondly, that these intellectuals had come to America embued with the general idealism of the Russian intelligentsia and the special mission of *Am Olam*. The failure of the colonies did not destroy this idealism, which was eventually channelled in new directions. The *Am Olam* pioneers became, in time, pioneers of the American Jewish labor movement.

Having accounted for the fact that the early 1880s witnessed the arrival in America of a rather sizeable number of Russian Jewish intellectuals (though they were, of course, vastly outnumbered by the "masses" of Russian Jewish immigrants) we must now consider more closely the political attitudes of these intellectuals. We have already noted their predeliction for radical views, but it is noteworthy that only a small minority were actually veterans of the Russian revolutionary movement. Among these veterans was Abraham Cahan, who had discovered an illegal revolutionary "circle" (*kruzhok*) while studying at the Jewish Teacher's Institute in Vilna. Cahan joined the group and, after his graduation, carried on socialist propaganda in Velich, a small town where he was employed as a teacher. In 1881, under police surveillance and agitated by the pogroms, he left for America.[16] Another Russian revolutionary activist who was to make a name for himself in the American Jewish labor movement was Isaac Hourwich, who participated in socialist circles in Minsk in the late 1870s and who came to America in 1890.[17] Phillip Krantz, editor of the famous London Yiddish socialist journal *Arbayter fraynd,* who in 1890 became editor of the New York socialist organ *Di arbayter tsaytung,* was active in the illegal circles of the Petersburg Polytechnical Institute in the late 1870s. And Michael Zametkin, a major figure in the Jewish labor movement in New York in the 1880s, had participated in revolutionary circles in Odessa in 1877–1878 and came to America to avoid incarceration.[18]

The historian is struck, however, by the fact that even the veterans were vague as to the ideological content of their radicalism. Thus Cahan admits that "I had no exact grasp" of socialist doctrine, and if this was true of a "circle" participant it was certainly true of the vast majority of other intellectuals. Khayim Spivakovsky (Spivak), a participant in the *Am Olam* movement, informs us that the Russian Jewish intelligentsia brought with it "no clearly defined political, social, and economic views;" and Morris Hillkowitz, who under the name Hillquit was to become one of the leaders of American socialism, remarks in his memoirs that ". . . my socialism was largely emotional and sentimental. My notions about the philosophy and practical program of the movement were quite vague." [19] In this Hillkowitz speaks for almost all his fellow intellectuals of the 1880s.

This ideological confusion is, of course, directly related to the state of Russian radical thought in the 1870s. While Marxist thought was beginning to make inroads among the radical intelligentsia it was still comparatively unknown, and only a few Jewish radicals who came to America in the 1880s were acquainted with the theories of scientific socialism. The prevailing theory was still populist, and here, surely, is the source of the vague radicalism of the Russian Jewish intelligentsia. For what the Jewish intellectuals acquired from their acquaintance with the Russian populist tradition—an acquaintance picked up, as we have seen, not so much through active participation in a circle as through reading and discussion—was a certain *mood* of revolutionary dedication and enthusiasm. The ideological content was, indeed, vague; what was clearly expressed was the revolutionary form, as manifest in the desire for rapid change, an end to oppression, a love for the "people," a hatred for authority. The typical Russian Jewish intellectual in America in the 1880s was more a revolutionary *type* than he was the bearer of a coherent ideology of revolution. William Frey, the Russian utopian socialist who was associated with those *Am Olam* members who established New Odessa in Oregon in 1883, has left us a most revealing portrait of the young intellectuals:

> All members were young Russians . . . thoroughly imbued with the individualism and revolutionism of our age. Like all Russian nihilists they stood for the extremes of individual liberty; they had aversion to everything pertaining to order and moral discipline. The

mere word "religion" was odious to them . . . The altruistic aim of
my friends was in flat contradiction with their individualistic theory.
Consciously they stood for anarchy, unconsciously they were led by
a strong instinct towards a harmonious brotherly social life. This
lack of unity, this combination of mean theory with a noble impulse
was the cause of all troubles in the community.

Despite their dislike for order, which was, in Frey's view, an obstacle to the creation of a harmonious community, their enthusiasm was most engaging: "If you be present," wrote Frey to a
friend, "at our meetings on New Year Day (a meeting specially
appointed to celebrate the festival of humanity) if you would see
their enthusiasm and the outburst of their best feelings, their wines
mixed with the tears of pure brotherly love—you would say you
are present at another descension of Holy Spirit." [20]

The process by which the Russian Jewish intellectuals assimilated the attitudes of the populist movement was not always identical, but certain recurrent patterns are clear. Most of them had
read certain classics of populist literature—the most commonly
read was perhaps Chernyshevsky's celebrated novel *What is to be
Done?* All knew of, and revered, the terrorists who had taken the
lives of many Russian officials and who were, in 1881, to assassinate Alexander II. And all had participated in fervent discussions with their fellow students on ". . . dimly understood high
themes with the oft-recurring refrain of 'Bazarov, Hegel, liberty,
Chernyshevsky, *v narod*' . . ." [21] The impression made by these
conversations and readings was deep and lasting. Emma Goldman,
the famous anarchist who came to America from Russia in 1885
was, at that time, "ignorant of the real meaning of socialism" but
nonetheless sought to pattern her life after that of Vera, the hero-
ine of Chernyshevsky's novel, who established a dressmaking shop
to aid the poor working girls of St. Petersburg.[22] Goldman's close
friend Alexander Berkman also found a suitable model in *What
is to be Done?*—that of Rakhmetov, the dedicated revolutionary.
"I am simply a revolutionist," Berkman writes in his memoirs, "an
instrument for furthering the cause of humanity; in short, a Rakhmetov." [23] Dovid Edelshtat, the Yiddish poet and anarchist, relates
in an autobiographical story how, at the age of fifteen, he encountered a populist named Vera who urged him to read the populist literature and added: "May Rakhmetov serve as a model for

your life." The revolutionary, who was eventually arrested, made a striking impression on the young boy:

> She not only preached that we must sacrifice all for the op-
> pressed and the down-trodden, but her whole heart, her soul, her
> every thought, her whole life was devoted to those who had been
> the victims, to those who had borne on their shoulders the yoke of
> tyranny and despotism.[24]

It was, indeed, precisely this heroic quality of populism which attracted the Jewish intellectuals, and which they sought, with all their heart, to emulate. In the words of Moissaye Olgin, himself a Russian Jewish intellectual who became a Communist in America, "They [the Russian radical intellectuals] stand out like so many pillars of fire in the desert. Their voices sound like beautiful music in a prison-house. Their eyes saw the dawn when dark reigned all around. And their call stirred the depths of young souls when all was apathy and gloom." And the Russian Jewish intellectuals who arrived in America in the 1880s saw themselves as the in-heritors of this glorious tradition, which represented everything good and noble in the world.[25]

Having arrived in the New World, the young idealists were faced with a severe problem—how to implement their ideals in a totally new environment. The problem was made especially acute by the general failure of the colonies, which were to serve as a sign of the redemption of a parasitic people. As one would-be pioneer commented, "If we can't be agriculturalists, why go to America?" Rather than engage in "unproductive" labor (as Man-delkorn termed his job as a clerk) some of the youths returned, disillusioned, to Russia.[26]

Most, however, stayed, and sought to find themselves in a world which seemed quite inhospitable to their ideals. The mem-oirs of a good number of these intellectuals testify to the extremely difficult early years. In the words of Khayim Spivakovsky (Spivak),

> After the stormy revolutionary life in Russia and the collapse
> of our ideals, we, the first Russian immigrants, spent our first years
> in America in a state of suspended animation. Without a goal in
> life, without ideals—in a word, we all felt like the *melamed* (tradi-
> tional Jewish teacher) without pupils.[27]

Kobrin's friend, Boris, found America to be "A land without a soul, and without a spirit," while Shmuel Garson, a graduate of the Vilna Jewish Teacher's Institute and one of the few intellectuals to have actually participated in the Russian revolutionary movement, was dismayed by the contrast between the "American spirit of materialism" and the "Russian spirit." The latter was ". . . what I had acquired from the Russian literature of my time —the spirit of compassion, the desire to build a society where there would be no oppressed or suffering." The belief in "going to the people," which Garson had received from his populist mentors, was not easily acted on in Boston, where he found himself in 1884.[28] And Phillip Krantz, too, the editor of *Di arbayter tsaytung*, confessed to the same feeling of alienation. The Russian revolutionary, he wrote in a letter to the Russian socialist journal *Znamia*, is hard pressed to maintain his revolutionary passion once he has left sacred Russia behind. "In a word, there is nothing sadder that the lot of the Russian intellectual abroad." [29] Emma Goldman and Alexander Berkman thought occasionally of returning to Russia, for "What could we hope to achieve in barren America? . . . In Russia we could engage in conspiratorial work. We belonged to Russia." [30] And Dovid Edelshtat wrote romantic poetry glorifying the Russia of his dreams, when

> Old Moscow is no longer seen,
> in the place of the ancient Kremlin—
> a great monument to Perovskaia
> erected by the Russian land! [31]

Alienation from American life and a romantic desire to return to an idealized Russia was the common lot of the Russian Jewish intellectuals in the 1880s. We now must consider the ways in which this alienation was eventually resolved.

In 1889 Michael Zametkin, one of the most notable of the Russian Jewish radicals in New York, wrote a letter expressing the dilemma of the radical intelligentsia in its new home:

> Some persecuted defenders of their country's [Russia's] rights found refuge in foreign countries. But the manly heart that beats in full accord with the interests of the unfortunate victims of universal plunder, tells its brave owner that here, too, there is work for him to do. And consciously and conscientiously he undertakes to fulfill his duty towards his brethren in his new country. But how changed the situation! How changed the environments. Free assemblage, free speech, self-government and many other things that stood as a leading-star and shone upon him who bravely fought

with the tyranny of a barbarian tzardom, these beautiful things,
they are already here.[32]

In other words, how does one retain that glorious revolutionary
purity, that legacy of Russian populism which the Jewish radical
intellectuals had adopted as their own, in a country where basic
freedoms are assured and the police is not particularly interested
in making martyrs out of radicals? The first reaction to this serious
dilemma was to cast doubts on the existence of American freedoms, to reject the "reformism" of American radicalism, and to
create, on American soil, societies and, indeed, a social life which
aimed at perpetuating the heroic and enthusiastic student life in
Russia. Even Zametkin, whose admission of the completely changed
American environment is an admission of the dilemma confronting the intelligentsia, asked: "Will the American hangman ever
force upon *Znamia*'s mind the deplorable fact that the difference
between tzardom and full-fledged plutocracy is but nominal after
all? That remains to be seen." [33] A poet in the anarchist journal
Fraye arbayter shtime noted that the old country was one of prisons
and blood but America is no better than "a free land of slaves;"
another correspondent, writing in 1890, made this comparison:
"The Russian regime suffocates its freedom fighters, the American
—well, I hope you have not yet forgotten the 11th of November,
when five freedom fighters were legally murdered in the Russian
manner." [34]

The general tendency to consider America no more free than
Czarist Russia—despite certain obvious but superficial liberties enjoyed in the New World—was accompanied by an attempt, in the
early years, to withdraw from American reality and establish a
self-contained Russian radical community. As Spivak recalls in his
memoirs, "Poor and lost we were here in the '80s, and friendship
and love were the only sources of refreshment and strength." [35]
And so the streets and cafes of the lower East Side in New York
were converted into islands of Russian student life; the mood is
well described by Morris Hillquit:

> They [the intellectuals] felt unhappy and forlorn in their work-
> shops, but at night on the roofs they again lived in a congenial at-
> mosphere. Once more they were students among students, forgetting
> the miseries of their hard and toilsome lives and enjoying the
> pleasures of freedom and companionship with the abandon and
> enthusiasm of youth . . . It was a slice of old Russian life that was

thus transported to Cherry Street by the uprooted young immigrants . . . Most of their evenings were spent in discussion. And what discussion! There was not a mooted question in science, philosophy, or politics that was not aired on the roofs in ardent, impassioned, and tumultuous debate . . . Communist anarchism, as it was then termed, was a simple creed and a romantic movement filled with thrilling conspiracies and acts of heroism and self-sacrifice. It had an irresistible attraction for the young and found many advocates on the Cherry Street roofs . . . It was amusing to hear these mild-mannered and soft-spoken boys and girls talk glibly about blowing up buildings and killing tyrants.

And Hillquit goes on to observe, "The fraternity on the roofs for a time was the main link between the idealism of my youth and the sordid realities of my new daily occupations." [36] It was, in a word, a method of resolving the deep feeling of alienation which seized the intellectuals in a country oblivious to their mission and their gifts.[37]

Along with informally structured efforts to recreate radical Russia in America went formal attempts to establish revolutionary organizations. A large number of these were founded in the 1880s —the "Propaganda Union," the "Russian Workers' Union," the "Russian Labor Lyceum," the "Russian Jewish Workers' Union," the "Jewish Workers' Union," the "Knights of Liberty," the "Pioneers of Liberty," the "Russian Progressive Union," and so forth.[38] Their names notwithstanding, these groups were, by and large, debating societies. In a clubbish atmosphere the Jewish radicals would meet to listen to lectures and to discuss various problems. Not surprisingly, a good deal of attention was paid to Russian problems (the language of these societies remained Russian though, as we shall see, attacks on this practice were soon forthcoming) and to the question of the Russian revolutionary's dilemma in America. Thus Abe Cahan, in a speech delivered at the Propaganda Union in 1882, had the following to say:

We find ourselves in a country which is relatively free. We are looking here for a new home. But we dare not forget that great struggle for freedom which we experienced in our former home. At a time when we are concerned only with ourselves, our comrades, our heroes, our martyrs struggle over there, or suffer in Russian prisons.

We dare not forget the struggle for freedom in our former home. We cannot do much from afar, but we can collect money.

> We must support that holy movement. The struggle of the Russian
> revolutionaries must remain deep in our hearts. We must not for-
> get the martyrs who martyr themselves in Siberia, at hard labor.[39]

This interesting speech, which demonstrates the urgent desire on
the part of Cahan and his colleagues to maintain their revolutionary credentials despite their having abandoned Russia (Cahan's
guilty feelings are readily apparent) set the tone for the activities
of this and the other societies. They established Russian libraries,
celebrated such great events as the anniversary of Alexander II's
assassination and, as Cahan had suggested, raised money for the
Russian revolutionary movement.[40] The "stars" of the Russian Jewish colony in New York appeared before these societies and lec-
tured, not only on socialist theory, but on such topics as "the family" and "the evolution of plants and animals." The organizations
stood apart from the masses, catered to the intellectual elite, and,
in the words of a contemporary, served as a "refuge" (*miklat*)
for the alienated intelligentsia.[41] Thus Shoel Yanovsky attended a
meeting of the "Russian Progressive Union" despite the fact that
". . . the actual aim of the meeting interested me very little; but
the fact that the meetings were held in Russian, that people were
coming to hear what others were saying in Russian, interested me
very much." The meetings, Yanovsky continues, ". . . took me
back, in my fantasies, to the old times, when I was still in Russia,
when I had such beautiful and wonderful dreams." [42] For Alexander Berkman, too, ". . . the Fridays in the little dingy hall in
the Ghetto, where bold imprecations are thundered against the
tyranny and injustice of the existing, and winged words prophesy
the near approach of a glorious dawn" served as a link between
past and present, and made the present more bearable.[43] Far more
important than the actual organizing achievements of these societies (we shall see that this amounted to very little) was their
social function, which was to shield the little band of Russian Jewish intellectuals from the harshness of the American experience.

Along with this voluntary segregation from American life,
quite naturally, went a rejection of American radical politics,
which the young populist-minded youths regarded with no little
scorn and condescension. Dovid Edelshtat, for example, made the
point (a point often repeated by his colleagues) that the American radicals were far inferior to their Russian counterparts:

When we consider the holy images of the Russian revolutionaries, full of self-sacrifice and immortal courage, and then we consider those who, in America, bear the name revolutionaries, what a sad comparison it is. At a time when the Russian revolutionaries amaze the world with their iron energy and holy spirit, our American revolutionaries offer empty phrases, with disgusting metaphysics, which they pass off as philosophy . . .[44]

Isaac Hourwich held similar opinions. Having personally known many Russian revolutionaries, and having participated in the movement in Petersburg and Minsk, he was contemptuous of American radicalism: "I have spent half my life in America," he writes in his memoirs, "where there never was and still is no revolutionary movement. Revolutionary declarations, which can be easily combined with daily business, I do not consider to constitute a revolutionary movement."[45] This attitude helps to explain why so many of the Russian Jewish intellectuals in the New World were attracted to the anarchist movement, which, at least in the early years of the Russian Jewish socialist movement, was its strongest faction. In this connection it is particularly instructive to quote the words of Leon Moiseyev (M. Leontiev) who came to America in 1891 and became active in the anarchist movement. When he arrived in New York, Moiseyev recalls,

My ideological orientation was Marxist: science, capitalist development, concentration of capital, proletarianization and revolution. My revolutionary education, my feelings, my tradition was incompatible with the variety of socialism as taught in Germany and America. I would go to listen to a social democratic speaker and everything would please me until the last ten or five minutes when he would . . . claim that only through politics and votes might the workers take power. I couldn't swallow that. When I went to hear an anarchist speaker and he would say the same thing with a bit more heart, but without mentioning voting, my heart would beat faster, though I knew scarcely anything about anarchism.[46]

As Alexander Berkman noted, describing the Jewish intellectuals, ". . . the fire of Russia still smolders in their hearts;" it is remarkable to what extent, throughout the 1880s, even those intellectuals who rejected anarchism continued to regard the Russian terrorists as, in Hillquit's words, "the best and noblest people in the world." [47]

The political sentiments of the intellectual immigrants, while shielding them from the "mainstream," if such a term can be used, of American radical thought, predisposed them towards making alliances in America with people who reminded them of their Russian heroes. A case in point was William Frey, whose remarks on the New Odessa pioneers have been quoted above. Frey, whose real name was Vladimir Geins, was born into the Russian gentry class in 1839; a typical "repentent noble" type, he became a populist and came to the United States in 1868 where he established several utopian societies. In 1881 he came to New York to lecture, and found a ready audience among the Jewish intellectuals of *Am Olam*. Mandelkorn, whose Odessa *Am Olam* group persuaded Frey to join them in New Odessa in 1883, found him to be ". . . an extraordinary character of his kind, a man of beauty and refinement of the old Russian military aristocracy," while Abe Cahan, despite his skepticism concerning utopian ventures, describes Frey as "one of the most remarkable people whom I have ever met. Such personalities appear on the earth only seldom . . . a few of us fell under his influence like disciples of a hassidic 'Rebbe.' " [48] Gregory Weinstein, an *Am Olam* member from Vilna, found Frey to be a "unique personality" while Hillquit remarks that his ". . . nobility of character and purity of life made a profound impression on the youthful members of the Russian colony . . ." [49] While the love-affair between Frey and the intellectuals did not last long—he managed to alienate even his most devoted supporters with his increasingly eccentric ways in New Odessa—the episode is a revealing one. For Frey possessed precisely what the intellectuals found lacking in American radicalism—that total devotion and dedication, that "holiness" (Mandelkorn actually describes Frey's family as the "holy family") which had characterized the fanatics of the populist movement.

Another political figure who excited the imagination of the intellectuals—and for the same reasons—was the German anarchist Johann Most. Emma Goldman, who was to become Most's lover, quickly fell under his spell and found herself "almost hypnotized." [50] Y. Benekvit converted to anarchism after hearing him speak, and Y. Kopelov, revealingly enough, found that Most resembled the "Rebbe" Leybele Kapitser, whose sermons he had heard in Bobruisk. He possessed "The same enthusiasm, the same devotion to his ideal and to his truth, and the same readiness to sacrifice himself for the ideal. Khayim Vaynberg, who also became a "Mostian," recalls that Most knew how "to hypnotize his audience so that they would follow him whenever he might call them to struggle on the barricades." [51]

The very refusal of men like Frey and Most to consider compromise and, indeed, to make the slightest effort to surrender to the American way of life, made them venerated figures on the lower East Side of New York. Their attractiveness to the intellectual immigrants had its roots in the same psychological need as did the attraction of the "society of the roofs" and the various organized "Unions" of the 1880s. And yet, this need to be sheltered from the new environment, this rejection of the environment, could not endure forever. The history of the radicals in the 1880s is, to a great extent, the history of their coming to terms with American life. Despite their occasional longing for the excitement and danger of Russia, the intellectuals came to realize that they had come to stay, and by 1891 Cahan had gone so far as to announce that "Yes, America is the new home, the only home of the Jewish people . . . America is the only place where Jews can find a little peace." [52] This process of "americanization" was, of course, a reflection of the simple passage of time—it is difficult to remain an "internal emigré" forever. But the process was a paradoxical one, for it was intricately involved with the intellectuals' discovery of the Jewish proletariat and their creation of a new movement which spoke, not Russian, and not English, but Yiddish. The creation of this Yiddish-speaking movement served as a final resolution of that alienation which was the hallmark of the intellectuals' condition in America.

We have seen that the Russian Jewish intellectuals who came to America were basically "populist," and initially rejected the practical socialism which they encountered in the New World. They were certainly not oriented towards the creation of a labor movement concerned with dollars and cents issues—Cahan tells us, for example, that the leader of the "Jewish Propaganda Union" considered labor organization "not dangerous enough" to interest a real revolutionary. [53] But as the years passed their attitude towards such activities changed. Central to this change was their "discovery" of the Jewish proletariat in New York and its desperate situation. Such a discovery was by no means inevitable and is to be

associated, first of all, with the important fact that the Jewish working class as it evolved in New York (as in London) struck the
radicals as being quite different from that which they had known
in the old country. They had never regarded the traditional Jewish *bal-melokhe* (artisan) in the Pale of Settlement as a worthy
subject for their energies, a view which their colleagues who remained in Russia continued to hold until the early 1890s.[54] But,
as Hillquit remarks in his memoirs, they found that, in New York,
the Jewish artisans ". . . evolved for the first time a solid proletarian block." The same point was made by the Jewish socialist
pioneer Morris Vintshevsky, who discovered in London (he did
not arrive in America until 1894) that the Jewish artisans from
Russia had been transformed into "a modern proletariat. . . .
What our little circle of propagandists had previously encountered
almost only in the literature now stood before our eyes."[55] Perhaps this modern proletariat, created by the great needle industries, might take the place of the Russian peasantry as a class
upon which the radical intelligentsia would lavish its attentions.

This all-important discovery of the Jewish proletariat was
made inevitable by an important change in the social situation of
the Jewish intelligentsia. In Russia they had, by and large, supported themselves by teaching. Isaac Hourwich had given lessons
to Jewish students seeking secular knowledge; Israel Mandelkorn
served in Odessa as a tutor to Jewish students hoping to enter
Gymnasium; Abe Cahan was a teacher at an elementary school
in Velich before coming to America. But in America there was
no need for this type of teacher, and since the radical immigrants
had to earn a living, they had no choice but to follow the "masses"
into the shops of the garment industry. They were obliged to remove their gymnasium uniforms and don the clothes of an American working man.[56] They therefore became, in America, not the
peasants which they hoped to become, but simple workers laboring for low wages in sweatshops.

The favorite trade of the intelligentsia was shirt-making, because it could be learned easily and was not particularly demanding. As Hillquit informs us, it was ". . . the favorite occupation
of the circle of young Russian intellectuals in which I moved . . .
the work was not exacting, and the surroundings were not uncon-
genial. The operators in the stuffy little workshop spent at least as

much time in discussing social and literary topics as in turning out shirts, and the whir of the sewing machines was often accompanied by the loud and hearty sound of revolutionary songs." [57] Among the more celebrated shirt-makers were Louis Miller and Michael Zametkin; Leon Kobrin, who remarks in his memoirs that he and his fellow intellectuals were "mama's boys" in Russia, became a shirt-maker because "one didn't need any special skills" and only took two weeks to learn.[58] Abe Cahan went to work in a cigar factory, where he converted the Jewish labor organizer Bernard Vaynshteyn to socialism; Shoel Yanovsky became a hat-maker, Emma Goldman made waists, and the radical poet Yoysef Bovshover became a furrier. Khayim Vaynberg became a cigar-maker, and Hillel Solotarov worked as a tailor. In this manner the Russian Jewish intelligentsia was "proletarianized" in the New World.

This "proletarianization" was of relatively short duration—many of the intellectuals—among them Spivak, Alenikov, and Solotarov—took advantage of American opportunities and became professionals. Abe Cahan and Louis Miller left the shops to become English teachers at immigrant schools. But we may assume that their exposure to working conditions made them more sensitive to the needs of the Jewish working class and presented to them the possibility of organizing this class into unions. Unlike the radicals who had remained in Russia, and who by their own admission were quite isolated from the Jewish masses, conditions in America brought the "people" and the intelligentsia together. And this led to extremely important results. We know, for example, from the account of Bernard Vaynshteyn, that the "intellectual proletariat" in the shirt-making trade established a union to improve working conditions in 1884—in 1888, when the United Hebrew Trades was established, this union was re-founded and became the "pride" of the Jewish labor movement because "The entire Jewish-Russian intelligentsia belonged to it." [59] Indeed, the United Hebrew Trades itself, which was organized in order to encourage the organization of Jewish labor, was conceived by Y. Magidov, an intellectual from Odessa who came to America in 1886 and worked as a shirt-maker. The first secretary was Bernard Vaynshteyn, who had come to America with the *Am Olam* and who had also worked in various factories.[60] We know that Michael Zametkin, who became a shirt-maker in New York, also became one of the leading union organizers in that city; and Shoel Yanovsky, despite his typical Russian radical background, became conscious of the extremes of proletarian exploitation only after his experiences in an American sweatshop.[61] We may assume that Hillquit's realization that the situation of the Jewish proletariat "fairly cried out for sympathy" was a result of his actual experience in the shop.[62]

To be sure, the proletarianization of the Jewish intelligentsia was not the only reason for its decision to "go to the people," the people now being the Jewish workers. There was, too, the very important influence of the German social democrats in New York. For Cahan, as for many of his colleagues, the *Volks-Zeitung* (the German social democratic organ) was a particularly important influence: "In each number we found Marxist explanations for daily events—food for new thought." Some of the leading German socialists became familiar figures at Jewish radical meetings—especially Sergei Shevich, whose Baltic German origins and knowledge of Russian made him a particularly acceptable figure.[63] But the German influence—which was also most instrumental in the founding of the United Hebrew Trades itself—was not as important as the discovery of the masses via proletarianization.

By the second half of the decade of the 1880s we detect a striking change in the ideas of the radical intelligentsia. In 1887 Nikolai Alenikov, the former leader of the Kievan *Am Olam*, made a speech urging Jewish Russian radicals to enter the Jewish labor movement; speaking at a meeting of the "Russian Progressive Union," held in 1887, another *Am Olam* alumnus, Rayevsky, made the point that the place of the Jewish intelligentsia was in the Jewish labor movement, and that the use of Russian should give way to the use of Yiddish.[64] In 1890 an unnamed socialist remarked in the pages of *Znamia* that the ". . . Jewish workers, who were looked upon up until this time as a hindrance to the workers' movement, can be extraordinarily useful in the ranks of the organized proletariat." [65] By 1890, Cahan informs us, "As speakers, agitators, and organizers we were closely connected with every important event in the life of the Jewish unions. We took part in every strike and in almost every settlement. We were in the center of all union activity." [66] From messianic politics and the worship of Russian terrorists, the intelligentsia had proceeded to trade union activities which nothing in their radical background had truly prepared them for.

The transformation of the intelligentsia into labor leaders also implied its transformation into a Yiddish-speaking group. Abe Cahan pioneered in the use of the people's language, and was the first to address (in 1882) a workers meeting in that language.[67] Yiddish was resisted by the intelligentsia at first, as was the notion of a specifically *Jewish* labor movement. The populist background of the intellectual radicals had definitely not included any recognition of the need for a Jewish movement—on the contrary, the russified intelligentsia was far from being interested in Jewish survival. And while the *Am Olam* was a movement dedicated to renewal through agriculture, it had, in fact, little Jewish content. This, at least, was the opinion of Israel Mandelkorn, who reports that the New Odessa group decided against the adoption of any specific Jewish characteristics. "The majority were far from Jewish life," he tells us, and the members regarded themselves as "a community of *workingmen*." [68] William Frey, while reporting that the Jews in New Odessa "are proud of their nationality" added that they had all abandoned their religion and did not even perform circumcision.[69] But if the intellectuals, having discovered the Jewish proletariat, were to have any success in organizing it, they must speak its language. Thus A. Ortman, who came to America in 1888, joined the Russian language branch of the American Socialist Labor Party, and participated in the journal *Znamia,* observed: "We became quickly convinced that in order to influence the masses we had to speak to them in their own language."[70] And Phillip Krantz, in a letter to the editors of *Znamia,* urged his fellow intellectuals to learn Yiddish; "Nothing is easier than to learn to write in Yiddish," he informs his colleagues, adding that he himself didn't know a word of the language five years ago but quickly learned.[71]

The Russian Jewish intelligentsia was therefore "yiddishized;" Dovid Edelshtat, a Russian poet in Russia, became a Yiddish poet in America so that his poetry might reach the Jewish working class; Leon Kobrin assiduously read the Yiddish press so that he could write short stories in the "jargon," as the language was affectionately (and also scornfully) called.[72] And the intelligentsia soon became not only users of Yiddish but its champion; as was the case, later on, within the ranks of the Russian Bundists, Yiddish came to be glorified as the language of the Jewish masses.[73] And, as is well known, the American Jewish labor movement gave enormous impetus to the flourishing of Yiddish culture in America.

Let us attempt a summary of the points made in this essay. The Russian Jewish intellectuals who came to America in the 1880s—whether on their own or as members of the *Am Olam* movement, were radicals whose political ideology was vague but populist-inspired. In America they sought to shield themselves against the strange environment of the New World by creating their own societies—formal and informal—which sought to perpetuate the Russian radical tradition as they understood it. For this reason many became anarchists, and many became followers of political leaders who reminded them of the martyr-heroes of the People's Will and the other populist factions. Gradually, however, this intelligentsia became "americanized," a process which was the result of their discovery of the Jewish proletariat and their acceptance of a new mission—to organize this proletariat and to uplift it economically and spiritually. This new orientation—the result of the passage of time, the influence of the German social democrats, and, above all, the proletarianization of the intelligentsia in the New World—was accompanied by a shift to Yiddish on the part of the intellectuals. They therefore gave up their essentially Russian orientation, though they certainly retained a sentimental attachment to the old country and to the politics of the Russian revolutionary movement.[74]

One final point must be made. While it is true that the intelligentsia was americanized, and largely abandoned its absolute devotion to messianic politics, it also retained the radical zeal of the Russian movement. This radical background, which was reinforced through the arrival of new intellectuals from the old country in the 1890s and, especially, following the revolution of 1905, imparted to the Jewish labor movement a radical orientation largely lacking in other labor movements in the United States. In other words, we have here a two-way process, whereby the Russian intelligentsia was americanized and therefore became concerned with trade unionism, while the Jewish labor movement was to a certain extent russified via the leadership of the Russian radical intelligentsia. This radical orientation has certainly been a distinguishing feature of the Jewish labor movement throughout its history.

NOTES

1 Aleksander Harkavy, *Perakim mi-khayai* (New York, 1935), p. 39; Leon Kobrin, *Mayne fuftsik yor in Amerike* (Buenos Aires, 1955), p. 20. Another intellectual immigrant of the period describes how he and his friends voyaged to America in a special cabin, apart from the other travelers; see Yisroel Iser Katsovitsh, *Zekhtsik yor lebn* (New York, 1919), p. 214.

2 In 1881 Jews constituted 12.3% of all Russian Gymnasium (High School) students—in 1863 the figure was 3.2%. See P. Marek, *Ocherki po istorii prosveshcheniia evreev v Rossii* (Moscow, 1909), pp. 166–167. Those Jews who attained a certain level of secular knowledge through self-education but were unable to finish Russian schools, were often called "one-half intellectuals."

3 Kahan, *Bleter fun mayn lebn*, II (New York, 1926), 34; see also pp. 82–83. Another intellectual immigrant describes his dress upon arriving in America; he had ". . . long hair, a pince-nez, a peaked cap and the uniform of the 'real school' (technical High School) . . ." Before applying for work he acquired "American working clothes," thus symbolizing his transformation from student-intellectual to proletarian; see "Iz vospominanii emigranta" in G. M. Prais, *Russkie evrei v Amerike* (St. Petersburg, 1893), p. 10.

4 There is an extensive literature on the Russian intelligentsia. A useful source is Richard Pipes, ed., *The Russian Intelligentsia* (New York, 1961).

5 Y. Kopelov, *Amol in Amerike* (Warsaw, 1928), p. 7.

6 Israel Mandelkorn, *My Recollections* (n.d., typescript located in the Frey Papers in the New York Public Library), p. 12.

7 Yankev Milkh, *Oytobiografishe skitsn* (New York, 1946), pp. 183–184; Shneyer Beyly, *Zikhroynes* (New York, American Jewish autobiographies, typescript, YIVO Institute, archives), p. 17.

8 Beyly, *op. cit.*, p. 17.

9 A group was also formed in Vilna, although the wave of pogroms did not reach Lithuania. The best general study of the movement is A. Menes, "Di 'Am Olam'—bavegung," in E. Tsherikover, ed., *Geshikhte fun der yidisher arbeterbavegung in di Fareynikte shtatn*, II (New York, 1945), 203–238. It should be pointed out that the reaction on the part of Russian radicals to the pogroms was mixed; some went so far as to praise the anti-Semitic excesses as "revolutionary" acts by the oppressed peasants. Some Jewish radicals shared this view, as is demonstrated by the following remarks of Isaac Hourwich, a pioneer of the Russian Jewish socialist movement and later an activist in New York: ". . . we in our revolutionary circle remained indifferent to the affair [the pogroms]. We were also under the influence of the theory that it was an uprising of the folk, and all such uprisings are good since they revolutionize the masses. As for the fact that Jews suffered—did not the Russian revolutionaries of gentry origin call upon the peasants to stage an uprising against their own fathers and brothers?" See

Yitskhok-Ayzik Ben Arye Tsvi Ha-Leyvi (Isaac Hourwich), "Zikhroynes fun an apikoyres," *Fraye arbayter shtime*, June 23, 1922. Yankev Gordin, the celebrated Jewish playwright, published an article in 1881 blaming the Jewish moneylenders ("protsentniks") for the pogroms; see Kalmen Marmor, *Yankev Gordin* (New York, 1953), pp. 36 ff. For a study of the reaction of Pavel Axelrod, the Menshevik leader, see Abraham Asher, "Pavel Axelrod: A Conflict between Jewish Loyalty and Revolutionary Dedication," *Russian Review*, XXIV, No. 3 (July, 1965), 249–265.

[10] "Iz vospominanii emigranta," *op. cit.*, p. 5.

[11] As quoted by Mandelkorn, *op. cit.*, p. 37.

[12] Katsovitsh, *op. cit.*, p. 211; Katherine Sabsovich, *Adventures in Idealism. A Personal Record of the Life of Professor Sabsovich* (New York, 1922), p. 13. Sabsovich was one of the leaders of the Odessa *Am Olam* and later the founder of the Woodbine colony in New Jersey.

[13] Beyly, *op. cit.*, p. 20; Moses Freeman, *Fuftsik yor geshikhte fun yidishn lebn in Filadelfye* (Philadelphia, n.d.), p. 199. In the words of a Russian Jewish colonist who reported back to Russia in 1886, "The only salvation for oppressed Israel lies in agricultural labor." See M. Zayfert, "Russkie evrei i zemledelenie v Amerike," *Nedel'naia khronika voskhoda*, No. 34, Aug. 24, 1886, p. 925.

[14] Mandelkorn, *op. cit.*, p. 65. For Bokal's views on the problem of establishing communistic colonies see Ben-Ami's report, originally published in 1882 and republished in *Tsherikover, op. cit.*, 471–474.

[15] The estimate is from Prais, *op. cit.*, 46. In 1886 Zayfert, *op. cit.*, p. 925, estimated that 344 Russian Jewish families, or 1,720 people in all, were settled in colonies.

[16] *Bleter, op. cit.*, I (New York, 1926), 386 ff.

[17] "Zikhroynes," *op. cit.*; for his description of the Minsk circle see *Fraye arbayter shtime*, March 16, 1923.

[18] On Krantz's revolutionary past see his remarks in *Di arbayter tsaytung*, I, No. 19, July 11, 1890 ("Mayne erinerungen vegn Grinevetsky"). For Zametkin's biography see the obituary in *Forverts*, March 7, 1935 and the *Leksikon fun der nayer yidisher literatur* (New York, 1960), III, 543 ff. Louis Miller, who together with his brother L. S. Bandes participated in revolutionary circles in Vilna, is another example. Miller came to America in 1886 and became one of the leaders of the Jewish socialist and trade union movement; he also worked on the Russian socialist paper *Znamia*, which appeared in 1889–1890.

[19] Kahan, II, *op. cit.*, 44; Kh. Spivak, "Erinerungen fun Kahan's grine tsaytn," *Yubileyum-shrift tsu Ab. Kahan's 50stn geburtstog* (New York, 1910), p. 33; Morris Hillquit, *Loose Leaves from a Busy Life* (New York, 1934), p. 8. Kopelov, *op. cit.*, p. 138, comments that "The majority of them [the intellectuals] knew very little about socialism and especially about various socialist factions."

[20] The first quotation is from an undated letter from Frey to an unnamed correspondent, presumably written in 1884 (Frey papers, New York Public Library). The second is from a letter by Frey to Edward King, dated Jan. 4, 1884. Frey is of the opinion, in this letter, that ". . . the Semitic race, which gave to the world the three grate (sic) religions of the past will be a leading race in the next religious revival." Frey, of whom more will be said below, was by this time an apostle of Compte's "religion of humanity."

21 The quotation is from Alexander Berkman, *Prison Memoirs of an Anarchist* (New York, 1912), p. 5. Berkman, who was from Kovno in Russia, came to America in 1887. Bazarov was the controversial hero of Turgenev's *Fathers and Sons*, while *v narod* ("to the people") was the slogan of the populist movement in the 1870s.

22 Emma Goldman, *Living My Life* (New York, 1934), pp. 9, 26. While still in Russia, she tells us, the populist terrorists ". . . became to me heroes and martyrs, henceforth my guiding stars." (28).

23 Berkman, *op. cit.*, pp. 9–10. In fact, he assumed the name Rakhmetov upon arriving in Pittsburgh to carry out his "deed," that is to assassinate the steel magnate Frick.

24 Dovid Edelshtat, "Vera," in *Dovid Edelshtat gedenk-bukh* (New York, etc., 1953), pp. 294, 293.

25 Moissaye Olgin, *The Soul of the Russian Revolution* (New York, 1917), p. 44. There is abundant material in the literature concerning the populist attitudes of the Jewish intelligentsia in America. The intellectuals whom Mandelkorn encountered in Odessa ". . . only offered me talk and disputes about the heroes of the novel *What is to be Done?* or Turgeneff's Bazaroff" (Mandelkorn, *op. cit.*, p. 12); Cahan's introduction to socialism was via the literature of the populist parties "Land and Freedom" and the "People's Will," as well as the inevitable *What is to be Done?* (*Bleter*, I, *op. cit.*, 386 ff.); Sh. Yanovsky was influenced by his reading of Dobroliubov, Belinsky, Pisarev, and the radical poet Nekrasov, who was also Edelshtat's hero (Shoel Yanovsky, *Ershte yorn fun yidishn frayhaytlekhn sotsyalizm* (New York, 1948), pp. 23–24; Kh. Rayevsky, who together with Cahan edited a Yiddish socialist paper in 1886, refers in a memoir to his "nihilist" past (*Yubileyum-shrift, op. cit.*, p. 15); M. Kats, a leading Jewish anarchist in America, is described by his biographer as having arrived in America in 1888 as a full-fledged *narodovoletz* (populist), (M. Melamed, "Kinder-yorn, ertsiung un der ershter aroystrit in der velt" in *M. Kats zamlbukh*, Philadelphia, 1925, pp. 5 ff.); Shneyer Beyly, *op. cit.*, recalls in his memoirs that he read the works of Mikhailovsky, Belinsky, Dobroliubov, and Pisarev; Leon Kobrin, who became a well known Yiddish writer, writes that he and his friends had no definite ideology but hated Russian despotism and believed simply in "revolution, whatever kind it might be." (*Mayne fuftsik yor, op. cit.*, p. 28.) In America among the favorite books of the intelligentsia was Stepniak's celebration of populist virtues, *The Career of a Nihilist*, which was serialized in *Di arbayter tsaytung* and, naturally enough, Chernyshevsky's *What is to be Done?* which was also published in the Yiddish socialist press (it appeared in *Der morgenshtern*, apparently in a translation by M. Zametkin).

26 The quotations are from Katsovitsh, *op. cit.*, p. 223, and Mandelkorn, *op. cit.*, p. 55. For information concerning the return of disappointed *Am Olam* members to Russia see Beyly, *op. cit.*, p. 20.

27 "Erinerungen," *op. cit.*, p. 31. For another description of the sad lot of the Russian Jewish intellectual in America see *Russkie evrei*, IV, No. 24, June 18, 1882, 926; the correspondent notes that the intellectual's ". . . Russian education doesn't do him any good, and no aid awaits him, for he is immediately seen to

the door with the words: 'be proud, you are an educated man, you must help yourself!' "

28 Kobrin, *op. cit.*, p. 122; memoirs of Shmuel Garson (typescript available at the YIVO Institute, American Jewish autobiographies collection), p. 34. On a somewhat different level, another educated immigrant was annoyed by the fact that Americans had no interest in his cultural achievements: "In the old home," he says, "I was able to speak with the Jews in Yiddish, with the local Germans in German (the author came from Courland) and in Russian with the intelligentsia, and now I find myself in a country where no one is interested in my knowledge and education in Hebrew, Yiddish, German, and Russian, so long as I don't know any English." (Memoirs of Philip Bernhardt, 1942, typescript available at the YIVO Institute, American Jewish autobiographies collection.)

29 *Znamia*, No. 3, Feb. 15, 1890.

30 *Living My Life, op. cit.,* p. 70.

31 *Fraye arbayter shtime*, No. 31, Jan. 30, 1891. Sofia Perovskaia was executed in 1881 for her role in the assassination of Alexander II.

32 The letter was published in the *Workmen's Advocate*, V, No. 8, Feb. 23, 1889, on the occasion of the publication of *Znamia*, a Russian-language socialist journal which appeared in New York.

33 *Ibid.*

34 R. Rozenblum, "Kenst du dos land?," *Fraye arbayter shtime*, No. 110, May 26, 1893; Yoysef Maytes, *ibid.*, No. 11, Sept. 12, 1890. The latter reference is to the execution of the anarchists involved in the Chicago Haymarket Affair of 1886, an event which made a great impression on the Jewish radicals. In *Di Nyu yorker yudishe folkstsaytung*, hereafter referred to as *Folkstsaytung*, a Yiddish socialist paper which began to appear in 1886, M. Zayfert published a list of thirteen "credos" (modelled after Maimonides' credo of Jewish faith) one of which reads as follows: "I believe that America is a free country, but only for the capitalist; he is free to suck the blood of the workers." (No. 4, July 16, 1886.) Abe Cahan's reaction to America was particularly interesting: "I felt America's liberty every minute. It seemed to me I could breathe more freely and more deeply than ever before. At the same time however I said to myself: 'But this is all a prison of capital.'" (*Bleter, op. cit.,* II, 90.)

35 Spivak, *op. cit.,* p. 31.

36 Hillquit, *op. cit.,* pp. 2 ff.

37 For an interesting description of another meeting place for the Jewish radicals—the home of Abraham Netter—see Michael Kan, "In Neters keler," *Dovid Edelshtat gedenk-bukh, op. cit.,* pp. 183–184. A description of a cafe on the lower East Side, to which Emma Goldman was taken in 1889 upon her arrival in New York, is found in her memoirs *Living My Life, op. cit.,* p. 5: "Everybody talked, gesticulated, and argued, in Yiddish and Russian, each competing with the other." This hot-house atmosphere was regarded by some observers as unhealthy; thus Anna Strunsky wrote to a young Jewish intellectual in 1897 urging him not to come to New York: ". . . there is even danger of your getting into bad society—for our Jewish socialist comrades who are ignorant and ill-mannered and who sit all day and night talking sophistry in the coffee-saloons or Labor Lyceum, make a very bad society indeed." (Edlin Papers, YIVO Institute.)

38 The general history of these societies is to be found in *Tsherikover*, II, *op. cit.*, 239 ff.

39 *Bleter*, II, *op. cit.*, 105. In 1887 N. Alenikov, the former leader of the Kiev *Am Olam*, spoke at the "Russian Progressive Union" on the "Duties of the Russian-Jewish youth in the United States." Alenikov urged the Russian Jewish intellectuals not to forget the Russian struggle; see *Folkstsaytung*, No. 30, Jan. 14, 1887. But Alenikov had another message as well; see note 64.

40 The best source for the activities of these various societies is the Yiddish socialist press of the 1880s, which clearly demonstrates their continued Russian orientation. Thus as late as 1889 the "Russian Progressive Union" announced the founding of a new Russian library "so that every worker, who understands Russian, will be able to read about and study social questions, for a small fee" (*Folkstsaytung*, No. 137, Jan. 4, 1889).

41 Kopelov, *op. cit.*, p. 174. See also, on the character of the early societies, Kahan, *Bleter*, *op. cit.*, II, 139. B. Vaynshteyn describes the "Russian Labor Union" as "aristocratic" in nature (*Fertsik yor in der yidisher arbeter bavegung*, New York, 1924, p. 45) but also notes that the "Russian Jewish Workers' Union" catered to the less educated because Yiddish was spoken there. Y. A. Benekvit, *Durkhgelebt un durkhgetrakht* (New York, 1934) attended, in 1887, meetings of the "Russian National League," which had been established by the intellectuals in order to protest the signing of a Russian-American trade agreement; he found that it had no connection with the masses (p. 55).

42 Yanovsky, *op. cit.*, p. 59.

43 Berkman, *op. cit.*, p. 207.

44 Dovid Edelshtat, "Eyn vort tsu di yidishe revolutsyonern," *Fraye arbayter shtime*, No. 5, Aug. 1, 1890.

45 "Zikhroynes fun an apikoyres," *Fraye arbayter shtime*, Nov. 11, 1921.

46 Leon Moiseyev, "M. Kats—der fareynignder element in der bavegung," *M. Kats zamlbukh, op. cit.*, p. 39.

47 Berkman, *op. cit.*, p. 84; *Di arbayter tsaytung*, No. 7, April 18, 1890. Hillquit also includes under this heading the Chicago martyrs of the Haymarket affair and the Paris communards. A. Mirovich, one of the founders of the "Jewish Propaganda Union," went so far as to name his son after one of the terrorists who had assassinated Alexander II; see Kahan, *op. cit.*, II, 139.

48 Mandelkorn, *op. cit.*, p. 62; Kahan, *op. cit.*, II, 123.

49 Gregory Weinstein, *The Ardent Eighties and After* (New York, 1947), p. 84; Hillquit, *op. cit.*, pp. 5–6. For information on Frey see Avrahm Yarmolinsky, *A Russian's American Dream. A Memoir on William Frey* (Lawrence, 1965).

50 Goldman, *op. cit.*, p. 38.

51 Benekvit, *op. cit.*, pp. 48 ff.; Kopelov, *op. cit.*, p. 114; Khayim Leyb Vaynberg, *Fertsik yor in kamf far sotsyaler bafrayung* (Los Angeles & Philadelphia, 1952), p. 26.

52 *Di arbayter tsaytung*, II, No. 21, May 22, 1891.

53 *Bleter, op. cit.*, II, 139.

54 Throughout the so-called "circle period" or the period of "propaganda," which lasted until the early 1890s, the Russian Jewish socialists active in the north-west provinces of the Empire did not consider the Jewish artisans of such

cities as Vilna and Minsk as a real proletariat; they changed their minds only with the transition from "propaganda" to "agitation." The "discovery" of the Jewish proletariat by the Jewish intelligentsia was made first in London, and then in New York.

55 Hillquit, *op. cit.*, p. 16; M. Vintshevsky, *Erinerungen* (Moscow, 1926), p. 170. Vintshevsky goes on to compare the Jewish proletarians in London, whom he regarded as true "wage slaves," with the journeymen of Russia who might be workers today, and owners of a shop tomorrow.

56 There is a description of this external transformation in "Iz vospominanii emigranta," *op. cit.*, pp. 10–11.

57 Hillquit, *op. cit.*, p. 32; see also Yanovsky, *op. cit.*, p. 53; Vaynshteyn, *op. cit.*, pp. 65 ff.

58 Kobrin, *op. cit.*, p. 28.

59 Vaynshteyn, *op. cit.*, p. 68.

60 On Magidov see *Leksikon, op. cit.*, V, 389–390. Vaynshteyn, *op. cit.*, pp. 75 ff.; see also Vaynshteyn, *Yidishe yunyons in Amerike* (New York, 1929), pp. 143 ff.

61 Yanovsky, *op. cit.*, pp. 54 ff. Yanovsky writes that the exploitation of Jewish workers in New York was far worse than anything he had known in his native city, Pinsk, where "The air in the workroom was fine and clear."

62 Hillquit, *op. cit.*, p. 17.

63 Kahan, *op. cit.*, II, 87–88. German, moreover, was an easier language for the intellectual immigrants than English; a good many had some acquaintance with it. See, for example, G. Weinstein, *op. cit.*, p. 23, and Benekvit, *op. cit.*, pp. 48 ff.

64 *Folkstsaytung*, No. 30, Jan. 14, 1887; *ibid.*, No. 40, March 25, 1887.

65 *Znamia*, No. 3, Feb. 15, 1890.

66 Kahan, *op. cit.*, III, 49.

67 *Ibid.*, II, 107 ff., and the description in Vaynshteyn, *op. cit.*, pp. 43 ff.

68 Mandelkorn, *op. cit.*, pp. 67, 68.

69 Frey, "Lecture to American Neighbors on Life at New Odessa" (1884?), Frey Papers, New York Public Library.

70 A. Ortman, "A bletl geshikhte (erinerungen, vi azoy di 'Tsukunft' iz gegrindet gevorn)," *Di tsukunft*, XVII, No. 1, Jan. 1912, 58.

71 *Znamia*, No. 3.

72 Another example was the case of Yankev Gordin, a russified intellectual from Poltava who, in America, became a celebrated Yiddish dramatist. Gordin was not involved directly in the labor movement but his first Yiddish writing appeared in the *Arbayter tsaytung*. See Marmor, *op. cit.*, pp. 47 ff.

73 See the interesting exchange between J. Finn, a Jewish radical from Boston, and Rabbi Solomon Schindler on the question of Yiddish in the pages of the *Workmen's Advocate*, No. 14, April 6, 1889. Schindler claims that Yiddish is a jargon "which only the *unintelligent* speak" while Finn says that ". . . I must say that the jargon is as much worthy of being called a language as the Roumanian or Bulgarian, so long as 6 millions of people speak it." In the next issue M. Kohn, a leading anarchist, writes: ". . . how do you [Schindler] know

whether our jargon is spoken by the unintelligent only, since you do not understand that tongue at all?" (No. 15, April 15, 1889).

74 Most of the radicals were, in later years, only too happy to lend their financial support to Russian radicals. Y. Kopelov, *op. cit.*, p. 454, writing on the occasion of a trip to the United States by a Russian social revolutionary emissary, confesses that "Every party which struggled against Czarism was dear and beloved to me." M. Kats aided G. Gershuni when the famous Russian populist came to America in 1907 (Kopelov, "M. Kats's tetikayt in der anarkhistisher un sots. revolutsyonerer bavegung," *M. Kats zamlbukh, op. cit.*, p. 28).

JEWISH SOCIAL CONDITIONS AS SEEN
BY THE MUCKRAKERS

By RUDOLF GLANZ

The group of American writers of the first decade of the 20th century who were characterized by President Theodore Roosevelt in 1906 as "muckrackers" had one thing in common: they engaged in social criticism of America solely by exposing conditions. Lacking a definite program, they attracted people of various ideologies. The muckrackers were not practical reformers. They certainly were not socialists. All they tried to do was to bring before the American public the inadequacy of the democratic process in coping with the explosive expansion of industrial capitalism in the United States. They succeeded in this task mainly because of the rapid expansion of the popular American magazines. Social criticism was introduced into the columns of these journals and at the same time the price of the most important magazines was reduced from twenty-five to ten cents. Circulation increased tremendously, and since these magazines were read by the entire family this meant also a correspondingly greater increase in the number of readers. It is safe to assume "that the muckrakers touched in one way or another the great majority of American citizens."[1]

Only a small percentage of the readers of the muckraker literature in the popular magazines were workers directly affected by the exploitation of American industry. The vast host of new readers whose interest was aroused by the social criticism of the magazines consisted of individuals who were still economically independent but who nevertheless felt themselves threatened by the process of industrial concentration and who projected their own apprehensions as a threat to the entire country.

[1] Regier, C. C., *The Era of the Muckrakers* (Chapel Hill, N. C. 1932) p. 197. For other literature on the muckrakers see: Faulkner, H. U., *The Quest for Social Justice, 1898-1914* (New York 1931) and Filler, Louis, *Crusaders for American Liberation* (New York 1939).

The opinions of the muckrakers regarding the Jews as found in these popular magazines were on the whole animated by entirely objective considerations. The enormous circulation which they enjoyed made them free from the pressure of advertisers and they did not, therefore, have to cater to the Jewish merchants who advertised in their pages. Nor did the muckrakers ever direct a special appeal to workers. They certainly could not have been concerned with the Jewish workers, who were predominantly recent immigrants and who were, for the most part, incapable as yet of reading an English paper. The Jewish group was conceived by the muckrakers as a completely outside group that still had to be integrated into the total picture of the country. Nor was there any Jewish influence within the muckraker group. All prominent muckrakers were non-Jews. All of them, however, attached special importance to the Jewish group in constructing their image of the future United States. In the words of Louis Filler, "The muckrakers were deeply infatuated with the Jews."[2]

I

The muckrakers displayed little or no interest in the Jewish groups of the "old immigration," those who had come from western Europe and who had by then attained a status of economic independence. Their chief preoccupation was with the compact masses of Jews who were coming from eastern Europe and who were creating new ghettos in the large cities of the United States. The Jewish ghetto became, for these writers, the great social group theme. The Jewish mass man was the classical example of the task at hand—the ghetto as a transformer. A writer in *Colliers Magazine* pointed out that "The Ghetto is perhaps best understood by those who regard it as a transformer of the human current from the Old World into the New—and especially so much of that current as is impelled toward this country by the European oppression of the Jews."[3] European poverty transplanted to America assumed here a completely new aspect because the new immigrant did not understand the factors governing the democratic life of the country. "The people are nearly all of them poor. Most of them are still in the alphabet of free government."[4] Thus the first experience of the immigrant in the new land

[2] *Op. cit.,* p. 118.
[3] "The New York Ghetto," in *Colliers,* Jan. 24, 1903, p. 10.
[4] *Loc. cit.*

was to find that among other unregulated sectors of social life, poverty, too, remained unregulated. What may have been adequate in Europe as poor relief was not even a palliative in America. As the first harbinger of a freedom not yet fully comprehended appeared human dignity, which declined favors that could no longer be of effective help. Thus the character of American, in contrast to European, poverty appeared radically different, and this difference found its classical expression in the ghetto.

> The Ghetto has taught intruding charity to seek other methods of satisfying itself and to send teachers and companions into the Ghetto instead of free soup and free claptrap talk. The pride of the Jew and the ambition of the Jew have vindicated themselves nobly in the face of the temptation which, above all others, must appeal to a Jew most subtly—that of getting substantial things for nothing.[5]

The value of concentration as a protective against the peculiar excrescences of the American political climate was also described by the keen eye of the muckraker.

> The folks of the Ghetto, [he wrote] who scarcely know enough English to understand the predatory demands made upon them by the grafters and the oppressors who always trail the weak, are quite helpless without the support which they get from living together by the thousands. The very thing which in a way keeps them down, their gregariousness, makes it possible for them to keep up the fight for existence.[6]

To the conception of concentration as a protective was added the additional function, namely, to serve as a basis for new creation. Freedom in its American manifestation at first presented a dilemma: the Jewish masses were at first helpless before the exploiting forces in the country until they were able to counter the brutal force of reality with an opposing force—that of the idea. This first rise of the social idea in the recent immigrant and its significance for the destiny of America, the muckraker saw in the first place and above all in the ghetto and he followed with the greatest eagerness the development of this idea among the other immigrants and its influence upon the rest of America. This special interest became a passion with him. "East Canal Street and the Bowery," wrote Hutchins Hapgood, "have interested me more than Broadway and Fifth Avenue."[7] And Ray Stannard Baker later wrote:

---

[5] *Loc. cit.*
[6] *Loc. cit.*
[7] *The Spirit of the Ghetto* (New York 1909) p. 5.

No one of the articles I wrote at that time more deeply aroused my interest and sympathy than the one I called "The Rise of the Tailors," which appeared in *McClure's* for December, 1904. It concerned the effort of a number of farsighted and idealistic labor leaders to organize the most poverty-stricken, unrecognized and undefended people in the country—masses of new immigrants who spoke little or no English, who were remorselessly exploited and cheated at every turn. They were the Russian Jews of the slums of New York, and Southern Italians, and Poles and Portuguese and Greeks who were workers in the garment industries.[8]

The same theme appeared in the muckraking fiction of David Graham Phillips. "Marx was a Hebrew—wasn't he? . . . Selma said: Yes, he was a Jew. Both were Jews . . . Marx and Jesus . . . And they were both labor leaders—labor agitators."[9] It was natural that the most famous of all muckrakers, Lincoln Steffens, came to see in all Jewish problems an incentive to activity. The articles that Steffens wrote on the East Side may well serve as an introduction to all later study of American social problems. These reports made him the teacher of an entire generation. Moreover, his personal contact with Jewish people in America, as he himself indicates, formed one of the most important moments in his biography.[10]

II

In the depth of their hearts the new social critics accepted the dynamic industrial development of America as a positive fact. They were merely ashamed of the fact that it created such distasteful human conditions. They felt the need of a sort of spiritual chivalry, at least toward the most obvious victims of the industrial Moloch, and the first object of this sentiment were the various minority ethnic groups among the new immigrants. Each one of these groups was studied sympathetically in terms of evaluation of its characteristics and of its potentialities in the development of the country. The compact Jewish group from eastern Europe however, challenged greater attention, than any other. Their conditions of life were unfamiliar to the Anglo-Saxon writer and were not covered by anything in his previous experiences with the European cultural world. Sec-

---

[8] *American Chronicle. The Autobiography of Ray Stannard Baker* [David Grayson] (New York 1945) p. 181.
[9] Phillips, David Graham, *The Conflict* (New York 1911) p. 62.
[10] See *The Autobiography of Lincoln Steffens* (New York 1931) and *The Letters of Lincoln Steffens* (New York 1938).

ondly, the Jews were the one group that was forced to migrate because of active persecution. The two decades of American newspaper reporting on the persecution of the Russian Jews served as a direct introduction to the subsequent critical evaluation of their adjustment in their new homeland. There is a direct line from the newspapers and magazines of the pre-muckraking era, with their penetrating reports on the Russian Jews, to the subsequent popular magazines of the muckrakers and their detailed and masterly studies of Jewish immigrant life.

Lincoln Steffens first came into prominence as a journalist with his articles on the East Side Jews in the New York *Evening Post*. As early as 1895 we find in this newspaper a description by him of the New York ghetto that may be considered the basis for all his subsequent observations. Steffens wrote as follows:

> It is estimated that between 111,000 and 112,000 Jews live in that part of New York west of the Bowery, bounded by East Houston Street, Ludlow Street and East Broadway. Of the number nearly half are children, and not more than 15,000 of the adults can speak English or even a foreign language fairly intelligible to other people. They come from Russia, Poland and Hungary, and the jargon most of them use is based upon Hebrew, and is made up of several languages and dialects and resembling no distinct European vernacular. Having been in this country but a short time, some of them only two or three years, very few more than twelve or fourteen, they have preserved their distinctive customs and practices almost inviolate, and are as orthodox and foreign to-day as when they first landed from the emigrant ships that brought them to these shores. By reason of their speech they are cut off from communication with the new world about them, their environments are Jewish, their acquaintances are Jews; if they buy and sell, their business associates and customers alike are of their own race. They recognize and understand no law but that dictated by their rabbis.[11]

Eight years later Steffens once again underscored the immobile and ethnocentric character of the Jewish ghetto population and even justified the expansion of the New York ghetto that had taken place.

> New York's ghetto people [wrote Steffens] are censured for not going into less thickly settled parts of the city. It is pointed out that they pay rent in Hester Street and Clinton Street and Norfolk Street and Chrystie Street which is far greater than the rent they would have to pay in much more comfortable parts of the city,

---

[11] "Customs in the Jewish Quarter," in the *Evening Post*, April 11, 1895, p. 2.

where they would be less crowded, where their children would have more room for recreation and where the air would be purer and the opportunity for earning money greater. But we might as well censure a blind kitten for not going out on its own initiative into the busy world.[12]

On January 1, 1895, the *Evening Post* published a report of the Hebrew Charities. Among the 7,508 applicants for aid, 1,486 came from Austria, 650 from Germany and 4,984 from Russia. *The Evening Post* added that the number of Jews in New York City exceeded 300,000.[13] These figures clearly show the complete predominance of eastern European Jewry, particularly Russian Jewry, and they are in accord with all other figures of that decade that are available. To this special group and its dramatic fate the popular newspapers turned their attention quite early. Departure of Russian Jews from their homes, their arrival in American ports, descriptions aboard the ship were frequent features of the newspapers and magazines. "More Jews to Leave Russia,"[14] meant the coming arrival of new immigrants, or "Jewish Exiles to be Returned,"[15] explained the prohibition of the landing of Siberian exiles in San Francisco. Such were the typical headlines of the period. At the very beginning of muckraking we encounter in the magazines illustrated reports, with scenes of Jewish immigrants aboard ship.[16]

Interest also turned at an early stage from the facts of eastern European Jewish emigration to its causes. Russia's treatment of the Jews was reported and discussed at length. "Treatment of the Jews in Siberia"[17] may be cited as a characteristic headline for a news story which linked all possible manifestations of Jewish persecution. Comprehensive studies of the treatment of Russian Jews were found in the last decade of the 19th century in those publications that later became representative of muckraking.[18] Simultaneously, concrete suggestions for aid to Russian Jews were discussed.[19]

An isolated voice against such aid appeared in a publication that later became a leader in muckraking—*The Arena.*

[12] *Collier's,* Jan. 24, 1903, p. 10.
[13] "Hebrew Charities," in the *Evening Post,* Jan. 20, 1895, p. 8.
[14] *Evening Post,* Nov. 21, 1893.
[15] *Evening Post,* Sept. 2, 1893, p. 1.
[16] "The Promised Land," in *McClure's Magazine,* vol. xx (1902-1903) 66-74.
[17] *Evening Post,* Nov. 11, 1893, p. 18.
[18] Hubert, Jr. T. G., "Russia's Treatment of Jewish Subjects," in *The Forum,* vol. xi (1891) 103-14.
[19] de Hirsch, M., "Refuge for Russian Jews," in *The Forum,* vol. xi (1891) 627-33.

The very dregs of foreign immigration [wrote Eva Valesh] always settle in New York, and the recent importation of the Baron Hirsch Jews can hardly be viewed in the light of philanthropy by this country. Their passage here is paid. They are taught the tailoring art in trade schools at twenty dollars per head. On leaving the trade school the sweat shop is the avenue of employment offered them. It is probably a cheap and expeditious method of disposing of this class, so far as Europe is concerned, but it is an additional burden to this country in a quarter where conditions were already well-nigh hopeless. Every industrial evil typical of the tenement quarter is aggravated by this new class of immigration.[20]

Such unfriendly voices, however, were exceptional.

Public sympathy was predominantly on the side of the Russian Jews and behind the efforts of world Jewry to rescue them by emigration. The few opponents of Jewish immigration among the muckrakers expressed their convictions much later, at a time when their social criticism was a thing of the past. An examination of the periodicals of the period provides the unmistakable impression that public discussion of the persecution of Jews in Russia came to the fore in those very publications that pioneered in American social criticism.[21] Their articles in these publications dealt with the Russian Jew as a human being, his circumstances, his striving for personal liberation from handicaps and his self-education and consequent success in the world. Simultaneously, there was elaborate exposition of the Americanization problems of the Jewish immigrant group as a whole.[22] These trends also coincided with fictional treatment of ghetto life in English by the first Russian-Jewish writers who had outgrown the milieu.[23] It is no mere coincidence that Abraham

[20] "The Tenement House Problem in New York," in *The Arena*, vol. vii (1892-93) 580-86.
[21] *Cf.* Yarras, Victor, "The Jewish Question in Russia," in *The Arena*, vol. iii (1890-91) 118-121; "Russia and the Jews," *ibid.*, vol. xxx (1903) 123 ff.; Weber, John B., "The Kishineff Massacre and Its Bearing upon the Question of Immigration into the United States," in *Collier's Weekly*, vol. xxxi (1903) 8; "The Massacres of Jews in Russia," *ibid.*, vol. xxxvi (1905-1906) 12-13; "The Massacres of Jews at Kishineff," in *The Outlook*, vol. lxxiv (1903) 203, 262, 298; "Jewish Persecutions in Russia," *ibid.*, vol. lxxv (1903) 381; "Persecution of Jews at Kishenev," vol. lxxvi (1904) 2; "The Result of the Kishinev Trial," p. 2.
[22] *Cf.* Poole, Ernest (as Told to Him by a Zemstvo Official in Southern Russia), "A Jewish Girl's Struggle to Rise in Russia," in *The Outlook* (1906) 125-31; "The Story of Manuel Levine," *ibid.* (1907) 413-19; Scott, Leroy, "A Daughter of the Russian Revolution," in *Everybody's Magazine*, vol. xvii (1907) 407 ff.; "Story of an Ambitious Russian Jew," in *American Magazine*, vol. lxvii (1908-1909) 236 ff.; "The Story of a Russian Jew," in *The Outlook* (1905) 376-78.
[23] Davis, Phillip, "Making Americans of Russian Jews," in *The Outlook*, (1905) 631-37.

Cahan's *The Rise of David Levinsky* first appeared in a muckraking magazine.[24]

The economic success of the Russian Jews in the United States suggested to some the thought that it was the function of the Russian Jew in America to maintain economic connections between the two countries by the establishment and advancement of Russian industries and by furthering trade relations between Russia and the United States.[25] At the same time these organs also directed their attention to the general and Jewish trends that animated the social organism of the new arrivals. One finds discussion of the relation to the general spirit of America as well as of the hotly contested problem: Zionism vs. Socialism?[26]

One aspect of the immigrant problem that had assumed a dominant place in the political discussion of the times was that of the immigrant vote. Was this vote a group vote, in the sense that certain immigrant groups as a whole were led by "national" politicians for special reward into the fold of the one or the other party? This became a vital question for both opponents and advocates of free immigration. It was even more crucial from the point of view of each of the national groups. Of all the objections raised against the "new immigration" the only one that was effective was the one grounded on the danger of the "foreign vote." Thus the *Evening Post* wrote:

> What is most remarkable in the discussion is the fact that little or no attention has been given to the undoubted, notorious, undeniable harm they do the country as additions to the voting population. This has been ignored in a most curious way by the champions of restriction although there is hardly a day in which it does not jump into our faces . . . The degradation of our city government is largely due to the readiness of the natives to let the immigrants sack the cities in return for their support in the Federal area . . .[27]

For a while the same danger threatened the Jewish immigrant group. The rise of politicians who pretended to be able to deliver or to influence the "Hebrew vote" was readily noted in the press.

[24] *McClure's Magazine,* vol. xl (1912-13) 92 ff.; vol. xli (1913) 73 ff.

[25] Ford, Alexander Hume, "The Russo-American Jew," in *Pearson's Magazine,* vol. x (1903) 233-39; "America's Debt to the Russian Jew," in *Collier's Weekly,* vol. xxxi (1903) 10.

[26] Baker, Edward M., "Judaism and the American Spirit," in *The Arena,* vol. xxxii (1904) 166 ff.; Beaumont, Saul, "Zionism or Socialism: Which Will Solve the Jewish Question?" in *The Arena,* vol. xxxix (1908) 54-58.

[27] "The Harm of Immigration," in the *Evening Post,* Jan. 14, 1893, p. 6.

> Most of the Hebrews who hold office in this city are men who are known as "professional Hebrews." They make their living by being Hebrews and making a pretence that they have great influence with their race.[28]

The following is an example of the treatment accorded to one such politician of the time:

> Harburger represents the east-side Hebrews of the lowest class, who followed the fortunes of Tammany until they saw better chances of plunder in the camp of the enemy. He has made his living out of public office nearly all his life, and he has obtained office on the strength of his supposed control of Hebrew votes. He is practically unknown to the prominent Hebrews of the city.[29]

In this political struggle the attempt was made to draw a line between the uptown and East Side Jews.

> The better class of Hebrews of this city are not proud of the men of their race who hold important offices. Some of them say that these men represent only the lowest Hebrew element and should not be regarded as representative Hebrews . . . It is a popular belief that these men are representative Hebrews, and that the race has been honored or "recognized" by placing them in public office. The fact is that Hebrews above the Baxter Street standard are ashamed of the men who have been put forward as their representatives, and would very much prefer no recognition at all to the kind they have received.[30]

Time rendered its clear decision. No "Hebrew vote" was established and consequently no one could boast of delivering it to a party. Moreover, the Jewish immigrant group demonstrated its political independence in a series of significant elections to a degree that pointed the way for the other immigrant groups. By the time the muckraking era arrived this development was already completed. Anxiety and doubt as to the political maturity of the Jewish immigrant had been overcome and the evaluation of this fact was undertaken in a comprehensive manner in the popular magazines of the muckrakers. Burton J. Hendrick commented as follows on this fact:

> Politically, the Jew's individualism is his saving grace. It prevents him from organizing in a mass. There is no such thing as the "Jewish vote" as there is an "Irish vote," and still, to a considerable extent, a "German vote." The Hebrews of New York are not controlled as a

---

[28] "Hebrew Office-Holders," in the *Evening Post*, March 4, 1895, p. 9.
[29] *Loc. cit.*
[30] *Loc. cit.*

unit by political leaders. They vote for one party at one election for another at the succeeding. Better than any other element, even the native stock, do they meet the two supreme tests of citizenship; they actually go to the polls, and when once there, vote independently.[31]

After a painstaking analysis of the results of the election on the East Side, the writer continued:

> Politically, therefore, it cannot be said that the Jews are a problem. In partisan politics their influence is decreased because of this very independence. Their leaders are unable to deliver their votes and thus are unable to demand much patronage. Of the thirty-five district leaders of Tammany Hall, in spite of the preponderance of the Jewish population, only one is a Jew. In all the East-Side districts except one, the Irish still control the party machinery.[32]

The difference in recreational and drinking habits between the new Jewish immigrants and the other immigrant groups also had important repercussions on the political situation. "The advent of Israel on the lower East Side of the metropolis," wrote James Creelman, "resulted in the closing of hundreds of bar-rooms."[33]

Or as a New York saloonkeeper put it in his memoirs:

> There were scarcely any Jews. Both Tye, the sales-agent, and Drugan, the later owner of the saloon, had dwelt on this last fact, saying that Jews are no drinkers and therefore n.g. for our trade.[34]

The saloon as a decisive factor in elections completely lost its function in Jewish neighborhoods or in sections in which Jews infiltrated. Gradually it became clear that it was impossible to master the new situation with the old means and personal influences.

> But beginning with the 80's the great Jewish and Italian immigration, which has overwhelmed the two earlier races, began to pour into the city. These people, especially the acute and intelligent Jews, could not be handled by the old time brutal, saloon-keeping Irish politician . . .[35]

The two ethnic groups of the "old immigration," the Germans

[31] Hendrick, Burton J., "The Great Jewish Invasion," in *McClure's Magazine,* vol. xxvii (1906-1907) 306-21.
[32] *Loc. cit.*
[33] "Israel Unbound," in *Pearson's Magazine,* vol. xvii (1907) p. 123-39; 239-60.
[34] "The Experience and Observations of a New York Saloon Keeper as Told by Himself," in *McClure's Magazine,* vol. xxxii (1908-1909) 308 ff.
[35] Turner, George Kibbe, "Tammany's Control of New York," in *McClure's Magazine,* vol. xxxiii (1909) 119 ff.

and the Irish, had actually used the saloons as centers of political machines. Political cartoons of the time frequently depicted their struggle as a fight between the German beer barrel and the Irish whiskey bottle. Things changed with the coming of the new Jewish immigrants. The serious attitude of the Jewish immigrant group toward the workaday problems made hopeless any attempt to regulate their political behavior from the saloon. Similarly the employment of gangsters against the Jewish population on the part of the local political machines was a total failure.

> These gangs were used, at first, fully as much for the intimidation of the Jewish voters as for "repeating." The Jew makes the most alert and most intelligent citizen of all the great immigrant races that have populated New York. He was a city dweller before the hairy Anglo-Saxon came up out of the woods, and every fall the East Side resolves itself into one great clamorous political debating society. In spite of all the efforts of the organized Jewish criminals in this district, it repeatedly gave a slight Republican plurality.[36]

In the final analysis, the influence of the Jewish population was felt, according to the critics, in their independence rather than in their closed vote.

> Not that the Jews of New York necessarily vote together, for they are recognized as a singularly independent and reform-seeking element in politics and it is this very independence which gives a growing importance to their voice in the civic affairs of the metropolis.[37]

Thus the writings of the muckrakers surveyed the salient features of a period in the development of American Jewry that was drawing to an end. By this time American Jewry consisted mostly of members of the "new immigration." The basis for this unfolding of new political powers in the American Jewish population was its integration in the economic life of the country, which was predicated upon the economic necessities and the abilities of the new immigrants, and led to a continual conquest of new economic positions. This process was seen by the muckrakers in all its acuteness and they appreciated its significance for the country as a whole. The problems of economic

[36] *Ibid.*, p. 121.
[37] Creelman, James, "Israel Unbound," in *Pearson's Magazine*, vol. xii (1907) 124.

and social adjustment of the new Jewish immigrants was thus brought
to the forefront of American public opinion by the social criticism
of the muckrakers.

III

The leading characteristic of the new social criticism of the muckrakers was its dispassionate description of social conditions. This was
true of their *belles-lettres* as well as of their journalistic reporting.
Their keen and observant eyes laid bare the living conditions of the
Jews in the ghettos of New York and Chicago. They paid special
attention to the tragic precocity of the life of Jewish children and
the weight of heavy responsibilities which they often carried. This
can be seen in the following masterly description by Lincoln Steffens.

> The children acquiring English quickly, with the adaptability of
> tender years, often assume the responsibilities that would rightfully
> belong to their elders. One girl of eleven habitually signs the
> checks and does all the writing necessary in transactions with cer-
> tain charitable bureaus that help her mother, and during her mother's
> illness undertook the cooking, washing, and general superintendence
> of five younger children, one of whom was an infant. When the
> baby had croup she doctored him herself, and on another occasion
> kept a paid position for her mother, proving an admirable sub-
> stitute until she could be relieved. This small maid is well up on
> the customs of her race, being able to give a fairly clear definition
> of the habit of wearing wigs . . . prevalent among east-side women,
> and answering questions in regard to other religious regulations with
> intelligent promptness.
>
> Another little girl is the real, although her mother is the osten-
> sible, janitress of a big tenement-house, the child conducting all the
> interviews with the Board of Health officials, the streetcleaners and
> other authorities, and personally conducting interviews regarding the
> renting of rooms, collecting, etc. She undertakes to make her bay-
> lodgers behave well and to enforce proper attention to the contracted
> area dignified by the term of "yard," generally coming off victor in
> the pitched battles in which she has to engage.[38]

All the earnestness of life seized the observer who had to evaluate
what he had seen on the East Side and register his impressions. Ray
Stannard Baker wrote:

> I can never forget my first visits to these workshops, the crowd-
> ed homes in slum tenements, the swarming, half-fed children—and

[38] "Customs in the Jewish Quarter," in the *Evening Post*, April 11, 1896,
p. 2. See also Darrow, Clarence, "Little Louis Epstine," in *The Pilgrim* (Dec.
1903) and Adams, S. H. *Blinky: A Story of the East Side* (New York 1897).

the sweat, the noise, the obscene poverty. It took hold powerfully
upon my sympathy and my imagination. I wanted to write an entire
book on what I found; I wanted it filled with pictures, both photo-
graphs and the finest available drawings, of what I had seen. But
there was no room—and no time—although the magazine did give
me generous space and used many good pictures.[39]

Descriptions by muckrakers of tenement houses and sweat shop
conditions were frequent and numerous.[40] But it was not the crushing
poverty nor the hard struggle for existence that impelled the in-
transigeant observers of new things in American life to the ghetto,
but a higher evidence of an entirely different kind, which reflected the
things perceived in a transcendental transfiguration. America saw here
for the first time an idealism arising from the struggle for existence
of the poor masses and a practical solidarity of all in the striving for
a better life built, in turn, upon a better organization of man's labor.

> What thrilled me most of all [wrote Baker] was the extra-
> ordinary idealism and patience with which these poor men and
> women came to their own help. They had to suffer everything, not
> only the loss of their jobs, but literally hunger and cold, in forming
> any organization at all. They kept at it for years, they struck again
> and again and when they were discharged and left homeless, other
> workers re-formed their lines and finally succeeded in organizing
> and re-creating the entire industry. The reform had come finally, as
> all great reforms must come, from within, from the men them-
> selves. . . .
>
> It seemed to me at times that this was the most remarkable
> exemplification of a true American and democratic approach to
> the solution of problems I had ever known. It seemed also an
> exemplification of the magic of the American system in lifting men
> into new freedom, new independence, and a new attitude toward life.
> All of these things I put into my article.[41]

It is difficult to conceive that the "rise of the tailors" could have
stirred the hopes of the most powerful group of American writers,
and even more, that their strikes could have become a herald of the
future America and thereby could have risen to symbolic significance
and become at times the only reality in which the socialist element
among the intellectuals sought solace. And yet these strikes were quite

[39] *Op. cit.,* p. 181.

[40] McKenna, M. J., *Our Brethren of the Tenements and the Ghetto* (New
York 1899); Markham, Edwin, "The Sweat-Shop Inferno," in *The Cosmopolitan,*
vol. xlii (1906-1907) 327.

[41] *Op. cit.,* p. 181.

different, something new, as can be seen in the contemporaneous analysis of Lincoln Steffens. The identification of the eastern European Jewish immigration with one major industry made it possible for all labor conflicts in that industry to appear in bolder outline.

> For years [wrote Baker] the fortunes of the East Side have risen and fallen with the garment-making industry. It is the typical trade of the tenements. No other industry in New York City, or in New York State, employs so many workers. Thousands of shops there are in the crowded districts below Fourteenth Street, and they produce over half the ready-made clothing used in the United States; a vast industry, supporting hundreds of thousands of souls, yet almost unknown to the outside world.[42]

And the union was the sole stay of the Jewish tailor. "He would hardly know that he was in free America were it not for the union."[43]

A decade before the flowering of the muckrakers the labor struggles of the Jewish tailors had been brought to the attention of the American public. Lincoln Steffens had reported on the tailors' strikes on the East Side of 1895-97.[44]

The era of the muckrakers saw also some of the worst defeats suffered by the striking Jewish tailors. Nevertheless it remained the opinion of the critics of the period that the successes of the workers achieved through the union could no longer be cancelled for they had become part of the public interests of American life. The belief in the solidarity of the Jewish workers, ready to bring the highest sacrifice for their principles, remained unshaken.

> These Jewish idealists, indeed, were prepared to risk everything —the high wages, the short hours, the excellent shop conditions they had secured after years of struggle—in order to maintain the principle they felt to be at stake.[45]

R. S. Baker told about the contributions made by the better paid workers for the benefit of their struggling brothers:

> What other class of men would contribute from fifteen to twenty percent of their wages to any cause whatsoever—and take the chances at that of being deprived of work entirely—with the dreadful alternative of the East Side staring them in the face? What

[42] Baker, Ray Stannard, "The Rise of the Tailors," in *McClure's Magazine,* vol. xxiv (1904-1905) 126-39.

[43] *Ibid.,* p. 129.

[44] *Evening Post,* August 10 and 12, 1895; July 11 and 22, 1896; May 17, 1897.

[45] "The Rise of the Tailors," in *McClure's Magazine,* vol. xxiv, p. 134.

religion would draw so much from its followers? No one can understand the meaning or the vitality of trade-unionism, or appreciate the depth to which its roots have struck into our soil, until he has seen a strike like this.[46]

Baker also described the change of feelings that came over the Jewish worker when he became an entrepreneur and noted the middle class traits of his private life.

And as a class these Jewish Garment-Workers are saving, frugal, progressive, eager to educate their children: tomorrow not a few of them will become employers and live in up-town houses, themselves troubled and probably bitter over the attitude of the union men whom they employ.[47]

Going beyond the fate of the Jewish immigrants, there now came into existence literary evaluations of American Jewry in all branches of economy, education and science.[48] Even Jewish agricultural colonization attempts were noted.[49] The special adaptability of the Jewish country merchant was stressed. In the South, for instance, his treatment of the Negro turned the scale in his favor. "If the Jew has a department store in a Southern City, he succeeds partly because he is so flexible in falling in with the peculiarities of blacks and whites alike. To say Miss or Mrs. to the colored purchaser is to get her trade."[50]

In the discussion of their positive contributions to American economic life the fact was stressed that in many economic sectors one Jewish group confronted another, e.g., entrepreneurs against workers. "They came with qualities and traditions so diverse that their competition among themselves (as between German and Russian Jews) is as relentless as it is against any other class of the community."[51]

A major theme of the muckraker's description was the monster of American capitalism. Included among the portraits of the outstanding captains of finance and industry which they drew were now

[46] *Ibid.*, p. 134.

[47] *Ibid.*, p. 132.

[48] See for example Herbert N. Casson's "The Jew in America," in *Munsey's Magazine*, vol. xxxiv (1905-1906) 381-95.

[49] Pincus, Joseph W., "A Significant Experiment with the Jews in Agriculture," in *The Independent*, vol. lv (1903) 2337-43.

[50] Brooks, John Graham, *As Others See Us* (New York 1908) p. 42 and p. 41.

[51] *Loc. cit.*

a number of Jews.[52] For the sake of comparison, the house of Rothschild was also included.[53]

The searching look of the muckrakers perceived the contrasts within the capitalist system that had nothing to do with capitalist interests but derived from the traditional position of the Jews. Thus Lincoln Steffens, in a study of the political power of American capital, wrote:

> None of the Jewish banking houses is "in it." Some financial critics include Kuhn, Loeb & Co., as Ryan did, and they show Jacob Schiff and other Jewish names in great directorates, but the Jews and the big insiders confirm my conclusion, and explain it. The Christians (so to speak) say the omission of the Jews is deliberate and personal; that Morgan has a race or religious prejudice against the Jews. The Jews themselves set aside this explanation in a very Christian spirit. One of the leaders among them attributed it to "an unfortunate experience Mr. Morgan had with a certain Jewish house" and the rest put it to "accident." Whatever the true explanation is, the "independence" of the Jewish interest is important. It is one more proof of the unintelligent innocence of the wickedness of the "money monster." No man who intended to put himself at the head of a perfect monopoly of money power would lock out the Jews.[54]

The results of this treatment of the Jewish capitalists were thus envisioned:

> They are powerful financially, both here and abroad; and they are good fighters. Slow to enter into a quarrel; once in they make it a war; they join hands all around the earth and, since they have sense, which other, younger peoples seem not yet to have developed, of their children's children unto the third and fourth generation, a financial war with the Jews might mean a divided Money Tower for generations to come.[55]

Another attempted explanation went back directly to the time when the German Jew entered the trade in securities and the interest groups of foreign capital marshalled their allies in the United States.

[52] "Captains of Industry (Charles Frohman, Joseph Pulitzer)," in *The Cosmopolitan*, vol. xxxiii (1902); "Captains of Industry (August Belmont, Jacob Schiff)," *ibid.*, vol. xxxiv (1902-1903); "Captains of Industry (Meyer Guggenheim and His Seven Sons)," vol. xxxv (1903); Lyle, Jr., Eugene P. "Founding the House of Guggenheim. The Guggenheims and the Smelter Trust," in *Hampton's Magazine*, vol. xxiv (1910) 256-67; 411-22.

[53] Phillips, David Graham, "The Empire of Rothschild," in *The Cosmopolitan*, vol. xxxviii (1904-1905) 501-15.

[54] "It. An Exposition of the Sovereign Political Power of Organized Business," in *Everybody's Magazine*, vol. xxiii (1910) 458.

[55] *Ibid.*

The Yankee against the Jew

The start of the Government's billion and a half refunding operation in 1871 marked one of the most interesting and important periods in the financial history of the country. For the first time in America, that great instrument of modern finance, the under-writing syndicate of security merchants (or private bankers), was to come into use; and, for the first time was to come that cleavage in American financial interests which has existed essentially ever since. On either side of the transaction were ranged the greatest traders of the Western world, the Yankee and the Jew.

The alignment was perfectly natural. The two parties represented, as they do to-day, the two great bodies of foreign capital invested here: the New Englanders the English; the Jews the German. Jay Cooke, the leading candidate for the refunding work, most naturally allied himself with the German Jews, who had come into business relations with him in their sale of Government bonds abroad. Drexel—early a friend of Cooke's, but since Cooke's overshadowing success a jealous rival—was his chief competitor. Side by side with Drexel fought the New Englanders—the old-time dry-goods dealers, the Morgans and the Mortons.[56]

Thus, after having brought the role of the Jewish worker to the attention of the American public, the muckrakers directed their descriptive analysis to the Jewish capitalist. In their extensive descriptions of general Jewish life they also included accounts of other phases of Jewish economic activity, such as petty trade, peddling and handicraft, woven into the general picture of the Jewish immigrant group.

IV

The visitor to the closed Jewish residential district was struck first by its surprising and absolutely novel character.

Striking east from Broadway and crossing the dividing line of the Bowery, in the neighborhood of Grand Street, the average New Yorker comes upon a country of whose habits he probably knows less and with whose inhabitants he certainly has much less in common, than if he had crossed the Atlantic and found himself in Picadilly or Pall Mall.[57]

This difference in kind found its classical expression in the young reporter Lincoln Steffens, who scrutinized all its details and oriented

[56] Moody, John and Turner, George Kibbe, "The Masters of Capital in America. Morgan: The Great Trustee," in *McClure's Magazine*, vol. xxxvi (1910-1911) 3-24.

[57] Hoffman, Katherine, "In the New York Ghetto," in *Munsey's Magazine*, vol. xxiii (1900) 608-10.

toward it his studies and personal habits. In his autobiography he tells us a few things about his reporting workshop, about the *mezuza* on the door of his East Side office, his fasting on Yom Kippur, his visits to synagogues, strike scenes and the conflict between the old and young generation. In his newspaper stories all this was presented in the simplest lines, as can be seen from the following example:

> Most of the older Jews, the kind who habitually wear long, black beards, a long black coat, shiny and shabby, buttoned across the breast, and a Russian felt hat, have calm, rather reverent faces, but the excitement of bargaining rouses them to unwonted animation, and they lose for the time their thoughtful, philosophical demeanor.[58]

Traditional religious practice helped to create the local character of the East Side, in the workaday as well as in the transformation that this part of the city underwent on holidays. On grey workdays one predominantly saw only petty trading.

> Peddlers are plentiful in the Jewish quarter; peddlers of candles, three in a bunch, to be used in religious rites, of artificial flowers, imitation peacock feathers and dyed grasses, peddlers of second-hand frocks and coats, of cooked and uncooked food, of combs, celluloid collar-buttons, and perfumery; but the most picturesque peddler of them all is he who sells packages of dirt, of genuine mother earth from Jerusalem, . . . Sales are managed on Oriental principles. There is always plenty of chaffering; the seller praises his goods, the buyer undervalues them. At length, after both parties have exhausted argument . . . a sale will be made.[59]

Business assumed an entirely different aspect in the pre-holiday season, when the need for all kinds of permanent goods came to the fore.

> This is the season also of the Hebrew book trade, for thousands of orthodox people who are forgetful of their prayer-books during the year and let them get lost, now find themselves in need of new ones. Then many of those who can afford it will want to appear in the synagogue in a new praying-shawl. The book-dealers, as a rule, sell these things and palm-branches and citrons as well as all sorts of religious publications. Nor are the clothier, the hatter, the shoe-dealer, and the jeweller left out of consideration, for who that is

[58] "Customs in the Jewish Quarter," in the *Evening Post,* April 11, 1896, p. 2.
[59] *Ibid.*

not out of work will fail to invest in a new suit, or a hat, or a pair of shoes, or a watch and chain for the greatest of holidays? . . Take it all in all, it is a money-making season as well as a money-spending one, at once the most solemn and the most cheerful part of the Jewish year.[60]

Old and new tendencies met in the preparation for the festival and yet conflict was avoided. Each one went his way.

And many of the irreligious ones relax their atheism on those days as on Yom Kippur, . . . "It is safe and does no harm," said a non-believer who scorned the ignorance of the orthodox and laughed as he told what his people do.
. . . All day to-day the East Side was busy preparing for the days of Rosh Hoshana. There was cleaning of clothes and of homes and the bathing-places were full. Hester Street and Essex and all the other market places were in commotion, the women and old men being out making purchases of fish at four cents a pound and rare fruits like pears and pineapples, or best of all, persimmons.
. . . "Don't you go to the concerts or theatres?" "Oh, I do," said a tailor, "I'm going to a ball uptown, but the others don't. They keep it holy." ". . . And where are you going to-morrow morning?" "Oh, most of our club are going bicycling out to— . . ."[61]

The preparations in the synagogue crowned all these activities. The entire organizational structure of the Jewish population was manifest above all in the manner in which such houses of prayer came into existence. The keen eye of the reporter discerned the essential.

Few orthodox congregations are large enough to afford a separate building for a house of worship. Most of them are small societies made up of fellow-townsmen and bearing the name of their native place. Almost every town within the pale of Jewish settlements in Russia, Austria, or Rumania is represented here by a synagogue. Accordingly, the average congregation must be content with a room and bed-room on the top floor of some overcrowded tenement-house, the smaller room usually being set aside for the female worshippers, who follow the chasan through the portieres. Most of these struggling societies sublet their rooms for weekdays to melamdim . . . who teach their scholars in the afternoon, when they come from the public schools. As a rule, a synagogue is also a kind of club-house, the more devout of the members coming to spend their leisure moments there, reading Psalms, swapping news of the old home, or exchanging notes upon the adopted country. In addition to the permanent

---

[60] "When the Shofar Blows," in the *Evening Post*, Sept. 25, 1897, p. 2.
[61] "The Jewish New Year," in the *Evening Post*, Sept. 7, 1896, p. 5.

congregation, of which there are several hundred in the Jewish quarter, at least as many temporary ones spring into existence for the great holidays. To accommodate these, every dancing hall and assembly-room, and many a sweat-shop is transformed into a synagogue, and every tailor or teacher of Hebrew who lays any claim to musical gift enters the list in competition for the place of cantor or chorister. The two large Jewish theatres of this city, the Windsor and the Thalia, are announced as houses of worship for the coming festivals, with some of the leading Jewish actors for chasans.[62]

The reporter was also well acquainted with the financial basis of the synagogue.

The net proceeds from the sale of seats are in many instances the main source of the congregation's income. Hence, the hiring of a good cantor is generally viewed in the light of an investment. . . . Some celebrities are paid for the four principal services of the Days of Awe as much as $1,000, but such virtuosos apart, $200 would be a fair average of the cantor's fee, although the humbler congregations cannot afford to pay more than $50 for the season. . . .

The wealthier synagogues engage their chasans by contract on a snug monthly salary, and often import them from some large city in Russia or Galicia; so that the Hebrew communities of those countries are said to have been drained of their best religious singers by their brethren of the New York Ghetto, who are by far the highest bidders in the world's cantor market.[63]

The transformation of the community of worshippers back to workaday existence appeared to the reporter as an incomprehensible metamorphosis:

To look at this whispering, gesticulating, nodding, ecstatic crowd, it was almost hard to imagine them in any other role than holding communion with their Maker or studying His sacred laws. But Minha over, each at once assumed a work-a-day air, and as they kissed the Mezuzoh parchment on the door-post in haste to get out into the noisy street, there was again before the observer a cluster of tailors, peddlers, store-keepers, each with the seal of wordly care on his face.[64]

The chief concern of all thoughtful critics of the period was Americanization—the education of the young as well as the adults among the immigrants to a proper understanding of American ideals. In respect to the Jewish immigrant, Americanization coincided with

---

[62] *Evening Post,* Sept. 25, 1897, p. 2.
[63] *Ibid.*
[64] "The Poor in Israel," in the *Evening Post,* Oct., 1897, p. 10.

the fact that a specific Jewish educational system had been transplanted from the Old into the New World, that Jewish parents discharged the duty of training their children through the establishment of schools with regard for the traditional values and that simultaneously they realized the importance of general education for the future of their children in the New World. Both, school scenes and general attitude to knowledge and education, Jewish as well as secular, formed the subject of description by the muckrakers in fiction and in reporting in the popular magazines.

Here is Lincoln Steffens' report on the East Side:

> These humbler Jews have certain distinct characteristics. They are born musicians, natural gamblers, abstemious, and earnest admirers of education and the benefits education confers. Among the ignorant of other nationalities the man of higher origin is oftimes regarded with distrust, but this is not so among the Jews; they are proud of their leaders being educated, and no matter how ignorant they may be themselves, though it is affirmed that the poorest among them can read and write in their native language, they crave education for their children, and strive to give them advantages.[65]

Thus the general atmosphere of the ghetto was set for youth organizations and their educational program and their lively activities.

> There are a number of boys' clubs in the district, in which the members take great interest, and try to improve themselves, taking part in literary debates and the discussion of current events in national and municipal affairs. Altogether it is plain that with the intelligence and activity displayed by the growing children of the race the Ghetto of New York must lose some of its Oriental characteristics in the next quarter of a century, but it will take a great deal of leaven to leaven such a compact mass.[66]

The same opinion was also expressed about the children of the group that attempted to settle on farms. A reporter on the Chesterfield Settlement, in Connecticut, had the following to say:

> This modern spirit is seen everywhere. It was a strange sight to me to see a group of typical little Jews gathered in the Chesterfield school house listening open-eyed to lessons from a Yankee schoolteacher from the next village, a girl who said that nothing could be more encouraging than the quickness with which these children learn. In six months after coming from Russia they talk English as

---

[65] *Evening Post,* April 11, 1896, p. 2.
[66] *Loc. cit.*

well as if they had been born here. On my way back to New London
I saw the Chesterfield base-ball club, composed of Russian lads, at
work with all the enthusiasm of our native born experts.[67]

The same we hear from Woodbine:

The Russian children are remarkably quick in learning English
and compare favorably with American scholars of the same age.
Fifteen of the older boys form a fire brigade, proud in the possession
of uniforms and a chemical engine upon wheels. In the evenings all
the year round there are classes for adults, the average attendance
this last spring have been forty.[68]

There are also other stories of the life of Jewish young people.
Lincoln Steffens attempted to give us the story of a Jewish girl who
strayed from the straight path.[69] In the general fiction of America
the story of the rising Jewish hero was as a rule accompanied by a
description of his apprenticeship years.[70]

General education in the direction of cultivating the taste was
attempted in the ghetto by means of art exhibitions. The results
varied, as Steffens wittily described:

It is grievous to report that notwithstanding a very appreciable
improvement in apprehension over last year, the interest of the
beholders centers more in the names of the owners than in those of
the artists or even in the pictures. The name of Mr. Straus or Mr.
Bloomingdale or Mr. Schiff is worth for their conjuring to such
names as Gerome, Schreyer, or Inness. The pecuniary end of the
whole business they also seek for with extreme diligence. "Are not
the pictures to be sold?" inquired an aged Jew of one of the custo-
dians, of his own race. Explanation was most difficult; but when the
old man finally understood, he piously and unexpectedly exclaimed
in jargon which may be translated: "Oh, that is grand! It will keep
many away from vice."[71]

In the study of Jewish character and of individuals steeped in
Jewish values, the muckrakers penetrated at last into the actual
spiritual life of the Jewish group, its spiritual movements and its relation to the position that Israel occupies among the nations. They saw
the problem of antisemitism in the light of the social contact between

[67] "Russian Jews as Farmers," in the *Evening Post,* Sept. 5, 1894, p. 5.

[68] "Russian Jews as Farmers," in the *Evening Post,* Sept. 6, 1894.

[69] "Schloma, the Daughter of Schmuhl," in *The Chapbook* (Chicago) vol. v
(1896) 128-32.

[70] Cahan, Abraham, *The Rise of David Levinsky.*

[71] "Paintings on the East Side," in the *Evening Post,* May 9, 1896, p. 12.

Jews and non-Jews in America as well as in the echo of the Dreyfus affair. Finally Zionism was also discussed.

Antisemitism in the various European countries had been discussed by the American press as far back as the end of the 19th century. A characteristic explanation of the time was that "it is safe to say that the spread of antisemitic feeling is a product, more or less direct, of the socialistic feeling which is now in the air in every country and seeking expression by all sorts of channels."[72] For local consumption, however, antisemitism was something altogether different. Its specific American function of excluding the Jew from social life was achieved in full precisely at a time when the economic rise had created an upper stratum of Jews. Cases of rejection of Jewish candidates for membership in various clubs became frequent, which enabled the daily press to establish fearlessly the existence of social antisemitism.

> The "Christian Place," or the Jew-free club, is a prejudice which in the main keeps Jews and Christians socially apart in nearly every city in the country, which excludes Jews more or less from all the leading summer hotels, and would probably prevent Mr. Seligman's entrance to any other non-Jewish club in New York. In fact, there is no social phenomenon of the day more familiar to all New Yorkers, and particularly to the philosophers of journalism, than this prejudice . . . as notoriously as the sun at noonday, and is of long standing. . . .[73]

In instances of the private social sphere the right of the club to exclude Jews was generally conceded. General prejudice, however, was fought strenuously by the popular magazines of the muckrakers. The attack on a funeral procession in the New York ghetto in 1902 was considered of general importance by the muckrakers and they recorded the reaction of the Jewish population to the incident.

> For their indiscriminate use of the nightstick the police have been criticized severely by the Jewish newspapers, and their readers have held mass meetings of protest against what they are prone to regard as an anti-Semitic demonstration to which the officers of the law lent their aid.
>
> On the Mayor's order, an inquiry into the whole matter has been started, and a vigilance committee of the Jews is at work.[74]

[72] "The Jews in Europe," in the *Evening Post*, Jan. 4, 1893.
[73] "Club Candidates," in the *Evening Post*, April 17, 1893.
[74] "A Riot in the Ghetto," in *Collier's Weekly*, vol. xxix (1902) 23.

The general study of the moving spiritual forces in America led to the perception of distant associations between historical Judaism and the foundations of American culture.[75] The critical appraisal of religious conditions in America was an important subject of the muck-raker. A study of parallel conditions in the Jewish community was made by R. S. Baker.[76] Gradually the development led to an understanding of the inner conditions of the Jewish people throughout the world. Zionism in its early stages had not aroused as much attention in America as an Europe. Yet precisely among the observers of the Jews of the ghetto there were such who properly recognized its moral impact for the Jews.

> Zionism represents, to me, all that is good in the Jewish ideals, and I have never found that a Jew who has no sympathy with Zionism has the moral qualities that entitle him to respect. Next to the Law, Zionism seems necessary for the life of Judaism.[77]

The magazines of the muckrakers opened their columns to the Zionist leaders,[78] and a number of articles appeared about the land of the future: Palestine.[79]

All in all, the end of the muckraking period left American Jewry with a solid diagnosis of its most important aspects by competent outsiders. The muckrakers contributed to the understanding of Jewish life in America no less than to the elucidation of other social conditions.

[75] Seward, Theodore F., "The Unity of Christianity and Judaism," in *The Arena,* vol. xxvii (1902) 351-66; Baker, Edward M., "Judaism and the American Spirit," *ibid.,* vol. xxvii (1904) 166 ff.
[76] "The Spiritual Unrest. The Disintegration of the Jews," in *American Magazine,* vol. lxvii (1909) 590-603.
[77] McKenna, M. J., *Our Brethren of the Tenements and the Ghetto,* p. 12.
[78] Nordau, Max, "The Zionist Movement," in *The Independent,* vol. lii (1900) 2191-92; Gaster, M., "The Truth about Zionism," in *The Forum,* vol. xxix (1900) 230-39.
[79] Meyer, Martin A., "The Jewish Colonies in Palestine," in *The Independent,* vol. liv (1902) 2347-53.

Un-American America
and the *Jewish Daily Forward*

By Tamara K. Hareven

> The *Forward* is the working men's organ in their every righteous
> fight against their oppressors; this struggle is the body of our
> movement. But its soul is the liberation of mankind—justice,
> humanity, fraternity—in brief, honest common sense and horse
> sense.[1]

In these phrases, Abraham Cahan, the creative editor of the
Forward, succinctly summarized his paper's philosophy. The *Forward* was the largest and most prosperous American foreign language newspaper and the most widely read Jewish paper in the
world. In the 1920's, its daily circulation reached 153,639.[2] A study
of its reaction to the restriction of liberties in the 1920's reveals the
views of a socialist-oriented ethnic and religious minority, including
large numbers of newly-arrived immigrants. The strain of nativism
and xenophobia underlying the Red Scare, the deportation of aliens
and the persecution of minorities, the restriction of immigration
and the revival of the Ku Klux Klan, held for the readers of the
Forward an unprecedented immediacy. To them American society
assumed the character of a nightmare which threatened them personally and which abused the ideals they cherished.

[1] Cahan, Abraham, quoted in Moses Rischin, *The Promised City* (Cam-
bridge, Mass., 1962), p. 159.
[2] Seldes, George, *Lords of the Press* (New York 1938), pp. 103ff. Abraham
Cahan was the first editor of the *Forward* in 1897. He then left and worked
as a reporter for Lincoln Steffens on the *Commercial Advertiser* and for the
Sun and *The Evening Post*. In 1902 he returned to the *Forward* and served
as its editor for the rest of his life.

The *Forward* was founded in 1897 by a small group of Jewish socialists on the East Side, as a non-profit paper. All its income was used for the publication of additional editions in Chicago and Philadelphia, for relief funds during strikes, for aid to labor organizations and for needy workers. Abraham Cahan was its first editor.

Under the editorship of Cahan over a period of nearly fifty years the *Forward* came to be more than a newspaper. *The New York Times* defined it later as "a newspaper, a party organ, an instrument for the building of labor unions and a popular university." [3] Jewish workers regarded it as the champion of their rights. They turned to it for advice and financial help in their struggle with employers. Gradually they began to refer to it their personal problems as well. The *Forward*'s readers were not only new immigrants and socialists, but also Americanized Jews who could read English papers, but who preferred the *Forward*, because of their sentiment for the Yiddish language and culture. In its pages they found the best coverage of those Jewish events which were overlooked by the general press. Moreover, the *Forward* inspired a sense of corporate belonging and provided ties with a past for which many still nurtured a nostalgic longing.

Ab. Cahan combined in his personality the intellectual, the novelist, the social worker, the socialist leader and the muckraker. He flavored all these with a deep sensitivity to human problems and with a philosophical, forgiving sense of humor. In his background, he merged the heritage of Judaic learning with the Western tradition of scholarship, letters and Marxism. Born in a small town near Vilna, he was educated in a typical Jewish Orthodox environment. He broke, however, with religious tradition and pursued a secular education in the Vilna Teachers Institute. Involvement in the revolutionary movement in 1882 drove him to the United States. His literary talent, his sense of reality, and his adaptability enabled him to absorb the culture of America quickly. His novels on the East European Ghetto and on immigrant life in the East Side brought him fame at the age of thirty-six. *The Rise of David Levinsky* became a classic immigrant novel. William Dean Howells compared Cahan's realism and achievement to that of Stephen

---

[3] *The New York Times*, September 1, 1951, p. 11.

Crane. Simultaneously with his literary activity, Cahan was an active member of the Socialist party and was instrumental in founding the first Jewish Tailors' Union.[4]

As a journalist, Cahan transformed the *Forward* into a mirror of everyday life and into a channel for the expression of the worker on the East Side. This was partly due to his apprenticeship under Lincoln Steffens on the staff of the *Commercial Advertiser*. Steffens taught him the trick of ruthless investigation behind the event. "Here, Cahan, is a report that a man has murdered his wife —a rather bloody, hacked-up crime. We don't care about that. There's a story in it. If you can just find what happened between the wedding and this murder...." [5] Later, when Cahan returned to edit the *Forward*, he applied this lesson. He changed the character of the paper, substituting lively realism for dialectical polemics and discarding stuffy high-brow articles, which rehashed Marxist ideology and class warfare slogans. He encouraged readers to contribute: "Under your tenement roofs are stories of the real-life stuff, the very stuff of which great literature can be made. Send them to us. Write them any way you can. Come and tell them to us." [6] Thus, the East Side began to read about itself.

At the same time, Cahan tried to maintain the didactic character of the paper and to develop it as an instrument of Americanization. From his editorials the readers learned about the structure of American government and received thorough explanations of the events. From 1921, Cahan published regular daily English lessons. Occasionally, he wrote articles teaching etiquette. In response to one of his columns, urging mothers to provide their children with handkerchiefs, indignant socialists asked sarcastically how this was connected with ideology. "And since when has socialism been opposed to clean noses?" came Cahan's reply.[7]

The simplifications appeared in language, as well. Cahan introduced a colloquial version of Yiddish as it was spoken on the streets, in the sweatshops and in the homes. Whenever one of his writers lapsed into long sentences or difficult German words, he

4 *Ibid.*, Professor Moses Rischin is now writing the long-awaited biography of Cahan.
5 Steffens, Lincoln, *Autobiography* (New York 1937), p. 255.
6 Quoted in Rischin, *op. cit.*, p. 131.
7 Cahan, quoted in Seldes, *Lords of the Press*, p. 105.

called the elevator man to see if he understood.[8] This, however, did not result in shallowness and intellectual sterility. Cahan was engaged in a continuous effort to develop his readers' taste. Hence, there was always room in the *Forward* for short novels and stories, book reviews and criticism of the theatre and the arts.

Although the organ of the Jewish members of the Socialist Party, the *Forward* was not committed to official socialist doctrine, nor was it restricted by the party's policy. Cahan preferred accurate information to propaganda and viewed socialism in human terms rather than as abstract dogma. He fought sweatshops, helped unions in their struggle and denounced all infringements upon liberty. His interest, however, was in factual information and education as much as in protest. "The *Forward* is a party paper," he wrote, "but it is first of all a newspaper. I think that party affiliations of newspapers are compatible as long as newspapers remember their primary purpose." [9]

From 1919 on and throughout the early 1920's, the *Forward* reflected the bewilderment and anxiety of its readers in reaction to the rising fever of the Red Scare and its ramifications. The readers' interest in the events, especially in immigration policies and in the Sacco-Vanzetti trial, was immediate and exceeded ideological commitments. True to its muckraking tradition the paper exploited every detail and involved the audience emotionally. As a socialist paper it presented the issues in class-warfare terms and rallied the readers to protest. Thus, the detailed debates around the Immigration Bills, the reports from Eugene Debs's prison cell and the proceedings of the Sacco-Vanzetti trial held greater attention than foreign affairs and presidential elections.

A typical illustration of the *Forward*'s stance was its coverage of the Amnesty Movement to free Eugene Debs and the other political prisoners who had been convicted under the Espionage Act. The *Forward* became the most important publicity vehicle among the Jewish workers. One of its reporters regularly accompanied the members of the Central Labor Bodies Conference for the Amnesty of Political Prisoners on their missions to the Presi-

---

[8] Park, Robert E., *The Immigrant Press and Its Control* (New York 1922), pp. 101–102.
[9] Cahan, quoted in Seldes, *Lords of the Press*, p. 106.

dent, the Attorney General and on their visits to the prison. Consequently, the *Forward* was the first to receive the news.[10] The case of Eugene Debs virtually monopolized the paper's headlines and editorials, overshadowing the fate of other political prisoners. The paper built an aura of martyrdom around the imprisoned Debs. When Woodrow Wilson refused to release him, the *Forward* came out with a vehement attack on the President. Attributing the refusal to personal hatred rather than to principle, it contrasted the "reactionary president" with the suffering idealist. Assuring its readers that Wilson could not possibly break the spirit of Debs, it construed the latter's ordeal in prison as the inevitable test every idealist had to face.[11]

Their attitudes towards Debs became the acid test for the President and his cabinet. Thus, despite his stand on other issues, the *Forward* hailed the newly-elected President Harding as a liberal, when he instructed the Attorney General to investigate the case of Debs and other political prisoners. By April 7, however, the *Forward* was disillusioned with Harding. Rallying its readers to a demonstration, it reminded them that Jewish workers had supported the amnesty movement from its inception. Here was their chance to manifest their power. "Let not one Jewish organization be left without representation." [12]

With the release of Debs on Christmas morning of 1921, the *Forward* celebrated its great victory. Abraham Cahan himself marked the occasion by writing the feature article. He hailed the event as a triumph for the labor movement, and as the end of an era of repression. Despite the joy, however, the *Forward* did not fail to note the limitations. Debs was deprived of his American citizenship; the other one hundred and eighty prisoners remained rotting in prison. This proved that the Government still responded to the pressure of "reactionary chauvinists." Nevertheless, there was

---

[10] *The Jewish Daily Forward,* December 26, 1921. Eugene Debs was arrested because of an anti-war speech which he made at the Ohio State Convention of the Socialist Party, at Canton, Ohio, in June 1918. He was tried, found guilty of violation of the Espionage Act and sentenced on September 12, 1918, to ten years imprisonment. The Supreme Court upheld the sentence. For an account of the activities of the Central Labor Bodies see Lucy Robins, *War Shadows* (New York 1922).

[11] *Forward,* February 2, 1921, editorial; February 19, 1921, editorial.

[12] *Ibid.,* April 7, 1921. The demonstration was organized by the Amnesty Committee of the Socialist Party.

hope that now that Debs was free, he would provide the needed leadership and engage in the struggle for freedom.[13] Earlier, a cartoon in the *Forward* had expressed this hope; it depicted an exhausted worker, stooping under the burden of strikes and exploitation, welcoming Debs at the prison door and saying: "Brother Debs, you returned at the right time. The workers of America need you now more than ever." [14]

If its identification with the political prisoners shows primarily the *Forward*'s socialist commitment, its stand on the United States' immigration policy presents it both as a socialist and ethnic paper. Pointing to a direct connection between the Johnson-Dillingham Act of 1921 and the Red Scare, the paper interpreted the closing of the gates as the Government's blow at radicals and as its official subscription to anti-Semitism.[15] The *Forward* protested especially the vicious attack on East European immigrants, voiced during the congressional debates and the implication that prospective Jewish immigrants could not make good American citizens. It warned against the dangers of such public slander. At a time when anti-Semitism was growing in the United States, official government bodies should not have abetted it by such statements.[16]

In protesting the National Origins Act of 1921, the *Forward* insisted that Jews were deliberately singled out. Only 12,000 Jews would enter the United States, in lieu of the 85,000 admitted in 1920. Furthermore, the Act allowed wives and children of American citizens to join them above the quota law, but barred families of aliens, even those who had already applied for citizenship. Not only was this cruel and inhumane, insisted the paper. What was worse, the quota could not be extended for the sake of broken families, but was flexible enough to accommodate business interests, since the Act of 1921 empowered the Secretary of Labor to authorize the entry of workers above the allotted quota. The *Forward* saw in this proof of the Government's subservience to business magnates.[17]

In criticizing the economic motives behind the immigration

13 *Forward*, December 26, 1921. *Ibid.*, December 25, 1921, editorial; December 27, 1921. *Ibid.*, December 24, 1921.
14 *Ibid.*, April 23, 1921.
15 *Ibid.*, April 20, 1921; April 21, 1921, editorial.
16 *Ibid.*, February 8, 1923, editorial.
17 *Ibid.*, April 20, 1921; April 24, 1921, editorial; April 26, 1921.

policy, the *Forward* attacked both big business for its interest in cheap immigrant labor, and the AFL for its fear of competition from the immigrant. The *Forward* claimed that the AFL was mistaken in its view of the economic danger presented by the immigrant. Unemployment and difficulties of labor were the products of the capitalist regime, and of the reactionary government, not of immigrant competition. The AFL should look for the real causes of the laborer's plight in the failure of America to adjust to industrialism. To substantiate this, the *Forward* brought statistical evidence proving that the number of those who had left the United States after the war was almost equal to the number of those who had entered.[18]

In trying to understand the paper's protest, especially the oversimplifications of its arguments, one must remember that its readers were personally affected by the restriction of immigration. Many of their relatives, uprooted by the war, were stranded in Europe waiting for visas, hoping to enter the "land of the free." The National Origins Act, in its deliberate attempt to limit the quota for East Europeans, was a slap in the face to the East Side Jew. Furthermore, since prospective immigrants came from the same stock as the American Jews, the Act was an insult to American citizens.[19]

Finally, the *Forward* warned that the immigration laws would shatter the faith of many in the American tradition of freedom and equality. The quota laws were discriminating against certain groups of people on the basis of race. Moreover, by placing the burden of proof of legal entry into the United States upon the immigrant, the amendment to the National Origins Act violated the prevailing legal principle that a person was innocent until proven guilty. The *Forward* suspected that many immigrants would not even have legal proof, because the Department of Labor might deliberately destroy their records. Likewise, the *Forward* bitterly opposed a bill requiring registration of aliens because it singled out a special group and authorized the search of residences of aliens without a warrant and made an immigrant who did not carry his passport subject to arrest. All these measures, wrote the

---

18 *Ibid.*, October 5, 1925, editorial.
19 *Ibid.*, December 17, 1921.

Forward, not only restricted individual freedom; they could be used by employers to punish labor. They were untraditional and un-American and marked the end of an era. The paper quoted Representative Bourke Cochran's statement in Congress that the restriction of immigration was the most crucial issue since the Civil War. If passed, it would mean the deliberate abandonment of the "policy which had fixed the position of this great Nation in the forefront of civilization, which had made it a bulwark of peace, a light of progress in the whole world."[20]

Regarding immigration restriction as symptomatic of the decadence of American ideals, the paper warned that closing of the gates would not guarantee the calm of the United States from within. Trouble was not imported; it grew at home, as the Jewish Congressman, Meyer London, said:

> The idea that by restricting immigration you will prevent the influx of radical thought is altogether untenable. You cannot exclude an idea by the most drastic legislation; you cannot confine it behind prison bars. The fact that there was almost no immigration during the war did not prevent us from importing any abominable idea from Europe.[21]

The *Forward*'s bitterness at the persecution of minorities culminated in its reaction to the trial of Niccola Sacco and Bartholomeo Vanzetti. The case of the two Italians turned into a drama which held the attention of the labor movement, radicals, disillusioned Progressives and liberals, for over a decade. Sacco and Vanzetti became symbols of the miscarriage of justice in the name of justice. The emotional integrity of a whole generation seemed to depend on their case. At the initial stage, at least, the *Forward* avoided the presentation of the two Italians as symbols. It described them as honest, innocent and simple workers, constantly stressing their devotion to the cause of labor. As it became exceedingly clear that they were the victims of a "reactionary regime," the *Forward* progressively treated them as heroic martyrs. At the same time, however, it tried to maintain their image as

---

[20] *Congressional Record,* 67th Congress, House of Representatives first session, April 20, 1921, p. 515; quoted in *Forward,* April 20, 1921.
[21] *Ibid.*

individuals, thus exploiting the human drama to the limits of endurance.[22]

Right from the beginning of the proceedings, the *Forward* was sceptical over the prospects of a fair trial; it doubted whether one could find a jury free from prejudice at a time when the police itself made every effort to keep the Red Scare alive.[23] Even the methods of identification were unconstitutional: the police did not permit the two suspects to shave. They lined them up in dishevelled clothes and roughed-up hair, placed them among uniformed policemen and forced them to aim guns. With no lawyer present, the two did not know that this procedure was illegal. Furthermore, the *Forward* stressed that the State Attorney and capitalist newspapers carried the Red Scare into the courtroom by spreading rumors about alleged anarchists' and communists' preparations to bomb the courthouse, which was constantly surrounded by detectives. The *Forward* described with great gusto how one morning, when searching all Italians in court for bombs, there was a triumphant gleam in the eye of a policeman who noticed a bulge in one man's pocket. The only bombs he found were eggs which the man had brought for his lunch. To make things worse, the court refused to pay the expenses of the witnesses for the defense, unless it submitted in advance the list of all its prospective witnesses. This the defense attorney could not do, however, because he suspected that the prosecution might intimidate the witnesses before their testimony.[24]

The shock came on July 15, when the verdict became known. Despite its earlier suspicions of the court's procedures, the *Forward* had refused to believe that the jury would actually find Sacco and Vanzetti guilty. From then on, the paper found only one explanation for the trial: Sacco and Vanzetti were tried because they were radicals, aliens and because of their devotion to the cause of labor. The *Forward* immediately launched a fund-raising campaign for the defense and issued a call to all workers to unite and defend the two martyrs and the labor movement.[25] It stressed

22 For details on the legal procedure and the impact of the case on literature see G. L. Joughin and E. M. Morgan, *The Legacy of Sacco and Vanzetti* (New York 1948), pp. 3–57.

23 *Forward*, June 7, 1921.

24 *Ibid.*, June 29, 1921.

25 *Ibid.*, July 21, 1921.

the similarity between this trial, the Mooney case and the case of Salsedo, the Italian anarchist, whose shattered body was found one day in front of the fourteen-story New York building in which he had been imprisoned. The *Forward* concluded that Sacco and Vanzetti were part of a long procession of martyrs for the cause of labor.[26]

In the period from July, 1921, to April 8, 1927, the defense made every effort to secure a new trial. Its arguments rested on the prejudice of the judge and on the grounds that the verdict was against the weight of evidence. Altogether, eight motions were presented before Judge Webster Thayer. After more than two and a half years of appeal to the Massachusetts Supreme Court and after using a whole new line of evidence, there was no legal recourse open. On April 9, 1927, Judge Thayer set the date for the execution.[27] The only hope left was clemency from the Governor. On August 3, 1927, following the recommendations of a special advisory committee, the Governor announced his conclusion that the trial was fair and that there was no proof of prejudice in Judge Thayer's conduct. The announcement created a wave of excitement and indignation which lasted until the day of execution. Since the Governor, the Judge, and the members of the committee came from old upper-class Yankee stock, even people who had no Marxist bias tended to view the trial as the crucial dividing line between two Americas.[28]

Weighing the Governor's conclusion against the insistence of millions of people on the innocence of Sacco and Vanzetti, the *Forward* concluded that the Governor was more interested in millions of dollars than in the opinion of millions of people. The *Forward* was sure that had a rich person been on trial he would have undoubtedly been acquitted. It drew the attention of its readers to the concern of the newspapers of all major cities for justice in the case, with the exception of Boston.[29] It suspected that Boston papers did not want the verdict changed, for they feared that a reversal of the court's decision would hurt the prestige of Massachusetts' judicial institutions. Thus, the *Forward*

26 *Ibid.*, August 16, 1921.
27 Joughin, G. L. and Morgan, E. M., *op. cit.*, pp. 116–158.
28 Leuchtenburg, William, *The Perils of Prosperity* (Chicago 1958), p. 82.
29 *Forward*, August 4, 1927, p. 1; August 5, 1927, p. 1.

claimed, a false patriotism made the judges blind to justice. They did not even realize that they were defeating their purpose by inflicting a lasting blemish on their state.[30]

The disillusionment of the *Forward* with the system of justice in Massachusetts shook its faith in American institutions and leaders. One writer referred to the Sacco-Vanzetti trial as "The American Dreyfus Case." He deplored America's transformation from the "land of the free and the mighty" into a terrorist regime similar to Czarist Russia. The Dreyfus case, at least, aroused Emile Zola's protest; America produced no Zola. The writer was frightened by the indifference of the "True American" to the abuse of justice. Most of the protest movements were led by Jews, Italians, and other "greenhorns." According to the *Forward*, the apathy of the American public did not derive from general indifference to justice, but from the absence of liberal leadership and from the individual citizen's indiscriminate reliance on politicians.[31] As one speaker at a mass meeting in New York said: "Had Lincoln been alive today, he would not have allowed the execution of Sacco and Vanzetti."[32]

In the meantime, what were Sacco and Vanzetti doing? During the drama of a seven years' struggle for justice, the *Forward* kept the public emotionally involved in the condition of the two prisoners. The paper stressed the differences in their personalities, as reflected in their reactions in crisis: Vanzetti signed the request for clemency, Sacco was too sceptical about positive results. Instead, he went on a hunger strike for twenty-six days until the prison physician forced him to eat. When the *Forward* quoted Vanzetti's letter to his comrades, in response to the Governor's refusal of pardon, "Governor Alvan T. Fuller is a murderer as are Thayer, Katzman, the State perjurors and all the others. . . . This is the way of plutocracy against liberty, against the people. Revenge our blood. We die for anarchy. Long life [sic] anarchy."[33]

The *Forward* pointed out the cruelty involved: "The devil himself could not have invented something more terrible than the

---

30 *Ibid.*, August 5, 1927, editorial; August 6, 1927, p. 1.
31 *Ibid.* August 9, 1927, p. 4.
32 Quoted in the *Forward*, August 11, 1927, p. 1.
33 Quoted in Francis Russell, *Tragedy in Dedham: The Story of the Sacco-Vanzetti Case* (New York 1962), p. 410.

keeping of people under the shadows of death for seven years."[34] The indifference of Judge Thayer to human life was even more painful than his biases. He stubbornly endorsed the preparations for the execution, even while the defense attorney discussed with him the possibility of an appeal. When Mrs. Sacco visited her husband in the "Death House," she witnessed the preparations for the electrocution.[35]

There was only one day left. "The shadows of death are closing around Sacco and Vanzetti, it is almost too late," wrote the *Forward* on August 9th. Two days earlier it had issued a call to all workers to resort to the last measure of despair—to join the Socialist Party and the leaders of the needle trades in a general strike, planned for August 9th.

> Let the workers remember today . . . that Sacco and Vanzetti are the better parts of their own body; that the struggle of Sacco and Vanzetti is part of the great struggle which the masses of workers wage for their liberation. Let the workers remember today that if Sacco and Vanzetti had not had the fortune or misfortune of being involved in radical movements, to support the struggle for more justice and more light for the laboring masses, probably they would have never been put on trial, and they would have been granted a new trial had they been found guilty.[36]

The protest of labor gained momentum from similar reactions in major European cities. There is no exact count of participants in the demonstrations in New York. The *Forward* anticipated a crowd of 500,000. According to Joughin, the estimates vary from 75,000 to 400,000.[37]

The first wave of excitement burst on August 10, thirty-nine minutes before the scheduled hour of execution. Then news arrived that the date was postponed until August 22. The last desperate efforts to free the two condemned, directed to the courts of Massachusetts and to the Federal Supreme Court, failed. Even attempts to enlist Justices Oliver Wendell Holmes and Louis Brandeis were abortive.[38] When the defense attorney told the defendants

[34] *Forward*, August 12, 1927, editorial.
[35] *Ibid.*, August 9, 1927, p. 1.
[36] *Ibid.*, editorial.
[37] *Ibid.*, August 8, 1927, p. 1; Joughin, *op. cit.*, p. 276.
[38] Justice Holmes declined the petition because he claimed to have found no legal justification for the interference of the Supreme Court. Justice Bran-

that all hope for a legal break was gone, Vanzetti lost his mind and shouted in a mixture of Italian and English: "I knew it! Get one million people, mobilize one million people!" During that night, the newspaper men, assembled outside the "Death House," could hear the voice of Vanzetti moaning: "Get a radio broadcasting station into my cell."[39]

The above descriptions in the pages of the *Forward* are typical of the paper's daily coverage of the last events leading to the execution. It said very little now in editorials. The major emphasis was on factual rendition, rather than direct propaganda. The *Forward* did not spare its readers any detail of the human tragedy. It reported Sacco's conversations with his wife, his letters to his son and finally, the execution itself. Leaving nothing to the imagination, it described the movement of each prisoner from his cell to the chair, counted steps, quoted last words; it even explained the technical procedure of the electrocution in elaborate detail. This form of protest was perhaps much more effective than editorials could have been. It was emotional and played directly on the nerves. Bringing thousands of readers into the cell, it forced them to face the electric chair.

The *Forward* was in no way unique in the forcefulness of its protest, nor in its arguments. It shared the feeling of despair of various liberal newspapers, of lawyers such as Clarence Darrow and Felix Frankfurter, and of writers such as John Dos Passos and Edna St. Vincent Millay.[40] This protest expressed more than an uproar against injustice. What made this case unique was the fact that legally everything could be justified and contained within a sound constitutional framework. Those concerned felt that they were facing the end of an era, that some cataclysmic event would destroy all the traditions they had trusted. The trial was a betrayal of American ideals. Sacco and Vanzetti became the test of a whole generation. If they were executed, nothing could be the

---

deis declined because members of his family were personally involved in the defense of Sacco and Vanzetti; Joughin, *op. cit.*, p. 25.

39 *Forward*, August 20, 1927, p. 1; compare with Joughin, *op. cit.*, p. 25; also, John Dos Passos, *Facing the Chair* (Boston 1927); for a recent analysis of the stand of the intellectuals, see David Felix, *Protest: Sacco-Vanzetti and the Intellectuals* (Bloomington, Indiana, 1965); for a reinterpretation of the case, Russell, *Tragedy in Dedham.*

40 On the literary protest record see especially Joughin, *op. cit.*, pp. 375–454.

same again. One of the writers for the *Forward* eloquently stated the execution as a point of no return:

> The hours are numbered. But one does not measure time with watches anymore; one counts it by the beat of human hearts. Do you hear their beat, tick, tack? . . . the century of Sacco and Vanzetti starts tomorrow . . . justice is dead. . . . It was murdered and buried in a graveyard named Massachusetts.[41]

*

From the *Forward*'s stand on the restriction of liberties in the 1920's a clear pattern emerges. The paper did not confine its protest to the issues discussed above. It denounced with equal fervor the Red Scare and crusaded against the Ku Klux Klan. It protested Negro lynchings in the South, the exclusion of socialist members of the New York legislature and the New York State law requiring an oath of allegiance from teachers in public schools. Above all, it devoted its effort to the struggle of labor for freedom to organize and to advance economically. It did not consider, however, these issues independently. Products of capitalist corruption and of persecution of the working class, they were all manifestations of decadence in a reactionary regime.

Thus, although the *Forward* criticized American society by universal standards of justice and freedom, it was unable to overcome its socialist bias. In this lay its major limitations. A Marxist interpretation could easily be applied to the struggle of labor against industry. It was more difficult, however, to explain the restriction of immigration in terms of class warfare. If the *Forward* attributed the immigration laws to capitalist persecution of radicals and to fear of Communists, how would it explain the opposition of the AFL to immigration? Did not the AFL represent the working class? How would this apply to the fact that industrialists supported immigration, because of their interest in free labor, as the *Forward* itself pointed out? Futhermore, by identifying nativism and anti-Semitism with capitalism, the paper denied its readers an understanding of cross currents in American society and an explanation of the role of Grass Root groups in the formation of nativism. Hence, in its use of slogans, such as "Capitalism" and "anti-Semitism" the *Forward* was just as fundamentalist and dogmatic as the reactionary movements which it criticized.

[41] *Forward,* August 9, 1927, p. 5.

Notwithstanding its socialist bias, the paper at no point opposed the basic structure and assumptions of American democracy. What it continually lamented was a violation and distortion of American ideals. Thus, when the socialist *New York Call* was proclaimed a potential promoter of revolutionary movements and denied cheap postal rates, the *Forward* invoked the principle of equality before the law.[42] Likewise, when the New York legislature discussed an amendment to its constitution, restricting the right to vote only to those literate in English, the paper cried out against this violation of American principles of democracy. "The United States always has been proud of the fact that every citizen had an equal right to vote."[43] The *Forward* did not want its readers to lose faith in America because of the events. It carefully reminded them that the persecutions they were witnessing were not characteristic of America; they were only grotesque caricatures. "This is not a normal time. . . . The war poison has settled in the souls of many Americans and a wild reaction now rules the state. . . ." It concluded that workers must remember the true ideals of America and stay loyal to them.[44]

The 1920's seemed to the *Forward* like a nightmare in which various groups paid lip service to certain principles and used certain slogans to justify measures which undermined those very principles. The American Legion, for example, distorted the true meaning of Americanism in the name of patriotism. Americanism, the *Forward* claimed, was not reaction, xenophobia, injustice, and restriction of individual liberties. Americanism was the tradition of democratic government and the people's right to criticize their government. It rested on the fundamental principles in the Constitution—liberty, justice, and humanity and in the supremacy of the will of the people over that of the politicians.[45] Americanism meant freedom; its personification was Abraham Lincoln. Freedom was more than political and civil rights. It had to include economic freedom, freedom from want. Meyer London expressed this concept before Congress, arguing that soup kitchens or arrests were

42 *Ibid.*, June 9, 1921, p. 6.
43 *Ibid.*, October 8, 1921, editorial.
44 *Loc. cit.*
45 *Ibid.*, March 29, 1921, editorial.

not solutions for poverty and unemployment: "Freedom without bread is no freedom."[46]

The *Forward* did not preach revolution or violence. It wanted its readers to develop a sensitivity to current issues, to realize when and why they were being deprived or wronged and how they should defend their rights. The solution it offered was political alertness and the exercise of the "most sacred right in a democracy"—the right to vote. Urging its readers to register for voting, it warned that only active participation by the citizens in their government could prevent America from becoming a Czarist Russia.[47]

In reading the *Forward's* reaction to American issues, one wonders to what extent it was affected by its Jewish identity. It was not affiliated with any Jewish religious organization and showed very little interest in the ritual. Unlike Jewish community papers, it did not post information pertaining to Holiday services or to Synagogue activity. This was so because the editors of the *Forward* did not identify with Judaism as a religion. They tended, rather, to stress its cultural heritage and to merge it with the ideals of socialism. As Rischin points out, to most Jewish socialists, socialism was "Judaism secularized." Cahan expressed this feeling in 1910: "The spiritual cheer which this ideal [socialism] creates is a living reward . . . a reward that Judaism promises the righteous in the world to come, but which laboring humanity attains in this world."[48] Sometimes the *Forward* criticized American society by Jewish ideals. For instance, in an editorial on Passover, Cahan wrote with bitterness that Jews should not rejoice over the "Holiday of Freedom" as long as the working class was in chains. He felt that a celebration of freedom was particularly out of place in the grim atmosphere of 1921.[49]

In addition to the cultural identification with Judaism, the *Forward* reflected ethnic solidarity. Even working class affiliation did not overcome the sense of belonging to a Jewish community and the pride in its achievements. In reality, it would be hard to distinguish how the readers on the East Side were primarily af-

46 *Ibid.*, October 19, 1921, p. 1.
47 *Ibid.*, October 8, 1921, editorial.
48 Rischin, *op. cit.*, p. 166.
49 *Forward*, April 19, 1921, editorial.

fected: as Jews, as workers, or as immigrants. In the 1920's, the problems were interwoven and derived from all three sources alike. Consequently, this question must be left open pending a comparative study of the *Forward,* both, with other Jewish newspapers and with other immigrant papers.

Notes on Contributors

ABRAHAM AIN, a native of Swisłocz, was a communal worker and leader in that town until his emigration to New York in 1921. Following World War II Ain devoted his energies to contacting and supporting survivors from his hometown. He helped disseminate a YIVO Institute questionnaire among refugees of Swisłocz and gathered material for *Yizkor l'kehilat Svislots*, a commemorative volume which was published in Tel Aviv in 1961, soon after Ain's death.

BERNHARD BRILLING, a German rabbi and scholar, was born in Posen in 1906. Before the start of World War II Brilling served as the archivist of the Breslau Jewish community and later worked as an archivist for the city of Tel Aviv. Since 1957 Brilling pursued various scholarly activities at the University of Münster, where he helped found a department for the study of German Jewish history. He published over fifty articles and books on Jewish history, including *Geschichte der Juden in Breslau von 1454–1702* and *Westfalia Judacia 1005–1350* (with H. Richtering). He received the Leo Baeck Prize in 1982.

PHILIP FRIEDMAN, a Polish Jewish historian, was born in Galicia in 1901. Friedman taught Jewish history in Łódź and Warsaw before World War II. After the war he organized the Central Jewish Historical Commission in Lublin. In 1948 Friedman came to the United States and served as director of the Jewish Teachers' Institute in New York and taught at Columbia University. He joined the staff of the YIVO Institute and directed the bibliographical series of the YIVO/Yad Vashem Joint Documentary Project. Friedman wrote several books on the Holocaust, including *This Was Oswiecim: The Story of a Murder Camp*, *Martyrs and Fighters: The Epic of the Warsaw Ghetto*, *Roads to Extinction: Essays in the Holocaust*, and *Their Brothers' Keepers*. He died in 1960.

RUDOLF GLANZ was born in Vienna in 1892. He studied history, education, and law at the Wiener Universität, receiving his doctorate in political science in 1918. Glanz studied at YIVO as an *aspirant*, pursuing his interests in Jewish history and philology. He emigrated to the United States in 1938. Glanz's work appeared frequently in the YIVO Institute's English and Yiddish scholarly publications. Active in the Poalei Zion, he served as director of its archives in the United States. Glanz died in New York in 1978.

TAMARA K. HAREVEN, an American social and family historian, is currently Professor of History at Clark University and Research Associate at the Center for Population Studies at Harvard University. Hareven has written numerous articles and several books on the history of the family and serves as the editor of the *Journal of Family History*.

LIEBMAN HERSCH, a statistician and demographer, was born in Lithuania in 1882. Hersch was a Bundist leader and publicist in Warsaw, contributing to the Yiddish, Polish, and Russian presses. Hersch was also active in the YIVO Institute and contributed articles to its scholarly publications. He wrote demographic studies in both Yiddish and English. Hersch died in 1955.

ABRAHAM JOSHUA HESCHEL, a renowned scholar, teacher, and philosopher, was born in Warsaw in 1907. Following a traditional Jewish education, he earned his doctorate at the University of Berlin and the Hochschule für die Wissenschaft des Judentums. He taught in Jewish academic institutions in Berlin, Frankfurt, and Warsaw before leaving Eastern Europe at the beginning of World War II. Heschel came to the United States in 1940 to teach at the Hebrew Union College in Cincinnati and joined the faculty of the Jewish Theological Seminary in 1945. Among his numerous articles and books on Jewish religion and philosophy are *Man is Not Alone, God in Search of Man,* and *The Prophets*. His article for the *YIVO Annual* on East European Jewry served as the basis for his book *The Earth is the Lord's*. Heschel died in 1972.

HORACE M. KALLEN, a philosopher and educator, was born in Silesia in 1882. His family emigrated to the United States in 1887. Kallen taught at Harvard, Clark, and the University of Wisconsin and was one of the founders of the New School for Social Research, where he taught and served as Dean of Graduate Faculties. Kallen wrote on a wide range of topics; his publications include *Zionism and World Politics*, *Individualism: An American Way of Life*, and *Liberty, Laughter and Tears*. He died in 1974.

JACOB LESTCHINSKY, a pioneer in the sociological, economic, and demographic study of Jewish life, was born in the Ukraine in 1876. An active Zionist and socialist, he researched the application of Marxist methodology in several early studies of the Jewish proletariat. Lestchinsky directed the economic and statistical divisions of the YIVO Institute in the 1920s and was also a foreign correspondent for the *Jewish Daily Forward*. In 1938 he came to the United States, where he worked at the Institute for Jewish Affairs. Lestchinsky's studies of the Holocaust include *Di Yidishe Katashrofe* and *Crisis, Catastophe and Survival: A Jewish Balance Sheet 1914–1948*. He died in Jerusalem in 1966.

RAPHAEL MAHLER, a historian, was born in Galicia in 1899. Mahler was educated at the Rabbinical Seminary and the University of Vienna and taught general and Jewish history in Poland until emigrating to the United States in 1937. In New York he continued to teach and also renewed his association with the YIVO Institute. In 1950 he moved to Israel, where he taught at the University of Tel Aviv. His publications include *Di yidn in amolikn Polyn*, *A History of Modern Jewry*, and *Hasidism and the Jewish Enlightenment*. He also edited *Jewish Emancipation: A Selection of Documents*. Mahler died in 1977.

EZRA MENDELSOHN is Professor of Contemporary Jewry and Russian Studies at the Hebrew University, Jerusalem. He is the author of *Class Struggle in the Pale*, *Zionism in Poland, 1918-1926*, and *The Jews of East Central Europe: Between the World Wars*.

DAN MIRON is L. B. Kaye Professor of Hebrew and Comparative Literature at Columbia University and Professor of Hebrew and Yiddish Literature at Hebrew University. His most recent publication is *When Loners Come Together: A Portrait of Hebrew Literature at the Turn of the Twentieth Century*. Miron is also the author of *A Traveler Disguised: The Rise of Yiddish Fiction in the Nineteenth Century* and *Imazh fun shtetl* (The shtetl image in modern Yiddish literature).

YEKHIEL SHTERN was born in Poland in 1903. Following a traditional Jewish education in Tyscowce, he attended the Yiddish Teachers' Seminary in Vilna. Shtern taught Yiddish and Hebrew in Poland until 1938 and in Canada until 1968. He wrote poems, stories, and articles on Jewish education and received the LaMed Prize for his book *Kheyder un bes-medresh*, published by the YIVO Institute in 1950. He died in Montreal in 1981.

ISAIAH TRUNK, a historian, was born in Poland in 1905. Trunk taught high school in Poland and was a research associate of the Jewish Historical Institute in Warsaw. In 1954 he came to New York and joined the research staff of the YIVO Institute. In 1972 he became the Institute's Head Archivist, a post he held until his death in 1981. Trunk's publications include *Ghetto Lodz: A Historical and Sociological Study* and *Judenrat: The Jewish Councils in Eastern Europe Under the Nazi Occupation*.